The Internationalisation Strategies of Small-Country Firms

NEW HORIZONS IN INTERNATIONAL BUSINESS

Series Editor: Peter J. Buckley
Centre for International Business,
University of Leeds (CIBUL), UK

The New Horizons in International Business series has established itself as the world's leading forum for the presentation of new ideas in international business research. It offers pre-eminent contributions in the areas of multinational enterprise – including foreign direct investment, business strategy and corporate alliances, global competitive strategies, and entrepreneurship. In short, this series constitutes essential reading for academics, business strategists and policy makers alike.

Titles in the series include:

Multinationals and Industrial Competitiveness
A New Agenda
John H. Dunning and Rajneesh Narula

Foreign Direct Investment
Six Country Case Studies
Edited by Yingqi Annie Wei and V.N. Balasubramanyam

Japanese Multinationals in Europe
A Comparison of the Automobile and Pharmaceutical Industries
Ken-ichi Ando

International Joint Venture Performance in South East Asia
Craig C. Julian

Governance, Multinationals and Growth
Edited by Lorraine Eden and Wendy Dobson

Institutions, Industrial Upgrading, and Economic Performance in Japan
The 'Flying Geese' Paradigm of Catch-up Growth
Terutomo Ozawa

European–American Trade and Financial Alliances
Edited by Gavin Boyd, Alan M. Rugman and Pier Carlo Padoan

Growth of New Technology Ventures in China's Emerging Market
Edited by Haiyang Li

Transformations in Global Governance
Implications for Multinationals and Other Stakeholders
Edited by Sushil Vachani

Emerging Economies and the Transformation of International Business
Brazil, Russia, India and China (BRICs)
Edited by Subhash C. Jain

Corporate Strategies in the Age of Regional Integration
Edited by Jong-Kil Kim and Pierre-Bruno Ruffini

The Internationalisation Strategies of Small-Country Firms

The Australian Experience of Globalisation

Edited by

Howard Dick, Professor,

Department of Management and Marketing, University of Melbourne, Australia

David Merrett, Professor,

Department of Management and Marketing, University of Melbourne, Australia

NEW HORIZONS IN INTERNATIONAL BUSINESS

Edward Elgar

Cheltenham, UK • Northampton, MA, USA

Published by
Edward Elgar Publishing Limited
Glensanda House
Montpellier Parade
Cheltenham
Glos GL50 1UA
UK

Edward Elgar Publishing, Inc.
William Pratt House
9 Dewey Court
Northampton
Massachusetts 01060
USA

A catalogue record for this book
is available from the British Library

Library of Congress Control Number: 2006937372

ISBN: 978 1 84542 212 7

Printed and bound in Great Britain by MPG Books Ltd, Bodmin, Cornwall

Contents

Contributors

Rodney Benjamin had a long and successful career in the insurance industry, during the course of which he found time to complete a PhD in economic history at the University of Melbourne.

Howard Dick is Professor and Co-Director of the Australian Centre for International Business in the Department of Management and Marketing at the University of Melbourne, Australia.

Paul Evans is a PhD candidate in the Department of Management and Marketing at the University of Melbourne.

Anne-Wil Harzing is Associate Professor in the Department of Management and Marketing at the University of Melbourne.

Geoffrey Lewis is Professorial Fellow at the Melbourne Business School, University of Melbourne.

David Merrett is Professor and Co-Director of the Australian Centre for International Business in the Department of Management and Marketing at the University of Melbourne.

Shey Newitt is a PhD candidate in the Department of Management and Marketing at the University of Melbourne.

Niels Noorderhaven is Professor in the Department of Organization and Strategy at Tilburg University, the Netherlands.

Thomas Osegowitsch is Lecturer in the Department of Management and Marketing at the University of Melbourne.

Frances Van Ruth is a PhD candidate in the Department of Management and Marketing at the University of Melbourne.

André Sammartino is Lecturer in the Department of Management and and Marketing at the University of Melbourne.

Robin Stewardson is former Chief Economist at BHP.

Robert Walters was up until June 2006 a Director of the Economic Analytical Analytical Unit in the Department of Foreign Affairs and Trade of the Australian Government.

Tatiana Zalan is Lecturer in the Department of Management and Marketing at at the University of Melbourne.

Acknowledgements

We are most grateful to Edward Elgar for his interest in the concept and support for the project as it evolved into the manuscript and to Alexandra O'Connell for her ready and sound advice at all stages, as also to our ever-helpful editorial assistant, Emma Gordon-Walker.

Early chapter outlines and then drafts were vigorously discussed at two workshops held at The University of Melbourne in November 2004 and November 2005. Both authors and editors benefited greatly from the critical comments of Gordon Boyce, Peter Liesch, Klaus Meyer and Simon Ville. Others who read, commented or advised on specific chapters are acknowledged therein.

In house at the Australian Centre for International Business, it was a team effort. Paul Evans, Shey Newitt and Eric Quintane provided careful and timely research assistance. Sheila Gowans assiduously copy-edited the whole manuscript and bibliography. The Centre's administrative assistant Jan Uhlhorn efficiently organised the two workshops and began the formatting, which was completed very capably by Virginia Atkins.

Melbourne September 2006

Conventions

$ denotes Australian dollars unless otherwise specified. Since 1983 the exchange rate has been floating. For annual average USD conversion rates since 1948 see http://fx.sauber.ubc.ca.

Abbreviations

ABS	Australian Bureau of Statistics
ACCC	Australian Competition and Consumer Commission
ACEA	Association of Consulting Engineers Australia
ACI	Australian Consolidated Industries
Adsteam	Adelaide Steamship Company
AG	Australia Group
AMATIL	Allied Manufacturing and Trading Industries Ltd
AMP	Australian Mutual Provident
AMSA	Australian Maritime Safety Authority
ANL	Australian National Line
ANZ	Australia and New Zealand Bank
ANZSIC	Australian and New Zealand Standard Industrial Classification
APM	Australian Paper Mills
APRA	Australian Prudential Regulatory Authority
ASEAN	Association of Southeast Asian Nations
ASIC	Australian Securities and Investment Commission
ASO	Associated Steamship Owners
ASX	Australian Stock Exchange
AUSFTA	Australia–United States Free Trade Agreement
AUSN	Australian United Steam Navigation Limited
Australasia	Australia and New Zealand
AWA	Amalgamated Wireless Australasia
AWAS	Ansett Worldwide Aviation Services
AWBC	Australian Wine and Brandy Corporation
BBWE	Beringer Blass Wine Estates
BHP	Broken Hill Proprietary
BICC	Building Industry Consultancy Council
BIE	Bureau of Industry Economics
BP	Burns Philp and Company
BRL Hardy	(Berri Renmano Limited) Hardy

BRW	*Business Review Weekly*
CCA	Coca-Cola Amatil
CCC	Coca-Cola Corporation
CEO	Chief Executive Officer
CMC Australia	Commercial Metals Company Australia
CML	Colonial Mutual Life
COAG	Council of Australian Governments
CRA	Conzinc Rio Tinto Australia
CSA	country-specific-advantage
CSIRO	Commonwealth Scientific and Industrial Research Organisation
CSL	Commonwealth Serum Laboratories
CSR	Colonial Sugar Refining
CUB	Carlton and United Breweries
DC	domestic company
DFAT	Department of Foreign Affairs and Trade
EDS Australia	Electronic Data Systems Australia
E(E)C	European (Economic) Community
EMEA	Europe, Middle East, Africa
ENR	*Engineering News Record*
EPG profile	Engineered Product Group
FSA	firm-specific-advantage
GE	General Electric
GF	Goodman Fielder
GHD	Gutteridge Haskins Davey
HCN	host country national
HRM	human resource management
HSBC	Hong Kong Shanghai Banking Corporation
IAG	Insurance Australia Group
IBM	International Business Machines
ICIANZ	Imperial Chemical Industries of Australia and New Zealand
IMF	International Monetary Fund
IMT	International Marine Transport
ING	ING Group
IPO	Initial Public Offering

LIC	Life Insurance Commission
LNG	liquified natural gas
LVMH	Louis Vuitton Möet Hennessy
M & A	mergers and acquisitions
MNC	multinational corporation
MWH Australia	Montgomery Watson Harza Australia
NAB	National Australia Bank
NAFTA	North American Free Trade Agreement
NASDAQ	National Association of Securities Dealers Automated Quotation
Newscorp	News Corporation
NML	National Mutual Life
NRMA	National Roads and Motorists Association
OECD	Organisation of Economic Cooperation and Development
OPSM	Optical Prescription Spectacle Makers
OTC	Overseas Telecommunications
P&O	Peninsular and Oriental Steam Navigation Company
PACCAR	Pacific Car and Foundry Company
PBS	Pharmaceutical Benefits Scheme
PCN	parent country national
PNG	Papua New Guinea
QBE	QBE Insurance Group
R&D	research and development
RBA	Reserve Bank of Australia
RTZ	Rio Tinto Zinc
SA Brewing	South Australian Brewing
SKF	Svenska Kullagerfabriken (Sweden)
TCN	third country national
TNC	transnational corporation
TNT	Thomas Nationwide Transport
UNCTAD	United Nations Conference on Trade and Development
Westpac	Westpac Bank
WMC	Western Mining Corporation

PART I

Perspectives

1. Introduction

Howard Dick and David Merrett

Globalisation is a universal experience which is integrating economies and business firms from economies large, medium and small. Multinational companies (MNCs) have been identified variously as 'flagships' and 'champions' of national competitiveness. If the world were indeed a 'level playing field', a firm's country of origin would make little difference to its success in international business. Other things being equal, firms from large economies would be more numerous but they would not necessarily enjoy superior competitive advantage beyond that arising from a large domestic market. Firms originating in small countries would enjoy equal opportunity in gaining access to the global market. Belgium, the Netherlands, Switzerland and the Scandinavian countries are classic examples of small countries that have turned smallness into an advantage.

Nevertheless, rankings of the world's multinationals and surveys of the leading firms by industry show that firms from the so-called triad economies of the United States (US), Europe and Japan predominate (UNCTAD, 2001; Rugman, 2005). Europe certainly includes a number of smaller countries but what about the rest of the world? Apart from Japan, there is minimal representation of multinationals from the rest of Asia, Central and Latin America, Africa and Oceania, which together constitute the major part of the world's land area and population. This is a problem. Countries whose firms struggle to establish themselves as multinationals are likely to be disadvantaged in the global market place, to be hosts to foreign direct investment (FDI) inflows rather than significant providers of FDI outflows. Continued progress in the liberalisation of trade and investment requires confidence that the benefits will be shared, which also means that firms from all countries have some – if not equal – opportunity to access world markets.

This book seeks to inform the literature by exploring the experience of Australia, an atypical case of a medium- to small-sized open economy. Australia enjoys the advantage of being an English-speaking country with a two-hundred-year history of trade relations with the rest of the world and fairly advanced technology. Australian MNCs are found among the Fortune 500 and a very few such as News Corporation and BHP Billiton are fairly well recognised. Nevertheless, in the late twentieth-century Australian firms seem to have faced greater obstacles to becoming successful multinationals than firms located in many other advanced economies, especially those from northwestern Europe. How much of this is due to geographic isolation, how much to resource base, and how much to institutions and policy regime? Australia's atypical case may be instructive.

This book offers a nuanced and layered view of the Australian experience of internationalisation since the 1980s. Many factors, both within Australia and overseas came to bear on what prompts firms to go abroad as multinationals. Some of those influences come from the state of the wider domestic economy, its prices and costs, its supply of skills, infrastructure and public knowledge, and economic policy in the broader sense. The structure, conduct and performance of the industries in which firms compete are important sets of situational factors. Additional factors, of equal importance, come from within firms, their accumulated competencies and capabilities. These economy, industry and firm factors affect the success or otherwise of ventures abroad. The following chapters focus on the experiences mainly of large firms. Within general and industry contexts, they seek to differentiate between the experiences and strategies of firms which succeeded and those which may be regarded to have failed offshore. From such diversity of experience, some general conclusions may be drawn.

This introductory chapter begins with a brief review of the new literature on non-triad economies. For non-Australian readers it then sets the Australian economy in comparative context by highlighting some of its key distinctive features. The following section gives an overview of the evolution of the Australian business environment with particular attention to those features which in the twentieth century led to the disengagement of Australian firms from the global economy and then, with the policy reforms of the 1980s, to re-engagement. The final section briefly sketches the theoretical parameters and then outlines the plan of the book.

BEYOND THE TRIAD

Few would argue with the proposition that the liberalisation of trade and investment over the past 25 years has been a key factor in raising productivity and living standards worldwide. Flows of FDI have been integral to the reallocation of resources across countries and the transfer of know-how between countries. However, it would appear that firms from a small group of countries have enjoyed a sustainable advantage in terms of the nature of the assets at their disposal, particularly in terms of patents and brands, and the capacity to deploy those assets across borders. Part of that ongoing advantage stems from being a multinational which, in the words of

Kogut and Zander (1993), has 'superior efficiency as an organizational vehicle by which to transfer ... knowledge across borders'. They have acquired, through experiential learning, the skills to offset the 'liability of foreignness' in the host countries in which they operate (Hymer, 1976).

While the flows and stocks of FDI have risen dramatically since 1980, multinationals from the triad nations have continued their dominance of global or regional industries. World Investment Reports from the United Nations Conference on Trade and Development (UNCTAD) show that the number of multinationals almost doubled from more than 36,000 in the early 1990s to nearly 62,000 a decade later. The number of subsidiaries has grown very much faster over the same period, from nearly 175,000 to 927,000 (UNCTAD, 2004: Annex table A.1.2, 273-5). The stock of outward FDI as a proportion of world GDP has risen from 5.8 per cent in 1980 to 23.0 per cent in 2003 (UNCTAD, 2004: Annex table B.6, 399). Yet the domicile of firms in UNCTAD's top 100 list has altered little. In 1980 firms from the USA, European Union (EU) and Japan comprised 95 of the 100 largest multinationals (UNCTAD, 1983: Annex Table II.3.1, 357-8). Nearly 20 years later the triad still provided 90 of the top 100 (UNCTAD, 2000: Table III.3, 76). The developed economies not only dominated at the top end of the scale but also were home to 76 per cent of the world's multinationals around 2000 (UNCTAD, 2003: Annex table, A.1.15, 222-3).

In the 1990s multinational firms were emerging from smaller and even developing and transitional economies not hitherto prominent as home bases for multinationals. However, these firms differed in a number of dimensions from their triad rivals. They were considerably smaller in terms of assets, sales and employees, both absolutely and adjusted for industry. They were found in low- rather than high-technology industries and had a much narrower geographic breadth. Moreover, foreign activities were a smaller part of the firm's overall operations (UNCTAD, 1998: xvii-xviii, 85-94; UNCTAD, 2004: 19-29). These data suggest that countries beyond the triad face considerable challenges in becoming breeding grounds for multinationals, especially in knowledge-intensive, high-technology global industries.

Large-country bias has been less remarked upon in academic literature than one might expect. The obvious reason is that English-language texts and journals in international business and strategy are dominated by the experience and cases of firms from the very large economies, notably the United States, Britain, France, Germany and Japan. The rest of both the Western and non-Western world studies the world economy and international business from a Euro-American perspective and increasingly, even in Europe and Japan, from an even more narrowly American one.

To the extent that the literature has addressed the prospects for firms based outside the triad it has focused on those from developing and transitional economies (Andreff, 2003). Multinationals from such economies have emerged by exploiting low-wage, labour-intensive technologies through foreign investment into other developing economies. However, if the north-south division of labour and the corresponding gap in per capita income is to be overturned, labour-intensive developing economies must lift their productivity. Some authors have argued that firms have travelled this path by using indigenous technologies upgraded by domestic R&D, while others have stressed the importance of technological transfers from the developed world, particularly via inward FDI (Andreff, 2003). Other researchers, notably John Dunning have argued that reaching a certain level of economic development in the home economy is a precondition for domestic firms to compete abroad. Rising incomes and the establishment of infrastructure and institutions supporting market exchange attracts inward FDI that in turn boosts the competencies and capabilities of local firms via spillover effects (Dunning, 1981).

Less attention has been paid to the progress of firms from smaller developed economies. A recent work to address this issue includes that edited by Daniel Van Den Bulcke and Alain Verbeke, *Globalization and the Small Open Economy* (2001), which focused on the experience of Belgium and the Netherlands. There followed Elizabeth Maitland and Stephen Nicholas, *Modeling Multinationals from Small, Open Economies* (2002), which focused on Scandinavian countries. Two key issues emerge from these studies, both highly relevant for Australia. The first is scale. Firms from such economies lack scale in manufacturing, particularly in domestic markets, and are therefore at a cost disadvantage. The second relates to policy regime. Firms originating in hitherto protected domestic economies which limited their involvement in the international economy face serious challenges when the barriers are removed. They struggle to compete with international firms in their domestic markets. Moreover, they must generate the organisational capabilities needed to manage across borders. Firms with limited prior experience are required to climb a steep learning curve. However, the international business literature is as yet too limited to generate broad-based and robust empirical findings that would explain why firms have been more numerous and successful in going abroad from some countries than from others. This is a huge gap in our knowledge of globalisation and the multinational firm.

AUSTRALIA IN COMPARATIVE PERSPECTIVE

The problem in dealing with small country cases is that they are both numerous and diverse. Countries differ enormously by location, economic size and level of economic development, industrial structure, political regime, and policy framework. Nevertheless, only from mining the richness of these cases can generalisations be drawn. Small countries have a great deal to learn from each other, and even large countries would benefit from greater awareness of these differences.

Australia is an awkward country to classify. In land area it is a vast continent of 7.7 million square kilometres, somewhat smaller than Brazil (8.5), the United States (9.3) and Canada (10), yet it sustains a population of only 20 million people (World Bank, 2005). By population it is equivalent to a middle-sized European country but on an Asian scale it ranks as small, even smaller than Malaysia (24 million) (Table 1.1).

In economic size Australia ranks surprisingly highly. By the conventional measure of GDP, in 2003 Australia stood thirteenth after the United States, Japan, Germany, Britain, France, Italy, China, Canada, Spain, Mexico, Korea and India (World Bank, 2005). If adjustment were made for purchasing power parity, inclusion of Brazil, Russia and Indonesia would push its ranking down to sixteenth. Nevertheless, the comparison may be better demonstrated using an exponential scale. Australia's economy is about one-twentieth the size of the United States and one-tenth the size of China, but dwarfs the world's numerous microconomies. Overall Australia may best be judged a middle-sized economy.

As a long-standing member of the Organisation for Economic Co-operation and Development (OECD), Australia is classified as a developed country. In terms of the standard measure of GDP per capita, in 2003 it ranked well below the richest European countries but only marginally below Ireland, the Netherlands and Belgium and well above Spain and Portugal and all the eastern European countries.

Within its own Asian region, Australia stands in elite company. Though well behind Japan, Australia's GDP per capita was almost the same as Singapore and well above fellow OECD member, Korea.

The feature that makes Australia almost unique among OECD countries is its remoteness: apart from New Zealand it is the only member in the southern hemisphere. From the main ports of Sydney and Melbourne it is 12,000 nautical miles by sea to northern Europe and about 10,000 miles to New York. By air, northern Europe or the United States are more than 24 hours flying time. Australia lies immediately adjacent to Southeast Asia, a region which has grown rapidly in recent years but, with the notable exception of Singapore, is still well behind OECD levels of development and income per capita. Australia's immediate neighbour, Indonesia, is by population the fourth largest country in the world but still one of the poorest.

Table 1.1: Nations ranked by economic size: GDP, population and GDP per capita (USD)

	GDP 2003 ($b)	Population 2002 (m.)	GDP p.c. (2000 $)
Canada	857	31	24,200
Spain	839	41	14,700
Mexico	639	196	5,800
Korea	608	48	12,200
India	601	1049	511
AUSTRALIA	**522**	**20**	**21,700**
Netherlands	511	16	23,000
Switzerland	320	7	33,800
Belgium	302	10	22,500
Sweden	253	9	28,000
Austria	250	8	24,200
Norway	221	5	38,300
Denmark	212	5	30,300
Poland	210	38	4,600
South Africa	165	45	3,200
Finland	162	5	24,200
Ireland	154	4	24,200
Portugal	148	10	10,300
Malaysia	104	24	4,000
Singapore	92	4	22,200
Czech	90	10	5,900
New Zealand	80	4	14,500
Chile	72	16	5,200

Source: World Bank Development Indicators 2003

Table 1.2: Nations ranked by GDP per capita with population and GDP

	GDP p.c. (2000 $)	Population 2002 (m.)	GDP 2003 ($b)
Norway	38,300	5	221
Japan	38,200	128	4300
Switzerland	33,800	7	320
Denmark	30,300	5	212
Sweden	28,000	9	253
Canada	24,200	31	857
Austria	24,200	8	250
Finland	24,200	5	162
Ireland	24,200	4	154
Netherlands	23,000	16	511
Belgium	22,500	10	302
Singapore	22,200	4	92
AUSTRALIA	**21,700**	**20**	**522**
Spain	14,700	41	839
New Zealand	14,500	4	80
Korea	12,200	48	608
Portugal	10,300	10	148
Czech	5,900	10	90
Mexico	5,800	196	639
Chile	5,200	16	72
Poland	4,600	38	210
Malaysia	4,000	24	104
South Africa	3,200	45	165

Source: World Bank Development Indicators 2003

The economies of the South Pacific economies, even Papua New Guinea, are miniscule. The prosperous northeast Asian countries of Japan and Korea along with the booming Chinese economy are 4 to 5 thousand miles away by sea or about ten hours by air.

All this has enormous implications for logistics and international business. Australia is not a way-port to anywhere else. One does not pass through Australia en route to anywhere else, except perhaps New Zealand, for beyond lie only the icy wastes of Antarctica and a lot of penguins. Australia is thus a great terminus of world trade and migration. Australia's involvement in world trade is therefore very different from other OECD countries of similar income per capita because it cannot trade across close neighbouring borders. Goods and people have to move across times and distances of more than transatlantic scale to reach other centres of the world economy. There is no European Union, no North American Free Trade Agreement (NAFTA). Australia has recently signed free trade agreements with the United States, Thailand and Singapore but its only close economic integration is with New Zealand, a micro-economy of only 4 million people or about the same size as Sydney, its largest city.

This unusual combination of vast land area, low density of population, high income per capita and extreme remoteness suggests that Australia is not representative of other small- to medium-sized economies. Australia is interesting not because it is typical but because it is atypical. From an international business perspective, it shares most of the features of a medium-ranking OECD economy but within an odd context. This experience may highlight some important features of the international business environment.

Australian experience may be of particular interest for four specific reasons. First, it is an OECD economy which enjoys all the advantages of being culturally part of the Anglo-American mainstream. Secondly, however, Australia lies at an enormous distance from the main centres of the world economy. By location it is on the periphery of the world economy, along with most of Asia, Central and Latin America, Africa and the rest of Oceania.

Thirdly, Australia shares with many developing or third-world economies a dependence upon commodity exports, a fact reflected in Australia's membership of the Cairns Group lobbying in the World Trade Organization (WTO) for the liberalisation of agricultural trade. As a commodity exporter, Australia has struggled to maintain its value share of world trade, which has fallen from two per cent in 1950 to 1.5 per cent in the mid-1960s and just one per cent in 2000 (UN, 2003). In 2003 exports of goods and services accounted for 19.5 per cent of GDP, a modest figure among OECD members though higher than Japan (12 per cent) and the United States (9.5 per cent) (OECD, 2005).

Fourthly, Australia has displayed some of the characteristics of a transitional economy, not in terms of regime change, by which the term is often loosely associated, but certainly in terms of a major shift in policy regime. In the 1980s this was identified as the shift from being an inward-looking to an outward-looking economy. The reorientation of Australian business also dates from this time.

Australia is therefore a curious case of an English-speaking OECD country at a great distance from the main centres of the world economy and with features of economic structure and policy regime that are usually associated with developing or transitional economies. In terms of FDI, Australia has long stood out as a host country, not as a source of outward FDI (Chapter 2). Several Australians have recently risen to become CEOs of leading American multinationals including Ford (Jacques Nasser, 1999-2001), Coca Cola (Douglas Daft, 2000-04) and McDonalds (Charlie Bell, 2004-04). Yet few Australian firms or even Australian brands enjoy international recognition. Is this an anomaly or a matter of scale, location and timing?

This book focuses upon Australia's mixed success in spawning its own multinationals. The reason is certainly not that Australia lacks large firms: Australia is represented by 37 firms in Forbes' list of the 2000 largest foreign companies compared with 67 for Canada, which is consistent with the relative sizes of the two economies (Forbes, 2005). Nevertheless, these large firms are not necessarily multinationals. Australia counts two non-financial transnational corporations (TNCs) in UNCTAD's ranking of the top 100 in 2002, namely media firm News Corporation (since 2004 relocated to the United States) and mining firm BHP Billiton, compared with four firms for Canada (UNCTAD, 2004: Annex A.I.4). However, by UNCTAD's performance index based on outward stock, in 2001-03 Australia ranked bottom at twentieth out of the top 20 economies, behind Canada (12), Malaysia (15) and Portugal (19) (UNCTAD, 2004: Annex A.I.9). Such figures are only indicative but they suggest a mixed performance. In outward FDI Australia seems to be punching below its economic weight.

The evidence that Australian firms have found it difficult to mature into multinationals/transnationals suggests that there may be some lessons for other developing or transitional economies with fewer advantages than Australia. To what extent are economies and firms at a distance from Europe, North America or northeast Asia able to transcend their disadvantage of location, not least in terms of information asymmetries? In this regard the Australian experience may be quite informative for other small- to medium-size economies in South America, Africa, the Middle East or Southeast Asia.

RECENT INTERNATIONALISATION IN HISTORICAL PERSPECTIVE

The internationalisation of Australian firms which we study in this book is a process that can reasonably be said to have begun in the 1980s. Some Australian firms did venture offshore in earlier decades but these cases, such as Burns Philp (Chapter 12), Nicholas Aspro and Kiwi (Chapter 13), are few and now little more than historical curiosities. For all practical purposes, Australian business has become outward looking only in recent times. Nevertheless, as Douglass North put it so succinctly, 'history matters'. It would be unwise to take the historical discontinuity of the 1980s as a starting point without some overview of the conditions that gave rise to that discontinuity. Why were Australian firms so reluctant or perhaps just uninterested to invest offshore before the 1980s? Was it primarily policy obstacles or market structures and business environment? And what did this isolation imply for the learning they would have to undertake when they did venture offshore? The answers turn out to be quite complex and reveal a twentieth-century experience of nationalism and protectionism that displays some of the features of a transitional economy.

Yet an even longer-term perspective reveals the important fact that Australian business was actually 'born global'. There were firms registered in Britain that did business in Australia, and there were firms registered in the self-governing Australian colonies under British law that had London offices and agents. Some principals did both at the same time, more or less according to convenience. By current practice, the former would now be regarded as inward FDI, the latter as outward FDI. In fact these firms were trans-national or, perhaps more meaningfully, empire firms. This identity was manifested through business networks. Leading business figures in the colonies had the advantage of being part of a global network, mediated through London, that gave access to capital, information and power. An important part of this empire network originated in Scotland (see also Chapter 8). Various authors have commented on the effectiveness of this network, in which informal understandings served as the basis for market arrangements.

The self-identification of even the local principals was therefore not so much Australian as British. This reflects the fact that before 1901 the self-governing colonies of Australia were proud members of the far-flung British Empire. Currency was the British pound and Imperial sovereigns, silver and copper coin were in circulation. The majority of the rapidly growing population had been born in the United Kingdom and, except for Irish Catholics, regarded themselves as indelibly British. Young Australians spilt blood for the Empire in two world wars and other localised conflicts ranging from Asia to Africa. Shipping and trade both ways flowed overwhelmingly between Australia and the United Kingdom. As late as the 1970s many older leaders of Australian business still moved comfortably in British circles, rather like successful foreign cousins.

What we observe at the end of the nineteenth century is colonial capital, a hybrid that was not quite foreign and not quite local. FDI from the mother country/metropole sometimes became localised, while colonial capital sometimes expatriated itself to the metropole. Families straddled the categories of foreign and colonial capital. Fortune seekers were often the second, third or fourth sons who, according to the old phrase, made their way to the colonies to seek their fortune. If successful, merchant, shipping or mining businesses were in time incorporated locally under British law and, especially in the case of mining companies, might float shares on local stock exchanges. Although local firms might be regarded derisively as colonial capital, being colonial did not of itself make a firm less international. Certainly distance from the London capital market was a disadvantage, necessitating London firms, offices and/or agents. However, local ports could often be a good basis for regional expansion, whether from Sydney, Melbourne, Bombay, Calcutta, Singapore, Hong Kong or Shanghai. There was no substantial legal or regulatory distinction between companies registered locally or those registered in London. Such colonial capital was not unique to Australia but a feature of any part of the British Empire, or for that matter the French, Dutch or American empires.

If nineteenth-century colonial firms were not 'Australian' in any substantive sense, by what process(es) did they become Australian? The two main aspects were the achievement of political sovereignty and economic de-internationalisation. Sovereignty determined the key date of 1901, the year of Federation, when the six self-governing colonies of Australia comprising the continent and the southern island of Tasmania came together to form a new nation, the Commonwealth of Australia, with the status of a dominion within the British Empire. Australian nationhood therefore follows a generation after the former British colonies of Canada (1867) and more than a century after the United States of America (1776). Moreover, even in 1901 nationhood was weak and qualified. For example, until World War II Australia did not maintain foreign embassies or conduct its own defence policy.

It follows that before 1901 there was also no semblance of a national economy. The various colonies held to different immigration and trade regimes. New South Wales was an open economy of free trade, the more prosperous Victoria committed to protectionism. Queensland allowed indentured labour migration from the South Pacific, which other states refused. There were customs barriers between the states and not even a common rail gauge. Passengers and freight moved by sea as though each state was a separate island, which to all intents and purposes it was, even after the 1880s when incompatible rail gauges met at the NSW, Victorian, South Australian and Queensland borders (Blainey, 1968). The concentration of population in cities and towns around the narrow coastline – Australian historian Geoffrey Blainey's 'limpet ports' – reinforced this pattern. The massive late nineteenth-century investment in railways was to move passengers and freight to and from coastal ports, not across colonial borders.

De-internationalisation was a consequence of the peculiar compact by which the self-governing colonies came together in the Commonwealth. Because the former colonies wished as constituent states to retain as much of their powers as possible, they agreed to a weak federation with powers only over currency, defence, immigration, customs and lighthouses. Defence, immigration and customs formed a policy triangle. Defence and immigration powers involved strict controls over non-white immigration to enforce what became known as the White Australia policy; customs powers were the basis not only of revenue but also of tariff protection for local manufacturing to underpin local employment and high wages. The Australian economy was therefore unified by a common currency and enclosed by the high walls of immigration restrictions and both tariff and non-tariff barriers to trade.

Federation therefore marked a decisive shift in the trade regime. Although Australia's prosperity had rested on the export of commodities, especially minerals (gold, silver, copper) and wool, the Australian economy now began to industrialise in a small domestic economy behind a tariff wall, a development path later followed by many other primary producing countries. This trade and policy regime did not suddenly wrench Australia away from the international economy as was later the case after World War II with many newly independent countries in Asia and Africa. In fact the export trades of wool, minerals supplemented by wheat, dairy products and fruit were very little disturbed. However, the market incentives for Australian firms or, for that matter, foreign investors, were not to develop new export markets and offshore ventures but to invest in the profitable domestic market with made-to-order tariffs and cosy cartel arrangements. Even had they the will to do so, Australian manufacturers could hardly compete because of the uncompetitive cost structures that flowed from high labour costs and inefficient scale. By the 1950s the inward-looking business environment had bred a new generation of business leaders who had lost much of their predecessors' entrepreneurial drive and, except perhaps in the 'mother country' of Britain and neighbouring New Zealand, had no cultural aptitude for offshore operations.

The process by which Australian capital became de-internationalised was therefore a mid-twentieth-century phenomenon. It was distinctive but not unique, for comparison might be drawn with British colonial capital in Canada, New Zealand and South Africa. Timing was important. Although the political turning point was 1901, the 1930s depression was decisive. The collapse of commodity markets was traumatic for a nation so heavily dependent upon a narrow range of primary exports and it gave impetus to the shift towards protectionism and Empire trade, impetus that was reinforced by

World War II and subsequent Keynesian full-employment policies which accompanied the postwar manufacturing boom. Here there are also some parallels with South American countries such as Argentina and Chile that switched in the 1930s from open to protectionist trade regimes and import substitution.

Australia's partial de-internationalisation was nevertheless of a different order from that experienced by those countries across Asia which received their independence after 1945. First, in most of these later cases independence was contested, which gave rise to nationalist and ethnic hostility towards 'white' colonial capital. Secondly, there was no smooth political transition. Consequent political turmoil badly damaged the business environment and discouraged new foreign capital inflow. Thirdly, these economies were mostly much smaller and enjoyed much slower economic growth through the 1950s and 1960s, so that the benefits of import substitution were so much less. Australia escaped most of these problems and from 1940 to 1974 enjoyed what Maddock and McLean (1987) refer to as the 'long boom' with a doubling of income per capita. In the 1940s the manufacturing share of GDP surpassed that of agriculture and mining together and reached a peak of 28 per cent in the 1950s (Maddock and McLean, 1987: 19).

Australia's economic tendency to become more inward looking was nevertheless moderated by far-reaching social changes. Australia's population growth had always relied heavily upon migration but after 1945 this program was broadened from the traditional source of the United Kingdom to embrace the whole of Europe. An initial influx of displaced persons was followed by large-scale migration from war-torn northwestern Europe. The migrant pool was soon widened to include southern Europe, especially Italy and Greece. Australia gradually took on the character of a multicultural society as immigration broadened to Asia, Latin America and Africa through a mixture of refugee, family reunion and skilled migrant programs. The rest of the world had come to reside in Australia. This foreign presence was augmented through inward FDI. Although this traditionally British inflow was now dominated by American capital, among the thousands of foreign firms were many other multinationals from Europe and Japan and later from elsewhere in East Asia (Chapter 2). These inflows of labour and capital underpinned the economic boom but also sowed seeds for later reorientation towards the world economy.

By the 1970s, however, the growth momentum had been lost. Import substitution had reached its limits and Australia found itself stagnating with a fragmented, high-cost manufacturing sector with very little export potential. The resources boom of the 1970s was a boon to exports but wage-price pressures made the manufacturing and service sector even more uncompetitive. Economists recognised that the only way forward was to dismantle the tariff wall, however painful that might be. As explained in more detail in Chapter 2, the Hawke-Keating governments of 1983-96 took on this challenge. Australia was in no sense a pioneer in opening up its protected economy, for similar processes were occurring in Europe and North America, but Australia reduced its protection unilaterally. This gave Australian business new freedom and incentive to pursue international business. The question was whether firms had the capabilities and the inclination (see Chapter 2). Most of them would face a steep learning curve.

STRUCTURE OF THE BOOK

Our approach may best be summarised as an eclectic blend of international business and strategic management theory informed by business history. International business is a fairly new body of theory that is grounded in models of the business firm as they inform its conduct and performance. It has particular relevance to the multinational firm and is a powerful means of explaining performance and outcomes in relation to both home country and host country environments. The interplay between the business environment and the firm is nicely analysed in terms of the framework developed by Rugman and Verbeke (1990), which distinguishes between country-specific advantages and firm-specific advantages (Chapter 2).

Strategic management takes a business policy perspective on the firm but in an increasingly rigorous way. We draw heavily on what is known as the 'resource-based view of the firm' for its insights into how firms mobilise resources and bundle them into capabilities giving rise to unique core competencies as the basis for sustainable competitive advantage. Resources are not only physical ones but also those associated with human capital, including tacit knowledge. Decision-making occurs within a broad environment and, after Michael Porter (1987), takes explicit account of competitive rivalry in the industry. Corporate-level strategy includes growth through vertical integration, diversification or geographic expansion. A critical issue is therefore how successful firms are in developing core competencies and leveraging from them to implement a viable strategy.

Business history elucidates the evolution of industries and the different paths taken by firms within them in the light of the changing business environment. In terms of strategic management, the notion of path dependency is taken up by Bartlett and Ghoshal's (1989) concept of 'administrative heritage'. Hence it is possible both to identify common patterns and to explain considerable diversity in firms' strategy and performance.

The book provides a cross-sectional and longitudinal study of the internationalisation experiences of Australian firms in three dimensions. Part I consists of overview and survey chapters that place the experience of Australian firms in historical and comparative perspective. Chapter 2 (Merrett) analyses trends in inward and outward FDI and applies the Rugman and Verbeke (1990) framework of country-specific and firm-specific advantages to analyse the impact of the changing policy regime. Chapter 3 (Zalan and Lewis) focuses on the administrative heritage of Australian firms from a management and strategy perspective. Chapter 4 (Zalan) then charts the differing experiences of industries and firms against various criteria for success or failure in international ventures. Chapters 5 (Walters) and 6 (Harzing and Noorderhaven) provide a cross-check on the business environment and performance of Australian firms by examining the experience of foreign firms investing in Australia and of American firms in particular.

Part II consists of a series of industry studies that examine the interplay between the home markets and policy environment from which investing firms originate and the host countries in which they choose to expand their business. It allows more detailed consideration of why firms in some industries such as retail, wine and professional services have been more successful than others such as financial services and shipping. To what extent have large and or innovative firms transformed their domestic industries to make them globally competitive? Or has it been smaller firms that have led innovation and expansion overseas?

Part III foreshortens the lens to the experience of specific firms and briefly identifies the elements of administrative heritage and strategy that have been the key to success or failure. Inevitably these experiences reveal a great deal of variation but certain elements can be distilled to suggest why Australian firms have struggled to establish themselves as multinationals, notwithstanding some outstanding successes. A brief conclusion suggests what can be learned and the implications for research and the prospects for firms in other small economies.

2. Australian Multinationals in Historical Perspective: 'Do you come from a land down under?'

David Merrett

An iconic Australian pop song[1] released in 1981 makes a play of the nationality of its vocalist, a young backpacker on the hippie trail who is immediately recognisable anywhere in the world. 'Do you come from a land down under?' is the question asked of him in all corners of the world. The Australian brand then revolved around a 'land of plenty', a 'vegemite sandwich', a place where 'women glow' and men drink too much beer. Australian men and women had gained international prominence in sports as diverse as tennis, squash, surfing, hockey, swimming, athletics, cricket and rugby. In contrast, its corporations and their brands were still little known on the world stage. Unlike the much travelled young songster, exploring the world in his 'fried-out [VW] combie [van]', few firms had yet made their mark abroad as multinationals (UNCTAD, various dates).[2] In this respect, Australia lagged behind other small OECD economies (Merrett, 2002a). Nevertheless, between 1980 and 2000 there was a dramatic increase in the value of the outward stock of foreign direct investment (FDI) by Australian firms; the total number of firms operating as multinationals did not rise but the composition of the group changed markedly. Did this enable Australian firms to catch up in the globalisation stakes?

At first sight, Australian firms were well placed to take advantage of the new opportunities presenting themselves in both the developed and developing economies, particularly those in the Asian region. Australia was securely placed in the developed economies club, enjoying one of the world's highest per capita incomes. Its firms had access to a skilled labour force, a sophisticated capital market and first-world infrastructure. In the decades after World War II there was slow and incomplete revolution in management. Many firms took on new organisational forms, began increasingly to seek the advice of US management consultants, overcame the old prejudice against hiring graduates and MBAs and adopted more sophisticated strategies, particularly diversification (Chenhall, 1979; Capon et al., 1987; Dunphy and Stace, 1990; Deveson, 1997; Wright, 2000). Leading industries, particularly mining and energy, manufacturing and financial services, attracted substantial inward FDI (Department of Trade and Industry, 1971; Department of Treasury, 1972; Brash, 1966; Australia-Japan Economic Institute, 1992; Merrett, 2002b). As a consequence, foreign firms were prominent in many industries and Australian firms could look to their subsidiaries with established capabilities to 'manage across borders' (Bartlett and Ghoshal, 1989). The presence of these foreign firms might also have been expected to provide positive spillovers to local firms, through technology transfer to local suppliers for instance, enabling the latter to develop stronger ownership advantages to be taken abroad.

In the 1980s and 1990s, many of Australia's largest firms made foreign direct investments, often for the first time. This chapter identifies the population of firms that were multinationals before 1980, and the different group that became multinationals thereafter, or those existing multinationals whose scale of outward investment increased significantly. A number of questions need to be considered in the light of this data. Why had Australian firms, particularly those in manufacturing, traditionally been reluctant to become multinationals before the 1980s? Much of the explanation for this phenomenon is to be found in a combination of Australia's comparative advantage in resource-intensive industries and government policies which shielded manufacturing from import competition. To what extent did Australian domiciled firms keep pace with the global upsurge in outward FDI flows in the 1980s and 1990s? What factors helped or hindered Australian firms in becoming multinationals and then operating successfully? A radical shift in government policy away from protection and intervention in the 1980s towards promoting competition provided both a stimulus and increased capacity to engage in outward FDI. Moreover, through trial and error many firms built the skill sets needed to operate effectively in foreign markets. However, the small scale of the economy and its geographic isolation remained a deterrent.

AUSTRALIAN MULTINATIONALS BEFORE 1980

Outward foreign direct investment from Australia is not a recent phenomenon. Australian firms have ventured abroad as multinationals since the nineteenth century. Banks, insurance companies, wholesale merchants, meat packers, shipping firms, a pastoral finance company, tin and gold miners and planters of tropical products such as sugar and rubber all operated offshore before World War I (Merrett, 2002a). The rapid increase in the importance of manufacturing within the Australian economy from the 1920s onwards, a consequence of trade protection, resulted in a small number of the burgeoning population of manufacturing firms becoming multinationals before 1980. For instance, by the middle of the 1960s, 99 of the country's 500 largest manufacturers had operations overseas (Block, 1967). By way of comparison, there were 872 manufacturing firms in Australian with foreign owned equity at that time (Department of Trade and Industry, 1971). Banks and insurance companies had maintained their traditional operations outside Australia, primarily in the City of London, New Zealand, Papua New Guinea (PNG) and Fiji. Twenty-six firms from the financial services industry were multinationals in the mid-1960s plus another 23 firms from a miscellany of service industries (Block, 1967).

The existence of these early Australian multinationals raises the question of whether outward FDI had been an important conduit between the Australian economy and international markets up to the 1970s. The available evidence suggests that it was not. Many of the first generation multinationals in tin mining, rubber, copra and sugar plantations, shipping and meat packing had divested their overseas operations or been acquired by other foreign firms (Merrett, 2002a). H.V. McKay, the agricultural implement manufacturer, merged with the Canadian firm, Massey Harris, in 1930, becoming H.V. McKay Massey Harris Pty Ltd. Just prior to the amalgamation H.V. McKay opened a subsidiary in Canada in 1930, the Sunshine Waterloo Company, which it continued to operate until the McKay's interest in the Australian firm was acquired by Massey-Ferguson in 1954 (Neufeld, 1969; McKay, 1974). Colonial Sugar Refinery's (hereafter CSR) Fijian operations, run by its subsidiary South Pacific Sugar Mills, were sold to the newly independent government of that country in 1973 (Moynagh, 1981). The writing was also on the wall for two of Australia's oldest and most successful multinationals, Nicholas Aspro and Kiwi International, manufacturers of global brands 'Aspro' and 'Kiwi' shoe polish (Smith & Barrie, 1976; Morgan, 1959; Kiwi, 1966). They sought refuge in a defensive merger in 1981 before falling into the clutches of the United States packaged goods giant, Sara Lee, in 1984.

The importance of overseas operations to the businesses of nearly all of the survivors and new multinationals was marginal. However, before 1987 Australian firms were not required to report the geographic distribution of their assets or sales. In the absence of proper measures of 'transnationality'[3] reliance must be placed in a number of very partial indicators. Island trading and shipping firms W.R. Carpenter and Burns Philp probably had the majority of their assets offshore in the late 1930s (Buckley and Klugman, 1983: 326-8). Banks and life-office firms, which reported to national regulatory bodies (so making it possible to estimate the disposition of their assets) had around a quarter of their assets offshore in the 1960s and 1970s, roughly in line with their numbers throughout the twentieth century (Merrett,

2002b). The average commitment of assets overseas by firms in the non-financial sector, particularly manufacturing, was probably much lower. There were outliers of course. The stock broking company, Ian Potter and Co., estimated in 1972 that over 80 per cent of Nicholas International's business was now conducted outside Australia. By comparison, the sugar refiner CSR had roughly 11 per cent of its assets[4] in Fiji and New Zealand in 1955 (Lowndes, 1956: 474-5). It is highly unlikely that any other manufacturing firm would have come anywhere near this modest figure.

Table 2.1: Australian multinational manufacturing firms, ca. 1965

Industry	Firms as MNE	Firms in industry	Export % turnover	Top 4 share sales	Offshore Distribution only	>1 host country
Food	22	4118	9.9	12	5	4
Textiles	3	797	12.2	24	0	1
Clothing	2	3227	0.7	11	0	0
Wood	0	5551	1.0	7	0	0
Paper	5	3131	1.1	20	4	2
Chemicals	12	980	4.8	27	3	4
Non-metallic	7	1311	2.7	25	1	3
Basic metals	3	508	19.3	71	0	1
Fabricated metals	10	453	2.4	12	2	4
Transport equipment	6	1316	3.8	52	0	2
Other machinery	24	4277	4.0	9	6	5
Misc	5	2545	3.7	28	2	1
Total	99	32291	6.5	10	23	27

Sources: Columns 1, 5-6: Block (1967: 186-263); Columns 2-4: Industry Assistance Commission (1974a: Table 4.1.2., 76-84)

Table 2.1 presents data about Australian manufacturing in the mid-1960s. An initial observation is that less than one per cent of the 32,000 firms had undertaken FDI. Nearly three-quarters of those 99 firms that were multinationals were concentrated in just four industry groups, namely food, beverages and tobacco; chemicals, petroleum and coal; fabricated metals; and the miscellaneous category. These were industries in which large-scale firms dominated in all developed economies by virtue of the exploitation of economies of scale and scope and the protection offered by patents and brands (Chandler, 1990; Chandler, Amatori and Hikino, 1997). Table 2.1

(column 4) also indicates high levels of seller concentration within industries even at a two-digit ANZSIC level, implying a degree of monopoly power. More detailed classifications within industries reveal much higher levels of concentration at the three and four-digit levels (Karmel and Brunt, 1962). Another defining characteristic of Australian manufacturing at this time was its concentration on the domestic market. Export markets were of little importance in aggregate. The basic metals and food beverage and tobacco industries were the stand-out performers. The lack of importance of exporting notwithstanding, a quarter of the firms which had undertaken FDI by 1965 had done so in distribution assets alone. The geographic scope of outward FDI was narrow in the extreme. It was concentrated almost exclusively in New Zealand, PNG, Fiji, and the United Kingdom (UK). Furthermore, only 27 of these 99 firms had undertaken FDI in more than one country.

The picture that emerges from the above data is corroborated by information provided by the Director of Industrial Services in the Department of Trade and Industry in 1965. The composition of his list of 35 companies, 31 of which were manufacturing firms, is instructive. The Director wrote that they had been chosen because these firms were ‘known to be active in overseas countries’ and while the list was by ‘no means exhaustive…it probably covers the more important developments that have taken place in this regard over recent years’ (quoted in Fitzpatrick and Wheelwright, 1965: 64-7). However, a number of the named firms had been long established internationally. CSR had operated in Fiji since the 1870s. Automatic Totalisators and Henry Jones IXL had both ventured abroad before World War I. The contingent that went abroad between the wars of Kiwi Polish, Nicholas Aspro, Hume Industries, ACI [formerly Australian Glass Manufacturers], James Hardie, Davis Gelatine and AWA were still prominent (Merrett, 2002a; Brown, 1991; Pratt, 1934: 132-3). However, it is not clear that any of these firms had significantly expanded the geographic range or extent of their investments after their initial foray overseas. The remainder, including firms in concrete products, earthmoving equipment and building materials, were small- and medium-sized enterprises that had gone abroad for the first time after World War II.

These data of Australian multinationals capture outward FDI by both Australian firms and subsidiaries of foreign firms. The limited information available about the nationality of Australian multinationals suggests that they were predominantly Australian-domiciled firms. For instance, five of the seven trading banks with branches in countries outside Australia in 1967 were local, as were all of the 19 insurance companies with foreign branches, 36 of the 42 firms that undertook FDI in plantations, resources and non-financial services, and 63 of the 95 manufacturers that had operations overseas (Block, 1967). Many foreign subsidiaries were denied a mandate by their parents to undertake FDI outside Australia (DFAT, 1994).

A more comprehensive picture of Australian multinationals can been drawn from the late 1970s because of changes in the government's collection of data relating to outward FDI. It had begun collecting data on investments being made overseas by Australian firms in 1947-48, identifying the country of destination (ABS, Catalogue 5305.0, various). The data were incomplete before 1954-55 as they relied on a survey of firms whose participation was voluntary. While the extent of the coverage improved from 1955-56 with compulsory participation, serious omissions remained. Most importantly, industry specific data were not collected before 1981-82, with the series being provided retrospectively back to 1976-77. The definition of flows and stock of outward FDI were changed on a number of occasions with major revisions in the early 1980s, particularly lowering the threshold of equity held in a foreign firm to be recorded as FDI from 25 to ten per cent, valuing equity in subsidiaries at market rather than book value, and converting the host country values back into Australian dollars at balance date, all of which make comparisons with earlier years problematic.[5]

Table 2.2: Australian multinationals by geographic spread, 1981-82

Country Host	Firms No.	Subsidiaries No.	Region share of subs %	Stock FDI $m	Region share of stock FDI, %	FDI per subsidiary $m
Americas	151	174	12.6	661	25.5	3.80
Europe	131	180	13.1	502	19.4	2.79
Africa	21	27	2.0	17	0.7	0.63
Asia	277	409	29.7	413	16.0	1.01
Pacific	468	586	42.6	997	38.5	1.70
Unspecified	1	-	-	-	-	-
Total	604	1377	100.0	2589	100.0	1.88

Sources: BIE (1984), Tables A2.2.1, A2.2.2 and A2.2.3, 84-86

By 1981-82 there were 604 multinationals operating from Australia with 1377 subsidiaries in many countries (Table 2.2). Close examination of the columns show that firms had subsidiaries in many countries and sometimes more than one subsidiary within a single host country. Most of the multinationals had subsidiaries in Asia and the Pacific, 277 and 468 respectively, compared to 151 and 131 in the Americas and Europe. There is a marked disparity between the number of subsidiaries and the value of the stock between the developed economies, represented here by the Americas and Europe, and the developing economies. Only a quarter of the subsidiaries operated in host economies in the Americas and Europe but 45 per cent of the value of the outward stock was deployed there. Asia and the Pacific hosts attracted 72 per cent of the subsidiaries but held only 54 per cent of the stock. It is likely that accumulation of assets by banks accounts for much of the above average value of FDI per subsidiary in the Americas and Europe (Merrett, 2002b).

AUSTRALIAN MULTINATIONALS, 1980-2000

Macro Measures

The scale and character of outward FDI flows from Australia changed dramatically through the 1980s and 1990s (Table 2.3). What is surprising is the static number of multinationals from Australia, oscillating between 600 and 740. This is in sharp contrast with the rest of the world, where the number of multinationals and their affiliates rose strongly in the 1990s (UNCTAD, 2004: Annex table A.1.2). The absolute growth in nominal values of the stock of Australian outward FDI over the last quarter of century is impressive, a rise from a little over $2 billion in 1980 to $117 billion in 2003. Comparison of those values with Australian GDP, shown in the third row, highlights the magnitude of the accumulation of assets offshore. In 1980 the stock of outward FDI was less than two per cent of Australia's GDP, a decade later it had risen to nearly ten per cent, another decade later the ratio was above a quarter. Two other measures indicate that Australia's performance was indeed unusual. First, UNCTAD's *World Investment Report* provides data on the ratio of outward stock of FDI to GDP of a group of developed economies, including Australia (UNCTAD, 2004: Annex table B.6). Australia's ratio was initially well below the average for developed countries, 1.4 per cent compared to 6.2 per cent. However, it caught up by 1990 and by 2000 had surpassed the average. Second, Australia's share of the world stock of outward FDI increased significantly, more than quadrupling between 1980 and 1990. It continued to grow until 1995, before falling back to 2003 levels.

The data on outward stock of FDI in Table 2.3 suggest that the engagement of Australian firms with the rest of the world was altering in dramatic fashion. Foreign firms had invested in Australia throughout its history. Many of its key industries were dominated by foreign-owned or controlled entities. The stock of inward FDI grew rapidly as a percentage of GDP from 1980 up to 2003, from eight per cent to more than 33 per cent. However, the stock of outward FDI as a percentage of GDP grew much faster up until 2000, rising from less than two per cent to more than 25 per cent. For the first time in its history Australia had achieved rough equality in its inflows and outflows of FDI.

Table 2.3: Australian multinationals and stock of FDI, 1980-2003

	1980	1990	2000	2003
Number of MNE	604	742	610	641
Outward stock	$2.3b	$30.5b	$89.7b	$117.1b
% AUS GDP	1.4	9.8	26.1	23.0
% DEV ECO	6.2	9.6	21.4	26.4
% World stock	0.40	1.74	1.65	1.43
Inward stock	$13.2b	$73.6b	$108.7b	$174.2b
% AUS GDP	7.9	23.7	28.7	34.3

Sources: Numbers of multinationals for 1980 from BIE (1984: Table 2.1, 6; 1993-94 from BIE: 1995a): Table 3.5. 35; 1998-99 from UNCTAD (2000): Table 1.4, 11-18; 2003, ABS, Catalogue 5495.0, Table 13, 21. Other data from UNCTAD (2004): Annex tables B.4.and B.6

The industry composition of outward FDI also changed in profound fashion. As shown in Table 2.4, manufacturing was the most important single category in 1980, accounting for a third of total stock. Mining followed in second place with 20 per cent. Collectively, the service sector comprised nearly a half of the total with finance and the wholesale trades being most important. By 2002, manufacturing's share had risen to 53 per cent, down from 58 per cent in 1992. Finance, having grown to nearly 33 per cent, was the other stand-out sector. Mining's share had fallen significantly to a mere five per cent. The rest of the services sector, construction, trade, transport and storage, and business activities, had all been swamped by the flow of FDI into manufacturing and financial services.

Table 2.5 shows the changing geographic destination of outward FDI. It altered significantly as Australian outward FDI flowed strongly to North America (mainly the US), and particularly to the UK. While the countries of destination might have been expected to diversify over time, in fact they consolidated. These two regions' share of the total rose from 45 per cent in 1982 to 80 per cent in 2002. The share of stock located in Asia remained roughly constant in the mid-teens through the 1980s and nearly all of the 1990s, then fell sharply after the Asian crisis. Another region to lose share was the once dominant Pacific, including New Zealand, PNG and Fiji. These close neighbours to Australia had nearly 40 per cent of the outward stock in

1982 but their share fell to 17 per cent a decade later and declined further to just 11 per cent in 2002.

Table 2.4: Outward stock of FDI by industry, 1982-2002 (%)

Industry	1982	1992	2002
Mining	20.4	7.6	4.4
Manufacturing	32.9	57.5	52.6
Construction	2.7	2.4	1.5
Trade	12.4	4.5	2.6
Transport	6.0	4.0	1.8
Finance	20.3*	20.5	31.8
Business activities	n.a.	1.2	0.9
Unspecified	5.3	2.3	6.2
	100.0	100.0	100.0

Note: *Includes property and business services

Sources: 1981: ABS, Catalogue 5305.0 (1982), Table 43, 45; 1992: UNCTAD online WID Country Profile, 2002, Australia, Table 14a

Table 2.5: Outward stock of FDI by geographic destination, 1982-2002 (%)

Region	1982	1992	2002
Americas	25.5	30.1*	51.9
European Union	19.4	31.2	28.6
Asia	16.0	16.8	3.7
Pacific	38.5	16.9	10.7
Other	0.7	5.0	5.1
Total	100.0	100.0	100.0

Note: *Omits data for Latin America and Caribbean

Sources: BIE (1984), Table A2.2.3, 86; UNCTAD (2002); WID Country Profile, Australia, Table 14a

While the bulk of the outward stock of FDI held by Australian multinationals shifted progressively towards the US and UK, the greater number of affiliates continued to be located much closer to home. Data in Table 2.2 for 1982 show that nearly 75 per cent of the affiliates were located in the Asia and Pacific regions while 55 per cent of the stock was in those host economies. By comparison, the Americas and Europe held a higher share of the stock, 45 per cent, than affiliates, 26 per cent. The average stock per affiliate was higher in the developed economies. This statement still held true 20 years later. A survey of 201 multinationals operating from Australia was undertaken in 2001 by the Productivity Commission (2002) which collected information about the geographic distribution of offshore affiliates. The results are shown in Table 2.6. Many of the reporting firms had affiliates in more than one host country. In all cases other than mining and mineral processing, the most common destination was New Zealand and Asia; between 70 and 100 per cent of the firms in manufacturing, construction, wholesale and retail trades, finance and insurance, and property and business services had affiliates in those markets. For mining and mineral processing firms, the key market was North America and 'Other', most likely Latin America. The dramatic increase in the share of outward stock held in the US and UK may have been driven by the actions of a small number of firms with large stocks of FDI.

Table 2.6: Regions of offshore operations of survey respondents, 2001 (%)

Industry	No. of MNEs	Affiliates					
		NZ	Asia	UK	Western Europe	USA	Other
Mining & processing	15	44	56	22	33	56	67
Manufacturing	56	71	71	11	14	37	23
Construction	11	71	100	29	0	14	57
Wholesale & retail trade	29	89	22	0	0	11	22
Finance & insurance	23	100	57	43	29	43	29
Property & business	32	73	73	18	9	9	18
Other	35	58	67	0	8	33	25
Total	201	71	66	14	13	31	30

Source: Productivity Commission (2002), Tables C.2 and C.14

By 2003 a more comprehensive analysis of the geographic distribution of affiliates became available with the publication of a new series by the Australian Bureau of Statistics (ABS, 2003). It estimated that there were 641 multinationals with 4,012 foreign affiliates operating in Australia, though this latter number was thought to be an over-estimate. Fifty-five per cent of these affiliates were located in three countries, the US (25 per cent), New Zealand (18 per cent) and the UK (12 per cent). Affiliates in these particular countries accounted for 55 per cent of the total value of sales of goods and 74 per cent of the sales of services. Four industry groups – manufacturing, finance and insurance, wholesale and retail trade, and property and business services – dominated both sales and employment with manufacturing being the leader in both sales (26 per cent) and employment (37 per cent).

Firm Studies

This transformation after 1980 in the level of outward FDI, the changing mix of industries and countries in which it was located was driven by a set of firms that for the most part had not hitherto undertaken outward FDI. In many cases these firms were amongst the largest in the land and operated in mature domestic markets in which they were corporate leaders (Fleming et al., 2004). For instance, Amcor, a leading manufacturer of paper and packaging materials, entered a range of markets in the late 1980s, including a number in Asia, the US, Canada and Europe (Sinclair, 1990). In 2000 Amcor divested its paper business to Paperlinx which has significantly increased its investments in international fine paper merchanting and production activities (Paperlinx, 2005). Another leading paper and packaging producer, Visy, entered the US market in 1989 before making further investments there in 1994 (Visy, 2005). Ansell, a firm specialising in healthcare barrier protection, which was acquired by Pacific Dunlop in 1969, built its first overseas plant in Malaysia in 1975. Up to and continuing past 2002, the year it resumed life as an independent company, it expanded its international operations to the point where its Australian factories were closed (Ansell, 2005). Other manufacturers of specialised medical products such as Cochlear (Cochlear, 2005), ResMed (ResMed, 2005) and CSL (CSL, 2005) have emerged more recently as successful multinationals. Orica, once part of the chemical giant ICIANZ, dates its transformation to a global company to the purchase of its UK parent's, ICI plc, global explosive business in 1998 (Orica, 2005).

In the resources industry, the mining giants, Conzinc Rio Tinto Australia (CRA) and Broken Hill Proprietary (BHP), brought their first overseas mines into operation in Bougainville in 1969 and at Ok Tedi in Papua New Guinea in 1984, respectively, after years of preparatory work (Oliver, 1973; Stott, 1992). BHP's international reach had increased dramatically in terms of both products and geographic breadth when it acquired Utah International in 1984 (Chapter 14). The company's moves offshore in the 1960s were to support exports of steel and these operations were quickly extended to the production and distribution of coated building products. Since 2002 when it was listed on the Australian Stock Exchange (ASX), BlueScope Steel, part of the steel division that was divested after the BHP Billiton merger, has made investments in new plants in a number of Asian markets (Stace, 1997; Bluescope Steel, 2005). The demand for other categories of building materials drew other firms to begin production overseas. The US rather than

Asia was a magnet for concrete and building products firms from the 1980s – first CSR and later Rinker, Boral, Monier and Pioneer Concrete, amongst others (Langdale, 1991; Korporaal, 1986b; Margo, 2000; Anon., 2000a; Murphy, 1984; Garden, 1992; King, 1999; Stace, 1997).

In the 1980s the local Coca-Cola bottler, Coca-Cola Amatil, acquired franchises in New Zealand, Fiji, PNG, Indonesia and the Philippines before expanding into central and eastern Europe, becoming one of the largest anchor bottlers in the world (Pringle, 1996). It remains an important multinational despite having divested its central European business and sold its business in the Philippines in 1998 and 2001 respectively (Chapter 16). Australia's two leading brewing groups, Foster's and Bond Brewing, both the products of mergers in the early 1980s, embarked on major overseas acquisitions in that decade (Merrett, 1998; Merrett and Whitwell, 1994; Langfield-Smith, 1991; Chapter 15).

Companies from the services industries showed a similar appetite for international expansion. The largest transport companies of the day, Brambles, Thomas National Transport – now part of the Dutch-owned TPG (Chapter 18) – and Mayne Nickless moved into Europe from the late 1970s (Langdale, 1991). The current leader in domestic logistics, Toll Holdings, has invested heavily in New Zealand since 2003 and in March 2006 expanded its reach into Asia by buying an initial 60 per cent of Singapore-based Sem[bawang]Corp Logistics (Toll, 2005, 2006). Leading construction firms Hooker, Lend Lease – which had acquired Civil & Civic that had previously made offshore investments – Jennings, Leightons and shopping centre managers Westfield also joined the exodus overseas, investing in Asia and the US (Langdale, 1991; Garden, 1992; Margo, 2000; King, 1999; Murphy, 1984; Anon., 1988; Chapter 19). News Corporation, which had a leading position in the local media, expanded offshore from the early 1960s, buying newspapers and print media in the UK before expanding into television, film and satellite and extending its geographic scope into the US and China in the 1980s (Langdale, 1991; Page, 2003; Chenoweth, 2001).

Australia's leading financial institutions made unprecedented acquisitions offshore in the 1980s. ANZ Bank acquired Grindlays Bank in 1984 and National Australian Bank acquired four small retail banks in the UK in the late 1980s, and later acquired Michigan National Bank and a mortgage originator, HomeSide Inc., in the US. Westpac also made a number of important acquisitions but in non-banking areas (Merrett, 2002b). More recent and successful newcomers as multinationals are the investment banks Macquarie Bank (Chapter 20) and its related entity, Macquarie Infrastructure Group (Macquarie, 2005) and Babcock and Brown. A number of Australia's leading insurers, Australian Mutual Provident, QBE, National Mutual and Colonial Mutual, also moved offshore in the 1980s (Langdale, 1991;

Blainey, 1999; Chapter 7). The partly privatised telecommunications corporation, Telstra, expanded its wings to operate in New Zealand and Hong Kong (Telstra, 2005: 19).

Small- and medium-size enterprises also undertook FDI in increasing numbers in the 1980s and 1990s. Accountants, architects and law firms opened offices overseas, particularly in Southeast Asia. For instance, Malleson Stephen Jaques, with offices in London, Hong Kong and Beijing, ranked the twelfth largest multinational law firm by number of lawyers in 2002 (UNCTAD, 2004: Annex table A.III.6). Australia's large mining industry spawned specialist mining exploration and service firms that came to operate globally (Alexander and Hattersley, 1981; Dun and Bradstreet, n.d.). Local firms engaged in infrastructure projects and construction, both large and small, also found work abroad (Jay, 1997; Anon., 1988). Manufacturers in industries as diverse as gaming equipment, Aristocrat (Aristocrat, 2005), and surfwear clothing, Billabong, are firms whose international operations are important. Village Roadshow, which began its business with a single drive-in movie theatre, owned movie screens in 16 countries by the late 1990s (Hubbard, 2000). Computershare runs share registries for stock exchanges around the world (Computershare, 2005).

Who made the largest investments overseas? A recent publication by the Department of Foreign Affairs and Trade (DFAT, 2002: 66-75) provides insight into the size distribution of investments made by Australian multinationals. It demonstrates that a few dozen firms dominated in terms of the value of Australia's outward stock of FDI. Moreover, the relative importance of these firms with very large offshore investments increased sharply in the 1990s. The study focuses on the top 100 firms ranked by total revenues. A sub-group of 26 firms, identified as ranking in the top 100 in terms of both assets and the number of employees, accounted for 84 per cent of Australia's total stock of outward FDI as of June 2000. ABS data quoted in the DFAT report show that in 2000 the stock held by the 25 largest investors comprised 90 per cent of the total stock (DFAT, 2002: 62). The largest five of this group would most likely have been the National Australia Bank, Australian Mutual Provident, News Corporation, ANZ Bank and Westpac. However, both NAB and AMP have divested significant international assets since that date. Moreover, News Corporation could be excluded from the list on the grounds that it is no longer an Australian-domiciled company. The nationality of a number of the largest companies, including Brambles, BHP Billiton, Rio Tinto and some of the large banks, is clouded by their dual listing on overseas stock exchanges.

How did these companies which began as multinationals in the last 25 years enter their host markets? Data published in the *World Investment Report* (UNCTAD, 2000) shows that cross border mergers and acquisitions

(M&A) were the primary form of entry, particularly into developed economies. Over the decade of the 1990s, the value of outward mergers and acquisitions by Australian firms was greater than outward flows of FDI (UNCTAD, various).[6] In the absence of any Australian statistics relating to the various types of entry mode – M&A, greenfield and joint ventures – recourse must be made to anecdotal evidence. A review of the history of international engagement of the companies listed in the above paragraphs suggests that merger and acquisition was the most common form of establishment. In financial services other than investment banking it was universal. In other industries there was some diversity. Resource firms negotiated with governments about exploration and development of major projects in which other firms often came in as partners. Firms that invested in the Asian region were more likely to have been involved in joint ventures with local partners to reduce risk in foreign business environments. Working with a local partner was mandatory in many developing countries, particularly transition economies such as China. The two dozen largest firms that held a disproportionate share of the outward stock, most of which was invested in developed economies, used merger and acquisition as their initial mode of entry and subsequent expansion in host markets.

MOTIVATIONS TO BECOME MULTINATIONALS

Why did Australian firms become multinationals? Australian firms were surveyed about this issue in the early 1980s and again in the early 2000s. Their replies provided an overwhelmingly consistent answer: access to markets (BIE, 1984: 22-3; Productivity Commission, 2002: 20-4). In both surveys, participants were asked to rank the importance of multiple factors and most firms nominated more than one. In the 1984 survey the greatest attraction, with more than a half of the total responses, was the expected growth of demand in host markets. Related influences were to overcome barriers to servicing those markets with exports such as import duties and high transport costs, or to take advantage of inducements offered by host governments. The incentive to 'use patents, know-how or expertise developed in Australia' (BIE, 1984: Table 3.1), capabilities that could give rise to what Dunning (1977) has called an ownership advantage, ranked a distant second. However, the ability to 'take advantage of lower unit costs in the host country' was an even less important consideration (BIE, 1984: Table 3.1). These conclusions were replicated by the Productivity Commission study. Access to global markets predominated over the inducement of operating in a lower cost environment (Productivity Commission, 2002: 22). The dominant attraction of new markets abroad implies that firms becoming multinationals faced less attractive growth prospects for their products and services at home.

Identifying the pull of new markets as a motive for outward FDI does not provide a full understanding of how so many Australian firms became multinationals in the last quarter of the twentieth century. I have argued elsewhere that before the policy reforms of the 1980s a host of structural conditions within the Australian economy reduced the likelihood of success of its multinationals compared to those from other small developed economies (Merrett, 2002a). The natural resource intensity of the economy gave Australia a comparative advantage in a range of commodities, wool, foodstuffs and minerals, most of which were exported in an unprocessed state. Australian producers were at the beginning of the supply chain. Only the mining companies integrated forward or undertook production in other countries. Manufacturing, whose expansion from the 1920s until the 1980s was a product of state-sponsored import substitution, was not internationally competitive. It was unable to achieve scale in a small and geographically fragmented market. Moreover, there was limited pressure on firms to seek competitive advantage through cost efficiencies and innovation as they operated in industries whose barriers to entry were raised by government regulation. Moreover, collusive behaviour among firms, particularly with respect to price fixing, was commonplace. As a consequence, few manufacturing firms had looked to foreign markets either as exporters or multinationals. Service firms, particularly in financial services and shipping, had gone abroad but tended to stay close to home. The economic reform process beginning in the 1980s coincided with a remarkable change in the strategic behaviour of Australia firms.

Country-Specific Advantages

The framework developed by Rugman and Verbeke (1990) helps disentangle the influences at work in motivating outward FDI. They distinguish between the nature and strength of country-specific advantages (CSA), which firms can enjoy, and the nature and strength of firm-specific advantages (FSA), the latter corresponding to a resource-based view of the firm (Barney, 1991). CSAs relates to the economic environment in which firms operate and FSAs to the competencies and capabilities of the individual firms. The interaction of both shapes firms' response to perceived opportunities to go abroad as multinationals and their likelihood of success.

CSAs derive predominantly from a country's resource endowments, both tangible in the form of natural resources and capital stock and intangible as represented by its stock of knowledge. The resultant country-specific advantages or disadvantages also reflect government policy, particularly in respect to investments in education, infrastructure and R&D. The efficiency with which resources are used by firms in industries in the home economy reflects the strength of industry 'diamonds' and 'clusters' that themselves contribute to CSAs (Porter, 1990, 1998).

Australia's CSAs have been altered since the 1980s in ways that strengthen the likelihood that firms will undertake outward FDI. Australian governments introduced a range of policy initiatives from the mid-1970s that increased the competitiveness of both product and factor markets. The influx of cheaper imports following the removal of high trade barriers increased competitive pressures. Deregulation of the financial system in the early 1980s stimulated price competition and innovation. The removal of exchange controls in 1983 to allow a floating exchange rate was of particular importance in facilitating the outflow of investment. A revised Trade Practices Act (1971) and (1974) brought about the end of price fixing and other forms of anti-competitive behaviours. A further structural reform in the 1980s and 1990s was the privatisation of the government-owned utilities such as rail, energy and water, communication providers, ports and other infrastructure, together with many state-owned financial services firms that brought large parts of the economy into the domain of market forces. A newly enunciated National Competition Policy extended the reach of the Trade Practices Commission, later the Australian Competition and Consumer Commission, into the operation of these previously monopolised utilities markets.

The motivation for what came to be known as 'microeconomic reform' was to make the economy more competitive and be better placed to engage in the global economy. An unintended by-product was that these same policies increased domestic competitiveness were in line with those advocated by UNCTAD and the OECD to promote outward FDI (UNCTAD, 1995: ch. 8; Brewer and Young, 1998). The list of countries with which Australia had a double-taxation agreement lengthened dramatically after 1969. Before agreements with Singapore and Japan in that year, Australia had agreements only with the UK (1946), the US (1953) and Canada (1957). Another 35 agreements were signed up to 2000, modelled on the OECD protocols of 1977 and 1992 (CCH Australia, 1982+).

The upsurge in outward FDI from Australia was in part a response to reductions by host governments in both developing and developed economies to many of the barriers which had been erected to limit inward FDI. This policy shift reflected the growing awareness, particularly amongst developing economies, of links between inward FDI, trade and growth (Jones, 2005a). An increasing number of national governments liberalised their policies towards inward FDI from the 1960s, with a marked increase in the 1990s (UNCTAD, 2000: 6-7). This policy shift mirrored multilateral agreements amongst the OECD group of countries, beginning with the Code of Liberalization of Capital Movements in 1961. In essence, it became easier for foreign firms to enter host markets, their ability to repatriate profits was guaranteed and they were treated no less favourably than local firms (Brewer and Young, 1998). However, many problems remained to face new arrivals in foreign jurisdictions. So much so that in 1979 the Law Council of Australia's Trade Law Committee created a document to 'identify aspects of the law on which information may be needed by an Australian lawyer in order to advise clients interested in investing overseas' (Trade Law Committee, 1979).

In general, however, the Australian government did not provide the type or level of support given by many other countries to promote outward FDI. Before World War II there was a lack of political will and administrative apparatus to promote exports, a key way of learning about opportunities in foreign markets (Tweedie, 1994). The situation improved subsequently, although the motivation of the government was primarily to correct the chronic deficit in the balance of trade (Deane, 1963; Crawford, 1968: 526-31). Eventually exporters, particularly manufacturers, were offered tax concessions, and specialist credit and insurance facilities (Pinkstone, 1992), palliative measures to offset the burden of tariff protection. However, studies of the impact of these programs at best damn them with faint praise (Report of the Committee for Review of Export Market Development Assistance, 1989). Those firms that did export struggled to make a success of it. One study in 1971 lamented the long list of the 'most common misconceptions which Australian firms have about exporting' and 'the most common complaints importers make about Australian export procedures and products' (Carew and Wilson, 1971: xx). While Australia did provide information and technical assistance to firms undertaking outward FDI (BIE, 1984: 40-5), in the early 1990s it was an outlier amongst the OECD countries in that it did not offer direct financial support or investment insurance (UNCTAD, 1995: Table VII.1). Respondents to a BIE survey (1995b: 129) felt that the gains from policies designed to aid outward FDI were partially offset by the negative impact of 'government-imposed limitations on domestic market dominance, unfavourable regulations [affecting domestic operations], declining levels of border [tariff] protection and relatively slow reform on the supply side of the economy'.

Australia's geographic isolation, combined with the higher costs in those parts of manufacturing and services where scale economies are important, has been a barrier to its engagement in commerce with the rest of the world. FDI provides a means of escaping the high cost of transport to distant markets and impediments to access resulting from tariffs and non-tariff barriers to trade. Moreover, it offers the possibility of operating at greater volumes in countries with larger populations. However, these inducements to undertake FDI counted for nothing as long as Australian business people remained unaware of opportunities in markets that were both geographically and psychically distant. The costs of the 'tyranny of distance' (Blainey, 1968) were significantly ameliorated in the late twentieth century by technological advances in communication and transportation. Knowledge about the world increased as a result of greater contact. A direct beam wireless service and overseas telephone services had begun to the UK in 1927 and 1930, respectively. The service was extended to many more countries in the postwar era but not until the 1960s and 1970s did usage grow dramatically, with the number of telephone calls from Australia to foreign countries rising from 47 million paid minutes to 415 million in the latter decade. The number of telexes sent overseas nearly trebled between 1979 and 1985, and the number of international leased services nearly doubled over the same time frame (Australia, *Year Book*, various; OTC Reports, various). Telecommunications were transformed by satellites, mobile phones and the internet (Clarke, 1992). The number of Australian residents departing the country to take short-term business trips rose from 17,000 in 1960, to 155,000 in 1980 and 572,000 in 2000 (ABS, various). Unlike earlier generations, almost everyone travelled by air – the number of passengers on Qantas international services rose from 790,000 in 1970 to four million in 1990 (O'Connor, 1995: Table 4.1), rather than by ship. Australians were becoming increasingly connected with the wider world.

Australia's knowledge of the opportunities available in other countries had been broadened in other ways. Large numbers of its young men had served abroad with the armed forces during World War II in North Africa, the Middle East and the Pacific theatres. Some stayed in Japan with the occupying forces and others fought in Korea, Malaya and Vietnam. They mixed with locals and troops from Britain and the USA and increasingly used American ordinance and communication systems. While war took Australians abroad, it also began a far greater reverse movement. Australia's postwar migration program was founded on the influx of displaced persons from Europe. These were followed with large numbers of migrants from war-torn Britain and Western Europe. The migrant pool was later widened to include southern Europe. Slowly Australia took on the character of a multicultural society with inflows of migrants from Asia, Latin America and Africa. The foreign presence was augmented through inward FDI, with thousands of expatriate managers working for the foreign firms operating in this market (Australia-Japan Economic Institute, 1992; Swedish Trade Council, 1999; Australian British Chamber of Commerce, 1997).

Changes in the machinery of corporate governance provided an important part of the link between changes in the regulatory structure of the economy and internationalisation (Merrett, 2002c). The success or otherwise of the broad package of 'microeconomic' reforms was contingent on there having been a 'sea change' in the nature of corporate governance in Australian firms. Large Australian corporations had been characterised by a separation of ownership and control since the end of World War II. Agency theory predicts that managers and owners have different objective functions and that managers have the ability to pursue their goals at the expense of the owners (Eggertsson, 1990; Jensen and Meckling, 1976). For a generation after 1945 managers of large Australian companies had been able to opt for a 'quiet life' in a heavily regulated environment. However, once the process of economic reform began they faced a radically different environment. Anticipating and reacting to changing market forces brought new challenges. Attempting to expand into overseas markets, a new experience for most Australian firms, meant even greater environmental turbulence and complexity. A significant shift in the pattern of corporate governance enabled a marked assertion of ownership rights. Owners came to possess a wider range of remedies through market instruments at a time when managerial performance was becoming more transparent.

This evolution in the system of corporate governance was not the consequence of premeditated or coherent policy. It was driven by many factors, some of which were unintended by-products of the process of economic reform, whose effects built cumulatively. One stream of reform was the rewriting of corporations and securities legislation in response to an upsurge in corporate malfeasance in the 1980s. These amendments improved the flow of information to the markets and defined duties and obligations of directors. The deregulation of the financial system in the early 1980s had powerful consequences for the development of a market for corporate control through providing funding for hostile takeovers and management buyouts. It also allowed firms greater freedom to raise investment funds offshore. Changes in the composition of the balance sheets of both corporations and households in the 1980s and 1990s magnified the importance of corporate performance in determining both cost of funding and return to owners. In particular, the shift in social policy towards self-funded retirement and the introduction of compulsory superannuation had important consequences. Insurance firms and funds managers, as institutional investors, became increasingly important owners of equity. Further, the proportion of Australian adults owning equities also rose dramatically. The privatisation of very large government-owned business enterprises and the demutualisation of large insurance and service corporations turned them towards profit-seeking enterprises. In addition, their initial public offerings (IPOs) added to the depth and liquidity of local equity markets.

These various changes combined to modify the system of corporate governance in ways that altered management behaviour, particularly in larger corporations with separation of ownership and control. Owners wanted profits and rising share values. By 2000 they were in a far stronger position to reward and punish managers than had been the case in the 1970s. Large corporations, many of whom already had dominant market share, faced constraints on expansion within the small and mature Australian market. Managers were increasingly prepared to explore and implement policies of internationalisation to preserve or increase returns. Reappraisal of strategy resulted in significant increases in internationalisation at the aggregate level as many firms dramatically increased their outward FDI.

A strong case can be made that the country-specific advantages (CSAs) facing firms operating in Australia strengthened significantly and in a variety of ways in the last quarter of the twentieth century. However, many of the forces driving Australia towards a more open and competitive economy were acting in a similar fashion in many other countries at the same time. Multilateral agreements with respect to trade and investment provided benefits to many national economies, as did participation in the expanding number of regional and bilateral trade agreements. While the Australian economy was more productive than it had been in the 25 years after the war, its improvement kept pace with those happening elsewhere. The ability of Australian firms to create sustainable competitive advantages in host economies would depend very much on their capabilities.

Firm-Specific Advantages (FSAs)

FSAs refer to a firm's distinctive capabilities that give rise to sustained competitive advantage as a multinational. These derive from the firm's unique resource-base, including its proprietary knowledge and the ability to economise on transaction costs through internalisation. They can be divided into two types: location-bound and non-location-bound, each of which draws on different aspects of its 'ownership advantage'. In essence, firms must have capabilities to manage across borders in two different dimensions. The first type of FSA sets the parameters to the ability of a multinational to operate in particular host markets. Markets that differ in significant respects from those of home present challenges to multinationals if they have to learn to be nationally responsive. International expansion usually requires the accumulation of country-specific capabilities. The costs associated with acquiring location-bound FSAs tie many firms to a restricted number of host locations. On the other hand, non-location-bound FSAs revolve around the capabilities of multinationals to integrate their value-adding activities across a number of host locations. Multinationals must decide on which countries to locate their particular activities and then set up internal systems that allow these activities to be coordinated in ways that will generate the greatest value (Rugman and Verbeke, 1991: 5-7).

It is difficult to generalise about FSAs on a national or even an industry scale. Recourse can be made to partial measures of success such as the longevity of firms which are leaders in their respective industries or the possession of a common set of behaviours amongst those firms (Fleming et al., 2004; Hubbard et al., 2002; Collins and Porras, 2000; Nohria et al., 2002). The question is whether Australian firms possessed or developed the requisite skills to be successful multinationals in the latter part of the twentieth century. Three sources of FSAs were identified above: capabilities leading to competitive advantages in domestic markets; abilities to coordinate activities internalised within the firm across borders; and the ability to operate across a number of host environments in ways that maximise differences in costs and productivity. Generalising from a large number of case studies, there is little evidence that Australia firms performed particularly well by any of these criteria.

A recent study of the rise of big business over the twentieth century identified numerous sources of competitive advantage that shifted over time, especially in the case of firms operating in maturing markets (Fleming et al., 2004). Most of Australia's largest firms in the 1970s had been amongst early adopters of new technologies in extractive industries, manufacturing and services, which allowed them to generate substantial economies of scale. Early-mover cost advantages over their rivals were reinforced over time by exploitation of economies of scope as they diversified into new products and new markets. The smallness of the local market meant that many industries were characterised by high levels of seller concentration from early in the century. High barriers to entry in the form of economies of scale, patents, brands and trade marks, and government regulations effectively blocked new entry, particularly via imports from foreign suppliers. Moreover, these dominant firms operated in an environment where competitive pressures were undermined by widespread collusion amongst producers in price setting and market sharing. As noted above, the micro-economic reforms instituted by the government in the 1980s and 1990s swept away these market failures. However, the administrative heritage (Bartlett and Ghoshal, 1989; Chapter 3) of many of the large companies that shaped their strategic thinking as multinationals had been forged in a non-competitive environment.

In manufacturing firms, particularly, the source of competitive advantage has shifted from scale economies associated with product and process technology to the ability to innovate. Australian firms were poorly placed in this regard compared with firms in the same industries in other developed economies. For whatever reason, Australian firms had been dependent on imported technology and spent little on their own R&D. In many industries, for example, automobiles, chemicals, petroleum, processed foods and distilling, the technological leaders were subsidiaries of foreign multinationals. The share of Australian firms in total spending on business enterprise R&D expenditure in developed economies between 1991 and 2001 rose from 0.64 per cent to 0.69 per cent. Between 30 and 41 per cent of this expenditure had been undertaken by affiliates of foreign firms operating in Australia (UNCTAD, 2005: Annex table A.III.2, 287 and A.IV.1). The Australian government had invested less in education, particularly universities, and offered less in the way of subsidies to industrial R&D than was the case in many of the OECD countries. Consequently, Australian firms went abroad with less valuable proprietary intangibles than their international rivals.

A survey of 45 Australian manufacturing and service multinationals conducted in the early 1990s illustrates the point. In response to a question about the sources of their competitive advantage, the most common response from manufacturing firms was 'superior management and staff' (30 per cent), well ahead of 'own technology' (19 per cent), 'copyrights and patents' (18 per cent), and 'trademarks and brand names' (16 per cent). The larger the asset base of the firm, the less the reliance placed on intangibles. The weighted results lifted the response rate to the source of competitive advantage being 'superior management and staff' to 43 per cent. The responses from service firms placed even more emphasis on 'superior management and staff' (62 per cent), and less on 'own technology' (13 per cent), 'trademarks and brand names' (11 per cent) or 'copyrights or patents' (4 per cent) (BIE, 1984: Table, 3.3).

The sources of competitive advantage derived from proprietary intangible assets would be considered non-location bound in the Rugman and Verbeke schema (1990). They can be transferred across locations without costly modification. However, operating in different host countries often requires considerable adaptation or local responsiveness. There is a range of circumstantial evidence to suggest that Australian firms struggled to make such adaptations. In the first place, Australian firms choose to enter markets with minimal psychic distance: the traditional hosts in the neighbouring region were former British colonies and dependencies in the South West Pacific, New Zealand, PNG and Fiji. After a brief flirtation in the 1970s with Asia as a destination, there was a dramatic shift towards investment in the US and UK. Those Australian firms investing in South East Asia in the 1960s faced challenges in meeting the language and cultural needs of local markets (Hughes, 1967). Hundreds of Australian expatriate managers in Malaysia, Singapore, Thailand and Indonesia reported a host of difficulties in managing within the subsidiary, dealing with local stakeholders and getting adequate guidance and support from head office (Thompson, 1981a, 1981b, and 1983; Thompson and Muir, 1982).[7] Many of the operational problems being confronted abroad stemmed from a lack of awareness of cross-cultural issues. Firms that stayed the course learnt how to adapt to these environments. A later study by Elizabeth Maitland and Stephen Nicholas (2002) found that 'contract choice and performance in each market [PRC, Indonesia and India] was critically dependent on prior overseas experience, especially skills in structuring, monitoring, and operating overseas contracts and [joint ventures]'.

While there was evidence of organisational learning within Australian multinationals, the nature of the relationship between head office in Australia and overseas subsidiaries appears to have changed little in the past 25 years. Australian multinationals continue to operate primarily as 'multinationals' or 'multi-domestics' rather than the alternative types identified by Bartlett and Ghoshal (1989) such as 'global' or 'transnational'. Surveys of multinational firms undertaken in the early 1980s, the mid-1990s and 2000 tell the same story (BIE, 1984 and 1995; Productivity Commission, 2002). In brief, firms went abroad to sell into host markets. Their subsidiaries facilitated exports into the host or there produced the same products as the parent produced in Australia. Very little investment was undertaken offshore for export from the host. Australian manufacturers did not exploit comparative and competitive advantages offered by the industrialising countries to its north to build global production platforms. A quarter of a century of experience had not led Australian firms beyond the simplest form of organisational design (Jones, 2005a; Johnston, 2005b). There is still a marked difference between affiliates owned by Australian firms and by foreign firms operating in Australia. Of affiliates of the Australian firms in 2000, 63 per cent were evenly spread across geographic regions. By contrast, foreign owned firms focused more heavily on the Asia-Pacific, suggesting that they were acting as regional headquarters (Productivity Commission, 2002).

Performance

Australian firms made very significant investments abroad after 1980. For the most part, the modest number of firms whose investments pushed up the aggregate value of outward stock were those taking their first steps as multinationals. We have discussed where they went, what they did and the relationship between head office and their subsidiaries. A critical issue is whether they added value for their shareholders. There are many stories of mistakes and failure culminating in divestment. The big banks, ANZ Bank, NAB and Westpac, all sold off large parts of their overseas acquisitions (Merrett, 2002b). The leading insurer, AMP, divested its disastrous UK operations, now trading as Henderson Global Investors, in 2005 (AMP, 2005). The list of firms who had written down the value of overseas assets or reported losses in the late 1990s and early 2000s lengthened to include the resources giants BHP Billiton, Rio Tinto and Pasminco, insurers HIH Insurance and QBE, the construction firm Lend Lease, brewers and wine makers, building construction firms, the leaders in transport and storage Telstra, and News Corporation. In all, an estimated $40 billion was lost over five years (Ferguson and James, 2003).

Do losses of this magnitude indicate that Australian multinationals are doomed to fail? Tatiana Zalan (Chapter 4) provides a comprehensive analysis of the offshore earnings of a large sample of multinationals in the 1990s and concludes that few were able to cover the cost of capital employed by their affiliates. A longer term view may be needed before we pass judgement. Australian multinationals have earned profits from their overseas operations in the past, CSR's Fijian sugar refinery or Nicholas Aspro's overseas operations, for instance. Statistics of reported income earned by overseas subsidiaries of Australian companies and the value of their assets in host nations is available from 1947-48 to 1996-97 (ABS, 2003). Over the half century the average ratio of income to assets was 9.7 per cent from 1948 to 1996-97.[8] These data also reveal a sharp decline through the 1980s and early 1990s. However, the tide seems to have turned in the past few years. Journalists and business analysts, once highly critical of overseas expansion, are taking a more sanguine view. They perceive that Australian firms have learnt from their past mistakes when going abroad (Hooper, 2005).

CONCLUSION

This introductory chapter has raised a number of themes that will be explored in the following chapters. They revolve around whether firms from developed economies which were late starters in the recent decades of the race to economic liberalisation and globalisation are placed at a disadvantage. The experience of Australian firms, particularly those that had dominated their domestic industries, with a history of exuberant early forays abroad and costly mistakes, would seem to support a view that the 'liability of foreignness' overwhelmed the 'ownership advantages' forged in a small, distant economy with a short history of competitive product and factor markets. A longer view, however, suggests a more optimistic stance. Firms learn from their experiences and mistakes. The whole experience of internationalisation is one of trial and error, experiential learning. Bartlett and Ghoshal (1989) have conceptualised the link between a firm's past and its present in terms of the influence of its administrative heritage. Present actions are tied to the past through a process of path dependency. Zalan and Lewis take up this approach in the next chapter when they explore the organisational characteristics leading Australian firms had acquired prior to their making very large offshore investments in the 1980s and 1990s. They argue that the collective administrative heritage ill-prepared them for international expansion and that path dependency drove the firms to make inappropriate strategic decisions.

NOTES

1. Copyright CBS Records.
2. Only three Australian firms have been included in the largest TNCs listed in the World Investment Report from 1980 until 2003: BHP (now BHP Billiton); CRA, (now Rio Tinto); and News Corporation.
3. The term refers to the ratio of overseas sales to domestic sales, foreign employees to total employees and foreign assets to total assets. UNCTAD (1983).
4. The figure has been calculated on the assumption that the value of the sugar refinery in New Zealand is the same as the average of the five in Australia lus itself.
5. The changes in definitions are reported in the Explanatory Notes of Foreign Investment in Australia, Catalogue No. 5305.0, various.
6. For an explanation of the construction of the two data sets and explanations of the differences between them see UNCTAD (2000): 10-14.
7. The tapes and transcripts of these hundreds of interviews are held in the University of Melbourne Archive.
8. The income figure is net rather than gross, roughly approximating profits earned.

3. The Administrative Heritage

Tatiana Zalan and Geoffrey Lewis

According to Bartlett and Ghoshal (1995), there are no 'zero-based' organisations: firms are invariably captives of their past. However, most managers of multinational corporations (MNCs) focus on their future strategies, forgetting that these strategies are constrained by their firms' 'administrative heritage'. Merrett (Chapter 2) has argued that Australia has a long history but only a weak tradition of foreign direct investment (FDI) and suggested that, at least until very recently, the performance of offshore ventures has been disappointing. This view is also found in the Australian media: '[i]f globalisation were an exam, Australia would have so far barely managed a pass' (James, 2005: 44). One way of analysing what appears to be systemic under-performance of Australian firms in international markets (see also Lewis, Jarvie and Zalan, 2004; Ferguson and James, 2003) is to explore their administrative heritage.

The concept of administrative heritage was developed by Bartlett and Ghoshal (1989) and extended by Collis (1991). Drawing on population ecology theories (Hannan and Freeman, 1984), Bartlett and Ghoshal (1995: 472) define 'administrative heritage' as a combination of organisational history, being the path along which a company develops, and its management culture, being its values, norms, and practices. Building on this concept, Collis (1991: 52-3) suggests that a firm's 'administrative heritage' consists of the cultural and physical heritage. The cultural heritage reflects the organisation's national culture, its management mentalities and leadership style; these intangible factors together distinguish a firm's culture and frame the administrative context of strategic decision-making. The physical heritage denotes the configuration of physical assets such as plant and office locations and communication systems which have resulted from the firm's strategies of growth and diversification. These two aspects of administrative heritage are part of the accumulated assets of the firm, influencing its organisational form and distinctive competencies. In a manner specific to each firm, they may enable or constrain strategy. In most cases, however, administrative heritage is a source of organisational inertia, limiting the speed and direction of strategic change.

Although administrative heritage is firm-specific, Bartlett and Ghoshal (1989) identified common patterns across firms of diverse national origins, resulting in four organisational models: international, multinational, global and transnational. Each of these models is characterised by distinct structural configurations, administrative processes and management mentalities. For example, in the most pervasive model, the multinational, key assets are nationally self-sufficient, decision-making is decentralised, headquarters-subsidiary relationships are overlaid with simple financial controls, and overseas operations are regarded by headquarters managers as a portfolio of independent businesses. By contrast, the global organisation model is based on a centralisation of assets, resources and responsibilities, and tight operational controls of decisions, resources and information whereby management treats overseas operations as delivery pipelines to a unified global market.

More recent work has extended Bartlett and Ghoshal's research by investigating exogenous influences on the firm's administrative heritage in the form of nation-specific socio-cultural, religious, political and legal institutions (Calori et al., 1997; Lubatkin et al., 1998; Carney and Gedajlovic, 2003). National institutions develop a distinct set of enduring routines that legitimises certain ways of organising and, at the same time, sets them apart from the accepted routines in other nations (Lubatkin et al., 1998). Thus three aspects of administrative heritage – cultural heritage, physical heritage and exogenous influences – inform the model of administrative heritage developed in this chapter. This approach nicely complements analysis of country-specific and firm-specific advantages (Chapter 2).

This chapter has two objectives: first, to explore the administrative heritage using a selected sample of Australian firms and, second, to discuss the implications of administrative heritage for the success or otherwise of firms' international strategies. Data are taken from a sample of eleven firms in four industries: mining and resources (BHP, Rio Tinto and WMC), integrated paper and packaging (Amcor and Visy Industries), wine (Southcorp, BRL Hardy and Foster's/Beringer Blass Wine Estates) and banking (the National/NAB, ANZ and Westpac) (Table 3.1). The selected firms are Australian-owned MNCs which are representative of the primary, manufacturing and services sectors and have good experience of internationalisation (Pettigrew, 1990). They are also large, ranking among the top 100 Australian companies by market capitalisation – Visy is a private firm but would rank in the top 100 if publicly listed. Given the high concentration of Australian industries, with two to four firms accounting for the majority of output, this research almost encompasses these four industries in their entirety.[1]

Both primary and secondary data were collected using a wide range of sources, including interviews with senior executives, internal company data, annual reports, analysts' reports, magazine articles and books. Quantitative performance data were collected for the period 1992-2001 in the following way: financial data were taken from the Connect-4 database of annual reports and other databases such as Aspect Financial; geographical segment profitability data were computed from annual reports and economic profitability data of international operations (returns in excess of the cost of capital) were taken from the study by Lewis et al. (2004).[2] Industry and firm case studies were written up and the data were analysed using standard approaches for grounded theory (Glaser and Strauss, 1967), longitudinal case study analysis (Pettigrew, 1990) and specific techniques as described in Miles and Huberman (1994).

In the first section of the chapter we look at the broad historical patterns of industry evolution driven by changes in the external environment. We then present the model of administrative heritage, discuss its constituents and draw out the implications for internationalisation. A brief conclusion summarises the findings.

PATTERNS OF INDUSTRY CHANGE

Despite differences in the timing and patterns of development of the four industries in the study, three common patterns can be established: (1) similar contextual pressures; (2) increasing concentration within each of the four industries; and (3) changing patterns of firms' growth. Trends in the national business and institutional environment and the evolution of Australian big business are summarised in the first two chapters in this volume and more detailed accounts of are available in Lewis et al. (1999) and Fleming et al. (2004). Here it is sufficient to note the salience for the firms' growth strategies of a sustained high rate of immigration, heavy regulation of the financial system, lack of anti-trust legislation and, most importantly, high levels of protection in a small and remote domestic economy as a result of government and trade union intervention (Karmel and Brunt, 1962). Under a pattern once described as 'protection all round', Australian manufacturers were protected by tariffs, employees by basic wage awards and farmers by marketing and price stabilisation schemes.

These externalities shaped the firms' strategic responses. One long-term response was the increasing concentration of economic power within each of the four industries, even though the specific timing and pattern of concentration differed across industries. The banking industry started its first round of consolidation during the depression of the 1890s, with rationalisation complete in the late 1980s when the 'Four Pillar' policy was introduced in 1990, imposing a regulatory ban on further rationalisation of what became an oligopolistic industry (Chapter 7). The mining and resources

Table 3.1. Study firms by industry, size, internationalisation and market share, 2001

Company	Industry	Mkt cap[a] $b	FSTS[b] %	FATA[c] %	Market share, domestic[d] %
Mining and resources					
BHP	Diversified resources	38.6	0.33	0.49	35
Rio Tinto/CRA	Diversified resources	16.9	0.58	0.55	27
WMC	Diversified mining	10.5	0.00	0.11	6
Total mining (i)					68
Paper and packaging					
Amcor	Paper and packaging	4.2	0.59	0.61	47
Visy Industries	Paper and packaging	n/a[e]	0.50[f]	n/a[e]	47
Total paper and packaging (ii)					94
Wine-making					
Southcorp	Diversified industrial	5.5	0.27	0.13	27
BRL Hardy	Alcohol and Tobacco –Vintner	1.9	0.63	0.27	21
Foster's/BBWE	Alcohol and Tobacco – Brewer	9.1	0.33	0.51	23
Total wine making (iii)					71
Banking					
NAB	Banks and Finance – Banking	53.8	0.51	0.45	31.5
ANZ	Banks and Finance – Banking	25.1	0.30	0.28	18.5
Westpac	Banks and Finance – Banking	25.1	0.25	0.20	17
Total banking (iv)					67

Notes:
a. Mkt cap = market capitalisation (2001).
b. FSTS = ratio of foreign sales to total sales (2001).
c. FATA = ratio of foreign assets to total assets (2001).
d. (i), (ii) and (iii) based on revenues; (iv) based on assets.
e. Private company, data not available.
f. Researcher's estimate.
Source: Based on company annual reports, Lewis et al. (2004)

industry exhibited more variation, depending on the commodity. Steel, for example, was monopolised by BHP after the late 1930s. In zinc, lead and aluminium refining, the Collins House Group (which included WMC) established a virtual monopoly after World War II, and by the late 1970s

WMC gained a dominant position in nickel. By the 1980s the resources industry had become an oligopoly. The paper and packaging industry was monopolised by Amcor (then known as Australian Paper Manufacturers, or APM) in the first 30 years of the twentieth century. After the entry of APM, Newsprint Mills and Visy Board, the industry became an oligopoly and then a duopoly, following exit of one of the major industry participants (Smorgon) in the late 1980s. The wine industry, by contrast, remained fragmented and family-owned throughout most of its long history, dating back to the early days of settlement in the nineteenth century. Not until the early 1990s did it assume an oligopolistic structure as a result of industry consolidation. Many firms in the study experienced rapid growth in assets, partially because of increased exports and the first attempts at FDI: Westpac's assets, for example, almost tripled in the brief period 1982-89. By the late 1980s, the industry structure of the Australian economy had become what was labelled as 'the land of the duopoly' or the 'Noah's Ark' economy (two players in every industry). The development of the firms in the study provides support for this characterisation.

Until the 1960s firms strategies had been quite similar but then began to diverge. The common initial strategy had been to accumulate resources, then to diversify into related product markets and to make the first modest attempts at internationalisation. In the 1970s and 1980s there emerged two new dimensions in corporate strategies, namely unrelated diversification and passive investments. The strategy of unrelated or conglomerate diversification was pioneered by Pacific Dunlop in 1969 (Chapter 17). Pacific Dunlop's CEO was renown for posing the question: 'Well, what will we take over this week?' (Blainey, 1993: 215), a question that captures the essence of this approach to corporate strategy (Porter, 1987). Following Pacific Dunlop, BHP, Elders, Amcor, Visy and S.A. Brewing (later known as Southcorp) also adopted this strategy of unrelated diversification in an attempt to maintain growth in the small Australian market. In the case of S.A. Brewing, which had few ideas about how to invest the cash flow from its core business into new activities, passive portfolio holdings in the mid-1980s represented nearly 70 per cent of the firm's total assets and its equity portfolio read like a *Who's Who* of South Australian business (Wetherel, 1988).

Unrelated diversification was not unknown in Australia before the 1960s but it gained legitimacy as a corporate strategy from the publicly listed conglomerates that became prominent in the US in the 1960s in response to antitrust laws limiting horizontal and vertical integration (Chandler, 1990). Conglomerates were less common in the UK and Germany and almost non-existent in Japan, where hostile acquisition was almost unheard of and considered 'bad manners' (Bengtsson, 1999; Wittington et al., 1999).[3] In

Australia, where legislative constraints were weak, unrelated diversification was largely motivated by the need to grow outside the firm's original business because of the small domestic market. Empire-building motives of managers might have been as much a factor as growth in shareholder value. Such 'irrational' motives were not unique to the firms in the study, and there is extensive empirical evidence in other settings to suggest that empire-building managers are often interested in maximising firm size at the expense of shareholders (Jensen, 1986; Eisenhardt, 1989; Hill, 1994; Collis and Montgomery, 2005). The Australian stock market at that time rewarded growth and some of the firms (Amcor, Elders and Southcorp) successfully exploited capital market imperfections by driving earnings-per-share growth through successive acquisitions. The agency problem was exacerbated by executive remuneration practices: in the mid-1980s, 90 per cent of the executive remuneration package was fixed and only 10 per cent was performance-based (O'Neill, 1999).

The outcome of these growth strategies was increased size and complexity in firms' operations in the context of the turbulent economic environment of the late 1970s to early 1980s. As a consequence of the aggressive economic reform of the early 1980s, firms had to deal with issues such as decreased tariffs, increased inward FDI as a result of deregulation, changes to the restrictive industrial relations practices and intensifying competition from foreign firms entering the Australian market (Lewis et al., 1999; Chapter 2).

THE MODEL OF ADMINISTRATIVE HERITAGE

Within the business and institutional context described above, the firms in this study developed a particular administrative heritage that was characterised by three aspects: (1) weak FDI traditions; (2) a domestic portfolio mentality, which in turn led to (3) reliance on strategic assets for competitive advantage (Figure 3.1). We explore each of these aspects, showing how they arose from the way the firms responded to their changing business environment.

Weak FDI traditions

Firms' weak FDI traditions were as much a function of the broader environment as of managers' mentalities. Because this issue has been well addressed by Merrett (Chapter 2, also 2000, 2002a, 2002b), discussion here can be kept brief. The overwhelming majority of Australian firms, including those in this study, internationalised through FDI late in their history. When the recent outflow of FDI began in the early 1980s, Australian MNCs had a narrow geographic focus, typically on just one country, with an average of only 1.6 foreign subsidiaries per firm. There was also a remarkable lack of expatriates, with nearly half of the subsidiaries having no expatriate managers

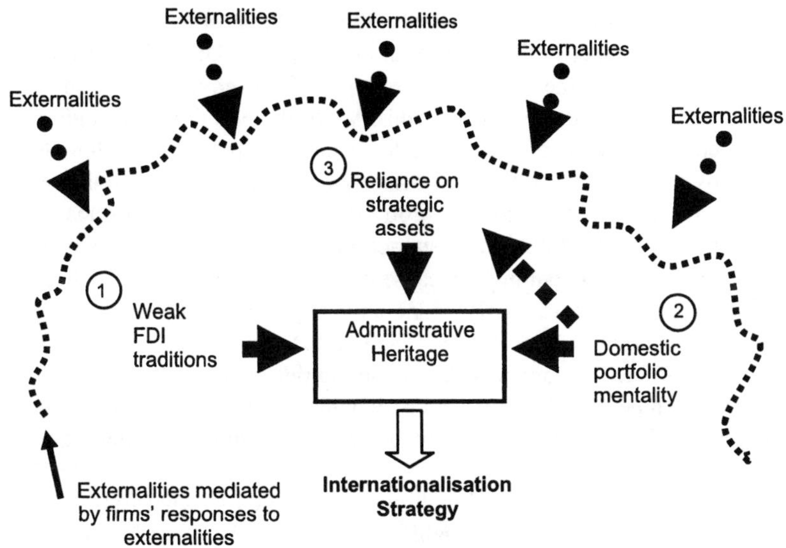

Figure 3.1: The administrative heritage of Australian firms

(BIE, 1984; Merrett, 2000). In 1990, Australia had only two MNCs – News Corporation and BHP – among the 100 world's largest non-financial corporations as ranked by foreign assets. Because News Corporation was by that time and until 2005 an 'Australian' firm only by registration – the place of business and a significant proportion of its assets were in the US and its CEO had become an American citizen – this left Australia with only one significant MNC. In 1990, BHP, known as 'the Big Australian', had only very recently engaged in FDI. Its first significant acquisition – of Utah International from General Electric in 1984 – was 'internationalisation by accident' rather than a deliberate strategy: BHP bought Utah for its Australian coal assets and 'picked up' a variety of offshore assets in the process.[4] Comparison of assets for all sample firms in 1990 and 2000-01 shows that the percentage of assets located in Australia over the decade remained virtually unchanged at 63-64 per cent. Clearly, FDI was yet to become part of the firms' administrative heritage.

A partial explanation for this late and limited entry of the Australian firms into international markets is to be found in the broader economic context.

Factors that may have impeded the internationalisation of Australian firms include small firm size, monopolistic, duopolistic and oligopolistic industry structures, the government's protection of local industries via trade barriers, physical isolation from major markets, and a wide and shallow range of manufacturing industries (Merrett, 2000). One of the most persistent themes cutting across the cases in this study was that of protection and government intervention. Perhaps the most vivid example of the government's role in our study comes from the resources industry. In the early years of industry development, legislation protected the local industry (particularly the steel industry) by imposing import duties, offering subsidies for gold mining and petroleum, restricting the exports of iron ore (thus providing a disincentive for exploration in Australia) and supported industrial relations practices based on centralised bargaining. Because of its importance to the Australian economy, BHP was particularly vulnerable to government pressure and interference in commercial decisions. The Federal government supported the development of BHP's monopoly in steel and in the early 1980s attempted to restore the fortunes of the steel industry with the five year plan. Such protectionism limited the steel industry's exposure to international competition.

This business and institutional environment resulted in what Bartlett and Ghoshal (2000) have termed 'liabilities of origin' which may have constrained the development of firms' competitive advantages. They identify three psychological factors that may hold back multinationals from the periphery of the global economy: (1) the gap between technical requirements and design norms at home and world-class standards abroad; (2) management that is either unaware of the company's global potential or too debilitated by self-doubt to capitalise on it; and (3) limited exposure to global competition. The last of these was especially relevant to Australia and left MNC managers either overconfident in their abilities or blind to the risks of overseas expansion. As noted by Brian Hartzer, a senior executive at ANZ Bank, a combination of arrogance and ignorance contributed to the poor record of internationalisation of a number of Australian firms.[5] We demonstrate later in this chapter that this context was conducive to the Australian firms competing on the basis of strategic assets and hence structural or positional advantages in the home market, rather than on the basis of distinctive and internationally transferable capabilities.

Besides these externalities, management mentalities also contributed to weak FDI traditions. After living a 'quiet life' for 25 years after World War II in a heavily protected and regulated environment (Merrett, 2002c), senior executives of Australian firms had few incentives to internationalise: the entire wine industry, for example, adopted in the 1980s a very opportunistic approach to exporting – FDI was not even on the horizon. Ray King, the former CEO of Mildara Blass (a premium wine company acquired by Foster's in 1996) used to contend that Mildara Blass was profitable because it was not in the business of low-margin volume growth in export markets.[6] Thomas Hardy, despite its long history of exporting, did not invest in its own distribution networks until acquired by UK distributor Whiclar and Gordon in 1989, while BRL started exporting only in the 1980s.[7] With the exception of the resources industry – which was international by nature of its world markets – firms often lacked commitment to international operations, as illustrated by ANZ's deliberations over whether it should divest its international operations in the early 1970s. Even within the internationally oriented resources industry, there were visible differences in management mentalities. Rio Tinto, majority owned by RTZ (UK), always had an external perspective, while WMC and BHP were much more focused on the domestic market. In the words of Barry Cusack, Rio Tinto's senior executive, the board and management in WMC and BHP until the late 1990s were 'very Australian' and, unlike Rio Tinto, did not enjoy the benefits of sharing information and knowledge about foreign markets with overseas shareholders.[8]

This lack of commitment to international activities is similar to the experiences of firms from other countries in the early stages of internationalisation, reflecting their 'international strategic mentality', when firms perceive themselves fundamentally as domestic companies with some marginal foreign operations (Bartlett and Ghoshal, 1995). This is not to say that Australian firms were somehow 'deficient'. Our argument is simply that, for understandable reasons, the firms in the study were late to internationalise via FDI. However, this 'lateness' was not in itself a reason for the poor performance of those firms' international assets in overseas markets. The other two determinants of administrative heritage – a domestic portfolio mentality and reliance on strategic assets – shed further light on why firms in the study had, in general, a poor record of internationalisation.

Domestic portfolio mentality

The second important observation from analysis of firm strategies is that they took a portfolio approach to corporate strategy. Porter's (1987) taxonomy, which includes three approaches to corporate strategy – portfolio management, restructuring and leveraging resources (transferring skills and sharing activities to capture what are commonly referred to as 'synergies') – helps to explain how value can be created at the corporate level through each of these strategies. In the period of the 1970s and 1980s portfolio management was the most common approach to corporate strategy among corporations worldwide (Porter, 1987), and the Australian firms in our study were no exception. Ten out of the 11 firms in the study (the exception being BRL Hardy, a single-business firm) pursued a portfolio management approach combined with some elements of restructuring. The strategies of some firms evolved over time, progressing from passive portfolio holding (such as Southcorp and Visy), denoting equity investments with no operational control, to a more active and aggressive portfolio strategy combining portfolio management with restructuring. In the late 1990s there was a shift to Porter's third and most sophisticated strategy of leveraging resources across businesses.

Each of Porter's approaches rests on a different mechanism by which the corporation creates value at the corporate level, and each requires quite different managerial and organisational arrangements (Collis and Montgomery, 2005). The portfolio management approach is based primarily on diversification through acquisitions. Business units are autonomous and are often categorised according to their potential and cash requirements (Henderson, 1979). A modest corporate office allocates resources and manages cash flows, acting as a 'banker' and 'reviewer' which necessitates superior financial and, to some extent, managerial corporate skills. Control focuses on monitoring the results of business units, or what is commonly known in the literature as financial or outcome control (Ouchi, 1979; Eisenhardt, 1989). The logic of portfolio management rests on the assumption that the acquired companies will benefit from the generic resources, usually capital and performance management processes, contributed by the new parent (Porter, 1987).

Portfolio management has two inherent limitations. First, this approach deliberately eschews any attempts to leverage resources across businesses, despite the claims to the contrary frequently made, at least in the 1990s and early 2000s, by managers of Australian companies. This was exemplified by Southcorp, whose CEO Graham Kraehe sought to justify the firm's conglomerate strategy on the grounds that it maximised cross-business synergies in the area of global communication system, a data network, group-wide purchasing projects and best practice transfer (Southcorp Annual Report 1997).[9] The second limitation – and simultaneous attraction – of the portfolio strategy is the very modest requirement for coordination between divisions of the firm, thus holding down headquarters costs. Portfolio management can succeed in creating shareholder value only under two conditions: if managers are aware that corporate costs and constraints have to be less than the modest corporate value added and in under-developed capital markets characterised by institutional voids (Khanna and Palepu, 1999, 2005). Portfolio-based corporate strategies may also incur significant opportunity costs in not pursuing a synergies strategy that potentially could add more value to the firm (Porter, 1987; Collis and Montgomery, 2005).

The restructuring approach to corporate strategy seeks out poorly performing firms on the threshold of significant structural change to strengthen the firm or to transform the industry (Porter, 1987). Typically the performance of the productive assets is enhanced by managerial improvements, after which the revamped businesses, often now within a restructured industry, are sold off. This strategy requires sophisticated financial and strategic management skills on the part of the corporate office as 'selector', 'banker' and 'change manager'. If well implemented, this strategy can generate a good deal of value at the corporate level: for example, Elders IXL, after the acquisition of Carlton & United Breweries (CUB) in 1983, restructured the conservatively run company, sold off its unproductive assets and improved management structures and reporting systems.

The banking industry represents another case of successful restructuring, consistent with Porter's (1987: 14) view that the best restructurers realise they are not just acquiring companies but transforming an industry. The banks' diversification in the 1960s and 1970s via acquisitions of non-banking institutions (merchant banks, hire purchase companies, credit cards and travel services operators) blurred the boundaries between various industry segments and redefined the industry as 'financial services'. As a result of such transformation, by the late 1980s the restructured Australian financial services industry became one of the most profitable in the world.

The limitation of the restructuring approach to corporate strategy, however, is that returns come largely from 'one-off' transactions rather than from a continuous creation of value. Our case data show that the diversification of the 1970s and 1980s into increasingly unrelated businesses precluded economies of scope except the trivial ones associated with administrative overheads. Firms were typically leveraging resources that were not much more than cash and general management skills. Such limited resources were too 'generic', which is to say common and easy to imitate, to generate value on a sustainable basis, even in the domestic market.

Nevertheless, the portfolio approach did create value for the firms in the context of inefficient capital markets and poor corporate governance and disclosure practices prevalent at that time. All over the world in the 1960s and 1970s, capital markets were rife with information asymmetries that enabled managers to misrepresent the value of the firm to investors. In Australia it was not until 1987 that firms were legally required to disclose their performance in terms of revenues, assets and profits by product and geographical segments. Thus even under the portfolio management approach pursued by the firms in this study hierarchical governance economies of the internal capital market variety potentially represented a source of value (Williamson, 1985; Hill et al., 1992; Hill, 1994). For example, Amcor's ability to successfully play the so-called 'chain letter' game of earnings per share (EPS) growth to inexpensively fund its domestic acquisitions and some international investments hinged on how the Australian equity market valued growth at that time. In the 1960s and 1970s the equity market rewarded growth, and high EPS growth was seen as highly desirable. As a result, firms with high EPS growth enjoyed high share prices relative to earnings. Many firms exploited this inefficiency in the capital market, thereby gaining access to low-cost capital.

Consistent with theoretical predictions, all firms in the study that pursued a portfolio approach, whether passive or aggressive, showed a bias toward divisional autonomy (Collis and Montgomery, 2005). Even Visy's vertically integrated operations in paper mills and corrugated divisions were run as essentially stand-alone businesses with few formal coordination mechanisms in place apart from financial controls. Lack of common systems to cost products was a major weakness for a company striving to become the lowest-cost producer at each stage of the value chain. WMC provides another insightful example. In the late 1980s, WMC was little more than a holding company trading in and operating mining assets: its corporate plan was an aggregation of the various budgets and operational plans and resident managers enjoyed a significant degree of autonomy and power. Only after 1994 did WMC move to becoming a more integrated firm organised along mineral products lines with strategic boundaries for each business unit and disciplined performance expectations.

The firms in the study typically employed outcome-based financial controls such as return on funds employed (ROFE), return on investment (ROI) or economic value added (EVA). Few mechanisms were put in place to foster the sharing of activities or the transfer of resources, whether formally or informally. Managers of autonomous units assessed on financial outcomes had little incentive – and in some cases even negative incentives – to cooperate and share resources, learning and knowledge (Collis, 1997). Administration of a portfolio approach required competition between divisions, whereas a 'synergies' approach would have required inter-divisional cooperation (Hill et al., 1992; Hill, 1994). Portfolio management was therefore incompatible with the realisation of scope economies. Amcor's strategy is a good example of such incompatibility. The 'scatter-gun' diversification of the 1970s had resulted in high decentralisation and an earnings-per-share mentality, given that the earnings-per-share metric was a key element of Amcor's performance system. Any move towards centralisation and more coordination from the corporate centre was destined to meet strong resistance from divisional managers (Lewis and Zalan, 2005a).

In short, a 'domestic portfolio mentality' seems an appropriate concept to capture the essence of the strategic approach which our firms pursued in the domestic market as part of their administrative heritage. For six firms in the study – BHP, WMC, S.A. Brewing/Southcorp, Elders, Amcor and Visy – the term 'conglomerate mentality' would be even more appropriate. In the 1970s and 1980s these firms were, in effect, holding companies which identified opportunities, traded assets, measured performance in terms of financial outcomes, undertook financial, rather than strategic, analysis, had poor accountability practices and were quite sure they 'knew what was best' for shareholders.[10] It could be argued that even Westpac, although technically not a conglomerate, would meet most of the above criteria. This conglomerate mentality characterised not only the firms in the study, but also many other Australian firms, such as Pacific Dunlop (Chapter 17), Burns, Philp (Chapter 12), TNT (Chapter 18), Bond Corporation, Adsteam and Qintex. Adsteam, which in the 1980s used to own brewer Tooth and Co. (later acquired by CUB/Foster's), Penfolds and Seppelt (wine companies subsequently acquired by S.A. Brewing/Southcorp) exemplified this conglomerate mentality at its worst: the earnings of these and other profitable operating businesses were mortgaged by Adsteam to raise debt used to finance takeovers or big share market gambles (such as investment in a tranche of 101 million BHP shares) (Sykes, 1994: 432).

After the deregulation of Australian capital markets in the 1980s, the corporate office role of portfolio manager was gradually subsumed by the market. Restructuring could and, in some cases, did create value, but was a one-off transaction. Once firms had consolidated and rationalised their industries, value-creation opportunities through restructuring were largely exhausted in the small Australian market. By the mid-1980s corporate strategies resting on portfolio management and restructuring in the domestic market had run their course. It is hardly surprising that the firms then began to look more seriously to international markets as a platform for further growth and value creation. With the exception of the banking industry, firms had diversified and consolidated in the domestic market prior to internationalisation through FDI. However, even the banks' activities before the 1980s were confined to correspondence banking (equivalent to exporting in manufacturing firms) and international trade finance carried out through representative offices and branches. It is, therefore, reasonable to conclude that firms in the study internationalised via FDI through the optics of portfolio management, if for no other reason than that in the domestic market they had yet to develop a more sophisticated corporate strategy and the associated systems and skills.

Reliance on strategic assets as a source of competitive advantage

The third pattern identified from our analysis is the nature of the competitive advantages that firms developed in the domestic market. Collis (1991) stresses the importance of understanding the nature of the domestic market for its impact on the outcomes of internationalisation. Because domestic factor markets are the easiest to access and cheapest in terms of transaction costs, they profoundly affect the development of a firm's distinctive competencies. Due to a combination of external and internal factors, the firms in the study tended to rely on strategic assets rather than capabilities for their competitive advantages. Building on the resource-based view of the firm and its extensions (Barney, 1991; Teece et al., 1997; Wernerfelt, 1984), we define 'strategic assets' as those resources that give the firm positional/structural advantages in the market. Examples include brands, market share (scale economies and market power), control of distribution and preferential access to capital and acquisitions. This concept combines what Williamson (2004) and Lasserre and Schütte (1995) refer to as resource-based advantages (access to low-cost raw materials and labour, preferential access to capital and raw materials, and government licences obtained through local relationships) and asset-based advantages (superior products, brands, distribution networks and efficient production facilities). Williamson (2004: 168) makes the point that these sources of competitive advantage are largely immobile or, in other words, location-specific (Rugman and Verbeke, 1992, 2003; Ghemawat, 2003).[11] Because they are typically associated with high barriers to imitation, these strategic assets, which take time to build and are a result of irreversible commitments, provide domestic firms with sustainable competitive advantages in their local market (Ghemawat et al., 1999).

One strategic asset often under-estimated by internationalising firms is the social capital they have created in domestic markets, broadly understood as resources embedded in social networks and used by firms to their strategic advantage (Lin, 1999; Nahapiet and Ghoshal, 1998). Social capital was an intrinsic element of the firms' domestic portfolio strategy as it underpinned their ability to obtain detailed information about an asset before its acquisition or to avoid a hostile takeover. To illustrate this point, Southcorp's entry into the wine industry, which in the early 2000s became its core business, was via a friendly takeover in 1984 of one of Australia's oldest winemaking enterprises, B. Seppelt & Sons Ltd, which was on the edge of bankruptcy. Social capital is a classic example of an asset which is highly valuable and inimitable but location-specific and non-transferable.

Capabilities are defined as bundles of resources that enable firms to undertake different activities or the same activities in a different and superior way (Porter, 1996). For example, if a strong brand is a strategic asset, superior brand-building skills are a capability; if a strong distribution network is a strategic asset, then the ability to find innovative new approaches to distribution is a capability. Capabilities to perform activities must be developed, rather than taken as given (Ghemawat et al., 1999). Williamson (2004: 169) refers to these sources of competitive advantage as 'system-based advantages' that leverage proprietary intangible assets like quality systems, marketing competence, technology and know-how.

The external factors of physical isolation, the small size of the economy and government protection which influenced the nature of firms' competitive advantages have already been discussed. Because for most of their history our firms were little threatened by competition from either new domestic or foreign entrants, the capabilities on which their original success was built gradually gave way to competitive advantages based on strategic assets. Few, if any, of these assets lent themselves easily to international transfer. Unlike strategic assets, capabilities are more readily transferable to new geographical markets and can be a source of competitive advantage internationally, providing the capabilities are competitively superior in these markets, and the internationalising firms have the skills and mindset to coordinate them across borders.

The example of Foster's entry into the Chinese beer market shows the pitfalls of overestimating the value of strategic assets and capabilities developed in the domestic market. Foster's continuing dominance and high profitability in the Australian beer market was based on its positional advantages: economies of scale, market share, product quality, control of distribution channels and national brand identity (with 'Victoria Bitter', 'Foster's Light Ice' and 'Carlton Cold'). These strategic assets were bundled with the capabilities of low-cost manufacturing processes and brand- and distribution-building skills. In 1993 Foster's entered China with the strategic goal of building a national brand in the then highly fragmented industry. This aimed to repeat Foster's success in transforming itself from a local to a national brewer in the Australian market. However, the ambition was at best naïve in light of the poorly developed infrastructure (particularly road transportation), highly fragmented distribution channels and regional variations in tastes. Skilled labour was hard to find and crucial raw materials had to be imported. None of the strategic assets were transferable to the Chinese market. Moreover, Foster's manufacturing, distribution- and brand-building capabilities, all sources of its competitive advantage in Australia, had little value in the Chinese market (see also Chapter 15).

THE IMPACT OF ADMINISTRATIVE HERITAGE ON INTERNATIONALISATION

Corporate strategy that relies on strategic assets and a portfolio approach are internally consistent but a dead end when applied to international business. Positional/structural advantages based on strategic assets in the domestic market do not readily translate into competitive advantage in international markets. Misguided attempts to transplant a portfolio approach to international markets explains much of the unimpressive international performance of the Australian firms in our study. Having pursued a portfolio approach to value creation in the domestic market, they sought to transfer this approach and associated organisational arrangements to international markets, thereby trying to run a portfolio of businesses spread across national borders. BRL Hardy, a single-business firm, is the only firm in the study for which the administrative heritage of a domestic portfolio strategy did not shape its approach to internationalisation. It may be pure coincidence, but BRL Hardy was also the only firm that performed well internationally: its returns from the international operations over the 1992-2001 decade were higher than domestic returns and it earned economic profits from international assets over the period 1997 to 2001.[12] Although technically ANZ and Westpac also had higher international returns than domestic returns, this reflected poor domestic profitability rather than superior international performance: the banks' domestic returns were well below the accepted one per cent net operating profits after tax (NOPAT)/Assets benchmark in banking.

The flaws in a portfolio approach to international strategy are clarified by Ghemawat's thesis on 'semiglobalisation', meaning the incomplete integration of product and factor markets (Ghemawat 2000, 2003). Two points are especially relevant. Firstly, the incomplete integration of cross-border markets highlights the critical role of location- and business-specificity of the firm's activities, resources and knowledge in determining the scope for single-business and multiple-business firms to pursue international strategies (Ghemawat, 2003: Table 5). Single-business firms must carefully assess the degree of location specificity of their resources, activities and knowledge. Diversified or multiple-business firms need also to consider the transferability of resources across their businesses.

The second key point is that incomplete integration of product and factor markets gives firms a choice of economic levers to add value: arbitrage, aggregation and transformation (the last also known as 'complex integration') (Yeaple, 2003). Arbitrageurs (vertical MNCs) reap advantages of specialisation and capitalise on differences across markets, for example by relocating labour-intensive activities to countries with low labour costs or making asset-seeking (rather than asset-exploiting) investments. Aggregators (horizontal MNCs) capitalise on similarities between markets and hence on international economies of scale, scope or experience, and are often required to make a trade-off between global integration and local adaptation. Complex integrators (firms that attempt to engage both in arbitrage and aggregation) try to exploit differences and similarities between countries simultaneously. Each of the economic levers for adding value requires well-developed coordination mechanisms and complex integration strategies, because of their multidimensional character, require very sophisticated coordination by function, geography and product (Ghemawat, 2000: 14).

The example of the National, a highly profitable, well-managed bank hailed as a paragon of international success by industry observers and academics, illustrates these points (Fung et al., 2002; Tschoegl, 2002). Like the majority of the firms in the study, before internationalising via acquisitions of New Zealand, UK and Irish banks in the late 1980s to early 1990s, the National had accumulated strategic assets in the domestic market. The bank pursued a portfolio management strategy, combined with industry consolidation, and had a decentralised organisational structure (with the exception of the centralised Credit Bureau). As an aggregator, the National was guided in its internationalisation decisions by the logic of dual relatedness of businesses (retail banks) and countries (the language, laws, corporate governance, culture and ethics had to be compatible with those in Australia). Given its administrative heritage, in the first few years after the acquisitions the bank's international strategy revolved around the concept of a 'federation of regional banks', or largely autonomous business units organised along regional lines and having individual functions and infrastructure, except in the areas of financial control and risk management. The bank's transition to a more synergistic organisation in the mid-1990s to early 2000s was based on convergence in global functions, products and IT platforms along core products and activities. In parallel with aggregation by product lines, the National engaged in inbound arbitrage with the acquisition of two financial institutions in the US – Michigan National (1995) and HomeSide (1997). This entry into the US seemed to be used as a learning opportunity, which was particularly pronounced in the case of HomeSide, one of the most efficient mortgage administrators in the world. The arbitrage was based on HomeSide's superior mortgage administration systems that could then be leveraged, via aggregation, across all retails banks.

For all its efforts at integration, even in the early 2000s the National was still suffering from a deeply ingrained portfolio approach to corporate strategy, evidenced by lack of the most basic coordination mechanisms such as common reporting and control systems in the UK. The divestment of

HomeSide in 2001 after $4 billion write-offs as a result of incorrect risk assumptions in the asset valuation model, demonstrated that the headquarters lacked effective controls over the actions of HomeSide's management, particularly in the critical risk management area. The bank, its management admitted, was a collection of silos lacking interdivisional cooperation (NAB Annual Report, 2004). After experimenting with the global structure, the Bank largely reversed back to regionally-based structure to build a more locally responsive organisation. Clearly, it remained beyond the National's reach to pursue a complex integration strategy based on concurrent replication of competitive advantages in new markets and creation of new advantages via inbound arbitrage, while trying to maintain superior financial performance in the absence of strong coordination mechanisms.

There is nothing inherently 'wrong' with a domestic portfolio strategy. As we have seen from the examples of the firms in our study, under certain circumstances, it can create value by exploiting market failure and institutional voids in the domestic market. In principle, the same could be true of an international portfolio/multi-domestic strategy, were it not for two interdependent factors. First, as already explained, there is limited transferability (non-fungibility) of firms' competitive advantages to international markets due to location-specificity of strategic assets. Secondly, there is a liability of foreignness, which involves increased costs of doing business abroad (Hymer, 1960; Zaheer, 1995). It can be argued that even if internationalising firms correctly estimate the attractiveness of foreign markets – and cases such as Foster's in China suggest that this is much harder than it seems – they are unlikely in foreign markets to gain preferential access to 'undervalued' assets or assets that have a good strategic fit. The main obstacles are unfamiliarity with the business environment and lack of social capital.

Based on what is known about the negative effects of acquisitions on corporate performance (Tichy, 2001), an international portfolio strategy is unlikely to succeed. Not only does the portfolio approach require serial acquisitions, which increases the complexity of the organisation, but also the task of integrating acquisitions becomes much more difficult when trying to operate across national boundaries. Empirical evidence such as the oft-cited KPMG (1999) study suggests that, although cross-border mergers and acquisitions are actually more successful than domestic acquisitions, 53 per cent of these deals decrease shareholder value, 30 per cent of deals leave it unchanged and only 17 per cent increase it. To create value in international markets in the 1990s, the firms in our study needed both capabilities that could provide competitive advantages in new markets (or be able to acquire such capabilities via inbound arbitrage) and coordination skills to manage arbitrage, aggregation or complex integration across markets. Their administrative heritage of relying on strategic assets and a portfolio approach to strategy meant that they struggled to develop these capabilities and skills.

CONCLUSION

This study of 11 large Australian-owned firms in four industries shows that they all had a distinct administrative heritage characterised by a domestic portfolio mentality and reliance on strategic assets for competitive advantage, together with weak FDI traditions. Such an administrative heritage predetermined and limited their value-creation opportunities internationally, because they tended without reflection to transfer their value-creation approaches and associated organisational arrangements from their domestic market to international markets. Our findings support the propositions advanced by Bartlett and Ghoshal (1989) and Collis (1991) that a firm's administrative heritage establishes unique constraints on future strategic choice.

This study has major implications for research and managerial practice. For researchers the clear path dependence between a firm's domestic and international strategy suggests that these two dimensions should be explored interdependently rather than separately, as has been the practice so far in most studies aiming at explaining the success and failure of MNCs in international markets (for an interdependent approach, see Meyer, forthcoming). International corporate strategy in diversified firms – as opposed to international business strategy and business and corporate strategies in domestic firms – requires very careful attention to the location- and business-specificity of firm resources. This domain of strategy is the most complex and, arguably, 'the one about which we currently know the least' (Ghemawat, 2003: 147).

The managerial implications of our study resonate with the arguments of resource-based theorists and international management scholars. Because history matters, managers of large Australian firms require a deeper understanding of the strengths and limitations of their administrative heritage. Normatively, such understanding is essential for the management of change (Collis, 1991). According to a recent report, Australian firms are at a critical juncture in their corporate development, with many firms having reached the saturation point in terms of market share in the domestic market, so that further growth must come from offshore operations (Hooper and Aylmer, 2005). Until managers move away from deeply ingrained 'portfolio mentalities' with little integration and coordination between business units and instead commit themselves to the development of synergies, capabilities and sophisticated mechanisms of coordination, there is little prospect of their firms succeeding in highly competitive international markets.

To what extent can the experiences of the eleven firms in this study be generalised to the larger population of Australian firms now undertaking FDI? Following upon Merrett (Chapter 2), we argue that this administrative heritage is typical of large firms from oligopolistic industries involved in the first big wave of internationalisation after 1980. Later chapters in this book will set out in more detail the administrative heritage of the financial services, shipping, wine and retailing industries and the specific cases of Burns Philp, BHP, Foster's, Pacific Dunlop and TNT, all of which fit nicely with this theoretical framework. Recent evidence of the first-wave survivors and their successors shows that firms have learnt from their failures and disappointments and are now applying more sophisticated strategies with much better performance outcomes. In short, administrative heritage is an important constraint on internationalisation, especially in the early phase, but it is not a straightjacket.

There are also some industries and firms to which our framework is not generalisable. For example, the consulting engineering industry (Chapter 11 below) is a niche global industry which has always had an international orientation and does not require large commitments in fixed assets. There is also a growing population of successful Australian 'born globals' such as ResMed (manufacturer of medical respiratory devices), Cochlear (manufacturer of hearing implants), Mincom (developer of enterprise planning solutions for asset-intensive industries), ThinkSmart (a financial services company specialising in high-volume transactions) and many boutique wineries which have different administrative heritages. Such highly focused firms have had a global mindset right from the outset and rely on superior internationally transferable capabilities. Nevertheless, many 'born globals' are exporters who are able to capitalise on cross-border differences in product and factor markets but are yet to make strategic foreign direct investments. Some of these 'born globals', such as boutique wineries, are unlikely ever to make the transition to FDI.

NOTES

1. The Commonwealth Bank, fourth major player in the oligopolistic financial services industry, was excluded because of its lack of internationalization and ownership by the government; Orlando Wyndham, the fourth major firm in the wine industry, was excluded because it is not an Australian firm, being owned by the French alcoholic beverages company Pernod Ricard.
2. From 1987 Australian firms were required to report business and geographical segment profitability but here we have not used geographical segment profitability for the recessionary period 1988-91 that followed after the 1987 stock market crash. The Australian economy was more stable over the period 1992-2001.

3. Japanese firms achieved similar outcomes through business groups known as *keiretsu*.
4. The alternative interpretation is that some senior executives within the company saw the acquisition as a primary path to internationalisation, with the Australian assets being an add-on to the Utah assets (Chapter 14).
5. Interview with Brian Hartzer, Managing Director Global Cards and Payments, ANZ Banking Group, 24 October 2001.
6. Interview with David Combe, former Senior Vice President, International, Southcorp, 5 March 2001. The situation changed with the departure of Ray King and the acquisition of Mildara Blass by Foster's, which brought in a much more sophisticated view about the value of exports.
7. Thomas Hardy and Berri Renmano Limited (BRL) merged in 1993 to form BRL Hardy. After the acquisition by Constellation Brands (US), BRL Hardy is known as Hardy Wines.
8. Interview with Barry Cusack, Managing Director – Australia, 21 August 2001.
9. In the late 1990s-early 2000s Southcorp divested its water heating and packaging businesses to focus on the wine business.
10. It should be remembered that Visy was a private company and the principal-agent (owner-manager) arrangement was different than that in the publicly listed companies.
11. Rugman and Verbeke (2004) extensively discuss the location-bound nature of knowledge but do not quite make the distinction between strategic assets (positional advantages) and capabilities and their international transferability.
12. The computations of BRL Hardy's cost of capital demonstrate that the firm did not earn economic profit from international operations in 1992-96, but improved its performance in 1997-2001, when the spreads became positive. In part, this improvement in performance of international assets is due to the exchange rate effect (the depreciation of the Australian dollar versus the British pound). On average, its domestic assets were less profitable than international assets, which can be explained by BRL Hardy's export orientation and heavy investments in the domestic market. Asset efficiency calculations (sales/assets) show that its international assets were significantly more efficient than domestic assets (1.79 vs 0.68). BRL Hardy's European trading business was highly profitable, with ROIC steadily increasing to almost 40 per cent in 1997 after the initial difficulties with the acquisitions in 1990-91.

4. Large Australian Firms: Empirical Evidence on Internationalisation

Tatiana Zalan*

The focus of this chapter is on the internationalisation experiences of large multinational corporations (MNCs). Large enterprises are the backbone of the Australian economy – they are big employers and income earners, dominate key industries (such as mining, retail trade, communications, building and construction, air transport and petroleum refining) and contribute significantly to Australia's exports and stocks of outward foreign direct investment (FDI). Of these enterprises, the role of the top 100 enterprises (ranked on the basis of worldwide revenues) is of utmost importance: they account for around 20 per cent of the nation's revenues and 11 per cent of the total workforce, some 70 per cent of the total capitalisation of the Australian Stock Exchange (ASX), 35 per cent of Australia's merchandise exports, 48 per cent of Australia's export of non-travel services, and over 90 per cent of the total stock of Australian FDI abroad. As a group, they derive almost a quarter of their revenues offshore (DFAT, 2002). Nine Australian firms are on the *Fortune Global 500* (2005) list: Coles Myer (235), BHP Billiton (241), National Australia Bank (269), Woolworths (289), Telstra (401), Commonwealth Bank of Australia (406), AMP (422), Westpac Banking Corporation (477) and ANZ (490).

Previous chapters have presented detailed accounts of the scope and character of outward FDI flows by Australian multinationals and their motivations to become multinationals, with reference to country-specific and firm-specific advantages. They have also discussed the strategic value of offshore assets and have elaborated on the administrative heritage of a population of Australian MNCs, which appeared to be a constraint on internationalisation. Earlier work on the international firm and the international competitiveness of Australian business has also significantly

---

* I am grateful to Klaus Meyer, Geoffrey Lewis, Tom Osegowitsch and Howard Dick for useful comments on the previous drafts of the chapter.

contributed to understanding the behaviour of Australian MNCs in international markets (Yetton et al., 1991; Industry Commission, 1996b; Morkel et al., 1999; Morkel and Osegowitsch, 1999; Merrett, 2000, 2002a; DFAT, 2002; Fleming et al., 2004). The prime purpose of this chapter is to systematise the available firm-level empirical evidence on the offshore activities of large Australian MNCs and to present new data on the nature and extent of firm internationalisation.

Our second objective is to contrast the experiences of large Australian firms with those of firms from other economies. As argued in Chapters 1 and 2, it makes sense to compare Australian firms with multinationals from other small open economies with similar levels of economic development and population size. However, given the data limitations, reference to other groups of MNCs will also be made. As a framework for this comparative perspective, we adapt the exhaustive study of contemporary MNCs by van den Berghe (2003). Acknowledging the complex, multi-faceted character of firm-level internationalisation (Welch and Luostarinen, 1988; Sullivan, 1994; Annavarjula and Beldona, 2000), the framework captures four different dimensions of internationalisation. These dimensions are: (1) the extent of firm internationalisation; (2) management and governance structure; (3) orientations (behaviours and attitudes) of managers to internationalisation, and (4) financial performance implications of internationalisation. Because the theme of Australian firms as 'late internationalisers' has been so prominent in much previous research (Chapters 2 and 3, also Bartlett and Ghoshal, 2000), we add a fifth dimension – the timing of entry into international market.

This chapter begins by documenting the timing of entry and then details the other four dimensions of degree of internationalisation, management and governance structures, orientations of senior managers and financial performance, concluding with a summary of insights and implications. The indicators for each dimension are summarised in Appendix 1.

FIVE DIMENSIONS OF INTERNATIONALISATION

Timing of Entry

It is often assumed that Australian MNCs, on average, are late internationalisers via FDI relative to MNCs in the triad countries. For example, Bartlett and Ghoshal (2000) refer to Australian firms as 'late movers' into global markets, together with emerging multinationals from Brazil, India, Korea and the Philippines. Merrett (2002a, 2002b; also Chapter 2) notes that Australian firms had been reluctant to become multinationals before the 1980s, citing a combination of Australia's comparative advantage and government policies as major contributing factors to this belated entry. Dick and Merrett (Chapter 1) allude to firms in Australia being reluctant or just uninterested in investing offshore before the 1980s, and Merrett (2002a,b) argues that this late entry puts Australian firms at a competitive disadvantage in foreign markets. Indeed, well-established MNCs, being early internationalisers, continue to shape current internationalisation patterns and are responsible for a large part of the world's FDI and trade flows (Tulder et al., 2001).

The Australian experience seems to be inconsistent with that of a number of firms from small open economies, such as Sweden, Denmark and Norway. Considerable evidence now exists that these MNCs demonstrate a high propensity to internationalise their operations, constrained by a small domestic economy combined with access to fewer location-specific advantages in the home market (Bellak and Cantwell, 1997; Benito et al., 2002). For example, internationalisation of many Swedish firms via FDI dates back more than a century: Sandvik, one of the four firms in the seminal study of the internationalisation process by Johanson and Wiedersheim-Paul (1975) established its first sales subsidiary in the UK in 1914 and its first manufacturing subsidiary in France in 1937.[1]

We believe, however, that the extent to which Australian MNCs were late movers is overstated. To start with, judgements as to whether Australian MNCs were late to internationalise via FDI should take into account the broader pattern of Australia's historical development (Lewis et al., 1999; also Chapter 2). For nearly two centuries, until the UK joined the EEC in 1973, trade with the former colonies was based on export industries which leveraged Australia's comparative advantages in resource endowments and import-substituting industries (PCEK, 1990). This system ensured that Australians enjoyed one of the highest living standards in the world. It is hardly surprising, then, that Australian firms had few incentives to internationalise via FDI.

Nevertheless, Australian MNCs were by no means 'outliers' in terms of their late entry into foreign markets: MNCs from developed countries as diverse as Finland and Japan were similar in this regard. Finland, being a small country with access to a large European market, should have provided an environment conducive to internationalisation, yet until the mid 1980s the amount and value of FDI by Finnish firms had been very modest. It was only from the mid-1980s that Finnish manufacturing firms internationalised at a rapid pace, with outward FDI flows in 1988-1990 exceeding the corresponding flows during the previous 20 years (Kallunki et al., 2001; Benito et al., 2002). Japanese firms' entry into international markets via FDI has also been quite recent, with the most dramatic period of expansion being the mid-1980s to the late 1990s (UNCTAD, 2000), largely driven by the rapid appreciation of the yen and the pressure applied by the US and Europeans governments in the form of 'voluntary' import quotas. Finally, a large population of European firms from formerly state-owned utilities (such as Spanish Telefónica and Electricité de France) had little or no international activities in the early 1990s and are now rapidly building up scale in world markets (Tulder et al., 2001). Internationalisation for firms from emerging and transition economies, such as Brazil, Russia, India, China, Malaysia, Taiwan and Thailand is yet to take place on a significant scale (Li, 2003).

Even if Australian firms are regarded as 'late movers' to international markets relative to firms from some small open economies, this does not mean that they will not be able to catch up by adopting 'accelerated strategies' that are resource- and knowledge-seeking rather than resource-exploiting (Dunning, 1995; Li, 2003; Young et al., 1996). Amcor Ltd is a telling example of a late internationaliser which not only caught up with other MNCs in the packaging industry but has recently become a world leader, with annual sales of around US$11 billion and 240 plants in 39 countries, it is now among the world's top three packaging firms by market capitalisation, sales and profits. Doz et al. (2001) argue persuasively that in the new environment where companies increasingly compete on their ability to discover, mobilise and leverage knowledge dispersed around the world, 'what matters is not where you are from but who you are'. While their proposition appears somewhat extreme – a firm's administrative heritage, as shown in Chapter 3, is equally important and may indeed prove a strategic constraint on internationalisation – late entry of Australian MNCs into foreign markets should not necessarily translate into competitive disadvantage.

Extent of Internationalisation

Ever since the Harvard Multinational Enterprise Research Project (Vernon, 1966), international business and strategy researchers have tried to unravel the nature and extent of international involvement of MNCs (van Tulder et al., 2001). Recent findings on the global scope of MNC activities are reported in two detailed studies by Tulder et al. (2001) and Berghe (2003). On a sample of companies from the SCOPE database (referred to as 'Core Companies'),[2] the researchers find that even well-established MNCs (those that internationalised well before the 1990s) have quite low levels of foreign assets (35 per cent) and foreign sales (45 per cent), while the composite Transnationality Index[3] of the 100 largest Core Companies is around 35 per cent (1998 data). In addition, at least 75 per cent of firm activity appears to be concentrated in only two regions of the world.

Perhaps the most comprehensive firm-level studies on globalisation are Rugman and Verbeke (2004) and Rugman's (2005) research into the largest MNCs drawn from the Fortune 500 list in fiscal year 2001. The researchers conclude that most of these firms are not global companies, in the sense of a broad and deep penetration of the triad markets of Asia-Pacific, Europe and North America. Adopting the extended triad concept of Ohmae (1985) and using the ratio of foreign sales to total sales as an indicator of multinationality,[4] Rugman and Verbeke establish that most large MNCs have an average of 80 per cent of total sales in their home triad region: only nine firms of the largest 500 companies are unambiguously global. For example, Wal-Mart, the largest Fortune 500 firm, with 94 per cent of its sales in North America, is a home-region oriented MNC. At the downstream end of the firms' value chain, most MNCs are trying to capitalise on similarities across markets. At the upstream end (including FDI-driven manufacturing), firms add value primarily through arbitrage, that is by exploiting differences across nations and regions. Rugman and Verbeke interpret these results as the outcome of a rational preference of managers for regionally based activities, resulting from a careful cost-benefit calculation. Like Ohmae, Rugman and colleagues are highly prescriptive in what MNC managers should do: for instance, Rugman and Collinson (2005: 271) assert that managers of European multinationals should 'forget about the need for a global strategy' and must not become 'overly concerned with markets outside of Europe'.

Using a similar method to Rugman and Verbeke (2004), we have calculated the degree of multinationality for the largest Australian firms in fiscal years 2004/05, supplementing these data with the proportion of foreign assets to total assets.[5] The sampling frame was the Business Review Weekly 100 list based on the Australian Stock Exchange (ASX) 100 list where firms are ranked by market capitalisation. Unlike Rugman and Verbeke, who include 54 purely domestic firms in their 'home regional' categorisation of multinationals (Osegowitsch and Sammartino, 2006), we exclude those companies that do not report foreign sales (assumed to be domestic firms).[6] The final list consists of 58 firms (Appendix 4.2). Based on the assets and sales data, Table 4.1 compares the distribution for Australian firms with Rugman and Verbeke's findings.

The conclusion from these calculations is that the majority of Australian firms with international operations are either bi-regional or home-region oriented, which is consistent with the Rugman and Verbeke study. Although direct comparisons with Rugman and Verbeke's study are fraught with difficulties,[7] the Australian sample reveals a much higher incidence of global and bi-regional firms. If the four Australian firms originally classified as bi-regional by assets but global by sales plus the one firm originally classified as global by assets and host-region oriented by sales, and the firm classified as global by assets and bi-regional by sales are added to this list (Table 4.1, explanatory note d), the number of global firms increases to ten, which is over 17 per cent of the sample. Similarly, if the three firms belonging to the

Table 4.1: Internationalisation of Austalian firms (2004/05) by comparison with Fortune 500 firms (2001)

Classification	Australian firms	Representative Australian firms	*Fortune 500* firms	Representative *Fortune 500* firms
Home-region oriented	30 (50.8%)[a]	ANZ, AMP, Coles Myer, Santos	266 (85.5%)[b]	Wal-Mart, GE, Total Fina Elf and Sumitomo
Bi-regional	9 (15.5%)	Westfield, Rio Tinto, Brambles Industries	25 (8%)	BP, Electrolux, 3M, Nissan
Global	4 (6.7%)	Amcor, Lend Lease, Babcock & Brown, and Sims Group	9 (2.9%)	IBM, Sony, Philips, Nokia, Intel, Canon, Coca-Cola, Flextronics, LVMH
Host-region oriented	1 (1.7%)	Paperlinx[c]	11 (3.5%)	News Corporation, ING Group, Royal Ahold, Honda
Mixed categorisation[d]	14 (24.1%)	BHP Billiton, National Australia Bank, CSL, Rinker Group, Ansell	N/A	N/A
Total	58		311	

Notes:

a. Percentage of the 58 firms included in the study.
b. Percentage of the 311 firms included in the study. These percentages do not match those reported in Rugman and Verbeke (2004: 7) because the 54 purely domestic firms in their study have been excluded to allow comparison with Australian firms.
c. The majority of sales and assets are in Europe.
d. Depending on whether sales or assets are used as a base. These included global by assets and host-region oriented by sales firms (Macquarie Infrastructure Group); home-region oriented by assets and bi-regional by sales (3 firms: BHP Billiton, Aristocrat Leisure, Zinifex); bi-regional by assets and home region-oriented by sales (4 firms: National Australia Bank, Centro Properties Group, DB REEF Trust and Flight Centre); bi-regional by assets and global by sales (4 firms: CSL, Computershare, Billabong International and Nufarm), bi-regional by assets and host-region oriented by sales (Rinker Group), and global by assets and bi-regional by sales (Ansell).

Source: Annual Reports

mixed category (classified as bi-regional by sales and home-region oriented by assets) were reclassified as bi-regional, which is consistent with Rugman and Verbeke's operationalisation of multinationality, there would be 14 bi-regional MNCs (24 per cent of the sample). Clearly, for a considerable proportion of Australian MNCs globalisation is no longer a distant goal, let alone a 'myth', as has been claimed by Rugman and his co-authors on many occasions (Rugman and Bain, 2003; Rugman and Girod, 2003; Rugman, 2005; Rugman and Verbeke, 2004).

Whether these firms exemplify best practice as benchmarks to be emulated by other firms, as Rugman and Verbeke (2004: 16) suggest, is another matter. It is dangerous to equate geographic spread of activities with global market success. The litmus test is whether being more global translates into superior performance. For example, of the firms classified as 'global' either by sales, assets or both, only one – Billabong International – is an outstanding performer, with returns on foreign assets of almost 40 per cent for 2005. Amcor, Babcock & Brown, CSL, Nufarm and Sims Group do not report the profitability of their foreign assets, while returns of Computershare (1.5 per cent), Macquarie Infrastructure Group (4.8 per cent) and Lend Lease (9 per cent) are unimpressive.

The robustness of Rugman and Verbeke's (2004) index of globalisation has been subject to criticism. Stevens and Bird (2004) offer a detailed critique, as also do Osegowitsch and Sammartino (2006). It is not our intention to contribute to this criticism but three limitations of the Rugman and Verbeke classification should be noted as affecting how we interpret the findings. First, like Stevens and Bird (2004), we question the rationale for selecting sales revenues as the only appropriate measure of globalisation for it is clearly driven by accounting rules. For example, Rugman and Verbeke (2004) do not specify how exports are treated in their study, that is, whether exports are reported as domestic sales or sales in foreign markets. If the measure of foreign sales to total sales captures exports from the domestic base, not sales by foreign subsidiaries, it will distort their findings and hence their recommendations.[8]

A second problem is that Rugman and Verbeke's classification seems to be biased toward the manufacturing sector and the triad countries. It does not make business sense that resource companies Rio Tinto and BHP Billiton, which have assets dispersed all over the world, including in non-triad countries in Latin America and Africa, and conduct active exploration on a global basis, are not classified as 'global'. Their exploration effort, being an upstream activity, internationalises far ahead of their production process and once the exploration effort is complete, the firm may or may not proceed with mine development. Such global exploration activity would not be captured by an index of foreign to total sales. Considering what we know about the strategies of BHP Billiton and Rio Tinto, it would appear odd to think of them as anything but global firms leveraging economies of scale, scope and experience, and arbitraging opportunities across markets (Chapter 14). Finally, the triad is operationalised so broadly that it loses all connection with the original conception of Ohmae (1985). The implication in the specific case of Australia is that firms that focus exclusively on Australia and New Zealand and those that have operations in the Asian region, often in countries characterised by significant economic, cultural and institutional differences, would both classify as 'home-region oriented'.

With all these caveats in mind, ideas presented in Rugman and Verbeke (2004), Ghemawat (2001, 2005), Kogut (1985) and Kogut and Kulatilaka (1994a, 1994b) could be a useful starting point to explore the normative implications of these findings to managers of Australian MNCs. Judging by our sample's high proportion of home-region oriented firms, we can hypothesise, consistent with Rugman and Verbeke (2004), that Australian managers – as well as managers of other MNCs on the Fortune 500 list – are often unable to leverage the competitive advantages of their firms beyond their home region. The Australian banking industry is a case in point. Three major banks (the National, ANZ and Commonwealth) have their operations primarily in the Asia-Pacific, with the National being a bi-regional firm in terms of assets (25 per cent of its assets are located in Europe). Westpac, the fourth largest bank, is essentially a domestic bank, after having made an unsuccessful attempt, starting in the mid 1980s, to become 'Australia's World Bank' (Chapter 7).

It is possible that Australian managers are not fully exploiting cultural, administrative, geographic and economic arbitraging opportunities in foreign markets, which limits their strategic repertoire of value-adding via FDI to exploiting similarities across markets at the expense of exploiting differences. Global strategy involves pursuit of operational flexibility which permits the MNC to exploit environmental uncertainty and volatility and create a broad opportunity set (see Kogut, 1985; Kogut and Kulatilaka, 1994a). Hence, it is likely that short-term orientations of Australian investors prevent senior executives from capitalising on flexibility and growth options inherent in investments in less familiar, distant and risky markets of Asia, Africa, Latin America and Central and Eastern Europe. It is equally plausible that managers of Australian MNCs are well aware of the negative consequences of extensive international diversification which have been widely communicated to the Australian business community (Ferguson and James, 2003).

Finally, Australian managers might realise that a good regional strategy, ranging from home-based strategies to inter-regional platforms, can create more value than purely global or purely local ones (Ghemawat, 2005). This point is well illustrated by Macquarie Bank, a profitable financial service institution which outperformed all ASX top 50 companies over the 1996-2005 period in terms of shareholder returns. In part this success is explained by a very selective international strategy. Even though its strategy seems to be focused on its home region (where it has 72 per cent of assets and 75 per cent of sales, Appendix 4.2), the bank has a much wider geographical footprint in Europe, the Middle East, Africa, the US and Asia. The bank seeks to enter only those markets where its skills and expertise deliver real advantage to clients (Macquarie, 2005: 7; Chapter 20).

Management and Governance Structures

A critical determinant of a firm's ability to successfully deal with internationalisation is its governance structure. Consistent with Sanders and Carpenter (1998), governance can be defined as the way in which a firm's top management team is rewarded, the composition of the top team, and board structure. Because it is a pervasive source of organisational complexity, internationalisation increases both the information-processing demands placed on top management teams and the difficulty for boards in monitoring senior executives. Research explicitly linking internationalisation and management and governance structures in various national contexts is very sparse. Exceptions are Sanders and Carpenter's (1998) study of US MNCs drawn from S&P's 500 list and Simeon's (2001) study of Japanese firms. Both studies focus on the structural variables of board membership (such as size of the top team or proportion of outside directors) that are associated with an increased degree of internationalisation. Thus, highly internationalised MNCs tend to have larger top management teams and separate the CEO and board chair positions. In the absence of equivalent studies for Australia, it is not clear whether Australian firms are different or similar from their overseas counterparts in this respect.

In an Australian context, the public debate on corporate governance has largely ignored the greater complexity faced by internationalising companies (Onto and Thomas, 1997). This debate has been hampered by sparsity of rigorous research. To our knowledge, there are only two studies – Onto and Thomas (1997) and Merrett (2002a) – that explicitly focus on the relationship between internationalisation and governance. Onto and Thomas (1997) explore board membership and corporate governance processes in an interview-based study of 25 Australian MNCs with a total of 255 directors. Several findings are particularly insightful. Firstly, geographic diversity at board level, even domestically within Australia, appears to be a low priority. In the words of a board chairman, '[i]f I had my choice, all members of my board would be from Melbourne' (Onto and Thomas, 1997: 9). Secondly, foreign shareholders are poorly represented, mainly because of the number of meetings held by Australian boards, the distance and time constraints, legal liabilities imposed on directors and the past negative experiences with foreign non-executive directors. Onto and Thomas (1997: 13) conclude that 'Australian boards do not come close to reflecting the diversity of the broader society of which they are a part, let alone the markets they are seeking to serve, nor we suspect their mix of shareholders'.

A longitudinal historical approach adopted by Merrett (2002c) provides insights into the changes in the Australian corporate governance system since 1980. Merrett argues that the introduction of competitive market forces in the late 1980s as a result of micro-economic reform placed new demands on managers. The complexity of international and domestic business environments gave rise to information asymmetries between managers and shareholders, allowing managers to under-invest in higher-risk foreign markets. Therefore, stronger incentives were required to motivate managers to go abroad. In order to take advantage of a more open, freer economy and internationalise, Australian firms needed to first reform their corporate governance structures to provide those incentives. Merrett's main contention is that there is a causal connection between the shift from a weak to a stronger form of corporate governance in the 1990s and the increased internationalisation of Australian business. In this way corporate governance reform was solving the problem of misaligned incentives that was preventing Australian firms from internationalising.

To obtain some sense of how boards of Australian MNCs have responded to the recent challenges of globalisation, we have collected new data on the board composition of the firms included in the original Onto and Thomas (1997) study.[9] These data, together with the data from the Onto and Thomas (1997) study (Appendix C: 31) are presented in Appendix 4.3. The figures (averages and proportions) indicate that the situation has changed considerably over the last decade. The proportion of foreign directors has increased from 6 per cent in 1996 to 17 per cent in 2005, even though the increase is attributable mainly to three companies – BHP, Pacific Dunlop (now Ansell, essentially based in the US) and Leighton Holdings. In the case of BHP, the higher proportion of foreign directors is undoubtedly due to the merger with Billiton (Chapter 14). It is also worth noting that the total number of directors remained either unchanged, as in National Australia Bank, or decreased, as in Amcor, BHP, Foster's and Mayne Nickless. This is quite surprising, given that these firms have increased the scope and, most likely, complexity of their overseas operations and appears to be inconsistent with the experiences of US and Japanese firms in the two studies by Sanders and Carpenter (1998) and Simeon (2001) cited above.

Attitudes and Behaviours

In addition to quantifiable measures, such as percentage of foreign assets overseas or listings on foreign stock exchanges, internationalisation can also be conceptualised as a 'state of mind' (Perlmutter, 1969). Thus, the orientation toward foreign people, ideas and resources in headquarters and subsidiaries, and in host and home environments, becomes a critical measure of internationalisation. In the words of Perlmutter (1969: 11), 'the more one penetrates into the living reality of an international firm, the more one finds it is necessary to give serious weight to the way executives think about doing business around the world'. This cognitive dimension of internationalisation is captured by 'the EPG profile' – ethnocentric (home-country oriented), polycentric (host-country oriented) and geocentric (world-oriented) attitudes. A test of such profile on a sample of US manufacturing firms from the 'Fortune 500' list was done by Kobrin (1994), who found that a geocentric mind-set is associated with broad geographical scope. One intriguing finding is that a geocentric mindset does not appear to be a function of the length of international experience, type of strategy (multidomestic, global or transnational) or organisational structure. To our knowledge, there is no systematic empirical evidence on the global orientations of Australian managers, but there is plenty of anecdotal evidence that such a mindset is indeed the key to successful internationalisation (for example, James, 1999).

In addition to these 'soft' attitudinal measures, 'hard' indicators, such as psychic dispersion of international operations or cultural distance, have also been commonly used to explain firms' internationalisation patterns. There is a well-documented tendency for companies, particularly at the early stages of internationalisation, to penetrate markets which are more familiar or less costly to service, and these are most commonly those which are closest in physical and cultural terms (Welch and Luostarinen, 1988). The concept of psychological (psychic) distance, popularised by Johanson and Vahlne (1977), has been operationalised and tested in many national contexts. 'Psychic distance' refers to the distance between the home market and a foreign market, resulting from the perception of cultural, institutional and language differences (O'Grady and Lane, 1996; Evans and Mavondo, 2002). A related narrower concept is 'cultural distance', operationalised by Kogut and Singh (1988), which refers to the differences in the values, norms and beliefs of one group or category of people from another (Hofstede, 1980; Harzing, 2003).[10]

Two multi-country studies (Luo, 2001; Pangarkar and Klein, 2001), which include a sub-sample of Australian firms, use cultural distance as a measure of multinationality. While these studies are useful in explaining the choice of entry strategy into foreign markets (between joint ventures and wholly owned subsidiaries, and between equity and non-equity alliances, respectively),[11] they are less insightful in establishing the reasons why Australian managers should choose certain markets in preference to others or, more generally, explaining global orientations of Australian managers. Two studies by Vicziany and Chatterjee (1999) and Chatterjee (1999) shed light on attitudes of Australian managers to international opportunities and emphasise the need for reorienting managerial mindsets, which they see as far more critical than considerations for design, product or distribution systems adaptations. The focus of both these studies is India, which makes them hard to generalise to other contexts.

Given the dearth of empirical studies focusing on either 'hard' or 'soft' indicators of managerial orientations, we have decided to deduce such orientations from what firms communicate about the importance of international operations to their overall strategy. Data were collected from publicly available secondary sources in the form of annual reports for 2004/05 and corporate websites for our sample of the 58 largest Australian MNCs. The firms' vision and mission statements and sections on strategy and objectives in annual reports appeared to contain most of the needed information, from which inferences were drawn on managerial attitudes and orientations to international markets. As a bonus, this approach allowed some triangulation of the Rugman and Verbeke (2004) classification scheme applied to these firms. Although these secondary data did not allow us to quantify managerial attitudes and behaviours according to accepted measures such as psychic distance or entrepreneurial orientation, subject to an element of subjectivity we could nevertheless draw conclusions on the global visions of senior executives. Table 4.2 sets out some illustrative examples.

Although the word 'global' is overused and likely to have different meanings to managers and academics, this analysis gives rise to some interesting findings. At least 31 firms (53 per cent) state their global aspirations as being in one or more businesses,[12] which is considerably higher than when the Rugman and Verbeke (2004) classification scheme is applied to the same data. However, there is still a significant proportion of firms (22 firms, or 38 per cent) that see themselves as having a narrow geographical focus predominantly on Australia, New Zealand and the Pacific. Examples include Westpac, Coles Myer, Coca-Cola Amatil (CCA), Promina Group and John Fairfax Holdings. For some of these firms, current home region bias appears to be a consequence of being badly burnt in prior forays in international markets. Back in the late 1980s Westpac's ambition was to build a profitable international presence to service an increasingly international customer base, leading to an aggressive expansion in the wholesale markets of the US and the UK. Although ill-considered international expansion was not what eventually 'broke the bank', some international activities (the European and the Americas divisions) nevertheless diluted shareholder value and were eventually divested or closed (Carew, 1997). CCA was also an aggressive internationaliser but, like Westpac, later retreated from international markets (Chapter 16).

Table 4.2: Global orientations of Australian firms: Illustrative example

Firm	Statement of global aspirations or vision
QBE Insurance	QBE's underlying business strategy is to maintain operations in key global insurance markets and to be a lead underwriter for selected lines of business setting rates and conditions in the markets in which it operates.
Foster's Group	Foster's Group is a premium global multi-beverage company delivering a total portfolio of beer, wine, spirits, cider and non-alcohol beverages. Our products inspire global enjoyment and are enjoyed by consumers all over the world.
Brambles Industries	Brambles is a leading global provider of support services, operating in almost 50 countries across six continents and employing approximately 28,000 people.
CSL Ltd	CSL Limited is a global, specialty biopharmaceutical company that develops, manufactures and markets products to treat and prevent serious human medical conditions.
Aristocrat Leisure	Aristocrat Leisure is the leading global provider of gaming solutions, namely world-class software, systems and hardware that consistently outperform the competition. Aristocrat's products and services are available in over 55 countries around the world.

Source: Annual Reports and corporate websites

Financial Performance

What ultimately matters to managers and investors in Australian MNCs is whether internationalisation creates value and improves the financial performance of the firm. The relationship between international diversification and performance (IDP) has been the focus of much recent empirical work in different national contexts. International diversification is identified as bringing economic benefits to a firm, such as increased capital and labour arbitraging opportunities, access to wider consumer markets, increased economies of scale, ability to amortise R&D expenditures across multiple markets, worldwide learning opportunities and access to specialised knowledge available in foreign markets (Ghoshal, 1987, Kogut and Kulatilaka, 1994; Doz et al., 2001). Pursuit of international diversification is also associated with significant costs. Geringer et al. (2000) give a detailed explanation of how costs influence MNC performance: examples include the 'liability of foreignness' or the costs of operating in an unknown business environment, and bureaucratic (governance) costs of managing a hierarchy (Hymer, 1960; Zaheer, 1995). The net effect of international diversification on performance is, however, not well understood from either conceptual or empirical standpoints (Hennart, 2005).

Empirical studies into the IDP relationship fall into two categories (Grant, 1987): comparative studies, which compare the performance of MNCs vs. domestic companies (DCs), and control studies, which explore performance effects associated with different levels of internationalisation while explicitly controlling for various variables, such as size and industry affiliation. Researchers who have tested the IDP relationship using the second approach have come to inconclusive results, showing a positive and negative linear, curvilinear (normal and inverted U-shape), S-shaped, or even no relationship (Ruigrok and Wagner, 2004). Recent comparative empirical studies are fewer in number, but they seem to suggest that either there are no statistically significant differences in the performance of MNCs and DCs, as is the case for firms from Hong Kong (Wan, 1998) or that DCs out-perform MNCs, as in Canada (Mathur et al., 2001). Two of the most comprehensive recent studies (Click and Harrison, 2000; Denis et al., 2002) have investigated the extent to which a firm's internationalisation is valued by investors, each using in excess of 40,000 US firm-year observations over a substantial period of time (1984-1997). Although the researchers use different measures of performance, both studies establish that MNCs are consistently valued at a discount relative to DCs, which, in their interpretation, represents an agency cost of internationalisation. Click and Harrison (2000) take the agency problem argument further to demonstrate that there is an inverse relationship between internationalisation and ownership of equity by MNC managers: the higher the degree of internationalisation, the less likely are managers to hold shares in the company.

Because most recent studies of Australia's outward FDI have been at the macro-level, the limited empirical evidence at the firm level has been either anecdotal (Ferguson and James, 2003) or based on single or multiple case studies (Lewis and Minchev, 2000; Stace, 1997). Interpretations drawn from this limited research of the financial performance outcomes of internationalisation seem to fall somewhere between two extremes. One view holds that a large population of Australian firms has chosen to stay domestic and those firms that did venture overseas did not succeed – a view often espoused by the popular business press (James, 1999; Ferguson and James, 2003; Roberts, 2004). This view is also supported by aggregate ABS statistics on profits earned by overseas subsidiaries of Australian companies in the 1980s to early 1990s, which show a sharp decline in profitability over this period (Chapter 2). The alternative view furnishes what could be an overly optimistic picture of internationalisation (Stace, 1997; Yetton et al., 1991; PCEK, 1990), possibly because financial performance has not been much of a concern in these studies.[13]

Four recent empirical studies provide much-needed evidence on the relationship between internationalisation and financial performance. Mangos et al. (2002) and Clarke et al. (2003), both belonging to the 'control' studies group, investigate the nature of the IDP relationship, but apply different theoretical lenses. Mangos et al. (2002), drawing on the resource-based view of the firm and transaction cost economics, suggest that initially an international firm is able to leverage its internal resources and capabilities across a wide range of international markets, but as a firm continues international expansion it experiences increased coordination costs. The researchers find that the relationship between internationalisation and performance is non-linear, being an inverted U-shape. Likewise, Clarke et al. (2003), who couch their conceptualisation in organisational learning theory, report a non-linear, horizontal S-shaped IDP and find that a firm's international experience has a significant effect on performance. Firms with limited international experience exhibit an initial performance decline, followed by performance increase and, subsequently, performance decline. By contrast, firms with extensive international experience enjoy an initial performance increase, followed by a performance decline and a performance increase. Both studies have enriched our understanding of firm-level internationalisation outcomes, but their generalisability is limited by sampling issues.[14]

Lewis et al. (2004) take a different approach to compare FDI experiences of large Australian MNCs and DCs in the period of 1992-2001.[15] Their three key findings are, first, that MNCs do not out-perform purely domestic firms, secondly that Australian MNCs destroyed economic value, and thirdly that they were not rewarded for internationalisation by the equity market. In addition, the returns from firms' foreign assets were generally lower than returns from their domestic assets. There was also some weak evidence that the performance of the firms' foreign investments improved in 1997-2001. These findings are broadly consistent with the findings of the Australian Bureau of Statistics (ABS) and the Templeton Global Performance Index (Gestrin et al., 1998, 2001). According to the ABS, three of the four biggest markets for Australian FDI in 2001-02 failed to produce returns above the bond rate of 4.75 per cent, the minimum requirement for an investment. In 2001, the return on Australian FDI in the US (42 per cent of the total) was only 2.66 per cent, from the UK 3.45 per cent (15 per cent of the total) and 1.69 per cent from Japan (6 per cent of the total). Only the return from

New Zealand (6 per cent of the total) was healthy, at 8.1 per cent (Ferguson and James, 2003: 40). The average returns on Australian firms' foreign assets reported in the Templeton Global Performance Index were even lower, at 0.31 per cent in 1996-1997 and at 1.51 per cent in 2000, which placed Australia in the last place in terms of performance in both years.[16]

A qualitative study by Zalan (2003) offers a grounded theory explanation for the lack of success using the experiences of 11 large Australian-owned MNCs in four industries. Two of the most important propositions advanced in the study are that Australian firms are unable to succeed in international markets due to two factors: resource asymmetry vis-à-vis foreign market incumbents and the firms' administrative heritage. Chapter 3 describes the administrative heritage of the firms in the study and explains its impact on internationalisation outcomes. Resource asymmetry is caused by several factors, but perhaps the most important one is the limited transferability of the sources of competitive advantages from the home market to international markets (Hu, 1995). Two complementary explanations of the limited transferability of competitive advantages are offered: the nature of advantages, that is, whether they result from positional/structural advantages or dynamic capabilities (Porter, 1980; Teece et al., 1997; Williamson, 2005) and the business and institutional context into which resources are transferred. The example of BRL Hardy illustrates this point: even though the firm developed positional advantages based on strong brands in its local market, consumer brand loyalty in the important UK market in the mid-1990s had to be built from scratch. Unlike the Australian market, where branded wine accounted for 90 per cent of sales, the UK market was dominated by supermarkets' own house brands and an almost indecipherable array of French, Italian and Spanish brands. The structure of distribution channels was also different: while in Australia wine was typically sold through hotels and bottle shops, in the UK wine suppliers sold wine to supermarkets and 'off licenses' (the equivalent of bottle shops). Under those circumstances, it was difficult to support a brand-driven strategy. Instead, BRL Hardy had to manage a progression from commodity, to commodity brand, to soft brand and then finally to hard brand, with distribution playing the key role at the early stage of this progression (Bartlett, 2000).

What broad conclusions can be drawn from this evidence on firm performance? It would seem that the first significant wave of FDI by Australian MNCs in the 1980s led to reduced returns on foreign assets. During the second wave of FDI in the 1990s, MNC performance in terms of economic profitability was also poor, with some evidence of improvement in the late 1990s. The third wave of FDI started in the late 1990s, but in the absence of firm-level data on the profitability of foreign operations it is difficult to judge whether there has been any learning or 'lag and lead' effect at work, when past investments are eventually starting to pay off dividends.[17]

CONCLUSIONS

Empirical research on large Australian firms, though frustratingly limited, presents the following picture. Australian MNCs are indeed late entrants into international markets via FDI, but firms from other economies, both developing and developed such as Japan, Korea, Taiwan and Finland are also quite late entrants. The significant proportion of global and bi-regional firms in our sample compared with the Fortune-500 sample leads to the conclusion that for many Australian MNCs globalisation is no longer an aspiration but, increasingly, a strategic reality.

Boards of some of the largest Australian MNCs have responded to the challenges of globalisation over the last decade by changing the composition of membership in favour of foreign directors. At the same time, the total number of directors has either remained stable or even decreased, which is surprising given the increased complexity of these firms' international operations. Over half of the largest Australian MNCs aspire to be global leaders and have explicitly stated their global ambitions. Finally, high degrees of internationalisation via FDI for Australian firms seem to be associated with reduced profitability, which is consistent with other recent non-linear 'control' studies in other contexts. Australian MNCs did not perform well in international markets and destroyed economic value in the 1990s decade, which is similar to the experiences of US firms in a comparable period. Although there is weak evidence that the performance of the firms' foreign assets has improved since the late 1990s, the jury is still out as to whether the high levels of internationalisation achieved by Australian MNCs relative to Fortune-500 firms are profitable and sustainable. Australia may well be an example of a country that tried to internationalise, failed, persisted and eventually learnt from past mistakes, but this will be better judged at the end of the decade.

Appendix 4.1: Five dimensions of internationalisation

Dimension	Measures
(1) Timing of entry	The year (decade) when firms started internationalisation*
(2) Extent of internationalisation	*single*
	Foreign Sales to Total Sales (FSTS)
	Foreign Assets to Total Assets (FATA)
	Export Sales to Total Sales (ESTS)
	Foreign Employment to Total Employment (FETE)
	Foreign Subsidiaries to Total Subsidiaries (FSUBS)
	Foreign R&D expense to total R&D expense
	Number of countries of operation
	Network-spread index:
	Sales spread
	Assets spread
	Employment spread
	Global Dispersion Index
	Global Market Diversification Index
	composite
	UNCTAD's transnationality index (TNi)
	Multinationality index
(3) Management and governance	*board and top management team composition*
	Number of non-nationals on the board
	Nationality composition of top management teams
	governance structure
	Number of foreign stock exchanges listed
	Number of foreign shareholders
	Use of international accounting standards
(4) Attitudes and behaviours	'*soft' indicators*
	Headquarter orientation
	Global mindset or global vision
	Entrepreneurial orientation*
	'hard' indicators
	Psychic dispersion of international operations
	Top management international experience
(5) Performance	*Financial*
	Single
	Return on Sales (ROS)
	Return on Assets (ROA)
	Return on Investment (ROI)
	Return on Equity (ROE)
	Foreign operating margins
	Foreign profits to total profits
	Earnings per share
	Market share
	Sales growth*
	Economic profit*
	Tobin's q
	Excess value*
	Composite
	Templeton Global Performance Index
	Operational
	Operating costs to total sales

Note: * are indicators not appearing on the original list
Source: Berghe (2003: 129)

Appendix 4.2: Classification of the top 100 Australian firms with international operations

No.	100 Rank	Company	Business	Revenues (A$m)	Assets (A$m)	FATA, %	North America % TA	Europe % TA	Asia-Pacific % TA	FSTS, %	North America % TS	Europe % TS	Asia-Pacific % TS	Type/ Assets	Type/ Sales
1	1	BHP Billiton	Diversified resources	23,513	31,179	67.8	NA	11.6	32.2	91.4	0.0	36.7	29.5	Home RO	Bi-regional
2	2	Commonwealth Bank (6/05)	Financial services	26,078	329,035	17.5	NA	NA	95.2	20.3	NA	NA	93.2	Home RO	Home RO
3	3	National Australia Bank (9/04)	Financial services	30,184	411,309	37.6	1.6	25.3	73.0	30.5	0.8	19.0	80.1	Bi-regional	Home RO
4	4	ANZ Banking Group (9/04)	Financial services	17,508	259,345	34.3	NA	NA	92.6	32.8	NA	NA	93.7	Home RO	Home RO
5	5	Westpac Banking Corporation (9/04)	Financial services	18,126	245,079	19.3	0	0	100.0	18.1	0	0	100.0	Home RO	Home RO
6	7	Westfield Group	Shopping centres	1,717	32,488	52.7d	48.0	4.6	47.3	56.3d	54.6	1.7	43.7	Bi-regional	Bi-regional
7	8	Rio Tinto	Diversified resources	13,323	16,609	38.7d	27.4	NA	61.3	50.4d	33.9	NA	49.6	Bi-regional	Bi-regional
8	9	Coles Myer (7/04)	Retailing	32,267	8,735	3.6	0	0	100.0	0.5	0	0	100.0	Home RO	Home RO

No.	100 Rank	Company	Business	Revenues (A$m)	Assets (A$m)	FATA, %	North America % TA	Europe % TA	Asia-Pacific % TA	FSTS, %	North America % TS	Europe % TS	Asia-Pacific % TS	Type/ Assets	Type/ Sales
9	12	AMP	Financial services	10,900	12,969	16.4d	NA	NA	83.6	0.6d	NA	NA	99.4	Home RO	Home RO
10	13	QBE Insurance	Insurance	10,424	25,102	75.3	8.4	25.4	30.1	76.4	17.4	53.2	29.4	Bi-regional	Bi-regional
11	14	Foster's Group	Alcoholic beverages	4,045	7,326	45.9	37.0	5.7	57.3	36.1	19.9	9.5	70.6	Bi-regional	Bi-regional
12	15	Insurance Australia Group (6/05)	General insurance	7,923	17,162	11.1	0	NA	100.0	13.1	0	NA	100.0	Home RO	Home RO
13	18	Brambles Industries	Logistics	7,802	9,298	88.6	30.9[a]	55.1	11.4	83.3	29.4[a]	51.5	16.7	Bi-regional	Bi-regional
14	19	Macquarie Infrastructure Group	Toll roads developer	4,439	12,404	65	30.3	35.0	34.8[c]	78.4	15.2	63.2	21.6c	Global	Host RO
15	20	Stockland (6/05)	Property & investment	1,762	7,655	3.2	0	0	100.0	1.6	0	0	100.0	Home RO	Home RO
16	21	Alumina	Aluminium mining	0	1,841	38.8	11.6	5.5	61.2	NA	NA	NA	NA	Home RO	NA
17	23	CSL	Health care	1,836	3,875	86.9[d]	21.3[a]	65.6[b]	13.1	68.9[d]	47.7a	21.2[b]	31.1	Bi-regional	Global

cont. overleaf

cont. overleaf

No.	100 Rank	Company	Business	Revenues (A$m)	Assets (A$m)	FATA, %	North America % TA	Europe % TA	Asia-Pacific % TA	FSTS, %	North America % TS	Europe % TS	Asia-Pacific % TS	Type/ Assets	Type/ Sales
18	24	Bluescope Steel	Steel fabrication	5,440	5,737	NA	15.3	NA	84.7	29.2	10.2	0.0	89.8	Home RO	Home RO
19	26	Qantas (6/05)	Air transportation	9,716	17,574	NA	NA	NA	0.0	31.1	NA	8.6	80.6	NA	Home RO
20	27	Coca-Cola Amatil	Beverages	3,591	5,585	35.8	0	NA	100.0	42.7	NA	NA	100.0	Home RO	Home RO
21	28	Amcor	Packaging	10,406	10,183	75.4[d]	29.0	32.5	28.8	75.7[d]	30.0	37.0	26.9	Global	Global
22	29	Newcrest Mining (6/05)	Gold producer	977	NA	NA	NA	NA	NA	90.4	NA	NA	100.0	NA	Home RO
23	30	Orica (9/04)	Industrial chemicals	4,735	4,153	31.7	17.0	NA	74.2	36.3	18.0	NA	72.8	Home RO	Home RO
24	31	Santos	Gas exploration & production	1,754	5,815	11.9	NA	NA	88.1[c]	6.9	NA	NA	93.1[c]	Home RO	Home RO
25	32	Promina Group	General insurance	4,659	10,492	19.4	0	NA	100.0	18.2	0	NA	100.0	Home RO	Home RO
26	33	Lend Lease Corporation (6/05)	Property development	9,267	5,778	71.8g	29.0[a]	39.0	32.0	80.0[g]	42.8[a]	33.0	24.1	Global	Global
27	35	Aristocrat Leisure	Gaming machines	1,142	930	24.6	6.4	0.0	91.5	74.6	32.3	0.0	65.9	Home RO	Bi-regional

No.	100 Rank	Company	Business	Revenues (A$m)	Assets (A$m)	FATA, %	North America % TA	Europe % TA	Asia-Pacific % TA	FSTS, %	North America % TS	Europe % TS	Asia-Pacific % TS	Type/ Assets	Type/ Sales
28	36	Macquarie Airports	Airport investments	1,650	5,679	48.7	0.0	48.7	51.3[c]	20.2	0.0	19.9	79.8[c]	Bi-regional	Bi-regional
29	37	Toll Holdings (6/05)	Logistics	3,877	2,482	29.4	NA	NA	100.0	18.2	NA	NA	100.0	Home RO	Home RO
30	40	Centro Properties Group (6/05)	Retail investments	580	6,565	30.0[e]	30.0	0.0	70.0	8.8[e]	8.8	0.0	91.2	Bi-regional	Home RO
31	42	John Fairfax Holdings (6/04)	Publishing	1,775	4,578	26.1	0	0	100.0	27.2	0	0	100.0	Home RO	Home RO
32	44	Lion Nathan (9/04)	Brewing	2,013	4,228	25.6	NA	NA	100.0	36.2	NA	NA	100.0	Home RO	Home RO
33	45	Boral (6/05)	Building products	4,297	4,928	27.1	17.0	NA	79.5	22.0	18.9	0.0	81.1	Home RO	Home RO
34	46	Multiplex Group (6/05)	Diversified property	57	2,010	6.0	0.0	0.0	100.0	11.5	0.0	0.0	100.0	Home RO	Home RO
35	47	DB REEF Trust	Real estate fund manager	1,036	6,997	22.6	22.5	NA	77.5	13.0	13.0	NA	87.0	Bi-regional	Home RO
36	49	Coal & Allied Industries	Coal mining & marketing	1,024	NA	NA	NA	NA	NA	96.5	0	8.4	89.9	NA	Home RO
37	51	Computershare (6/05)	Computer services	1,111	3,826	71.6[e]	64.4	7.2[b]	28.4	68.2[e]	42.4	25.8[b]	31.8	Bi-regional	Global
38	56	Rinker Group (3/05)	Building materials	6,005	4,915	75.2	74.5	0.0	25.5	78.6	77.6	0.0	22.4	Bi-regional	Host RO

cont. overleaf

No.	100 Rank	Company	Business	Revenues (A$m)	Assets (A$m)	FATA, %	North America % TA	Europe % TA	Asia-Pacific % TA	FSTS, %	North America % TS	Europe % TS	Asia-Pacific % TS	Type/ Assets	Type/ Sales
39	57	AXA Asia Pacific	Wealth management	4,945	30,176	26.9[f]	0	0	100.0	34.6[f]	0	0	100.0	Home RO	Home RO
40	59	Foodland Associated (3/05)	Groceries retailer	6,354	1,944	61.8	0	NA	100.0	61.6	0	NA	100.0	Home RO	Home RO
41	60	Leighton Holdings (6/05)	Construction & mining	6,367	3,395	17.6[g]	0	0	100.0	13.6[g]	0	0	100.0	Home RO	Home RO
42	61	Billabong International	Apparel & accessories	679	948	32.9[f]	20.6[a]	12.3	67.1	71.4[f]	47.6[a]	23.4	28.6	Bi-regional	Global
43	62	Macquarie Bank (3/05	Financial services	6,712	49,313	40.7	12.8	14.6	71.6	35.6	14.6	9.9	75.0	Home RO	Home RO
44	64	Mayne Group (3/05)	Healthcare & p'ceuticals	3,514	4,514	27.9	10.9[a]	5.6[b]	83.5	9.9	3.6[a]	5.8[b]	90.6	Home RO	Home RO
45	65	Babcock and Brown	Financial services	568	2,542	70.0[e]	26.9	43.1	30.0	74.6[e]	49.3	25.2	25.4	Global	Global
46	67	APN News & Media	Publishing & broadcasting	1,283	2,801	56.7[h]	0	NA	100.0	51.3h	0	NA	100.0	Home RO	Home RO
47	68	Soul Pattinson (7/04)	Diversified	529	1,415	15.3	0	0	100.0	17.5	0	0	100.0	Home RO	Home RO

No.	100 Rank	Company	Business	Revenues (A$m)	Assets (A$m)	FATA, %	North America % TA	Europe % TA	Asia-Pacific % TA	FSTS, %	North America % TS	Europe % TS	Asia-Pacific % TS	Type/ Assets	Type/ Sales
48	69	CSR (3/05)	Diversified	2,511	2,655	7.7	0	0	100.0	7.9	0	0	100.0	Home RO	Home RO
49	74	Macquarie Office Trust (6/05)	Property investment	245	3,262	38.2	38.2	0.0	61.8[c]	42.2	42.2	0.0	57.8[c]	Bi-regional	Bi-regional
50	75	Burns, Philp & Co	Food & beverage	3,355	4,144	25.1[e]	11.1	6.0	74.9	26.6[e]	14.7	5.0	73.4	Home RO	Home RO
51	80	Nufarm (1/05)	Crop protection chemicals	1,577	1,432	59.3[d]	16.7[a]	42.6	40.7	51.7[d]	27.9[a]	23.7	48.3	Bi-regional	Global
52	82	Macquarie Countrywide Trust (6/05)	Property investment	190	2,660	60.5	54.4	0.0	45.6	36.1	30.5	0.0	69.5	Bi-regional	Bi-regional
53	83	Paperlinx	Paper	6,226	4,740	62.6[d]	8.9	52.4	38.7	75.4[d]	14.5	58.2	27.3	Host RO	Host RO
54	86	Cochlear (6/05)	Hearing implants	319	137	81.9[e]	46.4[a]	35.4	18.1	82.3[e]	41.2[a]	41.0	17.7	Bi-regional	Bi-regional
55	89	Sims Group	Metal recycling	1,880	721	56.7	21.2	32.6	46.2	58.1	22.8	31.9	45.2	Global	Global
56	94	Ansell (6/05)	Rubber products	1,096	570.2	60.0[e]	34.5[a]	25.1	40.1	85.1[e]	48.1[a]	37.1	14.9	Global	Bi-regional

cont. overleaf

No.	100 Rank	Company	Business	Revenues (A$m)	Assets (A$m)	FATA, %	North America % TA	Europe % TA	Asia-Pacific % TA	FSTS, %	North America % TS	Europe % TS	Asia-Pacific % TS	Type/ Assets	Type/ Sales
57	95	Flight Centre (6/05)	Travel services	870	743	49.2	NA	27.6	62.6	36.7	NA	14.0	73.7	Bi-regional	Home RO
58	97	Zinifex	Zinc & lead producer	483	2,302	15.0	4.0	11.0	85.0[c]	31.5	9.9	21.6	68.5[c]	Home RO	Bi-regional

Notes: Ranking is based on market capitalization.

a. Refers to Americas.
b. Refers to EMEA: Europe, Middle East and Africa.
c. Refers to Australia only.
d. Indicates that domestic includes Australasia.
e. Indicates that domestic includes Asia-Pacific.
f. Indicates that domestic includes Australasia and Japan.
g. Indicates that domestic includes Australia and the Pacific.
h. Indicates that domestic includes Australia and other

NA=not available

Source: Data from annual reports at end 2004 unless otherwise stated.

Appendix 4.3: Board composition and domicile of directors

Firm	HQ city 05	Directors 05	Directors 96	Exec 05	Exec 96	Non-exec 05	Non-exec 96	Aus res 05	Aus res 96	HQ res 05	HQ res 96	NZ res 05	NZ res 96	Other 05	Other 96
Amcor	Melbourne	9	13	3	3	6	10	9	13	6	10	0	0	0	0
ANI (delisted)	Sydney		8		2		6		8		6		0		0
ANZ	Melbourne	10	12	2	3	8	9	8	10	6	8	1	2	1	0
BHP	Melbourne	10	13	2	4	8	9	4	13	3	9	0	0	6	0
Boral	Sydney	7	8	1	1	6	7	7	8	5	4	0	0	0	0
Brambles	Sydney		10		2		8		9		9		0		1
Burns,Philip	Sydney	5	8	2	2	3	6	3	8	3	5	1	0	1	0
Coca-Cola Amatil	Sydney	8	12	1	3	7	9	7	8	7	7	0	0	0	4
CSR	Sydney	6	11	1	2	5	9	6	11	4	8	0	0	0	0
Faulding (delisted)	Adelaide		7		2		5		7		6		0		0
Foster's Brewing Group	Melbourne	7	11	1	1	6	10	7	9	7	8	0	0	0	2
Goodman Fielder (delisted)	Sydney		9		2		7		8		6		1		0

cont. overleaf

Firm	HQ city 05	Directors 05	Directors 96	Exec 05	Exec 96	Non-exec 05	Non-exec 96	Aus res 05	Aus res 96	HQ res 05	HQ res 96	NZ res 05	NZ res 96	Other 05	Other 96
Howard Smith (delisted)	Sydney		8		2		6		8		7		0		0
James Hardie	No official HQ	9	8	1	2	8	6	4	8	3	6	0	0	0	0
Leighton Holdings	Sydney	12	11	2	3	10	8	9	9	8	7	0	0	3	2
Lend Lease	Sydney	7	13	2	4	5	9	5	10	3	7	0	0	1	3
Mayne Nickless	Melbourne	8	10	2	2	7	8	7	10	4	5	0	0	1	0
MIM Holdings (delisted)	Brisbane		8		1		7		8		3		0		0
National Australia Bank	Melbourne	14	14	3	1	11	13	10	13	6	8	0	0	1	1
Pacific Dunlop	Melbourne	8	11	1	3	7	8	3	10	1	7	0	0	5	1
Pioneer International (delisted)	Sydney		10		3		7		9		8		0		1
Southcorp (delisted)	Sydney		9		1		8		9		6		0		0
TNT Australia (delisted)	Canberra		8		1		7		7		7		0		1

Firm	HQ city 05	Directors 05	Directors 96	Exec 05	Exec 96	Non-exec 05	Non-exec 96	Aus res 05	Aus res 96	HQ res 05	HQ res 96	NZ res 05	NZ res 96	Other 05	Other 96
Westpac	Sydney	8	11	1	2	7	9	8	11	8	7	0	0	0	0
WMC (delisted)	Melbourne		12		3		9		12		6		0		0
Average		**8.53**	**10.20**	**1.67**	**2.20**	**8.00**	**8.00**	**6.47**	**9.40**	**4.93**	**6.80**	**0.13**	**0.10**	**1.27**	**0.7**
Total		**128**	**255**	**25**	**55**	**104**	**200**	**97**	**236**	**74**	**170**	**2**	**3**	**19**	**16**
Proportion		**100.00**	**100.00**	**0.20**	**0.22**	**0.81**	**0.78**	**0.76**	**0.93**	**0.58**	**0.67**	**0.02**	**0.01**	**0.15**	**0.06**

Source: Data from Annual Reports to end 2004

NOTES

1. Sandvik started exporting much earlier, in the 1860s, via representatives in foreign countries, which was an innovation at that time.
2. The SCOPE database covers financial and strategic information on the 200 world's largest enterprises and the 50 largest national enterprises in the US, Japan, Germany, France, the UK and the Netherlands.
3. The Transnationality Index is calculated as the average of three ratios: (1) foreign assets to total assets; (2) foreign sales to total sales; and (3) foreign employment to total employment. This index is adopted in UNCTAD's *World Investment Reports.*
4. The following cut-off points have been adopted for MNC classification: (1) home-region oriented firms have at least 50 per cent of their sales in their home region; (2) bi-regional MNCs have at least 20 per cent of sales in each of the two regions, but less than 50 per cent in any other region; (3) host-region-oriented MNCs have more than 50 per cent of their sales in a triad market other than their home region; (4) global firms have 20 per cent or more sales in each of the three parts of the world, but less than 50 per cent in any one region of the triad.
5. Multinationality, we believe, refers as much to the assets a firm has abroad as to their foreign sales. Therefore, consistent with much research which is concerned with the operationalisation of the multinationality/degree of internationalisation, including a ratio of foreign assets to total assets, this interpretation would seem justifiable.
6. It should be noted that some firms (e.g. Insurance Australia Group) report even marginal foreign sales/assets, well below the accepted 10 per cent cut-off point.
7. The 380 firms in Rugman and Verbeke's study included 120 firms with no data and 15 firms with insufficient data. Further, the study of Australian firms used *both* sales and assets as measures of multinationality.
8. In a recent study Rugman (2005) specifies that foreign sales are sales of foreign subsidiaries plus exports.
9. Most of the company data on board composition and directors' residence were collected from the database, Aspect Huntley Datanalysis for the year ending June 2005. Where data were unavailable, the company was contacted by phone, usually through the investor relations centre. Nine firms had been delisted since the earlier study, mostly as a result of merger and acquisitions. Data were incomplete for Brambles, which did not publish the data and were unwilling to provide information on residence of directors.
10. See Harzing (2003) for a thoughtful discussion of conceptual and methodological flaws of the 'psychic distance' and 'cultural distance' constructs. These flaws lead researchers who use these indices to overestimate their impact on managerial decision-making.
11. These two studies establish that cultural distance has no impact on the choice of entry strategy.
12. Businesses in diversified firms vary in terms of global orientations of managers. For example, Lion Nathan, a diversified alcoholic beverages company, has a vision of itself as an Australasian firm in beer, but having a global portfolio of brands in fine wines.
13. The studies by Yetton et al. (1991) and PCEK (1990) are concerned with exporting, not FDI.
14. Mangos and colleagues use 50 firms during 1993-1995, which results in 150 firm – year observations. Clarke and colleagues' study looks at 20 firms in a single year (2001).

15. This study is now being extended to include all Australian public firms in the Worldscope/Compustat databases. The original study included 64 largest Australian firms.
16. The Templeton Global Performance Index is based on a selected number of companies from various countries. Thus, in 2000 only five Australian firms were included in the index.
17. Many Australian MNCs stopped reporting profits earned from foreign assets. For example, out of 58 firms included in this study, 28 firms did not report profits in 2004-05.

5. Australian and New Zealand Subsidiaries: Victims of Geographic Isolation?

Anne-Wil Harzing and Niels Noorderhaven

INTRODUCTION

The subsidiaries of multinational corporations (MNCs) play an influential role in the Australian economy. In 2002/03 some 28 of the 100 largest companies in Australia were subsidiaries of MNCs (DFAT, 2002). MNC subsidiaries provide one in five jobs in the manufacturing sector. In New Zealand, FDI has risen from $9.7 billion in 1989 to $52.5 billion in 2003, while foreign-owned enterprises employ no less than 18 per cent of New Zealand's workforce (Scott-Kennel, 2004). As indicated in Chapter 2, foreign firms hold leading positions in many industries in Australia. Australian MNCs can learn how to 'manage across borders' from foreign firms present in their own economy. Local firms can also benefit from positive spillover effects which would allow them to develop stronger ownership advantages that may later translate into foreign direct investment (FDI). This chapter will therefore take a closer look at the role of subsidiaries of MNCs in the Australian and New Zealand economies. We will focus on two aspects of the Australian experience identified in Chapter 1: the fact that it is an English-speaking country and thus culturally part of the Anglo-American mainstream and the fact that it is so geographically isolated from the main centres of the world economy. We will explore how the latter impacts on the role and management of subsidiaries in Australia and New Zealand. In doing so, we will also discover that a shared language and culture are important attributes for subsidiaries seeking to play a larger role in the MNC networks.

In the last two decades there have been many studies of the role of subsidiaries in MNC networks, though most of them have focused on just a few countries. For example, Hedlund (1980) looked at Sweden, White and Poynter (1984) at Canada, Birkinshaw and Hood (1997) at Canada and

Scotland and Martinez and Jarillo (1991) at Spain. There are only three studies that have focused specifically on Australian subsidiaries and these unpublished studies did not provide a comparison with subsidiaries in other countries (Thorburn, Langdale and Houghton, 2002; Johnston, 2005a; Nicholas, Sammartino and Maitland, 2005). Such comparison is desirable because subsidiaries can play very different roles within their MNC network and this may have consequences for the economies in which they are embedded (Holm et al., 2003).

This chapter focuses on the role of Australian and New Zealand (henceforth Australasian) subsidiaries of MNCs in the wider MNC network in an attempt to determine whether their roles differ from these played by subsidiaries in other countries. A secondary question is whether they are managed by their headquarters (HQ) in a different way. Plausibly this may be the case because Australasian subsidiaries are generally geographically isolated from their headquarters and most other subsidiaries. More specifically, we investigate whether geographical isolation affects knowledge and/or material flows to and from Australasian subsidiaries. We also explore whether subsidiaries 'down-under' have more or less autonomy and whether they are controlled in different ways. Finally, we investigate how the capabilities of Australasian subsidiaries compare with other subsidiaries, how this is reflected in local production and R&D, and what is their performance relative to other companies.

This chapter will first discuss the most cited typology of subsidiary roles, namely Gupta and Govindarajan's (1991, 1994) typology based on knowledge inflows and outflows. This typology is applied to data from 169 subsidiaries from HQs in six different countries, after which we compare the role of Australasian subsidiaries with subsidiaries from other countries. A more detailed comparison of knowledge inflows and outflows is then provided in the four areas of product design, marketing, distribution and management systems and practices along with a comparison of intra-company sales and purchases, control mechanisms, capabilities, local production and R&D and performance. Despite some limitations this study provides the first systematic comparison of the role of Australasian subsidiaries with other subsidiaries worldwide.

Subsidiary roles and HQ–subsidiary relationships

Increasingly, the MNC is portrayed as a network of transactions that comprise capital flows, product flows and knowledge flows. It is knowledge flows that are argued to be the most important (Gupta and Govindarajan, 1991). By distinguishing two aspects of knowledge flows: the magnitude of transactions (whether or not subsidiaries engage in knowledge transfer) and their direction (whether subsidiaries are the provider or receiver of knowledge), Gupta and Govindarajan define four generic subsidiary roles: *Global Innovator* (high outflow, low inflow), *Integrated Player* (high outflow, high inflow), *Implementor* (low outflow, high inflow) and *Local Innovator* (low outflow, low inflow).

The Global Innovator (GI) subsidiary can be characterised as a fountain of knowledge for other units. It is a role that has become more important in recent times as more MNCs move towards a transnational model in which individual subsidiaries can act as a centre of excellence for specific product lines (Bartlett and Ghoshal, 1989). Integrated Players (IP) engage in knowledge transfer to other organisational units and also receive knowledge flows from HQs and other subsidiaries, making them important nodes in the MNC network. Subsidiaries with an Implementor (IM) role typically do not engage in extensive knowledge creation and as a result provide little knowledge to other organisational units. Nevertheless, they are heavily dependent on knowledge inflows from either HQ or other subsidiaries. Local Innovators (LI) are rather autonomous subsidiaries, who do engage in knowledge creation but do not transfer this knowledge to other organisational units, nor receive knowledge from them. This situation usually occurs when local knowledge is seen as too idiosyncratic to be of much use in other organisational units. Based on the geographical isolation of Australasian subsidiaries, we would expect a higher proportion of Local Innovators and a lower proportion to be Global Innovators and Integrated Players, because knowledge created locally might not be relevant to other subsidiaries. We would also expect intra-company sales and purchases to reflect this geographic isolation.

In addition to the level of autonomy granted to subsidiaries, HQs typically apply a range of control mechanisms to their subsidiaries. Following Martinez and Jarillo (1989, 1991) we distinguish between formal mechanisms – such as formalisation, planning and reporting – and informal mechanisms which, following Harzing (1999), we refer to as control by socialisation and networks. Control by socialisation and networks includes mechanisms such as participation of subsidiary managers in international task forces and international training programs, informal communication with other organisational sub-units and socialisation of subsidiary managers. Further, assignment of home country nationals to subsidiaries (expatriation) is often used as a way to control subsidiaries in formal or informal ways (Harzing, 2001). With regard to control, we would expect that the geographical isolation of subsidiaries 'down-under' leads HQ to grant a higher level of autonomy to these subsidiaries. Further, we would expect control mechanisms that involve physical movement of people such as expatriation, international training and international task forces to be lower in the Australasian context.

If subsidiaries in Australia and New Zealand are indeed more likely to fall in the Local Innovator category, we would expect the capabilities underlying any knowledge creation to be idiosyncratic to the local market. However, we have no *a priori* reason to expect subsidiaries 'down-under' to have a lower level of capabilities than other subsidiaries. Along similar lines, we do not expect significant performance differences.

Data and analysis

Data for this study were collected through a questionnaire survey (for details of the questionnaire development and sampling, see Appendix 1). The resulting sample of 169 subsidiaries represented nearly 50 different MNCs. Of these 169 subsidiaries, 46 were located in Australia and 13 in New Zealand. Subjective constructs in our study were measured with established multi-item scales as summarised in Table 5.1.

Forming knowledge flow clusters

Confirming Gupta and Govindarajan's (2000) study, the largest knowledge flows are seen to take place from headquarters to subsidiaries. The mean knowledge inflow from headquarters is virtually identical in both their study and our findings. However, all other knowledge flows are substantially higher in our study. It would seem that in the decade between the two studies – data for Gupta and Govindarajan's study were collected in 1991 – MNCs might have become less hierarchical and more interdependent.

Following Gupta and Govindarajan (1994), responses for the two types of knowledge inflow/outflow (from HQ and from other subsidiaries) were combined as a composite measure of knowledge inflow/outflow. A cluster analysis was subsequently conducted in order to verify whether a natural empirical pattern would emerge that confirmed Gupta and Govindarajan's theoretical model. A four-cluster solution provided the maximum differentiation between the types. As we can see in Table 5.2, this four-cluster solution fits the theoretical model very well.

As a further test of the validity of the clusters, we examined them for an industry-specific and home-country specific effect. This tests whether the clusters truly reflect the existence of different subsidiary roles within the same MNC, rather than a tendency for specific industries or home countries to have subsidiaries with a high level of knowledge inflows and outflows. We found no significant variation in the proportion of industries or home countries present in the four clusters.

Table 5.1: Measurement of the key constructs in this study

Construct	Source	Cronbach's alpha	Number of scale items and representative item
Knowledge flows to/from HQ and to/from subsidiaries	Gupta & Govindarajan (2000)	0.89, 0.71, 0.83, 0.82	4-item scales. To what extent does this subsidiary engage in transfer of knowledge and skills in the following areas? (Product design, marketing know-how, distribution know-how, management systems and practices.)
Autonomy	Otterbeck (1981)	0.82	6-item scale. How much influence would your headquarters normally have on the decisions given below? Six areas ranging from the selection of suppliers to design of advertising for local market.
Control by socialisation and networks	Harzing (1999)	0.65	4-item scale, measuring participation in international task forces and training, informal communication and shared values. *Sample item:* Some MNCs make extensive use of committees and task forces, made up by executives from different subsidiaries and headquarters. Such committees deal with issues such as new product ideas, resolution of internal conflicts etc. Please indicate to what extent this subsidiary's executives participated in international task forces in the past three years?
Formal control	Harzing (1999)	0.70	3-item scale, measuring the level of formalisation, planning and reporting/Enterprise Resource Planning. *Sample item:* Some MNCs have a high degree of formalisation in the relationship between headquarters and subsidiaries. This is apparent in very clear definition of policies, rules, job descriptions, etc. and in manuals that define standard operating procedures to be followed. Please indicate the degree of formalisation required by your headquarters.

Construct	Source	Cronbach's alpha	Number of scale items and representative item
Subsidiary capabilities	Holm & Pedersen (2000)	0.78	9-item scale. Please indicate this subsidiary's capabilities in the areas below relative to other subsidiaries. Nine functions ranging from R&D and logistics and to the management of international activities
Performance	New measure	0.77	8-item scale. Please evaluate this subsidiary's performance in comparison to other companies operating in the same industry. Separated into three areas: financial performance (market share, profitability, and sales growth), process performance (innovation, product quality, and productivity) and HRM performance (employee development and employee retention).
Intra-company sales and purchases	Harzing (1999)	N/a	Please give your best estimate of the percentage of this subsidiary's output/inputs (incl. parts/semi-manufactured articles) that is sold to/bought from: HQ, other subsidiaries in the same country or abroad and external suppliers (customers) in the same country or abroad.
Level of local production	Harzing (1999)	N/a	Please give your best estimate of the percentage of company products sold by this subsidiary that have been manufactured by/in: this subsidiary, HQ or subs in HQ country, other subs in this country, other subsidiaries abroad, external suppliers.
Level of local R&D	Harzing (1999)	N/a	Please give your best estimate of the percentage of R&D done for products sold by this subsidiary that is performed by/in: this subsidiary, HQ or subs in HQ country, other subs in this country, other subsidiaries abroad, external suppliers.
Expatriate presence	Harzing (1999)	N/a	Please indicate the nationality of the managers (local, HQ expatriate, other expatriate) heading the following positions? (managing director and eight functional areas).

Table 5.2: Knowledge balance (outflow-inflow) with HQ and subsidiaries for different types of subsidiaries on a scale of 1 (not at all) to 7 (very much)

Subsidiary type	Knowledge from HQ	Knowledge to HQ	Knowledge from subs	Knowledge to subs	Knowledge balance from HQ*	Knowledge balance from subs
Implementer	4.70	2.24	3.42	2.24	2.46	1.18
Integrated Player	4.89	4.78	3.92	4.41	0.11	-0.49
Global Innovator	3.42	3.69	2.71	4.28	-0.27	-1.57
Local Innovator	2.88	1.73	1.93	2.03	1.15	-0.10

*Note:**A positive balance means a subsidiary receives more knowledge than it provides, vice-versa for a negative balance

Source: Survey

Subsidiary roles of Australasian subsidiaries

Australasian subsidiaries were very comparable to subsidiaries in other countries according to basic characteristics. Australasian subsidiaries were slightly younger and smaller than other subsidiaries, but these differences were not significant. Industry distribution and entry mode did not differ significantly either. Australasian subsidiaries were more likely to have an assembly function, but other subsidiary functions (sales, service, production, R&D, country HQ) did not differ. The only characteristic by which Australasian subsidiaries differed systematically from subsidiaries in other countries was the percentage of subsidiaries with a headquarters in the USA. This percentage was nearly twice as high for Australasian subsidiaries, reflecting the dominance of US foreign direct investment in Australia and New Zealand (see also Chapter 6). As Australasian subsidiaries were not significantly different in other respects, we can be confident that differences between Australasian subsidiaries and subsidiaries from other countries are not caused by incomparable samples.

Table 5.3 shows the proportion of the different subsidiary types for Australasian subsidiaries compared with subsidiaries in other countries. As predicted, subsidiaries 'down-under' are more likely to be Local Innovators and less likely to be Global Innovators. However, contrary to our expectations, we did not find a lower proportion of Integrated Players. This is in contrast to the survey of 237 foreign-owned subsidiaries in Australia by

Nicholas et al. (2005). In their sample, active subsidiaries (comparable to our integrated players) accounted for only 12.4 per cent of the sample. However, it is likely that this difference was caused by differences in sample composition. On average, the Australasian subsidiaries in our sample were older (median 32 years versus median 24.5 years) and larger (median 100 versus median 87.5 employees) than the subsidiaries in this study. In the study by Nicholas et al. (2005) active subsidiaries were older (median 32 years) and larger (median 160 employees) than the other types of subsidiaries. Hence their lower percentage of active subsidiaries might have been caused by a focus on younger and smaller subsidiaries.

The difference in subsidiary roles cannot be explained by the over-representation of US headquarters in the Australasian sample. On the contrary, in comparison to MNCs headquartered in other countries, US MNCs are even more likely to have subsidiaries that are Global Innovators and less likely to have subsidiaries that are Local Innovators. Thus the predicted pattern would have been even more pronounced had subsidiaries of US MNCs not predominated.

Table 5.3: Proportions of different subsidiary types in different locations (%)

Subsidiary type	Implementer	Integrated Player	Global Innovator	Local Innovator
Australasian subsidiaries	21	22	23	34
Other subsidiaries	20	19	34	27

Source: Survey

Knowledge flows and intra-company sales and purchases

Table 5.4 compares subsidiaries based on knowledge and product inflows and outflows in the four different areas of product design, marketing, distribution and management systems and practices. Australasian subsidiaries do not differ significantly from subsidiaries in other countries with regard to knowledge inflows. Even though subsidiaries 'down-under' are geographically isolated, they seem to benefit from knowledge inflows from HQ and other subsidiaries just as much as MNC subsidiaries in other countries. The pattern of inflows for different functional areas is also broadly similar for both groups of subsidiaries. We find higher inflows for key generic activities such as product design and management systems and practices and lower inflows for locally specific support activities such as distribution. However, the two groups differ significantly on outflow of marketing knowledge. While the inflow of marketing knowledge is quite high for subsidiaries in other countries (even slightly higher than the inflow

Table 5.4: Detailed comparison of knowledge flows and intra-company sales and purchases for Australasian and other subsidiaries

Subsidiary characteristics	Australasian subsidiaries	Other subsidiaries	Sign. of difference
Knowledge inflows (7-point scale)	3.25	3.38	0.41
Product design	3.74	3.62	0.54
Marketing	**3.11**	**3.50**	**0.07**
Distribution	2.84	2.96	0.55
Management systems & practices	3.33	3.46	0.53
Knowledge outflows (7-point scale)	3.02	3.17	0.48
Product design	3.35	3.27	0.75
Marketing	3.22	3.30	0.76
Distribution	2.78	3.02	0.33
Management systems & practices	2.73	3.10	0.16
Inflow-outflow	0.23	0.21	0.92
Product design	0.39	0.35	0.88
Marketing	-0.11	0.20	0.28
Distribution	0.06	-0.07	0.62
Management systems & practices	0.59	0.36	0.42
Subsidiary inputs (%)			
Inputs from external suppliers locally	36	29	0.17
Inputs from external suppliers abroad	**12**	**19**	**0.01**
Inputs from HQ	28	27	0.91
Inputs from other subsidiaries locally	2	5	0.15
Inputs from other subsidiaries abroad	23	19	0.31
Subsidiary outputs (%)			
Outputs to external customers locally	**82**	**59**	**0.00**
Outputs to external customers abroad	**8**	**15**	**0.01**
Outputs to HQ	**4**	**9**	**0.04**
Outputs to other subsidiaries locally	1	3	0.13
Outputs to other subsidiaries abroad	**6**	**13**	**0.01**

Source: Survey

of knowledge relating to management systems and practices), for Australasian subsidiaries the inflow of marketing knowledge is more modest. This finding suggests that it is left to the Australasian subsidiaries to decide how best to market products in their own markets. The reasons for this might be that Australasian markets are both very distant from the home country of the MNC and very different from other countries. Some features that make marketing different in these countries are highly concentrated industries (which makes for very tough competition) and a widely dispersed and highly urbanised population.

Knowledge outflows from Australasian subsidiaries are slightly lower in three of the four areas, but none of these differences is statistically significant. However, Australasian subsidiaries do seem to show slightly more differentiation in their knowledge outflows, with particularly low outflows for distribution knowledge and knowledge about management systems and practices. The overall knowledge flow balance is again similar for both groups of subsidiaries, with the most important knowledge net inflow in key generic areas such as product design and management systems and practices, and low or negative net knowledge inflows in the more locally specific support activities marketing and distribution. Nevertheless, although Australasian subsidiaries show slightly lower knowledge inflows and outflows, they do not seem as isolated from the rest of the MNC network as we expected.

Table 5.4 also compares differences in intra-company sales and purchases. Australasian subsidiaries do not differ significantly from other subsidiaries in the extent to which they derive their inputs from HQ or other subsidiaries. Understandably, geographical isolation means that they are more likely to draw inputs from local suppliers than from overseas suppliers. The major differences occur on the output side: Australasian subsidiaries sell significantly more of their output locally and are also less likely to sell their output to internal customers. They are less connected with both other countries and other organisational units of the same MNC. Hence, the important differences between Australasian subsidiaries and subsidiaries in other countries lie in material flows rather than in non-material knowledge flows.

Management of subsidiaries, capabilities and performance

Table 5.5 shows a detailed comparison of Australasian subsidiaries with other subsidiaries in regard to autonomy, the type of control mechanisms, the

Table 5.5: Comparison of control mechanisms, capabilities and performance for Australasian and other subsidiaries

Subsidiary characteristics	Australasian subsidiaries	Other subsidiaries	Sign. of difference
Autonomy (5-point scale)	3.82	3.63	0.15
Accepting price increases from suppliers	**4.05**	**3.63**	**0.03**
Design of advertising for the local market	**4.19**	**3.85**	**0.04**
Pricing of products for the local market	**4.42**	**3.85**	**0.001**
Formulation of subsidiary's annual budget	**3.42**	**3.10**	**0.05**
Control by socialisation & networks (7-point scale)	4.19	4.22	0.88
Shared values	5.37	5.15	0.35
Informal communication	**4.71**	**4.29**	**0.05**
Participation in international training	3.59	3.67	0.77
Participation in international task forces	3.20	3.65	0.12
Formal control (7-point scale)	4.76	4.88	0.53
Formalisation	4.04	4.39	0.15
Planning	4.76	4.80	0.89
Reporting & ERP	5.49	5.45	0.85
Expatriation (%)			
PCNs in top management	**8**	**13**	**0.06**
TCNs in top management	7	7	0.98
Managing Director expatriate	35	44	0.25
Capabilities (7-point scale)	4.38	4.32	0.61
Capabilities in IT	**4.63**	**4.07**	**0.01**
Capabilities in marketing	**5.15**	**4.77**	**0.06**
Capabilities in production	**3.64**	**4.11**	**0.09**
Capabilities in R&D	3.14	3.49	0.19
Level of local production (%)			
sales manufactured by HQ	**28**	**18**	**0.06**
sales manufactured by this subsidiary	**33**	**50**	**0.02**
Level of local R&D (%)			
R&D in sales performed by HQ	53	44	0.17
R&D in sales performed by this subsidiary	26	33	0.28
Performance (7-point scale)	5.13	4.98	0.22
Financial performance	5.05	4.95	0.57
Process performance	5.22	5.07	0.27
HRM performance	5.10	4.88	0.18

Source: Survey

level of local capabilities, local production and R&D, and performance. Few differences are apparent with regard to control mechanisms. Confirming our expectations, Australasian subsidiaries are granted a higher level of autonomy than subsidiaries in other countries. This difference is not significant for the overall measure of autonomy but significant differences are found for individual decision areas. In particular, local decision-making relating to the pricing of products for the local markets is much more likely in Australasian subsidiaries than in other countries. This finding is consistent with the lower knowledge inflows pertaining to marketing. The same is true for the higher Australasian level of autonomy with regard to the design of advertising.

Only partial confirmation is found for our assumption that control mechanisms involving physical relocation of personnel (international training, international task forces and expatriation) are less likely to be used towards Australasian subsidiaries. While this is true for expatriation and in particular the use of parent country nationals (PCNs), differences for international task forces and international training are not significant, although participation in both is lower for managers in subsidiaries 'down-under'.

The difference in the level of informal communication with HQ and other subsidiaries, which is much higher for Australasian subsidiaries than for others, is striking. As US HQs are over-represented in the Australasian sample, we investigated whether this might explain this difference. We performed the analysis for US and non-US headquarters separately. When US HQs were excluded the difference was insignificant. On the contrary, for the sample of US MNCs only, the difference was even more significant. This led us to assume that it might be shared language and/or culture rather than geographical proximity that increases the likelihood of informal communication. A formal test of the difference of informal communication between two groups of subsidiaries – those that share the same language with HQ and those that do not – provided a highly significant difference. However, a correlation analysis between the level of perceived cultural similarity of the subsidiary and HQ countries and the level of informal communications did not show a significant relationship. Apparently, it is shared language rather than shared culture that influences the extent of informal communication.

As predicted, the level of capabilities relative to other subsidiaries is not significantly different between Australasian subsidiaries and other subsidiaries. However, Australasian subsidiaries seem to have higher levels of capabilities in support functions such as IT and marketing and lower levels of capabilities in primary functions such as production and R&D. The relatively high level of marketing capabilities can easily be understood in the light of our finding that HQs interfere little in the marketing of Australasian subsidiaries. In terms of IT skills, a recent study by research company Meta Group shows that US IT executives rank Australia and New Zealand second in the world after India as a location for IT outsourcing (NSW, 2005).

The lower level of production and R&D capabilities is also reflected in the lower level of local production and local R&D performed by subsidiaries 'down-under'. This confirms the results of the study conducted by Nicholas et al. (2003). They found low levels of R&D spending and staff numbers and few subsidiaries acting as centres of excellence in this area. It is important to note that the difference in R&D/production capabilities and local R&D/production is not caused by a differential distribution in subsidiary functions. As indicated above, Australasian subsidiaries in our sample are as likely to have an R&D or production function as subsidiaries in other countries. However, even though Australasian subsidiaries have been formally assigned these functions, apparently the level of local R&D/production and subsidiary capabilities in these areas do not match those of other subsidiaries. Years of under-investment in R&D in Australia and New Zealand in comparison to other OECD countries might explain the lower level of capabilities in this area.[1] Although Australia has moved up in the IMD World Competitiveness Ranking to fourth place overall in 2004 (IMD, 2004), anxiety over the threat of relocation of R&D facilities (and to a lesser extent production facilities) outside the country was quite high. The Miles Report warned that Australia must improve its performance as an innovative country or face a future as a 'branch office economy' (Miles, 2000).

Both our results and the results of the study by Nicholas et al. (2003, 2005) contrast rather strongly with the findings in the next chapter, which focuses on subsidiaries of US MNCs only and comes to much more positive conclusions with regard to the role of Australian subsidiaries. The key to this difference is that only 32 per cent (Nicholas et al. 2003, 2005) and 41 per cent (this study) of the subsidiaries in the first two studies were US-owned. Two thirds of all Global Innovators in our sample were subsidiaries of US MNCs and Global Innovator was the most frequent role for subsidiaries of US MNCs in Australia and New Zealand. We suggest that it might be the shared language and cultural background that explains the more important roles assigned to Australian subsidiaries of US MNCs.

Interestingly, the performance of Australasian subsidiaries is slightly better than the performance of other subsidiaries, though differences are small and non-significant. At first sight, this is difficult to reconcile with the fact that Australasian respondents do not rate their subsidiary's capabilities higher than other subsidiaries. However, we should realise that the performance questions asked the respondent to compare the subsidiary with *other companies in the same industry*, while the capabilities question asked for a comparison with *other subsidiaries*. In the first instance, most respondents will have compared their performance with other *local* firms and hence MNC subsidiaries in Australia and New Zealand appear to show higher levels of performance than local firms. This confirms an earlier study by Bora (1998), based on the 1995 Australian Workplace and Industrial Relations Survey. This study indicated that foreign subsidiaries in Australia were more productive than local companies. In addition, they were also more willing to embrace international benchmarks for productivity.

Australasian Integrated Players: A Class of Their Own?

A comparison of the management of different subsidiary types and their capabilities and performance showed some interesting differences. Although for most subsidiary types there were no differences between countries, Australasian Integrated Players differed significantly from the same type of subsidiaries in other countries on several aspects. As shown in Table 5.6, Integrated Players 'down-under' have a significantly higher level of autonomy than other integrated players and also have a slightly higher level of capabilities. In addition, they perform significantly better on all performance indicators than Integrated Players in other countries.

Table 5.6: Comparison of Australasian Integrated Players and other Integrated Players

Subsidiary characteristics	Australian/NZ Integrated Players	Other Integrated Players	Sign. of difference
Autonomy (5-point scale)	3.9	2.2	0.006
Capabilities (7-point scale)	4.6	4.4	0.360
Performance (7-point scale)	5.7	4.8	0.005
Financial performance	5.6	5.0	0.120
Process performance	5.8	4.6	0.003
HRM performance	5.7	4.8	0.020

Source: Survey

Knowledge outflows in Australasian subsidiaries are very strongly and significantly correlated with performance, while this relationship is negative though non-significant for other subsidiaries. The positive relationship holds for knowledge outflows in all areas (distribution, marketing, product design and management systems), but is significant only for financial and process performance. A linear regression including autonomy, capabilities and knowledge outflows as predictors of performance shows that for both groups a high level of capabilities is a highly significant predictor of performance, while autonomy does not have a significant impact for either group. However, for Australasian subsidiaries there is an equally positive and significant impact of knowledge outflows, while this effect is significantly negative for other subsidiaries.

These findings are not easy to interpret, whether for Australasian subsidiaries or for others. The negative relationship between knowledge outflows and performance of the other subsidiaries could be an indication that being a source of knowledge for the rest of the MNC has its costs. Perhaps the time and energy involved in transmitting information to other parts of the MNC has opportunity costs in terms of local performance. However, this explanation makes the findings for Australasian subsidiaries even more difficult to comprehend. One tentative explanation could be that Australasian subsidiaries, being more autonomous, are asked to contribute knowledge to the rest of the MNC network only if they demonstrate outstanding performance. As sample sizes are small and our results are cross-sectional rather than longitudinal, we should not attach too much importance to these differences, but the results are suggestive.

CONCLUSIONS

This study has shown that Australasian subsidiaries differ from other subsidiaries in their role in the overall MNC network. They are more likely to be Local Innovators and less likely to be Global Innovators, that is centres of excellence for the multinational firm as a whole. However, their levels of knowledge inflows and outflows did not differ significantly from other subsidiaries. The salient characteristic of geographical isolation therefore does not seem to inhibit knowledge flows. Given the availability of new communication technologies, perhaps this is hardly surprising. For Australia and New Zealand this finding is comforting, as it suggests that local subsidiaries can become well integrated in their MNCs despite their relative geographical isolation. Nevertheless, geographical isolation is reflected in a lower level of intra-company sales and weaker control mechanisms. Australasian subsidiaries are more likely to source from local suppliers and sell more of their output externally. Control mechanisms applied by HQs to some extent also reflected geographical isolation. Greater autonomy was given to Australasian subsidiaries in some areas and some mechanisms requiring physical relocation (e.g. expatriation, international task forces) were less likely for Australasian subsidiaries. Interestingly, the level of informal communication with other subsidiaries and HQ was significantly higher for subsidiaries 'down-under'. However, this was caused by the over-representation of subsidiaries from HQ located in countries that share the same language (USA).

Overall, subsidiaries 'down-under' showed a level of capabilities equal to that of their counterparts in other countries. They had higher capabilities in support functions such as IT and marketing, but lower capabilities in primary functions such as R&D and production. This was also reflected in the lower level of local R&D and local production in Australia and New Zealand. Yet performance relative to other firms in the industry was slightly higher for Australasian subsidiaries.

Several conclusions can be drawn with regard to management and competitiveness in Australia and New Zealand. First, Australasian subsidiaries seem to outperform local companies to a slightly larger degree than subsidiaries in other countries. It is not clear whether this is caused by superior performance of Australasian foreign-owned companies or by a lower level of performance of local companies. Certainly the presence of foreign-owned companies might offer opportunities for local companies to learn and improve their performance. Further encouragement of foreign direct investment into Australia and New Zealand, as well as the fostering of links between foreign-owned and local companies, would therefore seem likely to improve competitiveness in these countries. Inward FDI should be seen as a positive development, rather than something that is bad for the national interest, as is often suggested in the local press. In this respect our conclusion is identical to that reached by Thorburn et al. (2002), who claim that although the overall impact of MNCs in the Australian economy is positive, much more emphasis should be put on transferring their knowledge and skills to Australian firms.

Second, even though Australasian subsidiaries are as likely to have a production and R&D function or 'mandate' (see Chapter 6) as other subsidiaries, their relative capabilities in these areas do not compare favourably with other subsidiaries. This is also reflected in a relatively low level of local R&D and production. Investment in upgrading capabilities in these areas might therefore be seen as a priority for subsidiaries in Australia and New Zealand. This is particularly important because of the shift towards stronger intra-company knowledge flows, which we have observed comparing our findings with data collected in 1991 (Gupta and Govindarajan, 2000). Given our finding that the extent to which Australasian subsidiaries are not only receivers but also senders of knowledge streams is related to their performance, it is essential that these subsidiaries continue to perform well. Otherwise the danger looms large of becoming isolated not only in terms of physical flows, but also knowledge flows. Of course, even then local R&D and production might take a while to follow local capabilities because, once established in a particular location, these facilities are typically not easily redeployed (White and Poynter, 1984). Furthermore, development of strong capabilities might take time. Our data showed that Australasian subsidiaries were generally somewhat younger (though not significantly so) than subsidiaries in other countries. They also show a positive correlation between age and capabilities in both R&D and production for subsidiaries 'down-under', though no significant relationship was found for capabilities in other areas. It should be borne in mind that there is no simple explanation of the development of subsidiary roles. Enhancement of subsidiary capabilities is a necessary but not sufficient condition for a subsidiary to acquire a more important role within the MNC network (Hood and Taggart, 1999).

Third, as Hood and Taggart (1999) indicate, a critical element in creating a more significant role for a particular subsidiary is the quality and persistence of its local management. This depends upon continued investment in management education in the host country as development of subsidiary initiatives is unlikely to be a major priority of central MNC human resource development programs (Hood and Taggart, 1999). However, these HR development programsmight still play a role in developing subsidiary capabilities. Although managers of Australasian subsidiaries are less likely to participate in international training and international task forces, the relationship between participation in these activities and subsidiary capabilities is stronger and more significant for subsidiaries 'down-under' than for other subsidiaries. At the level of individual capabilities, participation in these development programs leads to a higher level of capabilities in marketing and sales and management of international activities for both groups of subsidiaries. For Australasian subsidiaries, participation in international training and task forces is also significantly related to higher capabilities in HRM and R&D. Subsidiary managers 'down-under' might therefore do well to lobby parent headquarters to allow them to increase their participation in these activities despite their geographical isolation. Thorburn et al. (2002) have also emphasised the importance of MNCs in exposing Australians to global training and skills development.

This chapter focused on a comparison of Australasian subsidiaries of MNCs headquartered in six different countries and used a survey as its main means of data collection. As such its results provide a broad-brush picture of the role of MNC subsidiaries in Australia and New Zealand. The next chapter will provide a more detailed assessment of the role of subsidiaries of US MNCs in Australia and is based on extensive interview data. As such it provides a more finegrained and in some respects different picture of the same phenomenon.

Appendix 5.1: Methodology

The questionnaire for this study was developed after an extensive review of the relevant literature on headquarters-subsidiary relationships. It was subjected to three rounds of pilot-testing with postgraduate students with extensive work experience as well as practising managers from different countries. The final questionnaire had a total of 149 questions, measuring a range of aspects of the headquarters–subsidiary relationship.

Questionnaires were mailed in 2002 to the subsidiary managing directors of 2754 subsidiaries of MNCs headquartered in the USA, Japan, Germany, the UK, France and the Netherlands. Subsidiaries were located in more than 50 different countries, but more than 80 per cent were located in developed countries in Europe, North America and Australia/New Zealand. The sample was drawn from the Dun & Bradstreet *Who Owns Whom* database. Four very different manufacturing industries were selected which included MNCs from most of the six home countries: motor vehicles and parts, chemicals, food and beverages and electronics. For each home country between three and five MNCs were selected, resulting in a total of 82 MNCs.[2] For each MNC, 30-50 subsidiaries were selected, taking care not to select more than five subsidiaries in each subsidiary country. Subsidiaries with fewer than 25 employees were excluded, as were pure service subsidiaries.

Of the 2754 questionnaires, 553 were returned undeliverable. After an initial mailing and one follow-up mailing, a total of 174 questionnaires were returned. Five of them contained more than 15 per cent missing values and were hence discarded, leaving a total response rate of eight per cent. Although very low, this response is not unusual for multi-country studies with high-level executives as respondents. Harzing (1997) reported that response rates for international mail surveys typically varied between 6 per cent and 16 per cent and key studies in the field (Ghoshal and Nohria, 1989) have been based on response rates of 15 per cent. Ghoshal and Nohria's data were collected nearly 20 years ago. Intensification of the pace of business as well as the increasing use of mail surveys is likely to have led to a substantial decline in willingness to respond to mail surveys.

The resulting sample of 169 subsidiaries represented nearly 50 different MNCs, with the number of responses per MNC varying from one to five. Of these 169 subsidiaries, 59 were located in either Australia (46) or New Zealand (13), reflecting the much higher response rate in these countries. Only six MNCs were represented by five subsidiaries and hence our sample is unlikely to be biased by parent company-specific characteristics.

Non-response bias was evaluated in several ways. First, we tested whether responses on the key variables in this study differed systematically between respondents in the original mailing and respondents in the reminder. In this protocol late respondents are treated as a proxy for non-respondents. No significant differences were found for any of the key variables in our study. Secondly, we compared responding and non-responding firms on size (number of employees), age, industry and country of headquarters. No significant differences were found on any of the variables. We can therefore be reasonably confident that non-response bias was not a problem in this study.

NOTES

1. A report by the Group of Eight universities in Australia (2002) benchmarked Australia's investment in R&D with that of other OECD countries and shows Australia's R&D expenditure as percentage of GDP has fallen well short of OECD average over the past decade. Australia ranked twentieth and New Zealand twenty fourth in terms of R&D intensity. (This ranking included selected non-OECD countries such as Israel, Singapore and Taiwan). Later figures are not available, but it is unlikely that this picture has changed drastically.
2. We were not able to completely balance the sample frame as the Netherlands has no MNCs in the motor vehicles and parts industry and few MNCs in the electronics industry and Germany has few MNCs in either the electronics or the food and beverages industry.

6. US Multinationals and the Internationalisation of Australian Industry

Robert Walters*

Australian subsidiaries of United States (US) multinational corporations have played an important role in Australia's economic growth and development since World War II. More recently, they have contributed significantly to the internationalisation of the economy that has occurred in the wake of the successive economic reform and deregulation programs put in place by the Australian Government since the early 1980s.

Many US subsidiaries are large firms in their own right. Most have both significant regional responsibilities within their global organisations as well as a significant reliance on exports. Many manufacturing sector firms have production or sales responsibilities, or 'mandates', beyond Australia, New Zealand and the South Pacific. A number of services sector companies also have broad-ranging regional or global responsibilities.

Australia is a favoured location for many US multinationals for the provision of services to affiliates throughout the Asia-Pacific region, particularly information technology and accounting functions. Many multinationals are also using Australia as an R&D hub, sometimes as a global hub and sometimes as a regional one for the Asia-Pacific area. In addition, many have facilitated the export business of their local Australian suppliers.

Some of these trends are expected to be reinforced by the Australia–United States Free Trade Agreement (AUSFTA), which came into effect in January 2005, although it will take some time for the full effects to show.

The primary focus of this chapter is on the role of US multinationals in furthering Australia's internationalisation.[1] It reports on the results of

---

* The views expressed are those of the author and are not necessarily those of the Department of Foreign Affairs and Trade.

interviews conducted around August-September 2004 with 54 of the largest US multinationals in Australia (see Appendix 6.1). Interviews were also held with a number of local companies that are successfully supplying or otherwise working with these multinationals.

A snapshot of the firms surveyed is provided in the first section. The second section provides a brief account of the significance of US multinationals in the Australian economy. The following section provides some insights into the degree of integration of the largest US multinationals in Australia with their corporations' regional and global strategies from three perspectives: their responsibilities within the global corporation beyond Australia's shores (their 'mandates'), their reliance on exports, and their involvement in R&D activities. This is followed by an examination of the role of US multinationals in facilitating access through their networks by local companies, including SMEs, to the US and other overseas markets. Two particular issues canvassed are the increasing importance of global and regional supply chains as well as the multinationals' outsourcing of services. The impact of the AUSFTA is then considered. Some implications are set out in the final section.

THE FIRMS SURVEYED

The firms approached for interview included all US multinationals on the *Business Review Weekly* (BRW) list of the top 200 foreign-owned companies in Australia plus ten other large US multinationals.[2,3] The survey response rate was 74 per cent. The 54 companies surveyed had combined revenues in 2002 in the order of A$62 billion. The median revenue of the firms surveyed was over A$600 million. The global corporations of around 60 per cent of the top 200 companies surveyed are in the *Fortune 500*.[4]

Almost half (24) of the companies interviewed were from the manufacturing sector.[5] Another one quarter (15) were from the wholesaling sector, although some of these have some local manufacturing activities. Five companies were from the property and business services sector, while the remainder were spread across other industry sectors.

Participating companies were particularly well represented in the field of information technology (three in property and business services and two in wholesaling) and pharmaceuticals (four manufacturers and two wholesalers). US businesses have built up a dominant position in the information technology sector. The income of majority-owned US information technology businesses exceeds that of Australian-owned information technology businesses (ABS, 2003). US companies are also a significant force in the pharmaceuticals sector, with the companies surveyed being amongst the largest participants in the sector.

Sixty per cent (33) of the firms surveyed had commenced operations in Australia before the 1970s, including all but six of the manufacturing sector firms. Overcoming high tariff barriers and other import restrictions at the time was a key motivation of many US manufacturing sector entrants. One-half of the 100 US companies engaged in manufacturing activities in 1962 surveyed by Brash identified tariff barriers as a motive for their establishing operations in Australia (Brash, 1966). Over 80 per cent of the firms have achieved their present scale of operations largely through greenfields investments and organic growth. Of these, 12 have commenced operations since 1970, half of which are in the information technology and communications sector. Six manufacturing sector companies have become US-owned through merger and acquisition activity since 1970. A number of companies have downsized their local manufacturing activity or ceased manufacturing altogether over recent years. At the same time, a number of companies have expanded their local activity over recent years, including some in the manufacturing sector.

THE SIGNIFICANCE OF US MULTINATIONALS FOR THE AUSTRALIAN ECONOMY

The United States is the world's largest economy, largest importer and largest investor. It is also of key importance to the Australian economy. For the year 2004, the United States ranked a close second to Japan as a trade partner. It was Australia's second largest market for goods exports, the largest market for services exports, and the largest source of imports of both goods and services.[6]

The United States is also Australia's largest source of direct investment. The operating income of all US businesses in Australia in 2000-01 was $110 billion (ABS, 2004b). US businesses accounted for over one-third of the operating income of all majority-foreign-owned businesses in Australia – almost double the share of the next largest foreign investor, the United Kingdom. They accounted for eight per cent of the operating income of all businesses in Australia (Table 6.1).

In addition to their direct contribution to the Australian economy, US multinationals generate considerable business activity and employment through their local supply networks. For example, while Merck Sharpe & Dohme (Australia)'s direct employment in 2000 was 850 people, Access Economics has estimated that its expenditure was responsible for creating an additional 4,600 jobs through its supplier relationships (Merck Sharp & Dohme, 2002).

Table 6.1: Importance of Large US multinationals in Australia

	$ billion
Operating income, 2000-01	
All businesses in Australia	1 373
Foreign businesses	311
US businesses	110
Revenues, 2002[a]	
BRW top 200 foreign companies	245[b]
US companies in top 200	75
US companies in top 200 surveyed	61

Notes:
a. There are minor definitional differences between the BRW revenue measure and the ABS operating income measure.
b. Some adjustments made for companies omitted from the BRW list.

Sources: ABS (2004b), BRW (2004)

THE INTERNATIONAL ENGAGEMENT OF US MULTINATIONALS'

Historically, most foreign multinational activity in Australia has been oriented to production purely for the Australian market or the Oceania region, or else the distribution of imported goods and services. In the manufacturing sector in particular, high trade barriers have in the past motivated much foreign investment activity.

Despite the opening up of the Australian economy over the past two decades, and the increasing tendency to organise multinational activity on a regional or global basis, concerns persist as to whether multinationals in Australia are integrated into their parent corporations' regional and global strategies (Nicholas et al., 2003). The present study finds some evidence that US multinationals in Australia – the larger ones at least – are today significantly integrated into their corporations' global networks and are also becoming increasingly export-oriented.

Roles within global networks

Many US multinationals play a significant role within their corporations' global networks. Virtually all the multinationals interviewed reported responsibilities beyond Australia of one type or another – a production/sales 'mandate', an R&D mandate and/or a mandate for the provision of other services functions. In a number of cases, however, production/sales mandates do not extend beyond New Zealand and the South Pacific. Similarly, a number of companies with R&D or other services mandates do not have a breadth of responsibilities consistent with a high degree of integration.

Nevertheless, over 40 per cent of the multinationals surveyed have significant production or sales responsibilities beyond Australia, New Zealand and the South Pacific, or are services sector companies with broad-ranging regional or global responsibilities.

Seventeen of the multinationals interviewed – around one-third – have production/sales responsibilities that extend beyond New Zealand and the South Pacific (Figure 6.1). Fully half the manufacturing sector firms have such responsibilities. The nature of companies' production/sales mandates varies. In some instances, Australian subsidiaries face few constraints in their export activities, at least in Southeast Asia or the Asia–Pacific region. This is more likely where they do not compete with other affiliates, because of clearly differentiated goods and services or because of a clear competitive advantage in supplying to the region. In other instances, the markets that a multinational is allowed to enter may be more heavily constrained, with its competitiveness vis-à-vis other affiliates the key determining factor. Its ongoing supply into those markets will be subject to its continuing ability to maintain a competitive edge. In some cases, arrangements may be highly structured, with so-called 'centres of excellence' for different activities scattered around the globe, including in Australia. Such affiliates will tend to be highly integrated into their corporation's global activities.

Reflecting Australia's extensive research capabilities and very good R&D infrastructure, 22 (40 per cent) of the companies interviewed are using Australia as a research hub. In two-thirds of the companies this mandate is global or for the Asia–Pacific region or Southeast Asia. This is suggestive of a significant degree of integration into their parents' global R&D networks, at least in certain fields of activity.

Twenty-seven (50 per cent) of the companies interviewed have an 'other services' mandate that extends beyond New Zealand and the South Pacific, mostly for the Asia-Pacific region. Seven services sector companies have broad-ranging regional or global responsibilities demonstrating a significant degree of integration within their corporations' global networks.

Reflecting Australian capabilities, a number of companies handle a range of IT functions for affiliates across the Asia-Pacific region. Several also provide accounting services for the Asia-Pacific region. Eight companies have a procurement role which extends beyond the immediate region. Altogether three-quarters of the companies surveyed have an R&D or other services mandate.[7]

Subsidiary mandates can change over time. Responsibilities can be extended into related product, market or functional areas. Mandates can also be lost as well as won, underlining the need for subsidiaries to adapt their

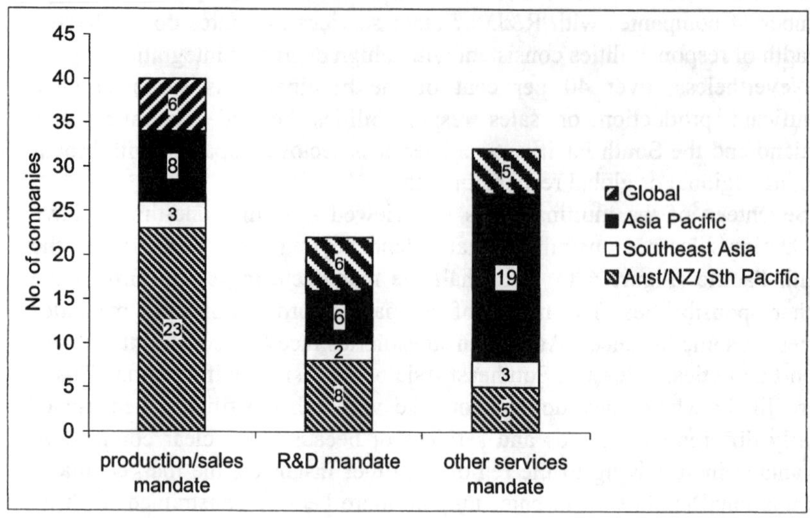

Source: Survey results

Figure 6.1: US multinationals: wide-ranging responsibilities

capabilities as market opportunities shift (Birkinshaw, 1996). The mandates of fully one-third of the multinationals surveyed in the present study have changed over the past five years, some enhanced and some reduced. Australian subsidiaries thus need to continually demonstrate their relevance if they are to retain or secure wide-ranging responsibilities.

US multinationals and exports

US multinationals are also significant contributors to Australia's overall export effort. In 2002-03, majority US-owned 'major exporters' (businesses exporting A$1 million or more of goods or services) contributed A$17.6 billion in exports, representing 13 per cent of Australia's total exports of goods and services (ABS, 2004a). This is appreciably higher than their eight per cent share in all Australian businesses' operating income, although majority UK-owned major exporters recorded a still greater export intensity.

Exports are an important source of income (more than 10 per cent of total revenues) for 60 per cent of the multinationals involved in export or some 40 per cent of all the multinationals surveyed. Nine companies are focused primarily on export markets with exports contributing more than 50 per cent of total revenues.

The companies surveyed include some of Australia's largest exporters. Five companies account for close to half the exports of all majority US-owned companies in Australia: Alcoa World Alumina Australia (exports of A$2.6 billion in 2003), Australia Meat Holdings, a subsidiary of Swift & Co. (towards A$3 billion for year to May 2004), General Motors Holden (A$1.2 billion in 2003), IBM Australia (over A$650 million in 2004), and Pfizer Australia (over A$600 million annually).

Southeast Asia is a major market for some three-quarters of the multinationals (29 companies) involved in export (Figure 6.2). The South Pacific including New Zealand is a major market for around 60 per cent and the sole major market for a quarter of these. North Asia is a major market for over half the companies. The United States is a major market for just over one-third of the companies. Around one in five of the exporters export worldwide.

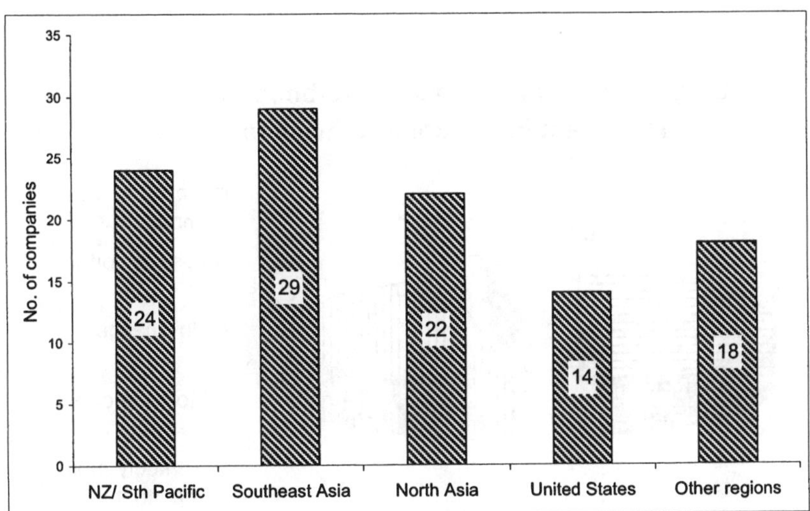

Source: Survey results

Figure 6.2: Major export markets of US multinationals in Australia

Exports are also becoming more important for many US multinationals. Over the past five years, exports have become more important for most of the multinationals surveyed that are involved in export. Most expect this trend to continue (Figure 6.3). The increasing importance of exports – mainly to the Asia-Pacific region – is consistent with Australia being drawn more into the integrated regional and global production strategies of US multinationals.

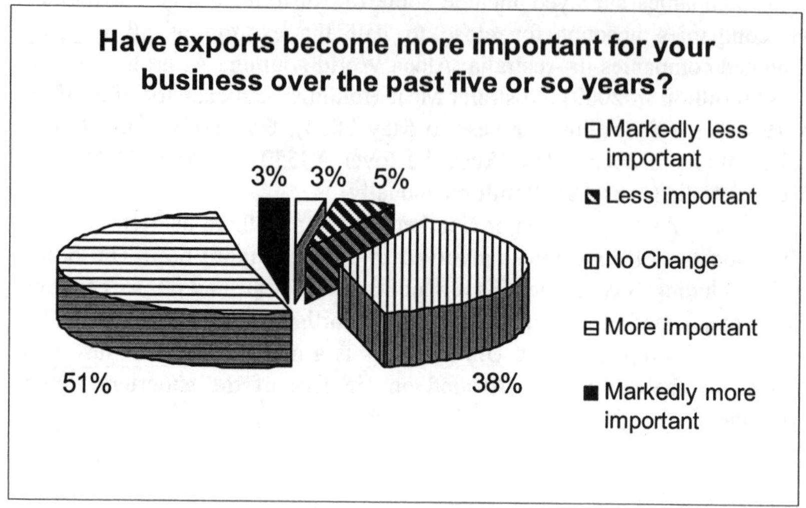

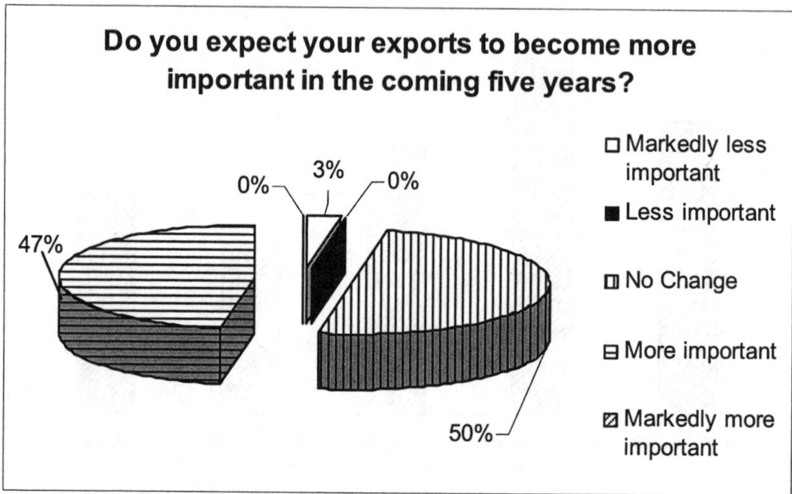

Source: Survey results

Figure 6.3: An increasing export profile

US multinationals and R&D

Innovation is a critical driver of economic growth. A study undertaken by the Department of Industry, Tourism and Resources (2002) underlines the significant contribution multinational enterprises make to the national innovation system through their own R&D activities in Australia, through technology diffusion from their parent corporations, and through their interactions with local firms and institutions.

Over one-half of the R&D of all foreign-owned businesses in Australia – and over 20 per cent of the R&D undertaken by all businesses – is undertaken by US companies (ABS, 2002). At the same time, the intensity of R&D undertaken in Australia by US multinationals is more modest by comparison with that undertaken by US affiliates in many OECD countries. In 2001, R&D expenditures by US affiliates in Australia were 1.5 per cent of their value added, which is less than that of US affiliates in Belgium, Finland, Switzerland and the Republic of Korea for example (US Bureau of Economic Analysis, 2003).

Similarly, Harzing and Noorderhaven have found that Australian subsidiaries of multinational manufacturing corporations from the United States and five other countries have lower capabilities in R&D compared with their overseas affiliates (Chapter 5). At the same time, they have found few significant differences between Australian and other affiliates in the extent of two-way knowledge transfers, although Australian subsidiaries were less likely to be 'global innovators' (characterised by high knowledge outflows and low knowledge inflows) and more likely to be 'local innovators' (low knowledge outflows and inflows).

The extent of R&D undertaken in Australia by US multinationals varies considerably from company to company. Holden headed the list of corporate spenders on R&D in 2002/03, with outlays of A$227 million, followed by Ford Motor Company of Australia at A$93 million (Intellectual Property Research Institute of Australia, 2004).

Around 30 per cent of interviewees said their companies spend three per cent or more of their revenues on R&D, with a handful reporting spending of over five per cent.[8] At the other end of the spectrum, over 40 per cent of the companies surveyed spend less than one per cent of their revenues on R&D. In half of these companies, R&D tends to be highly centralised in their organisations, with no R&D undertaken in Australia.

Some companies' R&D activities in Australia are focused on product modification for the Australian market. While studies by Thorburn et al. (2002) and Nicholas et al. (2003) have identified modification of products or services for the local market as a key, if not principal, focus of R&D undertaken by multinationals in Australia, some two-thirds of interviewees said their companies conduct R&D in Australia that results in product sales into overseas markets. In some instances, this R&D is incorporated into customers' overseas product sales. Some companies also have a significant R&D mandate within their organisation.

US MULTINATIONALS AND THE INTERNATIONALISATION OF LOCAL COMPANIES

Global and regional supply chains

The survey revealed that US multinationals in Australia have maintained high levels of local procurement despite an increasing contestability of purchasing decisions arising from the trend to global or regional purchasing decisions by multinational corporations. Most multinationals also did not expect their reliance on local suppliers to change noticeably over the coming five years.

One reason for the trend to global and regional procurements not impacting in a major way on local procurement levels is that local subsidiaries have often retained reasonable flexibility in their sourcing. Local sourcing has the advantage of avoiding shipping costs and delays associated with foreign sourcing. Shipping delays can be important where just-in-time manufacturing is being undertaken, product life cycles are short or demand responsiveness is important. Relationship building is also easier in the case of suppliers close at hand, as is legal recourse in the case of non-fulfilment of contract terms. Some multinationals also recognise that nurturing local procurement helps build the capabilities and competitiveness of the local supplier base.

Australian suppliers nevertheless face a challenging environment. While most US multinationals surveyed have found that the capabilities of local businesses have improved over the past five years, the capabilities and competitiveness of businesses in Asia are also improving. Australian companies therefore need to continue to sharpen their competitiveness and move up the 'value chain'. Australian companies may also need to look to getting into global or regional supply chains if they are to achieve sufficient scale (CEDA, 2004).

With multinationals increasingly turning towards e-commerce, local companies also need e-commerce capabilities. The multinationals surveyed are increasingly expecting their suppliers to bid for contracts by electronic means, as well as to engage in electronic payments systems.

Ongoing business opportunities both in Australia and overseas can arise if local suppliers are able to gain pre-qualification or 'preferred supplier' status for business with multinationals and their overseas affiliates. Some local companies have succeeded in qualifying as preferred suppliers for global or regional procurements and are winning contracts.

Participation in global or regional supply chains brings new considerations into play. Suppliers need to adapt their products or services, provide regional or global product and service support, and work or partner with other supply chain participants, both in Australia and overseas. The sharing of risk is also a much more important dimension of these supply chains compared with the traditional arm's-length contractual relationships that have existed between supplier and customer.

Australian suppliers are likely to be advantaged where the Australian affiliate has a procurement role extending beyond the immediate region. Some of the multinationals interviewed have such responsibilities.

Similarly, if Australian companies are to secure and maintain involvement in global supply chains for large projects undertaken in Australia and overseas, they need to demonstrate capabilities beyond delivering competitively priced, quality products to site within tight project schedules. A number of factors take on greater importance, such as sophisticated business systems (including e-commerce capabilities), an ability to take on project risk, relationship-building with key players and innovation.

Outsourcing

There is an increasing trend amongst US multinationals to focus more narrowly on core competencies, whether these be production processes, technology development or marketing. At the same time, they are looking more to developing partnerships with key suppliers and also to contracting out some operations. Such operations are being spread internationally, with location decisions dependent on costs and logistics (UNCTAD, 2002). The outsourcing of services is an important part of this trend.

There is increasing reliance on local outsourcing of services by US multinationals in Australia, which is creating opportunities for Australian service providers. For almost half the multinationals interviewed, local outsourcing has become more significant over the past five or so years. And local outsourcing is expected to become still more significant for just as many over the coming five years (Figure 6.4). Services that are outsourced will tend to be related to a multinational's non-core activities. Two prominent examples of services outsourced are warehousing and distribution. Information technology services is another. This expanding local business activity has occurred in spite of the growing tendency for large companies to consider the option of 'offshoring' IT and IT-enabled services.

For some multinationals, the focus has been less on outsourcing but more on the centralisation of 'back-office' services functions within the corporation at either the regional or global level. The Australian subsidiaries of a number of multinationals have been beneficiaries of this centralisation. A number of multinationals said that some functions, mostly lower-skilled functions such as payroll processing, were now handled by affiliates in Asia.

Some multinational corporations have instead 'offshored' services to unrelated parties.

Helping local company participation in procurement

US multinationals have identified a diverse set of ways in which they have helped local company participation in their procurement. More than one-third of the companies interviewed have developed partnerships and long-term relationships with their key suppliers. Other mechanisms have included inviting and facilitating local involvement in tenders, providing information, and helping suppliers streamline their processes and procedures. Such assistance can help suppliers in their other business activities, both here and overseas. Other studies have pointed to similar benefits arising from supplier relationships with multinational firms (see Thorburn et al., 2002,[9] PA Cambridge Economic Consultants, 1995).

The 'spillover' benefits multinationals bring to the broader economy can be substantial (UNCTAD, 2001). These may include enterprise spin-offs, demonstration effects, competition effects, and the mobility of trained labour. In recognition of this, there are a number of government and government-supported programs to help promote partnerships and links between the multinationals and local industry. Most prominently, the Industry Capability Network facilitates business partnerships for the purpose of local supply, access to global supply chains and local business growth.

Facilitating local company exports

Over 70 per cent of the US multinationals surveyed are exporters. Many of these companies depend on inputs from local suppliers and, in this sense, these suppliers are also exporters.

Established links with multinationals can help suppliers and contractors directly enter or expand export markets through the multinationals' overseas networks. Multinationals may refer their proven suppliers to their overseas affiliates. Moreover, export-oriented multinationals will have a good knowledge of overseas market conditions and preferences, which they may be willing to share with their suppliers. They may also be able to provide marketing channel assistance.

Any offshore business generated may be one-off, intermittent or more regular. Ongoing business opportunities can arise if a local supplier is able to gain pre-qualification or 'preferred supplier' status for affiliate business. Any business secured with overseas affiliates can in turn lead to introductions to other affiliates or third parties in overseas markets. Australian companies gaining overseas consulting business may also be able to draw in other local

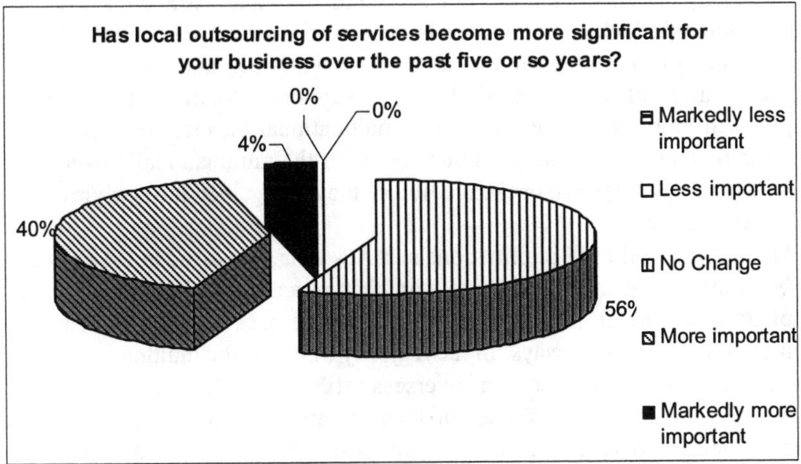

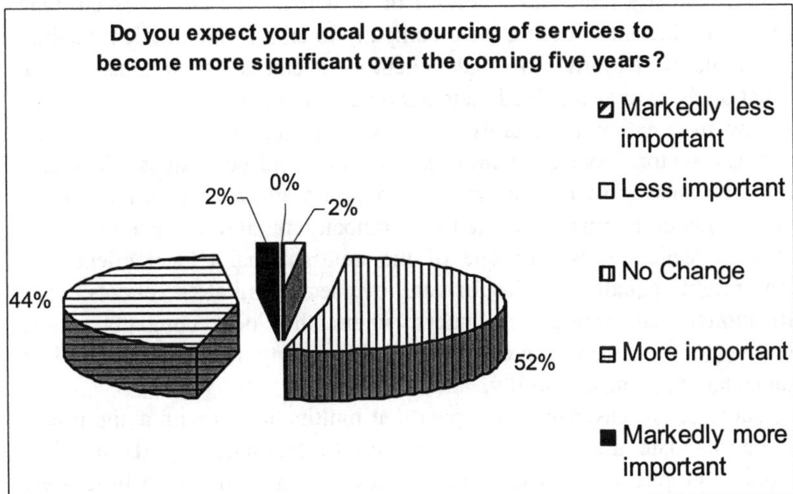

Source: Survey Results.

Figure 6.4: Outsourcing is becoming more important

people. This trade facilitation role can be mutually beneficial. The multinationals can benefit to the extent that their suppliers stand to derive greater efficiencies and competencies as a result of a greater scale of operations and exposure to this export trade.

However, very little study has been undertaken to date on these market access 'spillovers', or the channels of transmission (Blomström et al., 2000).

One study by Raines et al. (2001) of the Scottish oil and gas and electronics sectors, both of which are dominated by foreign-owned multinationals, found that multinationals had been instrumental in initiating and extending the export business of a number of their key suppliers. Nearly half of these suppliers in both sectors followed their multinational business partners into overseas markets, or else secured business with the multinational's overseas affiliates through referrals, or the credibility they had gained in supplying the multinational locally.

Around half of the US multinationals in Australia canvassed in the present study – both manufacturers and non-manufacturers alike – have helped local suppliers to export in their own right (refer Table 6.2). This assistance has been provided in various ways. In the majority of cases, the multinational has introduced local suppliers to their overseas affiliates or otherwise facilitated trade with their overseas affiliates or their clients. In a couple of instances, multinationals have facilitated trade or on-the-ground business with overseas operations directly under their control or in which they are involved. One multinational has introduced a local company to an Australian client leading to technology exports to that client's overseas operations. Some multinationals have also helped their customers to export.

A few multinationals, notably in the information, communications and technology sector, have gone into export with local companies. This may involve the sharing of technologies to create an attractive solution for the export market or, alternatively, the local company might develop a process or technology which works for one of the multinational's local clients but which might equally work for an overseas affiliate's clients. The multinational can provide customers whom the local company would otherwise not access and can offer the local company backing by way of its financial strength and credibility.

It would seem reasonable to expect that multinationals with a significant offshore mandate are in a better position to facilitate exports by their Australian suppliers, not least because they are more likely to be closely linked into their global organisations in terms of two-way knowledge and other information flows. However, there was no marked difference in the extent to which multinationals with a significant mandate have facilitated exports by their suppliers compared with the other companies interviewed. Nor was there a marked difference in the extent to which multinationals involved in export have facilitated exports by their suppliers compared with the non-exporting companies interviewed. However, seven of the eight companies with a procurement role beyond the immediate region have helped their local suppliers to export.

THE AUSTRALIA–UNITED STATES FREE TRADE AGREEMENT

With its entry into force on 1 January 2005, AUSFTA is delivering significant new benefits and opportunities for Australian exporters. They have gained immediate, free and open access to the US market for almost all manufactured goods and services. Duties on over 97 per cent of US tariff lines for Australia's non-agricultural exports (excluding textiles and clothing) have been eliminated. Australian agricultural producers will also enjoy substantially improved access into the US market over time. Tariffs on 66 per cent of agricultural lines were reduced to zero on day one and a further 9 per cent of tariff lines will be cut to zero by the end of 2008.

Enhanced legal protections that guarantee market access and non-discriminatory treatment for Australian service providers in the US market have been achieved with only limited exceptions. Full access has also been secured for Australian goods and services to the A$200 billion market for US federal government procurement.

Table 6.2: Some examples of US multinationals facilitating local business exports

US multinational	Nature of export facilitation
General Motors Holden	Holden commissioned Monash University Accident Research Centre to undertake a research program investigating vehicle crash and injury risk in connection with Holden's vehicle exports to the Middle East. The Centre has as a result established a close working relationship with the United Arab Emirates University.
Campbell Arnott's	Amcor (packaging) has been able to leverage its supply relationship with Campbell's in Australia to open up new opportunities for sales to the firm in Europe and North America.
PACCAR Australia	Air Radiators' reputation with PACCAR Australia for truck radiators suited to harsh conditions has led to its securing some ongoing export business with KenMex (PACCAR Mexico).
Alcoa World Alumina Australia	Hofmann Engineering was winning most of Alcoa's tenders in Australia for valves for both operations and new projects and the relationship it had built up helped it to secure a global contract for three years. Hofmann has since provided valves for the upgrade of Alcoa's Jamaican refinery, as well as follow-up orders.

US multinational	Nature of export facilitation
Yum! Restaurants Australia	Yum! Restaurants – part of Tricon Global Restaurants, Inc. – has helped Australian suppliers secure business with Yum! franchisees in Asia and the Middle East. It provides supplier introductions and sometimes assists suppliers secure contracts.
Honeywell Australia	The knowledge and expertise which some key subcontractors have acquired in the process of working with Honeywell Australia has been instrumental in their obtaining work in connection with Honeywell projects in Asia.
Eli Lilly Australia	Eli Lilly Australia has established local collaborations with local biotechnology companies as well as some of Australia's leading medical research institutes; the resulting innovation and expertise has been exported throughout the world.
EDS (Australia)	EDS Australia facilitates the export efforts of Australian IT companies through their 'Global Partner Solutions' program. The aim of the program is to support local SMEs by helping them with the marketing of their products and services throughout the EDS global network of clients and industries.
CMC (Australia)	Commercial Metals Company has assisted Pacific Coal Processing, a start-up business in Newcastle, to sell coke domestically as well as through CMC international marketing offices. Pacific Coal Processing shareholders own the coke production facilities while CMC provides the working capital to purchase the coal, and funds the marketing cost and accounts receivable.

Investment liberalisation, including significant changes to Australia's investment screening and the greater certainty and protection accorded to investors, should also act as a spur to inward investment. More broadly, the dynamic gains from the Agreement should yield significant long-term benefits for the Australian economy. The Centre for International Economics has projected annual GDP gains of A$6 billion within a decade (Centre for International Economics, 2004).

Given their two-way trade with their US affiliates and their being linked more broadly into global networks, the Australian operations of many US multinational corporations are also in a good position to benefit through both an expanded level of domestic business activity and a stronger export performance. The membership of many of the parent corporations of the companies interviewed (as well as some of the companies themselves) of coalitions or business associations which came out strongly in support of the Agreement, points to anticipated benefits for their operations in Australia.

Over one-quarter of the multinationals surveyed that are involved in export anticipated that AUSFTA would lead to a significant increase in their overall exports. This is broadly comparable with results of other surveys undertaken at the time. For example, according to the November 2004 survey of exporters undertaken by DHL in conjunction with Austrade, 25 per cent of exporters believed AUSFTA would have a 'positive' impact on their business (DHL, 2004).

This represents a conservative indicator of longer-term export gains for it takes time for multinational corporations to weigh up the full implications of the Agreement, especially where these might point to major investment decisions and/or shifts in regional/global responsibilities of subsidiaries. Indeed, 37 per cent of exporters participating in the May 2005 DHL survey believed that the agreement had also had a positive impact on their business (DHL, 2005). The survey response is also unlikely to capture the effects of the harder to measure dynamic productivity gains on the multinationals' export competitiveness.

The boost AUSFTA will provide to the Australian operations of the multinational corporations will in turn lead to greater business opportunities for their suppliers and other business partners.

The Agreement will enhance Australia's attractiveness as a destination for US investment. Increased investment will, in turn, spur greater linkages and synergies between firms in the two countries, and encourage best practice in both the private and public sectors as the economies integrate further. The Agreement should also serve as an incentive for US investors to use Australia as a base for operations in the Asia-Pacific region, particularly Southeast Asia.

US investors will come to see Australia as a still more attractive base to service the region if other free trade agreements (FTAs) currently being negotiated by Australia – an ASEAN–Australia New Zealand FTA, an Australia–China FTA and an Australia–Malaysia FTA – come to fruition.

CONCLUSIONS

Many US multinationals play a significant role within their corporations' global networks, with responsibilities for production/sales and services beyond New Zealand and the South Pacific. Many also have a significant reliance on exports. These findings are encouraging, as they underline the key role these firms play in integrating Australia into the global economy.

Many local companies and institutions, including SMEs, have developed successful business with the multinationals. Many have also been able to develop export business through the overseas networks and connections of multinationals. As well as providing direct business opportunities for their suppliers, multinationals can be a force for bringing about the improved competitiveness of suppliers. This can lead to business openings with other companies, both in Australia and overseas.

However, some important changes are taking place in the way that multinationals are conducting their business, which present both challenges and opportunities for Australian suppliers. In particular, multinational companies are increasingly looking to global and regional sourcing options as well as the outsourcing and offshoring of services.

US multinationals can be demanding customers. To secure their business generally necessitates good capabilities, continuous improvement and cost competitiveness. Characteristics that can set successful companies apart from other suppliers include innovativeness, responsiveness, focusing on core areas of expertise and skill sets, keeping up with technology, and benchmarking against competitors here and overseas. Local suppliers also need to be prepared to take on a share of the risks if they are to retain and extend their business dealings with the multinationals.

AUSFTA brings the prospect of expanded business activities by the US multinationals in Australia and, for many, a stronger export performance, in turn creating greater business opportunities for their local suppliers and other business partners. More US investors might be encouraged to use Australia as a base for operations in the Asia-Pacific region, particularly Southeast Asia.

Opportunities for US companies stand to be heightened should regional and other bilateral free trade agreements be concluded, notably with the Association of South east Asian Nations (ASEAN), Malaysia and China. In particular, Australia would offer added attractions as a base for operations in the Asia-Pacific region.

Appendix 6.1: US multinational companies interviewed

Company	BRW 500 ranking*	Parent corporation Fortune Global 500 ranking	Company	BRW 200 ranking*	Parent corporation Fortune Global 500 ranking
ExxonMobil Australia	1	3	Philip Morris (Australia)	109	30
Holden	3	2	Cisco Systems Australia	117	247
IBM Australia	9	19	John Deere Australia/ New Zealand	132	-
Alcoa World Alumina Australia	11, 106	216	Heinz Wattie's	134	-
Australia Meat Holdings	n.l.	-	Yum! Restaurants Australia	143	-
Newmont Australia	12	-	Cummins Engine Company	155	-
GE Australia & New Zealand	18, 84	9	Wyeth Australia	157	340
Hewlett-Packard Australia	29	40	PACCAR Australia	159	-
Masterfoods Australia New Zealand	30	-	MCI Worldcom Australia	160	-
Caterpillar of Australia	36	223	Sun Microsystems Australia	161	404
Citigroup Australia	38, 118 245	13	3M Australia	169	291
Owens-Illinois (Australia)	39	-	CMC (Australia)	173	-
Arnott's Biscuits Holdings	40	-	Bristol-Myers Squibb Australia	180	252
Tyco Services	44	91	Honeywell Holdings	183	197
EDS (Australia)	45	-	Dow Chemical (Australia)	185	145

cont. overleaf

Company	BRW 500 ranking*	Parent corporation Fortune Global 500 ranking	Company	BRW 200 ranking*	Parent corporation Fortune Global 500 ranking
Kimberly-Clark Australia	59	370	Manpower Services (Australia)	186	475
CSC Australia	62	448	DuPont (Australia)	194	172
Johnson & Johnson	63	101	Millennium Inorganic Chemicals	195	-
Hardy Wine Company	65	-	Baxter Healthcare	196	-
Cargill Australia	67	-	Eli Lilly Australia	199	456
McDonald's Australia Holdings	70	321	Abbott Australasia	224	263
Boeing Australia	81	43	Lucent Technologies Australia	238	368
Pfizer Australia	82	106	Collins Foods Group	242	-
Kraft Foods (Australia)	98	30	Monroe Australia	255	-
Merck Sharp & Dohme (Australia)	105	50	Dunavant Enterprises	304	-
Apache Energy	107	-	ChevronTexaco Australia	n.l.	15
Bechtel Australia	108	-	Sara Lee (Household & Body Care segment)	215	266

Note: * n.l. not listed

Sources: Survey; '*BRW*', 12–18 February 2004; *Fortune* Global 500, 21 July 2003

NOTES

1. The paper draws from the recently published Economic Analytical Unit report, Australia and the United States: Trade and the Multinationals in a New Era (2005).
2. Two companies omitted from the BRW list, Australia Meat Holdings and Chevron Texaco Australia, were also approached.
3. As an indicator of the situation and perspectives of the top 200, a small amount of survey bias would result from the fact that the non-participating companies

would overall be somewhat less oriented towards international activities than participating ones. In addition, the 10 other large companies in the survey frame were for the most part selected on the basis of an apparent significant involvement in international activities.

4. Fortune Global 500, 21 July 2003.
5. Industry classification is according to the *BRW's* list of the 'Top 200 Foreign Owned Companies', and is the industry where the major proportion of revenues are derived.
6. China has since eclipsed the United States as a merchandise export and import market for Australia.
7. An R&D or other services mandate is akin to a 'regional headquarters' role.
8. Based on a comparison with IBISWorld data on R&D expense incurred, there was some observed tendency to over-reporting of R&D intensity at interview.
9. Thorburn et al.'s study of 56 SMEs supplying to both multinational and Australian customers found that the suppliers' multinational customers in Australia were more likely to train or certify them to meet product quality and service standards than were their local Australian customers.

PART II

Industry Dynamics

Part II: Industry Dynamics

In this second part of the book our focus shifts from broad surveys of the Australian business environment and the characteristics and performance of Australian multinationals to specific industries. So far we have concentrated on those firms which have escaped the constraints of the domestic economy and considered the extent to which they conform to the model of a successful multinational. The parameters for this sample have been international ones. An industry focus shifts the sample frame back to the domestic economy. Here the issue is what differentiates firms undertaking FDI from other firms in the local industry. Are they market leaders, aggressive new entrants or just typical firms? Is there a definite industry pattern or a set of diverse outcomes? Another issue raised in the first three chapters is the extent to which the domestic business environment creates country-specific advantages and disadvantages and how these are affected by changes in policy regime. Finally, to what extent are country-specific advantages and disadvantages moderated by industry structures? Plausibly, some industries are more conducive to globalisation than others and, as argued in Chapters 5 and 6, may have been more or less impinged upon by inward foreign investment. These three issues all call for industry-level analysis.

Of necessity our industry coverage has to be very selective. We have chosen just five industries, namely financial services, shipping, retailing, wine and engineering services. Each justifies its place, but so could many other industries. Multiplication would nevertheless result in diminishing returns and an unbalanced book. What these five industries share in common is a sectoral bias towards services (apart from wine) and an historic bias towards the domestic market (apart, perhaps, from engineering services). In other respects they are very different. Financial services (banking and insurance) and shipping are old, well-established industries that trace back to the nineteenth century when they emerged and flourished in the heyday of the British Empire, then after Federation in 1901 consolidated and turned inwards. In recent decades their history has been one of erratic and very partial re-internationalisation. Their interwoven but subtly different stories give the book its necessary, very long-term perspective. Retailing as such is also an old industry but in its modern, highly concentrated form of retail chains does not predate the 1970s. Here is an industry that has innovated and adopted modern business structures yet, as a virtual duopoly, been almost indifferent to internationalisation: those retail chains which have internationalised have been small, niche players. The wine industry can also trace its origins back to the late eighteenth century but in its modern oligopolistic form is a product of the 1990s: in this case industry consolidation and internationalisation have gone hand in hand. Engineering services consist of smaller firms which in many cases are not even incorporated: it is a nice example of more flexible modes of internationalisation that are now being observed in the service industries. The diversity of these five industry cases is a means of stretching and testing the arguments of Part I before the highly individualised firm cases of Part III.

7. Financial Services: Banking and Insurance

Rodney Benjamin and David Merrett

The marked upward shift since 1980 in the ratio of Australia's outward stock of FDI to GDP owed much to decisions made by the country's leading banks and insurers in anticipation of and in response to the sudden deregulation of 1983. Although Australian financial institutions had long been internationally networked and held strategic foreign assets, this new surge of outward FDI was on an unprecedented scale. More importantly, it represented new strategic directions for domestic financiers. This was particularly the case for Australia's largest banks, two of whom acquired large branch networks beyond their traditional confines of New Zealand and the southwest Pacific. New investment banks emerged, including Macquarie Bank (Chapter 20), which found niche markets in the emerging infrastructure industry. Life and general insurers moved aggressively, with very different levels of success, to become important international players.

Yet for all these changes, there was a strong element of continuity. History and administrative heritage still mattered (see also Chapters 2, 3). From initial European settlement Australia's financial system had been 'open', allowing entry to foreign firms and permitting local firms to seek business offshore. However, while the door through which entry and exit took place was generally open, for several crucial decades in the mid-twentieth century it had remained shut. Banks and insurers became inward-looking and highly conservative, which hampered their ability to internationalise in response to sudden deregulation at home and trade liberalisation abroad. Not that they failed to do so, for indeed their strategies were very aggressive. Rather it was sheer lack of skills and experience that resulted in very uneven trajectories. Close examination of the data relating to banks, life and general insurers shows quite different stories for each industry. The large investments made by the trading banks were not sustained over the longer haul as financial pressures brought about divestments. The life insurance industry also retreated in terms of outward stock when Australian Mutual Provident (AMP) sold off its UK business.

Only in the general life industry was outward FDI maintained, which reflected the experience of a single firm, QBE Insurance Group.

This chapter contextualises developments since 1980 by taking a chronological approach. The internationalisation of Australian financial services is a story of four parts, each characterised by a distinct set of environmental factors that impinged on the attractiveness and possibility of domestic firms going abroad or foreign firms coming to Australia. Local firms adapted to each environment in ways shaped by their administrative heritage. What they carried forward from the past shaped their ability to cope with new circumstances. The most recent phase of internationalisation was achieved by a good deal of organisational learning.

FROM THE BEGINNING TO 1890: BANKS AND INSURERS

The structure of Australia's financial system owed much to its strong British connection. From in the early 1800s as the penal colony transformed into an economy, there was a demand for a range of financial instruments – currency, credit, deposits, settlement of debt by cheques and bills of exchange, and trading in foreign currency. Insurance was also needed against a variety of risk, including fire, marine, accident and death. Domestic suppliers emerged but from the 1830s were supplanted by an influx of British banks and insurers. British overseas banks quickly came to dominate banking in Australia, as they did in most other parts of the world that fell within the orbit of Pax Britannia (Jones, 1993). However, by the 1860s the influx of new British banks had run its course. An increasing number of local banks quickly emulated the 'Anglos' in all respects, including opening branches in London (Merrett, 1990). By 1890, Australian-domiciled banks not only outnumbered the British banks 21 to 7 but held 68 per cent of total assets within the country (Butlin, Hall and White, 1971: Table 7(i), 131). Three banks, two 'Anglos' and one local, had taken the British model of overseas banking further abroad by setting up branches in New Zealand and Fiji. Roughly a quarter of the assets of Australian trading banks where held in London offices and branches elsewhere by 1890 (Merrett, 1995).

A similar story was repeated in bold outline for the insurers (Raynes, 1948). In the nineteenth century, British life and general insurers sought out overseas markets, particularly in the United States and elsewhere in the Empire. They came to Australia where they competed with local firms and a handful of New York-based life offices. However, by century's end, the largest Australian life offices – mutual societies rather than joint-stock companies – had captured the lion's share of the attractive Australian market (Gray, 1977: Table 3.1, 22). Both the British and American life offices had vacated the field in the 1880s and early 1900s respectively, largely in response to regulatory changes in their home countries (Gray, 1977: 23, 122-24). In contrast, British companies came to dominate the fire and marine business in the 1890s and 1900s. The ranks of the locals were decimated by the price-cutting of the 1880s and losses associated with the depression of the 1890s, to the extent that there were only seven left by 1912 (Pursell, 1968: 453). Once in command, the British companies formed a cartel, known as the 'tariff', which seriously dampened price competition until the 1960s (Pursell, 1968).

In similar fashion to the banks, Australian life offices ventured abroad from the late nineteenth century. There were two principal destinations, London and New Zealand. Three firms dominated the outward movement: Colonial Mutual Life (CML), National Mutual Life (NML) and Australian Mutual Provident (AMP). Within 12 years of its establishment in 1874, CML had branches in Fiji, South Africa, New Zealand and London (Gray, 1977: 54). NML opened branches in New Zealand, South Africa and the United Kingdom before 1900, then added agencies in Egypt, Sri Lanka, Fiji, India and Singapore early in the new century (Gray, 1977: 54). However, the major figure in overseas expansion was AMP. Like the others it had been in London since the late nineteenth century, first using an agency before opening a branch in 1908. What set AMP apart was that it continued to invest heavily in the British home market, expanding its presence through regional offices.

Being smaller, general insurers had been less inclined to go abroad than either the banks or life offices. Early attempts to venture offshore were short-lived. For instance, in 1882 the Sydney-based Pacific Fire and Marine Insurance, a specialist marine insurer, opened an office in London, the world hub for marine insurance. After a bright beginning, it retreated back to Sydney in 1885, needing to make calls on its shareholders and to sell its Sydney office building to meet the losses. Undeterred, the directors revived the London operation in 1889 but further losses sent the company into bankruptcy in 1892 (Benjamin, 2004).

By way of comparison, one company has had a long-term and large scale engagement in many foreign markets, QBE. In 1886 Burns Philp (Chapter 12) established the North Queensland Insurance Company to take over insurance of the risks that had been assumed by its internal insurance fund managing its extensive shipping, plantation and trading businesses. By 1890 the insurance company had over 36 agencies in the Pacific Islands, New Zealand, Singapore, London and Hong Kong. In 1904 it opened a branch in London plus branches in Auckland and Wellington. In 1907 the name of the company was changed to the Queensland Insurance Company. Premium income from its overseas business in 1919 was nearly a half or 'not far short of that done within the Commonwealth' (Gunn, 1995: 95). QBE broadened its business with acquisitions of the Bankers' and Traders' Insurance Company in 1922,[1] and continued to open overseas branches and agencies in the inter-war period.

BARRIERS 1890-1930: PRIVATE CARTELS AND GOVERNMENT PROVISION

The 1890s depression had important longer term consequences for the strategic positioning of the banking industry. The collapse of fringe banking institutions involved in a speculative property boom in the city of Melbourne undermined confidence in all banks. One of the largest banks, the Commercial Bank of Australia, closed its doors on 6 April 1893, sparking a general panic. Customers rushed to withdraw their deposits. Only a few banks were insolvent, but illiquidity forced 13 banks to stop payment (Merrett, 1989).The trauma of the 1890s haunted Australian bankers for a generation. The public's confidence having been shaken, they shifted in droves to state-based government owned and guaranteed savings banks, or 'thrifts', and to the Australian government's Commonwealth Bank of Australia, which opened in 1911. The Government bank's share of total banking assets rose from nine per cent in 1890 to more than 33 per cent by 1913 and reached 43 per cent by 1939 (Butlin, Hall and White, 1971: Table 7(i), 131-2, Table 53(ii), 502-4). This spread of state and Commonwealth government bank branches across the country lessened the options for any foreign bank contemplating entry.

After the ordeal of the 1890s, the private banks, like the general insurers, sought comfort in a cartel. Agreements on interest rates and commissions, so often broken before the 1890s, became the order of the day. Between 1913 and 1931 a flurry of amalgamations reduced the number of banks from more than 20 to just nine. Balance sheets were restructured to reflect the self-imposed prudential standards of high liquidity and conservative lending. Stability became the watchword of the industry with steady profits coming from industry agreements rather than innovation. In this stultifying environment no Australian bank sought to undertake new investments abroad. To provide international services to their customers, including arranging payments and collections, they relied upon a worldwide network of correspondent banks (Merrett, 1995).

The possible entry of new foreign banks was always a matter of material concern to the incumbents. From the late nineteenth century, banks from France, China, Japan and America displayed interest in the Australian market. Nationals from those countries were important purchasers of Australia's commodity exports, particularly wool. These banks were altogether different from the foreign banks already in Australia, in that they did not want to raise deposits. The Comptoir National d'Escompte de Paris opened in Sydney in 1880, followed much later by the Bank of China in 1912, and the Yokohama Specie Bank in 1915 (Butlin, Hall and White, 1971: 106). The presence of these small banks was tolerated. However, any further challenge to local dominance of the lucrative foreign exchange market, particularly from American banks, was actively resisted. The local banks behaved in predatory fashion, refusing to open accounts and lobbying the government to use its authority to refuse entry. The de facto prohibition of the 1920s became official policy from the war-time regulations until 1986. The spur of competition from foreign banks had been blunted (Merrett, 1990: 73).

From the 1920s the Australian financial system turned increasingly inward in a number of respects. The growing influence of government banking has already been noted. Government entry into general insurance began in 1915. The intention was to offer price competition to private insurers for the new compulsory workers' compensation insurance. Five offices were opened between 1914 and 1926. In Queensland workers' compensation became a government monopoly in 1916 (Thomis and Murdoch, 1986). The government offices also played a significant role for compulsory motor vehicle third party insurance, eventually having a monopoly of this field when premiums were held at uneconomic levels for private insurers. All but the Victorian State office entered into competition for general insurance business (James and Murray, 1997). By 1980 state offices controlled 37 per cent of general premium income and by 1990 this had grown to 45 per cent (ISC). This percentage fell during the following decade when workers' compensation and motor third party insurance were replaced by state no-fault legislation and the remnants of the state offices' businesses were sold to private insurers. These important providers, unlike private firms, had no mandate to extend beyond state borders or to go overseas.

The growth of private insurance from the 1920s was attributable to the popularity of the motor car. The race for this business was won by local motoring clubs, who enjoyed a clear price advantage by direct marketing to their members (Broomham, 1996; Smith, 2002) and Lloyd's brokers (Benjamin, 1988: 96-102). At home this was a successful business model. However, the directors of these motoring clubs, like the managers of government insurance bodies, had no mandate from their members to take it abroad, or even interstate.

The 1920s also saw the beginnings of a more general withdrawal by Australian firms from the international economy through the imposition of a series of policies to 'protect' local producers and their workers, particularly in manufacturing and rural industries, from the free play of market forces (Chapter 2). Financial services had followed a different route but arrived at much the same destination. Barriers existed to prevent a further influx of foreign banks or insurers, either through covert government policy or government provision of both banking and insurance services. The British firms which had entered the market in the middle third of the nineteenth century and their local 'competitors' had settled down to a life of quiet domesticity.[2] There was no price competition in banking or insurance and precious little innovation in terms of product or process.

With some exceptions to be discussed below, there was little evidence of internationalisation being an important part of the business plan of any of the players in the financial services industry. The early international momentum, albeit of modest proportions, had been lost. For instance, three of the four Australian banks that had entered New Zealand, two of which were British-owned, had done so in the 1840s and 1860s.[3] Twenty years elapsed before the Union Bank opened a branch in Fiji in 1879 which it later sold to the Bank of New Zealand in 1895. There was a similar delay before the Bank of New South Wales opened a branch in Fiji in 1901 and one in Papua New Guinea in 1910 (Holder, 1970: 509). Apart from two short-lived forays into New York (Skully, 1980: 205), there was no additional offshore presence anywhere in the world for the next half century.

Financial institutions were captives of a 'sea change' in domestic policy that dampened the prospect of further internationalisation either outwards or inwards. As a heavily-indebted commodity producer, Australia suffered in the 1930s from the dual calamities of falling prices and a closure of international capital markets. The austerity measures adopted to restore external balance in the early 1930s gave way to a form of Keynesian demand management in the post-World War II decades. This highly interventionist macro-economic policy continued through to the 1980s. To their consternation Australian private banks, having narrowly avoided nationalisation in 1949, found themselves participants in a highly regulated monetary system (Merrett, 2002b). They were told how much they might lend and for what purpose and at what rate of interest. Similar restrictions applied on the liability side of their balance sheets. The authorities required banks to hold certain proportions of their assets in government bonds and as deposits with the central bank. All these directives squeezed bank profitability, as did competition from an aggressive government-owned Commonwealth Bank of Australia. Rather than make substantial alterations to the policies affecting banks, the central bank reluctantly permitted the trading banks to enter new markets such as savings banking, hire purchase, merchant banking, stock broking and insurance to restore their earnings (Schedvin, 1992). For three decades after the end of the war, the overwhelming strategic concerns facing the private banks were those within the domestic markets.

BARRIERS 1930-1970: PUBLIC POLICY AND PRIVATE CAPABILITIES

From the 1930s, the 'door' between the Australian financial system and that of the rest of world had almost closed. Controls restricting entry of foreign banks were strengthened. The Bank Act of 1945 contained an effective prohibition on the entry of foreign banks by permitting the Treasurer to refuse them a banking licence. However, many foreign banks operated beyond the reach of the legislation from the 1950s by opening representative offices or trading as a merchant bank. The key in the lock was capital controls, which were in place from 1939 until December 1983. Foreign residents were not permitted to hold Australian currency accounts in Australian banks; the reverse also applied with a prohibition on Australians holding foreign currency accounts outside the country. However, foreign insurance firms were neither banned from entering the market nor discriminated against, making Australia one of the more accessible markets in the world (Carter, 1990).

Closing the Australian markets to foreign entrants was part of a world-wide phenomenon. Up to the 1920s there had been few restrictions imposed on foreign banks and insurance companies entering foreign markets, especially in those developing countries that were colonies or fell within the sphere of influence of the United States, the leading European powers or Japan (Jones, 1993; Stern, 1951). Such freedom of entry ended with the economic maelstrom of the 1930s and conflict of World War II. There was little improvement after the war as the rise of the communist bloc cut bankers off from markets in China, Russia and central Europe. Some of the newly independent countries in Asia and Africa nationalised foreign banks and refused others entry for fear of economic domination. Barriers to entry faced foreign banks and insurers in nearly all of the non-communist countries until the 1980s (Pecchioli, 1983; Carter, 1990).

By mid-century there was little reason to believe that Australian financial institutions would have either the motivation or capacity to extend their reach abroad. The most common destination for outward FDI, New Zealand, was a very small and slowly growing economy. No other markets beckoned in which a branch network could be built. Australia's almost bilateral trade with the United Kingdom had kept it and its banks firmly in the sterling block.

Australian financial services firms possessed little in the way of ownership advantages to take abroad. There had been earlier sparks of product innovation from the life offices in the nineteenth century when they led the world in the liberality of policy conditions, particularly non-forfeiture, and endowment policies (Gray, 1977: ch. 5). However, the leaders quickly reverted to being followers with the introduction of well-established industrial insurance (Gray, 1977: ch. 7). General insurers had been compelled to follow new forms and prices of insurance introduced by Lloyd's brokers now operating in Australia (Benjamin, 1988: ch. 8 and 9), the motoring organisations and government offices. They lost out in this new competitive market, so much harsher than the comfortable cartel they had previously enjoyed.

The lack of potential international competitiveness is more readily apparent when considering the range of products that Australian banks offered clients before the onset of government regulations in 1939 (Walter, 1985: 23-7). Their core international business was plain vanilla-flavoured, although highly profitable, trade-related collections and payments and foreign exchange trading in Australian currency for local clients. Banks in other countries offered more. For instance, Australian banks did not offer futures contracts for currency or trade in physical markets for gold or other commodities. They did not engage in sovereign lending, or issuing, underwriting and dealing in corporate securities. Neither did they raise deposits offshore to fund activities in other countries and currencies. Australian banks had been far more adventurous in the nineteenth century, raising loans for colonial governments and buying and selling gold and other commodities on commission and their own account. Many had raised significant amounts of deposits in the United Kingdom market in the 1880s to fund domestic lending. These activities had simply faded away after 1900. Most of their overseas assets were committed to retail branch banking in New Zealand.

There was little reason for them to look farther afield. United States banks had been encouraged to follow their multinational customers abroad. Australian companies, island trader Burns Philp (Chapter 12) and sugar-producer CSR, had applied pressure to the banks to open in Fiji and PNG in the late nineteenth century. However, this type of motivation dissipated quickly in the new century as few Australian firms became multinationals of a size that would warrant such a response or were located in a country that was not already well served by European or American banks.

The more critical issue was that Australian banks did not possess the necessary capabilities to be competitive as international banks. Ingo Walter (1985: 28-47) discusses the potential sources of competitive advantage in a post-Eurocurrency and partially deregulated world in some detail. Australian banks were too small to enjoy the economies of scale available to their faster growing European, American and Japanese competitors after World War II. Access to market-sensitive information and the ability to process it and respond more quickly than other banks was identified as a source of competitive advantage. Once again, geography placed Australian banks at a disadvantage because of their isolation from the world's key financial markets. This weakness was only partly addressed by the telephone, telex and faster air travel.

Bringing the world to Australia: an international financial centre

Australia's remote geographical position and its small volume of global trade made it a poor contender as an 'international financial centre'. Before World War II London, New York, Amsterdam and Paris stood at the apex of a hierarchy of such centres (Jones, 1992: 405). They were the world's great markets for currency and credit tied to flows of trade and investment. Smaller centres serving narrower regions and sub-regions formed a constellation below them (Reed, 1983). As nodal points for payments and collections related to trade and investment flows, these cities enjoyed exceptionally high levels of international clearing activity. The correspondent balances held by local banks enlarged the pool of funds available at the centre and *pari passu* stimulated foreign currency transactions. A centre had to be able to attract 'relatively large amounts of foreign financial liabilities' (Reed, 1983: 229), either through trade payments or by having local banks accept foreign currency deposits. A final requirement for a city to become a final centre was that there should be excellent communications linking it with counter-parties overseas.

Australia failed to meet any of these three conditions. First, its share of world trade was too small to generate the float of money awaiting settlement to fund other market activities. In practice, this float was further reduced because Australian trading banks used London offices to direct the bulk of their trade collection business there. Second, the banks did not seek foreign currency accounts for individuals or corporations from the neighbouring region, though doing business with some of them through representation within those countries. By contrast, Shanghai, Singapore and Hong Kong were already regional centres attracting business from non-residents and foreign banks (Jones, 1992: 406-8). Finally, Australia's distance from other financial markets reduced its ability to be 'an active and influential participant in managing the world's portfolio of financial liabilities and assets' (Reed, 1983: 229). New communication technologies, cables and telexes, speeded up the transmission of information but the difficulty of face-to-face contact remained an issue. Besides these handicaps, Australia's small financial market suffered the further disadvantage of being split between the almost equally sized rival cities of Melbourne and Sydney.

Yet the greatest weakness of Australian banks was their human resource management. During the nineteenth century they had all developed internal labour markets that continued to operate until they began to break down in the 1960s. There was a single port of entry, a junior clerk, for workers whose remuneration was linked to length of service, most staying until retirement with pension entitlements, and rank achieved by promotion based on merit. This system provided on-the-job training and job matching that delivered significant operational efficiencies and allowed high level of monitoring of individual workers (Merrett and Seltzer, 2000; Seltzer and Merrett, 2000).

The system worked best in an environment that required no adjustments in the products the banks offered, the back office procedures being used or the markets they served. Branch office staff simply complied with the extraordinarily detailed and comprehensive sets of rules or 'procedures' prescribed by head office. In the longer term, the rules stifled entrepreneurship and adaptability. The cohort which became senior managers in the 1950s had spent more than 30 years acquiring skills that would be largely irrelevant in international markets or in a deregulated domestic market. They suffered a similar atrophy to the British clearing banks, whom Lord Franks, chairman of Lloyds Bank, described in the 1950s as being 'anaesthetised – [living in] ... a kind of dream world' (Cassis, 2002: 47). Thus during the 1970s when the government of Singapore was vigorously promoting Singapore as a world financial centre and Hong Kong was emerging into greater prominence, Australia's leading banks were still fixated on domestic markets.

INTERNATIONALISATION POST-1980: FEWER RULES AND CROSS-BORDER PENETRATION

The acceleration of growth in global GDP after World War II was driven by the expansion of world trade and investment flows. Both exports and investment responded to progressive relaxation of the restrictive policy regimes that had been in place for many decades. Bankers and insurers faced rising demands for their services at home and abroad. They were able to respond in part because the barriers that had previously blocked them from doing so were broken down. The initial push to open the 'door' was the renewed internationalisation of leading banks from the United States in the 1960s. Frustrated by highly restrictive policies at home and anxious to follow their multinational customers abroad, US banks increased their presence in London (Sylla, 2002). Markets in Eurodollars grew quickly to provide a pool of wholesale funds, boosted by recycled petro-dollars in the 1970s and 1980s, which fuelled the growth of international banking. Reformist policies in national financial markets and the application of new information technologies from the 1980s led to the global integration of once segmented domestic markets for currency, capital and financial intermediation (Solomon, 1999).

This phase of internationalisation of financial services differed from what had gone before in a number of respects. First, the scale of the trade in financial services and the stock of outward FDI by financiers were unprecedented both in absolute and relative terms. Moreover, the trade and investment flows were increasingly between the leading industrial economies rather than between the developed and developing worlds as had been the case before the 1930s (UNCTAD, 2004: Annex table A.III.4, 321; Carter, 1990: Table 12.1, 207).

Banks

Australian banks were swept along by these global developments. Their London offices provided the opportunity to trade in euro-currency markets, raising liabilities in inter-bank markets, and participating in syndicated lending. The shift in Australia's merchandise trade towards Japan and the United States enabled the banks to follow those funds held with correspondent banks. Table 1 (Merrett, 2002b: 383) shows the dramatic shift in the value and distribution of assets held offshore between 1975 and 1987.

Table 7.1: Assets of Australian banks overseas offices, 1975 and 1987

Country	1975[c] $m	1975 %	1987[d] $m	1987 %
UK[a]	1,452	52	25,351	31
United States[b]	-	-	17,372	21
Singapore	-	-	10,337	13
Hong Kong	-	-	6,585	8
New Zealand	979	35	8,207	10
Japan	-	-	2,793	4
Other	348	13	10,313	13
Total	2,779	100	80,958	100

Notes:

a. Includes Channel Isles
b. Includes Cayman Islands.
c. 1975 data exclude amounts owing in respect to forward exchange contracts.
d. 1987 figure includes inter-bank and inter-office loans. Includes assets of restricted branches, subsidiaries and representative offices as well as full branches.

Sources: RBA (1981): Table 2, 417 and RBA (1987): Attachment 2, 23

By the mid-1980s, however, there had been a significant change in the size, direction and nature of offshore activity by Australian banks. The number of countries in which they had representation rose from 16 in 1978 to 50 within a decade (RBA, 1981: Attachment W, 3.26; RBA, 1987: Attachment 1, 21-2). Moreover, the aggregate value of offshore assets rose very sharply from a low base, doubling the share of these assets in the total assets of the major trading banks between 1975 and 1987 (RBA, 1981: 417 and 1987: 17). There was a dramatic shift in the geographic distribution of assets. Initially almost 90 per cent of banks' overseas assets were in Britain and New Zealand with nearly all of the rest in Papua New Guinea and Fiji. However, by 1987 the share of Britain and New Zealand had fallen to 41 per cent. New locations such as the United States and Japan and offshore banking centres in Asia had increased their share from zero to nearly a half.

Deregulation of the Australian financial system as part of the trend towards reduced global barriers to trade in financial services also permitted entry of foreign banks to Australia, which threatened to increase competition at home (Perkins, 1989: 49-51). Australian bankers feared that foreign banks would have a competitive edge, especially in corporate banking. Anticipating the opening of the domestic banking market to foreign banks following the release of the Campbell Report (Australian Financial System Inquiry, 1981) and government approval of its deregulatory reforms, Australia's leading banks sought to reinforce and secure their competitive position. In 1982 a round of pre-emptive mergers culminated in the ANZ Bank standing alone and two new larger entities emerging as National Australia Bank or NAB[4] and Westpac.[5] Bigger did not mean better as half a century of cartel agreements had left them all with significant operational inefficiencies, reflected in higher than the OECD average ratios of non-interest expense to income (Revell, 1980; OECD, 1991). Their ability to compete against foreign banks within Australia or in foreign markets was contingent on a significant reduction in their cost structures. This was achieved slowly through a combination of closing branches and retrenching staff, investing in electronic distribution systems and overhauling back-office procedures (OECD, 1991 and 2002).

The new deregulated environment provided Australian bankers with unaccustomed freedoms. They behaved aggressively and rashly, partly in anticipation of competition from the new foreign banks. Collectively they tapped into international wholesale markets to fund rapid increases in lending to local 'entrepreneurs', who went of a binge of mergers and acquisitions. Nearly all of these heavily indebted conglomerates failed after the stock market crash in November 1987. The end of the property bubble in the early 1990s, funded by loans by banks' subsidiaries, later added to the banks' woes. Both ANZ and Westpac recorded losses for the first time in their long histories.

After the dust had settled it became apparent that the large Australian trading banks had grossly overestimated the challenges they would face from the newly licensed foreign banks, especially in retail markets. The share of assets of these foreign banks, swollen by the absorption of merchant bank subsidiaries into their balance sheets, rose quickly in the 1980s to reach about 10 per cent of all financial assets. However, it has grown little over the past 15 years (RBA, 2004). More than half of the foreign banks that entered the market have since left. Those that stayed have tended to occupy niche markets.

After the policy reforms on the 1980s, the Australian government belatedly established Offshore Banking Units in 1988 in an attempt to establish an international banking centre. The factors that had prevented the organic evolution of such a centre before World War II still operated. From 1939 to 1983 capital controls had blocked the development of what Arndt (1988) describes as 'cross border bank credit'. Their removal was insufficient in itself to change the situation, given Australia's want of any 'natural' competitive advantage in trade in financial services (Arndt, 1988). The small tax benefits given to participants were insufficient to woo customers away from the well entrenched regional centres (Skully, 1997: 32-3, 59; Jüttner, 1998: 219-21).

Overseas acquisitions in the 1980s by the three private Australian banks (Westpac, ANZ and NAB) were the key driver of these changes in the geographic scope and character of overseas banking operations (Table 7.1). Each followed a very different path. With aspirations to turn Sydney into the financial centre of the western Pacific, Westpac purchased firms in Britain and the United States dealing in bullion, foreign exchange and US government securities. ANZ acquired Grindlays Bank plc in 1984, an old British overseas bank that conducted the bulk of its business outside Britain, predominantly in India, the Gulf and East Africa (Jones, 1993). Offices and branches in international banking centres around the world, including a branch in Tokyo, had been added to the colonial heritage. NAB purchased a string of regional retail banks in Britain and Ireland. In the 1990s it entered the US market buying Michigan National Bank and a mortgage originator, HomeSide Inc. (Merrett, 2002b).

The decades of the 1980s and 1990s saw a second and smaller wave of FDI into New Zealand and the Pacific Islands. ANZ, NAB, the Commonwealth Bank and two of the smaller government-owned state banks all made acquisitions in New Zealand, resulting in complete foreign ownership of that country's tier-one banking assets. The Australians expanded their operations in the Pacific islands by buying branches from other multinational banks. For instance, NAB bought the South Pacific operations of Hong Kong and Shanghai Bank (HKSB) and the New Caledonian business of Banque Indosuez (Tabart-Gay and Wolnizer, 1997: 203). Australian banks also sought banking licences in emerging markets in Asia, particularly Vietnam and China (Merrett, 2002b).

Table 7.2 shows the net effect of these acquisitions and the divestments on the internationalisation of the four largest domestic banks. ANZ, NAB and Westpac all made substantial investments abroad before 1987. NAB continued to invest throughout the 1990s while ANZ had stopped doing so and Westpac made significant divestments. By 2005, the three old private banks had all made a strategic withdrawal[6] from multinational banking while the newly (1997) privatised Commonwealth Bank had 16-17 per cent of its assets outside Australia.

Table 7.2: Assets outside Australia by individual banks, 1987, 1997 and 2005 (per cent)

	1987	1997	2005
ANZ	42	44	33
Commonwealth	N/A	16	17
NAB	22	37	33
Westpac	38	29	18

Source: Annual Reports

Collectively, these leading banks confronted obstacles of unimagined proportions in trying to become multinational banks. Their experiences before 1980 had been similar, that is running a wholesale business through a London office, having representative offices in other international financial centres, and replicating Australian retail banking in New Zealand and the south-west Pacific. The administrative heritage of the century-old bifurcation of their wholesale international business and the retail domestic business, run in London and Melbourne or Sydney respectively, proved to be a considerable handicap. The banks did not possess the human capital to manage foreign subsidiaries undertaking new types of business in unfamiliar markets (Merrett, 2002b: 388-92). Failure to undertake rigorous due diligence before acquisitions cost them dearly. Moreover, head offices struggled to develop organisational structures that allowed appropriate lines of reporting and the required transfers of information and resources.

In short, focus on international banking had been lost amongst the other competing areas of sprawling financial conglomerates. Serious losses in domestic non-bank divisions of both ANZ and Westpac during the recession of the early 1990s were to have serious implications for their international presence. Westpac sold its US business to shore up its balance sheet (Carew, 1997; Davidson and Salsbury, 2005). Following losses from securities fraud in India and the Asian financial crisis, ANZ sought to extricate itself from Grindlays, which it saw as an unacceptably high risk international business. In 2001 NAB sold its high risk HomeSide mortgage production and servicing operations business that had been adversely affected by falling US interest rates. In the longer term, new senior executive teams of foreign bankers, from Britain and the United States, and American management consultants took charge in all three banks.

At the beginning of the twenty-first century Australian banks occupy a minor role in the current world of global banking. The financial services industry has been characterised by consolidation at the top end over the past two decades (Wasserstein, 1998). A small number of the world's largest banks and insurers from the United States, the EU and Japan, now have a presence in dozens of countries (UNCTAD, 2004: Annex table A.III.9 and A.III.12). Moreover, these large institutions dominate markets for global products such as foreign exchange (Kimbell, Newby and Skalinder, 2005) Many of these banks now combine the operations of commercial banks, investment banks and insurers (Grosse, 2005). Australian banks have not gone so far down the road of becoming *allfinanz* institutions. Moreover, despite domestic mergers and international acquisitions, they have fallen behind the global leaders in terms of size. Their customer base remains firmly anchored to the modest Australian economy.

Public policy prohibits further mergers between Australia's largest banks. A proposed merger between ANZ Bank and insurer NML in 1990 was stopped by the Treasurer who extended the ban to include all four main banks and the big insurers, a policy known as the 'six pillars'. Despite numerous calls for its abolition, the embargo has been continued, although it now translates into the 'four [bank] pillars'. The current policy maintains the status quo of having four mid-scale banks on a global scale. It is highly unlikely that the government would allow a large foreign bank to take over a domestic target. The banks are protected from external predators but hamstrung in an attempt to achieve global scale.

From 1980 onwards banks around the world have greatly increased the value of loans made to and deposits accepted from non-residents (IMF, 1995). Australian banks have participated in this wider movement and greatly increased the volume of their assets and liabilities held in other countries from the mid-1980s (IMF, 1995; ABS, 1999). Their international assets were the equivalent of 23 per cent of GDP in 2003. However, this figure pales into insignificance when compared to world financial centres: 558 per cent in Singapore, 330 per cent in Hong Kong and 237 per cent of the United Kingdom. Moreover, the international liabilities of Australian banks outweighed their assets by two-to-one. The rest of the world is being used to fund domestic lending. Australian branches and subsidiaries in foreign countries operate primarily within those countries. Nearly 70 per cent of their total overseas claims are receivable in the currency in which the loans were made, predominantly in New Zealand, the UK and Ireland. Only 30 per cent of their claims on counterparties arose from the cross border transfers of funds raised in one currency and lent in another (RBA, 2004). All in all, Australian banks play a minor and passive role in the international banking system.

Insurance

In the last two decades of the twentieth century Australian insurance firms faced a different set of challenges to the banks. The attractiveness of the local market was changed decisively by government policies. Concerns about the cost of providing tax-funded pensions to an ageing population led the government to promote self-funded retirement. The first reform in the 1980s was to offer taxation incentives for superannuation contributions, but the key reform was to make superannuation compulsory for both employees and employers. Under the Superannuation Guarantee Levy 1991, employers would be required to contribute nine per cent of their worker's salaries into a superannuation fund. Funds held by superannuation funds rose from $35 billion to over $350 billion between 1983 and 1998 (ISC, 1997-98: 69). Life policies became less attractive investments whose annual premiums fell from $1 billion in 1999 to only $400 million by 2004.

Banks and foreign insurers aggressively entered this lucrative superannuation market, either trading on their own account or by buying out existing firms. The three mutual life offices had de-mutualised in the 1980s so they could increase their funding. Building scale to fund new opportunities came at a heavy price. They were vulnerable to take over: NML was acquired by the French giant AXA in 1995 and CML by the Commonwealth Bank in 2000. Their international assets disappeared into the balance sheets of their new owners. There was a dramatic decline in the sums insured abroad by local firms, falling from 15 per cent of the total in 1987 to six in 1997 and less than two per cent in 2003 (ASIC, various; APRA, various).

A significant part of the decline reflects decisions taken by the largest life office, AMP. That firm had extended its already substantial UK operations in dramatic fashion in the late 1980s by acquiring two British insurers, London Life in 1989 and Pearl Assurance a year later (Blainey, 1999). However, large losses ensued, partly because of a lack of due diligence before purchase of the latter firm. After boardroom battles and the appointment of a new executive team, AMP signalled its intent to downsize its international business. Its United Kingdom business, Henderson Global Investors, was spun off and sold in 2003-04.

The domestic life insurers, many of whom now combined life and general business,[7] struggled in competition with foreign firms for life business. Foreign firms increased their share of premiums from 18 per cent in 1970 to 27 per cent in 1989 and 31 per cent by 2004 (LIC, 1978: 20; 1986: 24; ISC, 1989-90; APRA, 2004).

The general insurance industry underwent a comprehensive restructuring that has had its impact on the internationalisation strategies of local players. The stable order of government offices and state-based motor clubs was overturned in the 1990s by the privatisation of the former and demutualisation of the latter. New entities emerged from amalgamations that crossed the previous boundaries. For instance, the insurance arm of the Sydney-based National Roads and Motorists' Association (NRMA) reemerged as Insurance Australia Group (IAG), incorporating several government offices and other insurers. IAG has acquired part of Norwich Union's Australian general insurance business as that company, renamed Aviva, now focuses on life and wealth management products. IAG has extended its business to New Zealand and has announced plans to expand into Asian markets (AFR, 8/2/06). Other leading domestic firms, Suncorp Metway and Wesfarmers, are products of recent amalgamations whose business is firmly centred on their home states of Queensland and Western Australia.

Foreign firms continued to play a key role in the general insurance market, taking between a third and a half of premiums from the 1970s onwards (ABS, 1972-73; 1983-84; APRA, various). However, leadership passed decisively from the British to the Germans together with Swiss, French and US companies in Australia, as it did worldwide following catastrophic losses suffered by British firms from the 1970s (Hodgson, 1984). By 2002, there was only one British company in the top 20 insurance firms operating in Australia.

Only two general insurers have sought to build substantial overseas markets in recent years. QBE still stands alone amongst Australian general insurers in having a truly international focus. As early as 1980 its overseas premium income exceeded that of the Australian side, 55 to 45 per cent (Gunn, 1995: 379). It has continued to build the overseas side of its business since then by using locally registered companies rather than branches (Gunn, 1995: 392). In 2004 QBE operated in 38 countries and was in the top 25 general insurance and reinsurance companies in the world. Its expansion has been by the acquisition of more than 80 companies during the past 20 years.

It has even become the largest syndicate at Lloyd's of London (O'Halloran, 2004).

HIH Insurance Limited, which had become Australia's most diversified general insurer and major player after acquiring FAI Insurance in 1999, had also moved aggressively offshore. However, it enjoyed a very different outcome to QBE. In 1987 HIH had entered the US workers' compensation market by setting up a new company in California. It sold the business in 1994 for US$119 million, then bought it back two years later for US$60 million less than the sale price. However, management failed to undertake proper due diligence of the understated outstanding claims or the changed regulatory environment, resulting in a loss of $620 million. HIH collapsed in 2001 with losses of $5.3 billion, the result of incompetence and malfeasance on a grand scale (HIH Royal Commission, 2003: vol. II, para. 13.2.3; Main, 2003: 79-84). The Royal Commissioner drew attention to the abuse by HIH of financial reinsurance to mask underwriting losses. Human failure was the cause of this disaster rather than any problem of being headquartered in a small and distant economy.

CONCLUSION

Australia's financial services industry has always been international to a greater or lesser degree. For the past two hundred years foreign firms have had a presence in domestic markets, bringing with them what Goldsmith (1969: 367) calls 'financial technology'. Yet for all their advantages, foreign firms have never supplanted their domestic rivals, who have doggedly held the lion's share of the local market. Moreover, from the mid-nineteenth century local firms have sought markets abroad. While there was no acceleration of the advance offshore over the inward-looking decades of the 1900s to the 1970s, neither was there a retreat. Australian trading banks held roughly a quarter of their assets offshore throughout the twentieth century and the insurance industry's share, while subject to more fluctuations, was an important part of its business. In their early ventures both banks and insurers opted for safe havens, known locations that were thought to be safe such as London and New Zealand. Yet as the barriers to international trade and investment in financial services came tumbling down, both took much greater risks in terms of where they went and what they did. Expensive mistakes were made that prompted tactical withdrawals. Yet the allure of foreign markets, particularly in China and Southeast Asia, has not diminished. International business remains an important part of the corporate strategy of domestic financial institutions.

The difficult questions are counterfactual ones. Could Australian banks and insurers have become genuinely international banks had they moved to internationalise sooner and more aggressively? Would they have remained Australian-owned had they succeeded? Would more successful financial internationalisation strategies have assisted other Australian firms to internationalise? Or was it the weakness of the international customer base that held back financial internationalisation? This chapter has suggested some tentative answers, without being able to quantify the sources of disadvantage. Perhaps an indirect answer can be found in the performance of banks from other countries in the western Pacific. Despite being in balance sheet terms among the largest banks in the world, Japanese banks have struggled to internationalise independently of their customer base among Japanese MNEs. No single bank from the world financial centre of Singapore, neither government-owned nor private, has yet become a global competitor, notwithstanding efforts towards regional diversification. Hong Kong banks have enjoyed a large and adjacent offshore market in China, yet have also struggled to become global competitors. The one outstanding success has been the Hong Kong and Shanghai Bank, which has established a strong regional presence with a foot in the United Kingdom/Europe. The fact that HKSB is the only genuine transnational player from the region suggests that the global playing field is still a great deal less level than is usually recognised.

NOTES

1. In 1959 it added the final letter E to QBE with the acquisition of the life company Equitable Probate and General.
2. Of the British banks trading in Australia in 1931, the Bank of Australasia had entered the market in 1835, the Union Bank of Australia in 1838 and the English, Scottish & Australian Bank in 1853.
3. The Commercial Bank of Australia was the outlier, having entered in 1912.
4. NAB was the product of the 1982 merger of the National Bank of Australasia and the Commercial Banking Company of Sydney. NAB later changed its name to the National.
5. The Bank of New South Wales and the Commercial Bank of Australia adopted the Westpac (West Pacific) name after their merger in 1982.
6. NAB sold its Irish bank in 2005.
7. AMP had a banking licence.

8. Shipping

Howard Dick*

The shipping industry is a fascinating case of 'the dog that did not bark'.[1] After the mid-nineteenth century, Australia became on a world scale a large generator of export cargo as well as a significant destination for imported goods and immigrants. Unlike many other commodity-producing regions, the resources and the technical and organisational capabilities to sustain a modest international shipping industry were all available in the form of large domestic shipping companies. By the early 1900s the leading Australian shipping companies – Adelaide Steamship, AUSN, Burns Philip, Howard Smith, Huddart Parker and McIlwraith McEacharn – were not just shipping companies but also agents, stevedores, forwarders, insurers, energy producers, marine engineers, sugar millers, salvors, and much else besides. In differing degrees, they were both vertically and horizontally diversified and, as such, may be classified as conglomerates. They ranked alongside the trading banks and pastoral houses as pillars of the Australian business world. If there was one global industry in which Australia might have been expected *a priori* to have achieved a sustainable competitive advantage, it was shipping. Yet until the emergence of TNT and BHP Transport in the 1980s, Australia could boast only one substantial private shipping company that was international in the scope of its operations. This one exception was Burns Philp, which from the 1890s had built up a significant regional shipping network across the South Pacific and into Southeast Asia. Nevertheless, Burns Philp closed its liner services in 1970, marking the decline of the old rather than the emergence of the new (Chapter 12).

The puzzle of the Australian experience is highlighted by the very different experiences of the other British dominions, New Zealand and Canada. Despite its much smaller population, New Zealand gave rise to two important shipping firms. The New Zealand Shipping Company Ltd was founded in Christchurch in 1873 to carry migrants and cargo between Britain

* I am grateful to David Hancox, Peter Morris and Tom Stevens for comments on previous drafts.

and New Zealand with a fleet first of sailing ships; in the 1880s it switched to steam but in 1887 liquidity problems resulted in control passing to a London board (Laxon et al., 1997). The Union Steam Ship Company of New Zealand Ltd – 'The Southern Octopus' – was founded in Dunedin in 1875 and, although initially a coastal operation, by expansion, merger and acquisition rapidly extended to Australia, the Pacific Islands, the west coast of North America, India and, in 1912, to the United Kingdom (McLean, 1990). Control of both firms was taken over by the British P&O group during World War I, though management of Union Steam Ship remained locally based. Canada boasted the Canadian Pacific Line, which from 1891 provided a liner service from Vancouver to East Asia and, after 1903, from the East Coast across the Atlantic.

This chapter seeks to unravel this puzzle by looking two ways, backwards for 'the dog that did not bark' and forwards to the indifferent results of attempts at internationalisation since the late-1960s: the cases of the Australian National Line, BHP Transport and Howard Smith are considered here and TNT in more detail in Chapter 18. There appears to be no simple explanation for the inability of Australian firms to carry more than a tiny fraction of the country's own two-way trade, a failure that stands in marked contrast to the success of Qantas in air passengers and freight, although it should be noted that Qantas has enjoyed consistent government support. This conundrum cannot be attributed specifically to lack of capital or expertise, or to the cabotage restrictions of the Navigation Act, or to British shipping cartels, though all of these factors were significant.

Colonial Capital and De-internationalisation

In the nineteenth century the Australasian shipping industry exemplified the fluidity of colonial capital. Barriers to entry were very low. British shipmasters like Captain William Howard Smith in 1854 could bring a ship out to Australia and simply place her in the coastal trade (Farquhar, 2002). As capital was accumulated, new ships could be built or acquired in the United Kingdom and sailed out. Most founders of early Australasian shipping companies had been born there, James Mills of Dunedin (Union SS Co. of NZ) being a rare exception (McLean, 1990). Regardless of their port of registration, Australian ships continued to be classified as British until long after World War II. Not until the Shipping Registration Act 1981 did the Commonwealth Government establish an Australian Register of Ships, which at last formalised separate nationality (AMSA, 2006).

As the investment of the founding partnerships increased, so did the attraction of limited liability status. Some companies were registered in London, such as McIlwraith, McEacharn & Co. (1875), Australasian United

S.N. Co. Ltd (AUSN) (1887) and the Scottish Line Ltd London (1891). Others were registered in the colonies, including:

1875 The Adelaide Steamship Co. Ltd, Adelaide
Union Steamship Co. of New Zealand, Dunedin
1883 Wm. Howard Smith & Sons Ltd, Melbourne
1883 Burns, Philp & Co. Ltd, Sydney
1889 Huddart, Parker Ltd, Melbourne
1891 McIlwraith, McEacharn & Co. Ltd, Melbourne

Of these, Howard Smith, Burns Philp and McIlwraith McEacharn all had London offices.[2]

The nationality of the principals was more ambiguous than the legal identity of their corporate offspring. One example shows how international were family networks. The McIlwraith family came from modest merchants in Ayr, Scotland. The eldest son John (1828-1902) arrived in Australia and set up a plumbing supplies business as John McIlwraith & Company; he served as alderman of the City of Melbourne from 1870 to 1882 and was mayor in 1873-74 but died suddenly on a visit back to Ayr.[3] Thomas (1835-1900) went out to Australia in 1854, entered Queensland parliament in 1870, served as premier of the colony from 1879 to 1883 and briefly again in 1888 and 1893 before retiring to England. Their younger brother Andrew (1844-1932) in 1874 moved to London and set up in partnership with Malcolm McEacharn as commission and shipping agents, in 1876 winning an immigrant contract and building a fleet of sailing ships to serve Queensland. Andrew visited but never resided in Australia, though he was on good terms with fellow Ayshireman Andrew Fisher, who served three terms as Prime Minister of Australia between 1908 and 1915. His business partner McEacharn (1852-1910) was elected to Melbourne City Council in 1893, served as mayor from 1897 to 1900, became a member of the Federal Parliament from 1901 to 1903, then Lord Mayor of Melbourne in 1903-04 before retiring to England. These four Scotsmen not only constituted a substantial accumulation of capital with solid London connections but also represented political constituencies in two colonies (Victoria and Queensland) as well as in Federal Parliament. They all died in Britain but their local businesses eventually became completely Australian in management and scope of operations.

Nevertheless, until 1921, when the Navigation Act 1912 finally came into force, after having been delayed by World War I, there had been no cabotage restrictions and no legal distinction between foreign and domestic shipping (Bach, 1982). Thus, British-registered ships could trade freely on the Australian coast and 'Australasian' ships registered in colonial ports under the British flag could engage in international trade. Ships of homeward lines carried passengers and cargo around the coast insofar as there was excess capacity to do so. Australasian-flag ships engaged in the homeward trade and, more notably in the inter-colonial trade, to India, China and the Pacific coast of North America, as well as shipping coal throughout the Pacific. That this did not happen to a greater extent was due to logical market segmentation and the increasing barriers of cartel (conference) arrangements.

The Navigation Act was a protectionist measure to reserve the coastal trade for ships which employed Australian crews. By then the few Australian deepsea shipping companies had already seen the writing on the wall and made other arrangements. Australian-crewed ships were recognised to be uncompetitive in deepsea liner or tramp trades, not only because of higher real wages but also because of inflated manning scales. The Melbourne-based firm of Archibald Currie & Co. P/L, which traded to India with a fleet of five ships, sold out in January 1913 to the mighty British India S.N. Co. (BI) and the local firm was wound up (Laxon, 2002); in the same year McIlwraith McEacharn also sold its one ship and interests in the India trade to BI, leaving the Union Steam Ship Co. of New Zealand as the only Australasian firm in the trade.

The one substantial deepsea venture to survive application of the Navigation Act was the Commonwealth Government Line, known derisively after the prime minister as Billy Hughes' Navy. It began in 1916 with a fleet of captured German ships and was expanded by secondhand purchases (McDonell, 1976). At the end of World War I the Government attempted to place the line on a sound commercial footing by ordering five passenger-cargo ships from British yards for the immigrant trade, plus two large cargo carriers from the government-owned dockyard at Cockatoo Island, Sydney. They were all fine ships, but built at high wartime prices and manned by expensive and strike-prone Australian crews. The losses mounted steadily until the line and its ships were sold to rival British lines in November 1927.

The debacle of the Commonwealth Government Line confirmed a view – by the 1950s entrenched in the public mind – that Australian-owned ships could not compete in international trades, notwithstanding a large and well-established coastal shipping industry with a significant pool of trained ship managers, officers and crew. Among Liberal-Country Party governments this perception became dogma, reinforced by left-wing maritime unions which had frequent resort to strikes.

Nevertheless, the argument that the Navigation Act prevented the development of Australia's deepsea shipping is poorly conceived. Certainly the Act had the unintended consequence that Australian-manned ships became unprofitable in deepsea trades, but that did not shut out Australian companies or principals. Throughout the interwar and early postwar years, private Australian-based firms continued to engage in deepsea shipping, albeit with ships manned by foreign crews.

An overview of the main ventures in chronological order gives some sense of scale, scope and continuity:

- Colonial Sugar Refining Co. Ltd (CSR): from the late-nineteenth century until 1972 employed ships in the sugar trade from Fiji to New Zealand and Australia, backloading with stores and provisions (Log, 8/76)
- Wm Crosby & Co. Ltd, Melbourne (agents, brokers, charterers and shipowners): from 1900 provided ships for the phosphate trade initially from Ocean Island and then also from Nauru, extending this trade in the interwar years to shipping wool to the US west coast and flour to East Asia (Log, 2/76)
- Burns Philp & Co. Ltd: from 1902 to 1964 employed two ships (registered in London) on a monthly line from east coast Australia to Java and Singapore and Malaya, also from 1935 to 1941 two ships to Manila and Hong Kong; these lines were in addition to local shipping and trading to and within PNG, the Solomons, Gilbert & Ellice Islands, the New Hebrides and Fiji (Wilkinson and Willson, 1981)
- Yuill & Co. (Australian-Oriental Line): from 1912 to 1960 employed two ships (registered in Hong Kong) on a monthly passenger-cargo line to Manila and Hong Kong (Log, 8/74)
- China Australia Mail Line (principal William J. Lumb Liu, Sydney): from 1917 to 1923 employed two ships in a monthly line from Sydney to Hong Kong and Shanghai (Yong, 1977; Log, 11/78)
- Western Australian Government: From 1921 to 1938 employed one ship in a regular line from Fremantle to Java, Singapore and Malaya (Stephens, ca. 1977)
- Austral-China Navigation Co. Ltd: from 1926 to 1930 employed two ships in a monthly line from Sydney to Hong Kong and China, returning via the Philippines and Sandakan (Log, 2/86)
- Wesfarmers: from the early 1930s employed chartered ships in a line from St Lawrence ports in Canada and in the late 1930s in another line to Europe (Log, 2/87)
- W.R. Carpenter & Co. Ltd (South Pacific traders and copra producers): from 1934 to 1947 (and thereafter until 1967 as Pacific Shipowners Ltd of Suva) operated a line from Sydney to the west coast of North America (Log, 11/70)

- H.C. Sleigh & Co. Ltd, Melbourne (shipping agent and principal of Golden Fleece Petroleum): in 1950 set up the Singapore Navigation Co. Ltd of Singapore to own tankers carrying crude oil to Australia refineries, then in 1960 the Dominion Nav. Co. Ltd of Nassau (later also Hong Kong); in 1962 Dominion diversified into liner trades with two ships under Chinese crews trading from east coast Australia to Hong Kong and Japan; in 1965 the line became a joint venture with Hong Kong-based Jardine, Matheson & Co. Ltd; from 1968 to 1976 the joint venture also operated two vehicle-deck ships before selling out to the Australian National Line (Log, 8/79; Dick and Kentwell, 1988).

Most of these Australian firms registered their ships under the British flag in London, Hong Kong, Singapore or even Suva, which allowed them to employ Australian officers and Asian crews in line with British manning scales. They also usually drydocked and repaired their ships overseas. Overall their cost structures were not out of line with other British-flag operators serving the same routes, some of which also found it practical to employ Australian officers and engineers.

Although only Burns Philp may be rated as a substantial and long-lived business (Chapter 12), the number of players suggests that Australian principals were not lacking in entrepreneurship or capabilities. Something more than the Navigation Act is required to explain why Australian shipowners de-internationalised in the interwar years and were so unadventurous in following decades.

The key is the changing nature of the local industry. In the late nineteenth century the coastal shipping market was characterised by low barriers to entry and cut-throat competition for coverage and market share. In 1902, after extended negotiations, a secret pool agreement known as 'Collins' came into effect and lasted until 1911, when it was dissolved under pressure from the anti-trust provisions of the Australian Industries Preservation Act (1906); eight years later with government approval the pool was reformed as the Associated Steamship Owners (ASO) and remained in force until 1960 (McKellar, 1977). Under a system that pooled costs and distributed the surplus, the profitability of member companies came to depend not upon their efficiency and innovation but their skill in playing a game of byzantine complexity. In the words of McKellar (1977: 641), they 'enjoyed a complacency to which they were never entitled'. The dynamic entrepreneurs of the nineteenth century gave way to committee men of small imagination, who either refused to admit that their industry was slowly dying of attrition from rising costs and falling demand or, if they did perceive it, were incapable of an entrepreneurial response.

A clear example of the lack of entrepreneurial drive was the failure of members of the ASO cartel to see the opportunities for more efficient carriage of bulk cargoes in response to postwar growth and industrialisation. Beginning in 1952, British shipowners began taking delivery of wide-hatch bulk carriers without cargo-handling gear for long-term charter to the British Iron & Steel Corporation (Harrison, 2003). The Australian coast had a similar need for such vessels for both the coal and iron ore trades. Yet the ASO missed the market. Instead the initiative was taken by steel producer BHP, which expanded its own fleet, and by the government-run Australian Shipping Board, reorganised in 1957 as the Australian National Line (ANL) (Riley, 1992; Clark et al. 1982). It took ten more years and much agonising before the ASO joint-entity, Bulkships P/L, took delivery of a pair of bulk carriers modeled on the original British designs, by which time ASO had ceased to exist (Stevens, m.s.).

The decline of the main coastal shipping companies over the period between the eve of World War I and 1970 is illustrated by Table 8.1. The year 1960 was decisive, because it marked the suspension of the ASO coastal freight cartel. AUSN liquidated almost immediately. Huddart Parker was taken over in 1961 by McIlwraith McEacharn, which in 1963 merged its shipping interests with those of Adelaide Steamship to form Associated Steamships (Stevens, 1984): even with the affiliated Bulkships, the combined fleet in 1970 was considerably smaller than in 1939. Howard Smith remained staunchly independent with a fleet of prewar size, albeit with much fewer ships. Except for the small state-owned West Australian coastal fleet, all the postwar growth was in the dedicated fleet of specialist steel producer BHP and the state-owned Australian National Line, which had not even existed in 1939. It is a damning summary of a private sector industry stagnating not through lack of resources but through sheer lack of vision and initiative.

To the extent that there survived some entrepreneurial spirit, the leading coastal shipping companies had no reason beyond sentiment to invest retained earnings or borrowings back into the underperforming shipping industry. For example, the Adelaide Steamship group, after hiving off its shipping division in 1963 into the joint venture Associated Steamships, aggressively pursued non-shipping interests. In the 1980s under CEO John Spalvins, the group engaged in a highly leveraged takeover spree that transformed it into Australia's largest industrial and retail conglomerate, only to collapse in 1991 with debts of $6.4 billion against shareholders' funds of just one billion (Sykes, 1994: ch. 13). Conglomerate Howard Smith retained some shipping interests, most notably harbour towage, but over time came to identify its core business as domestic hardware distribution (see below).

Table 8.1: Main Australian-flag shipping fleets, 1 January 1939 and 1970

Company (abbreviated name)	1939 No.	1939 Gross tons	1970 No.	1970 Gross tons
Adelaide Steamship	30	72,800	)	
McIlwraith McE.	12	40,100	) 13 [a]	128,700[a]
Huddart Parker	11	39,900	)	
Howard Smith	19	39,700	4	44,700
BHP	8	32,200	13	140,235
AUSN	11	25,327	liquidated 1961	
Melbourne SS Co.	7	21,020	to Howard Smith 1961	
W.A. Government	4	13,020	7 [b]	23,300 [b]
ANL	-	-	34	295,500

Notes:
a. Now Associated Steamships, Bulkships and McIlwraith McEacharn
b. Trading as 'Stateships'

Source: LRS (1938), DST (1970)

Re-internationalisation since the late-1960s

Australian shipping firms faced barriers to entry into the deepsea liner trades from the resistance of the British-dominated cartels (known as conferences) and their resort to predatory tactics (Bach, 1982). These barriers were high, but not insurmountable, especially in earlier decades, as the periodic new entry of British and foreign lines continued to demonstrate. Back in the 1890s there had been some 'Australian' initiatives. Andrew McIlwraith, who was both an outward loading broker in London and a shipowner in Australia, ordered several ships which appear to have been associated with a putative deepsea line; in the event his interest became a minority stake in the formation of the London-based Federal Steam Navigation Company and the ships were deployed on the Australian coast (Stevens, m.s.). In 1893 James Huddart, partner in Huddart Parker & Co. but here acting on his own account, placed two fast new ships in a subsidised Canadian Australasian Royal Mail Line between Sydney and Vancouver: this venture in opposition to the Union Steamship Company of New Zealand was a financial debacle that destroyed him (McLean, 1990: 127-30). It may be that other Australian principals noted such experiences, as well as the difficulties of non-conference lines in other trades, and considered that the likely returns from a deepsea line did not justify the large risk capital that would be required. By the interwar years conference membership had stabilised. Australian marketing boards gained some influence in the 1930s in strengthening the bargaining power of shippers vis-à-vis the liner cartels, but only occasionally did they direct cargo to the benefit of Australian charterers or shipping lines, as in the case of Wesfarmers. Timely concessions by the conference lines usually obviated the threat of new entry.

Beginning in the mid-1960s, however, the new technology of containerisation revolutionised the economics of liner shipping. The huge capital requirements of new fleets of ships broke down longstanding conference arrangements, obliging independent firms to combine into larger consortia. The Australian liner trades followed two different technological paths. On the one hand were fully cellular containerships which served the Australia/Europe trade; on the other hand, as in the East and Southeast Asian and Trans-Pacific trades, were vehicle-deck ships that combined lift-on/lift-off with 'roll-on/roll-off' capabilities. During the 1960s Australian coastal shipping firms, especially the Australian National Line, had built up world-class expertise in the latter mode of operation (Clark et al., 1982).

Technological change was reinforced by bipartisan policy change as more nationalistic governments overturned decades of Federal Government hostility towards Australian involvement in deepsea shipping. The initiative was taken by John Gorton, Liberal-Country Party Prime Minister from 1968 to 1971, and long-serving Minister for Trade John McEwen to put pressure on the new consortia and liner conferences to accept the entry of Australian-flag carriers. After 1972 the Whitlam Labor Government keenly followed up this policy with initiatives to take the Australian National Line into deepsea bulk trades as well.

A second wave of policy reform began in 1982 with the release of the Crawford Report on revitalisation of the Australian shipping industry. The incoming Hawke Labor Government in 1983 promptly implemented the recommendations for a more internationally competitive maritime tax regime in return for manning reductions on new ships (ANMA, 1989). This was followed up by a second package in response to the tripartite Maritime Industry Development Committee report of 1986, which recommended a seven per cent taxable investment grant in return for further manning reductions (Dick, 1992). These reforms brought the costs of Australian-flag shipping into line with OECD levels and made it commercially viable with best-practice technologies and operations.

Deepsea liner shipping: the Australian National Line

In October 1956 the ill-assorted fleet of the Australian Shipping Board was transferred to the Australian Coastal Shipping Commission trading as the Australian National Line (ANL) (Clark et al., 1982). Though government-owned, ANL was well managed by experienced master mariner (Sir) John Williams and his successors and proved to be more far-sighted and innovative than the tradition-bound private coastal firms. Seeing little future in the general cargo trade and responding to the need for faster ship turnaround, it pursued a large investment program that from the late-1950s concentrated upon vehicle-deck ('roll-on/roll-off') ships and bulk carriers of increasing size. By the mid-1960s it operated the largest fleet on the Australian coast.

The deepsea liner and bulk shipping interests of the ANL were built up from 1968 on the initiative of the nationalistic Gorton-McEwen government. Nevertheless, Australia's first significant overseas shipping line since the sale of the ill-starred Commonwealth Government Line in the 1920s was less a strategic diversification than a set of minor, rent-seeking stakes in global cartels. Given that ANL's entry had government backing, the liner conferences were obliged to allow entry, at least of one token ship per trade. The benefit to the incumbents was that ANL came in with Australian manning scales as a higher cost operator, which helped to protect intra-marginal rents for lower cost lines, as well as securing government endorsement for the continued operation of the cartels. It follows that, despite its state-of-the-art ships and government support, ANL was never able to build up scale and thus develop a sustainable competitive advantage. When non-conference operators began to erode conference rates and split open the longstanding cartels, ANL's deepsea ventures became unprofitable. There was no possibility of ANL becoming a significant force in its own right.[4] The ships were sold off as they reached the end of their economic life.

In deepsea bulk shipping, ANL was unable to repeat its success on the coast. Unlike BHP (see below), it had no control of cargoes. In addition, it was handicapped from the outset because the four very large bulk carriers delivered in 1976-77 for the Australia-Japan iron ore trade had both high capital and high manning costs. Although their carrying capacity of 120 to 140 thousand tonnes was best practice, they were built by expensive European yards at the peak of the construction cycle and under pressure from Treasury were then refinanced on terms disadvantageous to ANL. Their accumulating operating losses were another significant factor in the deterioration of ANL's financial position, leading to its eventual demise in 1998.[5]

Deepsea bulk shipping: BHP Transport

Broken Hill Proprietary Co. Ltd (BHP) began in 1885 as a mining company that soon diversified into smelting and in 1915 opened a steelworks at Newcastle (NSW) (Chapter 14). In the early years it met its shipping requirements by chartering but in 1917, under pressure of wartime shortage, the company reluctantly became a joint-venture investor with its former shipping managers (Riley, 1992: 23). In 1921 BHP set up its own Shipping Department with a manager and marine superintendent and during the interwar years gradually built up a core owned and managed fleet for the carriage of iron ore, coal and products. The balance of requirements was still met by chartering in from private coastal shipowners. In 1935 BHP took over the new Port Kembla plant from Australian Iron & Steel and became the monopoly domestic steel producer. The opening up of iron ore mines in northwest Australia led to construction of a new class of ships designed and built by the company's own shipyard at Whyalla. In the late 1950s the first true bulk carriers followed. By 1970 BHP was the second largest Australian-flag shipowner after ANL (DST, 1970). Soon it was employing ships as large as 100,000 tonnes in the coastal iron ore trade, as well as smaller ships in coastal limestone and product trades.

BHP's first ventures into deepsea trades were incidental. Pig iron was shipped to Southeast and East Asia in one-off voyages, while from 1967 two ships were employed for some years carrying pelletised iron from Whyalla to Japan (Riley, 1992: 82-3). The turning point was the recession of 1982, which underlined to BHP how completely it was exposed to the Australian economy. A strategic review led in 1984 to the takeover of Utah International Inc. with its coal, iron ore and copper mining interests (Chapter 14). Utah's shipping department Utah Marine was merged with BHP's new Transport division based in Melbourne and injected a much more vigorous and outward-looking attitude (Riley 1992: 104, 106-8). At the same time, the Crawford Report recommendations to reduce the manning scales on Australian-flag ships and to bring the depreciation and tax provisions more into line with international practice, substantially improved the cost-competitiveness of Australian-flag ships.

In this new environment, it was possible for John Prescott as General Manager Transport to tackle two problems simultaneously. First, as BHP became a genuine multinational, there was the incentive to gain greater control over the shipping costs of low-margin raw materials, traditionally sold on a free on board (f.o.b.) basis with the buyer arranging shipment. Secondly, there was the longstanding problem of how to secure backloading for the huge bulk carriers now employed in the NW Australia-NSW iron ore trade. A partial solution was 'triangulation'. This involved building several large new bulk carriers to carry coal from the former Utah mines in Queensland to Korea or Japan, returning in ballast to NW Australia to load iron ore for Newcastle and Port Kembla (Riley, 1992: 109). Korean steel mills readily agreed on the basis that the vessels would be built in Korean yards; the Japanese steel cartel resisted until the Australian Government invoked a clause of the 1976 Basic Treaty of Friendship and Cooperation (Nara Treaty) (Morris, pers. comm.).

A second initiative was taken in 1989 when BHP Transport's break-bulk chartering interests were hived off as International Marine Transport (IMT) with a head office in Oakland, California. BHP-IMT moved into non-conference, breakbulk liner shipping between the Pacific coast of North America and the east coast of Australia, providing cost-efficient logistics for BHP's steel exports back to the United States. Albeit under direct control of BHP Transport, in 1991-92 the company's steel product shipments from Australia to New Zealand were integrated with those of New Zealand Steel into a regular, two-ship trans-Tasman service (Riley, 1992: 124-5).

By 1991 when BHP's fleet operations were concentrated in BHP Transport in Melbourne head office, BHP had become a substantial ship-owner, operator and charterer in its own right. Although the capabilities had been nurtured in-house over more than 70 years and were still ancillary to the mining, steel and oil industries, the takeover of Utah International had given rise to international competencies in deepsea shipping, both bulk and break-bulk. BHP was by then Australia's largest shipping company with its own Australian-flag fleet of 1.2 million tonnes capacity, plus four part-owned and managed liquified natural gas tankers and another 0.6 tonnes under foreign flags, totaling 2 million tonnes excluding tugs, drillships and charters (Riley, 1992). The future seemed bright.

In the subsequent decade, however, the tide turned. The company had to write off over $A2 billion in the over-priced purchase of Magma Copper and a technically troubled investment in a hot briquetted steel plant in NW Australia (Chapter 14). Market capitalisation suffered. In 2001 BHP merged with South-African mining company Billiton to form the giant resources entity BHP Billiton.

Meanwhile in 1996 there had been a change of Commonwealth government. The new government, a conservative Liberal-National Party coalition, was hostile to the maritime industry as a perceived bastion of trade unionism and, abandoning the Labor government's efforts to assist Australian-flag shipping to achieve international competitiveness, sought to relax domestic cabotage and reduce the size of the Australian-flag fleet. At the same time, the shipping industry worldwide was moving towards separation of shipowning (financial risk), ship management (crewing, maintenance) and ship operation (chartering-in).

Thus, as a result of both a changing industry environment and internal crisis, the ship management business of BHP Transport, including management of all owned, joint-venture and third-party ships and tugs, was contracted out to Canadian-based global ship management firm Teekay Shipping Corporation in February 2003 (Log, 2/03: 45). In effect, this turned the clock back prior to 1921 when BHP outsourced its shipping requirements to local agents Scott Fell & Company. While BHP Billiton Freight Trading

& Logistics still engages in maritime-related services, especially in the fixing of cargoes, its head office is in The Hague. The group's operational maritime capabilities and associated human resources have largely been dissipated.

With hindsight, BHP Transport's internationalisation of the 1980s and 1990s was a commercial success – arguably the best conceived and best performed of the international ventures discussed here – but it was not sustainable under a very different company structure and in a much more competitive industry. The parent BHP Billiton adapted to changed circumstances without, as seemed possible in the early 1990s, using its impressive operational capabilities to consolidate its own place in the global shipping industry. Instead, like rival mining firm Rio Tinto, it now uses its bargaining strength from control of cargoes to obtain the best prices that it can from suppliers of marine services.

International towage: Howard Smith[6]

Howard Smith Industries P/L was a conglomerate firm that had diversified from its original interest in coastal shipping into stevedoring, coal, sugar, metals and engineering. Its modest diversification into international towage was not a failure in terms of profitability but turned out to be a distraction from its core business.

In 1960 Howard Smith withdrew from the coastal shipping cartel, phased out general cargo shipping and moved aggressively into coastal bulk shipping, tankers and port towage as well as stevedoring. Around 1980 the firm undertook a number of exploratory international ventures. First, experience in operating coastal oil tankers led to the acquisition of one and later two larger ships for deepsea trading; this was very much a niche operation. Second, the group's interests in coal mining and export through Coal & Allied led to various tie-ups with Ube Industries of Japan, one of which involved building the specialist bulk carrier *Howard Smith* for the carriage of steaming coal to Ube, back-loading with limestone and tar (Jay, 1994).

The offshore venture with the greatest potential, however, was towage. Trade Practices Commission rulings against mergers with fellow duopolists in Australian ports restricted further opportunities in the profitable domestic market. The first offshore move was a one-tug joint venture known as South Pacific Towage in Fiji in 1979. Acquisition of Offshore Maintenance Services in 1980 led into offshore rig supply vessels, subsequently converted into a joint venture with P&O Australia in exchange for a share in P&O's towage interests in Western Australia (D. Hancox, pers. comm.). In 1987 Howard Smith went well outside the region to buy a 75 per cent controlling interest in the North British Maritime Group Ltd of Hull. In 1990 Howard Smith sold out its interest in Offshore Maintenance Services to joint-venture partner P&O and extended its towage interests in the United Kingdom by acquiring the Medway towage interests of J.P. Knight (Rochester) Ltd. In 1993 this was followed by acquisition of The Alexander Towing Co. Ltd, the largest operator in the United Kingdom.

Well satisfied by these results, in 1995 Howard Smith decided to withdraw from all other shipowning to concentrate its shipping interests in towing and salvage. In most Australian ports towage was either a monopoly or a cosy duopoly offering steady profits, while the United Kingdom and overseas seemed to offer good opportunities for expansion. In 2000, having sold off its sugar, coal, general shipping, stevedoring and engineering interests, Howard Smith Industries P/L in fact became Howard Smith Towage P/L.

In 1994 the Howard Smith group had bought out the domestic BBC Hardware chain from ailing Burns Philp, another former shipping and trading company which had sought to go back onshore (Chapter 12). As the BBC Hardware stores prospered, the incompatibility with port towage, especially in the United Kingdom, became increasingly apparent. From a managerial point of view, there was also the reality that towage delivers few network benefits because each port is more or less an independent operation. Accordingly, in 2001 Howard Smith sold its entire Australian and United Kingdom towage operations to its former domestic joint-venture partner, Adsteam Marine Ltd, for $0.5 billion.[7] Within a few months Howard Smith itself was swallowed up for $2.25 billion by conglomerate Wesfarmers (Bunnings), its main rival in hardware distribution (see also Chapter 9). Ironically, the towage interests, through their entanglement with the recalcitrant maritime unions, may hitherto have been a 'poison pill' that had frightened off potential predators.

Adsteam Marine Ltd, a good business spun off in 1997 from the wreckage of the failed conglomerate, Adelaide Steamship Company, is a specialist harbour towage, offshore supply and salvage firm (Adsteam, 2006a). Until 2001 it had shared the Australian towage industry in a virtual duopoly with Howard Smith, with whom it had been a joint-venture partner in Sydney and other main ports. Thereafter Adsteam became the dominant firm. At the end of 2005 its operations divided into Australasia (including New Zealand, Papua New Guinea, Fiji and agencies in India) and the United Kingdom with earnings before interest, tax and depreciation in the ratio of about two to one respectively (Adsteam, 2006b). Thus Adsteam is now substantially diversified offshore and from a solid base has had some success in contracting for services not only in harbour towage but also in the highly competitive North Sea oil-LNG market. How long it will survive takeover remains to be seen.[8]

CONCLUSION

Studied over a long period back to the late nineteenth century, the 'Australian' shipping industry is a story neither of success nor of failed internationalisation. Its origins in British Empire days were international. After Federation in 1901 and in particular from 1921 after the delayed imposition of the cabotage provisions of the Navigation Act, the industry was, with a few minor exceptions, nationalised. The recent phase of internationalisation is therefore part of the wider story of the re-acculturation of Australian management and the revival of entrepreneurship in response to the gradual weakening of the regime of high protection with all its delightful rent-seeking opportunities and the comforts of a sheltered life.

The earliest attempts at internationalisation during the Gorton-Whitlam era, most notably by the Australian National Line, were an extension of the protectionist regime into international shipping. As the designated national carrier, ANL was able to enjoy the rights and privileges of a conference line, albeit as a tolerated minor player. These efforts foundered when liner shipping was exposed to non-conference competition. Ultimately ANL was no more viable in the nasty, competitive world than the high-cost private shipping firms that it had supplanted for a brief period in the 1960s and 1970s.

The next wave of international ventures was more genuinely entrepreneurial and were all the result of private initiative. They benefited from the opening up of the Australian economy by the Hawke-Keating government but were not immune from the heady overconfidence of that time. International business seemed easy. TNT rushed in to do deals, created on paper an impressive multi-modal network, but failed to lay solid foundations for an internationally competitive business, at least not under Australian management (Chapter 18). Howard Smith more wisely targeted its offshore acquisitions in a defined core business, namely port towage, but found itself with a set of discrete franchises rather than a real international business. After a few modestly profitable years, it sold out to concentrate on more profitable hardware distribution, only to be promptly swallowed up by a larger and more hungry rival. If this was failure, it was a failure of corporate strategy rather than business strategy. Whether Howard Smith's successor, Adsteam Marine, will build a more viable international business remains to be seen.

BHP Transport was the firm that most systematically built upon solid capabilities and created genuine and potentially sustainable core competencies in international liner and bulk shipping. Both corporate and business strategy were sound. What had not been anticipated was the loss of financial momentum by the BHP group, the consequent restructuring that included the hiving off of the transport-intensive steel industry, and the eventual merger with Billiton. All these events left BHP Transport stranded, reducing its internal cargo base without the option of hiving off. The increasingly harsh operating environment for the Australian-flag shipping industry was also a problem. As BHP Billiton became more international, it was logical that transport management would be shifted away from Australia, except for local operations that were contracted out anyway.

A final observation would be that the struggles of Australian firms to build international competitiveness in the shipping industry were part of a much wider industry restructuring in the domestic economy. On the eve of World War II Australia's main shipping firms were all 'blue-chip' companies, giants of the corporate landscape. By the 1960s Australian-flag shipping was no longer profitable without massive investment in new technologies. Restructuring was therefore essential. Huddart Parker, McIlwraith McEacharn and Union Company were eventually swallowed up in the ill-fated TNT empire and disappeared from the corporate landscape. Adelaide Steamship and Burns Philp came under the control of corporate adventurers, driving the former into liquidation and exposing the latter to a near death. Howard Smith, which remained until quite late under family influence, was more conservative and the most successful, but ultimately failed to maintain its independence.

If the shipping industry is a story of failure, it is therefore not simply a failure of internationalisation, which would imply that firms remaining in the domestic economy would somehow have led a safer and quieter life. There is no evidence for this corollary. Eventually Schumpeter's 'gale of creative destruction' swept all firms away. The few names that survive as corporate labels are no longer linked with maritime capabilities. With the notable exception of the revived Adsteam Marine, the Australian shipping industry is now but a shadow of its former self. Given that the same thing can be said of the once mighty British shipping industry, this should perhaps be no surprise. Australia's huge cargo base nevertheless continues to give rise to business opportunities in maritime-related services and in inter-modal logistics.

NOTES

1. Conan Doyle, Arthur, 'The Silver Blaze' (1892). The dog, of course, should have barked.
2. For sources, see the company histories by Buckley and Klugman (1981, 1983), Farquhar (2002), Huddart Parker (1926), McKellar (1977), McLean (1990), Page (1975) and Stevens (m.s.).
3. I am grateful for permission to draw on a manuscript history of McIlwraith, McEacharn & Co. by Mr T.S. Stevens.
4. Some years ago I was told by the late C.K. Jones, Minister for Transport in the Whitlam Government, that in the period leading up to dismissal of the

government in November 1975 there had been highly secret negotiations to buy out one of the main conference lines trading to Australia. Most likely this was Port Line, part of the Cunard/Trafalgar House group and a large stakeholder in the ACTA container consortium. Had the bid succeeded, ANL would have gained a larger stake in the cartel but remained a minority interest heavily dependent upon the Australian government for any leverage.

5. ANL's financial position can be followed in its annual reports, which from 1977 to 1996 are summarized and analysed in *The Log* (1978-97). The trading rights to the ANL name were bought by the French liner shipping group CMA CGM in 1998 (ANL, 2006).
6. Details in this section are taken from the excellent chronology of Farquhar (2002a: 55-63) with some further details by courtesy of David Hancox.
7. In the domestic joint ventures there had been a longstanding 'Savoy clause' that allowed either party to trigger a sale to the other.
8. In July 2006 Adsteam became the target of a $0.7 billion bid by the SvitzerWijsmuller towage and salvage group, a subsidiary of the world's leading shipping group, Danish-owned A.P. Moller-Maersk A/S. The British Office of Fair Trading referred the bid to the Competition Commission for determination in February 2007 (SMH, 23/9/06; SvitzerWijsmuller, 2006).

9. Retail

André Sammartino

INTRODUCTION

Retailers are late arrivals on the global business scene (Alexander, 1997; Alexander and Myers, 2000; Vida, 2000). Although Godley and Fletcher (2001) have recorded a raft of typically small foreign firms entering Britain over the period 1850 to 1964, most of the large-scale internationalisation in the developed world has occurred in the last three decades of the twentieth century. As Dawson (2003: 190) asserts:

> With a few notable exceptions, the operation of shops internationally by large firms, other than as a token presence, in another country, is a relatively new phenomenon associated with the globalisation trends in economies.

The relevance to Australia is twofold. Firstly, local retailers have been little affected by competition from overseas firms. A very geographically dispersed and isolated retail environment, which modernised concurrently with the most likely sources of FDI, has not proven attractive to international retailers. Of the world's 250 largest retailers, only 16 operate in Australia, of which 13 are foreign-owned firms (Table 9.1). Of these, several operate on a very small scale and all but two have arrived since the late 1980s. Secondly, this isolation and lack of competitors has allowed various retail sectors to consolidate into tight oligopolies and often duopolies. These retailing behemoths have proven ill-suited and reluctant to seek out expansion through FDI, instead preferring further consolidation and domestic diversification. Two Australian retailers, Coles Myer and Woolworths, now rank among the 30 largest retailers in the world (Deloitte, 2006), yet their businesses extend no further than New Zealand.[1]

Table 9.1: Retail firms in Global Top 250 operating in Australia (2006)

Firm (and Australian brand name(s) if different)	Global ranking	No. of Countries	Country of Origin	Format[a]	Number of Australian stores	Date of entry[b]
Aldi	10	12	Germany	F	100+	2001
Ito-Yokado (7-Eleven)[c]	23	16	Japan	F	359	1991
Woolworths (Woolworths, Safeway, Big W, Tandy, Dick Smith Electronics, Dan Murphy)	29	2	Australia	F, G, S	1700+	1924
Coles Myer (Coles New World/Bi-Lo, Myer, Target, Kmart, Officeworks, Harris Technology)	30	2	Australia	F, G, S	1900+	1900
Ikea	44	33	Sweden	S (Homewares)	6	1975
Toys'R'Us	58	32	US	S (Toys)	32	1993
Gus (Burberry)	60	22	UK	S (Luxury)	5	2002
Metcash (IGA, Jewel, Campbells Cash & Carry)	81	11	South Africa	F	n/a	1988
Blockbuster	110	26	US	S (Video)	404	1991
Footlocker	118	19	US	S (Sporting)	82	1989
Pick'n Pay (Franklins (NSW))	123	6	South Africa	F	78	1974

Firm (and Australian brand name(s) if different)	Global ranking	No. of Countries	Country of Origin	Format[a]	Number of Australian stores	Date of entry[b]
Foodland (Action) [d]	148	2	Australia	F	80	1926
LVMH (DFS Galleria)	150	22	France	S (Luxury)	3	2000
Borders	159	6	US	S (Books)	14	1998
HMV [e]	173	7	UK	S (Music)	31	1989
Hachette (Newslink, Virgin, Relay, Bijoux Terner, Hub)	197	17	France	S (Airport)	53	2004
Bunnings	200	2	Australia	S (Hardware)	194	1952
Luxottica (OPSM, Sunglass Hut, Laubman & Pank, Budget Eyewear, Watch Station)	208	17	Italy	S (Eyewear)	300+	2003

Notes:

a. F=grocery, G=generalist, S=specialist
b. Into retailing in Australia
c. Initial 7-Eleven entry was by US firm Southland in 1977
d. Foodland was acquired by Metcash in Dec 2005 (its NZ assets were on sold to Woolworths)
e. HMV Australia was sold to Australian retailer Brazin in Sept 2005

Sources: Deloitte (2006), company websites and annual reports

Despite the recent incursions into the Asian region by the world's largest retailers such as Wal-Mart, Carrefour, Metro AG and Tesco, the trans-Tasman option has been the extent of the overseas adventures of Australia's largest retailers.

Nevertheless, Australia is not a retail backwater. On the one hand, the leading domestic retailers have copied and sometimes led international best practice. On the other hand, several smaller-scale specialists, such as Barbeques Galore, Flight Centre, Cash Converters, Cartridge World and OPSM have identified gaps in the market to prosper domestically while, often simultaneously, expanding offshore. Although the literature has tended to focus on the global majors, these cases demonstrate the scope for niche players from small, but modern retail environments to build significant international operations. They also serve as valuable lessons for other Australian retailers concerned with diminishing returns from domestic expansion or reluctant to sit and watch while foreign firms spread their business networks.

This chapter opens with a discussion of the nature of competitive advantage in the retailing sector. The following section gives an overview of the internationalisation of generalist and grocery retailers. It is argued that Australia has been relatively untouched in these areas, and that two giants have emerged locally, but ventured little from their home. The final section explores the experience in the specialist sector and argues that this has been the most fruitful area for Australian retailers in the international domain.

RETAILING AND COMPETITIVE ADVANTAGE

At a functional level, retailing is merely one mode of product distribution, a mode that sees the firm distributing their own or, more typically, other firms' products, through some consolidated means to individual non-business consumers (Betancourt, 2004). The distinction is often made between those firms that focus solely on this business-to-consumer distribution task and retail mode, and others that also engage in activities further back along the value chain. Firms in this study are chosen so that the majority of their value-added occurs in the retail function, either through direct sales or through income received for a franchise. Fast food and restaurant chains are not considered.

Competitive advantage in retailing develops on multiple fronts. Successful firms may achieve micro-level location advantages by securing prime geographic sites with high volumes of customer traffic. Such locations are clearly finite in number. There are obvious rewards for first-movers and from access to ready capital to fund leases/purchases of such premises. These firms may build valuable, rare, inimitable and non-substitutable assets

– that is, hold resource advantages or firm-specific advantages (FSAs) – in terms of significant and unique networks of stores and locations (Rugman and Verbeke, 1992; Barney, 1995). Firms that develop larger networks of stores may secure FSAs from economies of scale in purchasing, logistics and distribution, and marketing. Buying economies, in terms of lower costs, may derive from the simple preferences of suppliers to sell in bulk. More significantly, the large retailer's capacity to offer considerable market reach or share will play out as enhanced bargaining power over suppliers. This same logic flows through to advantages in dealing with providers of logistics and distribution services. However, these are not *ex ante* sources of firm-specific advantage, but *ex post* and path-dependent outcomes of early market entry and success. The more fundamental FSA is some unique product mix or distribution process – what Godley and Fletcher (2000: 396) identify as '...advantages in supply-chain activities (such as superior products or logistics) or...novel merchandising techniques or formats, or...both'.[2]

Over time the key shift in retailing has been toward greater returns to scale. The early part of the twentieth century saw the emergence of department and then chain stores, with their respective capacities to attract large volumes of customers and achieve economies in buying, logistics and marketing (Chandler, 1977). The self-service supermarket emerged first in the US in the 1920s, later in the United Kingdom, Europe, Australia and beyond (Zimmerman, 1955; Chandler, 1977; Godley and Fletcher, 2001; Shaw et al., 2004). The post-World War II shift to suburban living and the general adoption of the automobile increased the advantages of scale in the grocery sector. Tjordman (1995: 18-19) argues that as retailing has evolved, each new major retail format has had a shorter period before maturity. Department stores took 100 years (1860-1960), variety stores 40 years (1930-1970), supermarkets 25 years (1965-1985) and large specialist stores perhaps 15 years (1980-1995).

Internationalisation as discussed in this chapter is, in the parlance of Dunning (1993b: 58), 'market-seeking'. The extant literature can be summarised by the claim that retailers are '...pulled into other markets through the international relevance of the product and service which they offer' (Alexander, 1997: 4) and pushed by factors such as '...high levels of competition, format maturation and heavy regulation' (Alexander and Myers, 2000: 336). Significant differences often exist in regional and national buying preferences, which may derive from cultural peculiarities and/or path dependent historical idiosyncrasies. These factors of micro-level location advantages and macro-level national differences play into the hands of domestic incumbents, being those that were early movers in introducing more effective retailing processes. As such, it is not clear how country-specific advantages (CSAs) come into play. Firms will be attracted to larger markets, if they see untapped potential. Firms will be drawn to countries that share some similarities in buying behaviour, and/or that are geographically convenient. Retailers from modern, high-income, and less idiosyncratic home markets may find it easier to transplant their home FSAs into new environments.

Data sources

Throughout this chapter the size of firms is calculated according to their ranking by sales on Deloitte's *Top 250 Global Retailers* (2006). This list demonstrates how much national boundaries still matter in the world of retailing. Of the 250 firms listed, 104 had no operations outside their domestic market, and a further 39 only operated in two countries. Over half of the 90 US firms, and 60 per cent of the 40 Japanese firms, had no overseas outlets. Rugman and Girod (2003) arrived at a similar result when looking at the 49 retailers in *Fortune* magazine's 'Global-500'. They found 18 of the 49 firms were solely domestic. Distinguishing between Europe, North America and Asia-Pacific, they identify only five firms that earned more than 20 per cent of their sales outside their home region.

GENERALIST AND GROCERY RETAILERS

The first large retailers – generalist department stores and variety and discount chain stores – achieved economies of scale advantages by different strategies. Department stores offered a 'complete' shopping experience and an unprecedented range of items, thus acting as a magnet to consumers across a wide geographical area. Chain retailers shifted the products to the consumers, building a network of stores and increasing the incidence and convenience of shopping (Hayward and White, 1928). In both instances, first and/or rapid movers built advantage due to the scarcity of available properties. Incumbency and access to capital to fund further expansion became key determinants of success. Late arrivals, at least those with second-rate or bypassed locations, with poor product offerings or with insufficient volume to secure and maintain advantageous supply relationships, either faded away or became the targets for consolidation.

Shifting demographics, especially the flight from inner urban areas to the suburbs and the development of new residential areas, played into the hands of the variety chains. Department stores began to decline, particularly from the 1960s on. A new format emerged in the postwar period – the supermarket. Like the chain store, success with this format relied on building a sufficient network of locations and on mastering what has become known as supply-chain logistics. These logistics were more specialised due to the perishable nature of goods. Again a race was on to build sufficient economies of scale.

Internationalisation

In terms of internationalisation, department and chain stores displayed little initiative. Among the US pioneers, the more ambitious ventured across the northern and southern borders. Large-scale variety chain Kmart (#33 on Deloitte's list) ventured into Canada in 1929, department store Sears Roebuck (#20) entered Cuba in 1942, Mexico in 1947 and Canada in 1952 (Brown, 1948). And there expansion typically stalled. Protectionism in most domestic markets made it difficult to leverage FSAs arising from logistics and supply relationships in geographically distant and disconnected markets. Leading firms saw greater promise in domestic consolidation or diversification. Europe produced very few international department store or pure variety store chains because firms chose to modify their format to meet competition from supermarkets, or developed their own domestic supermarket brand. Whether in the US or Europe, department stores have remained country-bound: only four firms on the Deloitte list operate department stores in more than two countries.[3]

The supermarket story is one of geographic bifurcation. The immense size of the United States precluded the quick emergence of large national players. Instead, the format was developed and adopted almost simultaneously in various states across the country by a large number of firms of varying sizes and strengths. Subsequent growth outside home states/regions was severely hampered by two major legislative restrictions, which inhibited price discrimination and cross-border mergers (Seth and Randall, 2001).[4] It took until the 1990s before the long-expected consolidations started to occur, with big players such as Kroger (#6) Albertsons (#14) and Safeway (#19) and the Great Atlantic & Pacific Tea Company (now part of German conglomerate, Tengelmann, #25) picking off smaller players, while under pressure from emerging phenomenon Wal-Mart (#1). In the interim, few stepped offshore.[5]

The European supermarket experience was considerably different. The format was not adopted until the late 1950s but then evolved quickly. Within a decade, national players had emerged in several countries. More densely settled and stable urban environments along with a range of institutional constraints allowed the development of several innovative business models, such as the deep discounting (Germany's Aldi, #10 and Lidl, #11), and hypermarket (France's Carrefour, #2) formats. Successful domestic players in Europe actually faced considerably lower barriers to expansion than firms in North America. As the European Community steadily reduced barriers to trade, goods flowed more easily across national borders and the shorter distances restrained logistics costs. The potential saturation of domestic markets pushed retailers to expand into geographically contiguous markets despite linguistic, cultural and institutional differences. Carrefour ventured into neighbouring Belgium (1969) and Spain (1973). Germany's Metro AG (#4) expanded into the Netherlands in 1964, while Aldi headed into Austria in 1968. Expansion continued into less sophisticated Mediterranean markets, and later, transitional Eastern Europe markets. Both Royal Ahold (The Netherlands, #9) and the Delhaize Group (Belgium, #32) entered Czechoslovakia in 1991 (Drtina, 1995). Carrefour entered Poland in 1997 and the Czech Republic in 1998, and subsequently moved into Slovakia and Romania (Seth and Randall, 2005). Britain's Tesco (#5) entered Hungary in 1995, and Poland, the Czech Republic and Slovakia in 1996. These firms have clearly developed and leveraged non-location-bound FSAs by seeking out environments where no substantial incumbents held sway.

Two European firms – Royal Ahold and the Delhaize Group – took the more atypical step of entering the US in the mid-1970s. Several others followed such as Britain's Sainsbury's (#27), who entered in 1983, but withdrew in 2004 via a sale to Albertson's (#14). Royal Ahold and Delhaize are now two of Rugman and Girod's bi-regional firms, with both earning more than fifty per cent of their global sales in North America.

European grocery retailers have, via an environment of considerable competition, and the repeated experience of expansion, built considerable capabilities in internationalisation. They have ventured into new, underdeveloped markets such as South America (France's Groupe Casino, #26 and Carrefour) and the Middle East (Carrefour, Marks & Spencer, UK, #46). Carrefour opened its first Asian store in Taiwan in 1989, and soon ventured into Malaysia (1994), China (1995), Thailand, South Korea (all 1996), Singapore (1997) and Indonesia (1998). Tesco entered Thailand and Taiwan in 1998, South Korea (1999), Malaysia (2001), Japan (2003) and China in 2004.[6]

The Australian experience

Large retailers emerged quite early in the Australian economy, within the more densely populated states and main cities. As noted by Fleming et al. (2004, Appendix C), department stores such as David Jones, Farmers', Myer and Mark Foy's were the early forces on the retail scene. The middle half of the twentieth century was a period of both growth and consolidation. By 1952, two variety chains – G.J. Coles and Woolworths – had emerged which would soon move into the supermarket industry with stunning success. The period from the mid-1950s was one of consolidation. The newly emerging suburbs fuelled growth in supermarkets, and in the capital cities single firms had increasing opportunities to open multiple department and variety stores in new stand-alone shopping centre complexes. The traditional single-state generalist retailers either collapsed or were consumed into the larger Myer empire (Kingston, 1994). Eventually the supermarket and department/variety giants converged into one highly concentrated sector. Coles Myer was the result of a merger between G.J. Coles and Myer in 1985.[7]

As Fleming et al. (2004: 61) calculate, by 1998 the grocery component of the retail sector could be technically classified as a duopoly with Woolworths (36 per cent) and Coles Myer (30 per cent) holding over two-thirds of market share.[8] The major source of growth for both was domestic diversification within the broader retail/service sector. Over time they developed (and at times, divested) extensive holdings across multiple retail lines including electronics, fashion clothing, fast food, travel, removals, autocare, office supplies, liquor and petrol. They have often adopted and adapted innovative ideas from overseas for the Australian market, or had the capital to acquire those firms that have.[9] As noted by Schmidt and Lloyd (2003), they appear to have pursued the breadth of activities undertaken within the US by Wal-Mart. Such expansion is viable as the firms leverage their significant economies of scope into new consumer segments. The prospect of testing the location-boundedness of any FSAs has not proven attractive.

Inward FDI

For most of the twentieth century, there was little significant inward FDI into generalist retailing in Australia. As noted, potential entrants from the regions with the most comparable level of retail development (the US, UK or Western Europe) were preoccupied with their own industry consolidation. No international entrant could utilise advantages in purchasing from existing networks of suppliers to outmanoeuvre incumbents because many products were purchased from protected domestic producers.

US department store Sears Roebuck did enter in 1954 via a joint venture with local firm Waltons but soon exited. Kmart is credited with introducing the large-scale discount store into Australia through a 1968 joint venture with G.J. Coles (Wolf, 1997). The joint venture was bought out by Coles a decade later (McLaughlin, 1991). Japanese department store Daimaru (#105) opened a store in downtown Melbourne in 1991 and on the Gold Coast in 1998, citing a desire to 'undertake a case study of a western market' (Clarke and Rimmer, 1997: 378). The firm never achieved desired results and closed both stores by mid-2002.[10]

The supermarket sector saw more prolonged investments. US firm Safeway entered in 1963 and developed considerable coverage across the eastern states. Woolworths acquired Safeway's Australian subsidiary in 1985 (Murray, 1999). Hong Kong's Dairy Farm International (#157), a subsidiary of British conglomerate Jardine Matheson, purchased discount grocery chain Franklins in 1978 and built the brand into Australia's third largest supermarket group before encountering financial difficulties in the 1990s. The Franklins empire was slowly divested, with Dairy Farm quitting Australia in 2002. South Africa's Metro Cash & Carry (#81) acquired Australian grocery wholesaler and minor retailer Davids in 1998 alongside a broader expansion into Africa. A 2005 local management buyout removed Metcash Australia from South African hands, and closed the book on what has been described in the Australian business press as 'one of the worst takeovers of the 1990s' (Ries, 1998: 52). Metcash Australia has increasingly extracted itself from direct competition with Coles Myer and Woolworths by concentrating on wholesaling. South Africa's Pick'n'Pay (#123) made a furtive entry into Australia in 1984, quickly left and returned in 1998 via the acquisition of almost half of the Franklins stores from Dairy Farm.

Perhaps the most significant inward FDI was the entry of German deep discount giant Aldi in 2001. By late 2005 they had opened over 100 stores and achieved market shares of around five per cent in the main NSW and Victorian grocery markets (Taylor, 2005). Unencumbered by share market scrutiny, this privately-held entity appeared to have the deep pockets necessary to take on the big duopolists. Commentators cited their presence as a key driver in both Coles Myer and Woolworth's shift to increased private branding (Aston, 2005).

Outward FDI

Outward FDI initiatives by the major Australian retailers were startlingly infrequent. Even the shift across the Tasman proved difficult for the major players. Woolworths had several variety NZ stores by the early 1930s. They introduced no particular innovations, however, and NZ customers had to wait for independent stores to introduce self-service supermarkets. The Woolworths brand was sold to local firm L.D. Nathan in 1979. Woolworths bought back the brand (and its stores) in 2005 with the Australian CEO proclaiming 'Woolworths believes that it will be able to leverage its retail experience and scale into New Zealand' (Woolworths, 2005). As discussed below, Woolworths has recently made some very tentative steps beyond Australasia with its electronics business.

Coles Myer entered NZ in 1988 by acquiring Foodtown (supermarkets), 3 Guys (discount food) and Georgie Pie (family restaurants). Over the next two years they launched Kmart and Katies (fashion) stores. The grocery components were sold off by 1993. This FDI has been roundly condemned as unsuccessful (Scherer, 2000). In 2001 Coles Myer unsuccessfully attempted to sell its Kmart stores to NZ rival The Warehouse Group.

Despite the noted expansion of European retailers and Wal-Mart into Asia from the 1990s, neither of the large Australian generalists has made any attempt in the region.

SPECIALIST RETAILERS

Speciality retailers seek to exploit consumers' discretionary spending with items such as homewares, hardware, stationery, fashion clothing and entertainment. Large-scale speciality chains began to emerge in various countries from the 1960s as entrepreneurs responded to increased income levels and more sophisticated demand by offering innovative new product mixes, store formats and service experiences. Often these retailers sold products in competition with department and variety store chains (in electronics, furniture and homewares for example), or 'mom-and-pop' atomistic concerns (hardware, stationery, sporting goods). Firms, tagged as 'category killers' established economies of scale advantages by building 'big box' outlets for products previously lacking significant range (Fernie and Fernie, 1997; Spector, 2005). Examples of the 'big box' model included Home Depot (#3) and Lowes (#17) in hardware, Office Depot (#72) and Staples (#65) in office products, Borders (#159) in books and music, PETsMART (#196) in pet care, Circuit City (#63) in home electronics, and Toys'R'Us (#58) in toys.[11] Sweden's Ikea (#37) transformed consumer expectations of what constitutes home furniture, shifting construction duties to the buyer along with the cost savings of flat-packing. Various clothing retailers such as Spain's Inditex (#102) and Sweden's H&M (#93) considerably reduced 'time-to-market', thus pioneering 'fast fashion'. Other specialists sought a more standardised but very recognisable product range in diverse markets such as clothing (Gap, #38, Italy's Benetton), videos (Blockbuster, #110), sporting goods (Footlocker, #118, France's Decathlon #145) and eyeware (Italy's Luxottica, #208).

The source of advantage here was often the capacity to identify and exploit gaps in the existing marketplace. Firms built specialised knowledge and tapped into the desire of suppliers to break the stranglehold of the large department stores and variety chains, as well as to develop deeper product offerings.

Internationalisation

Specialist retailers in many countries quickly exhausted the opportunities for domestic expansion. Furthermore, they were trading on the uniqueness of their concepts. If the gaps in the market were universal or at least consistent across several markets, then they needed to get to these consumers quickly, before someone else imitated them.

Table 9.2: Geographical breadth of specialist retailers

Company	Global ranking	Country of Origin	Speciality	No. of Countries (Continents)	Date of first FDI	Location of first FDI
Home Depot	3	US	Hardware	5 (1)	1994	Canada
Gap	38	US	Clothing	6 (3)	1987	UK
Ikea	44	Sweden	Home furnishings	22 (4)	1958	Norway
DSG International	51	UK	Electronics	13 (1)	1972	Holland
Toys'R'Us	58	US	Toys	32 (5)	1984	Canada
Staples	65	US	Office supplies	7 (2)	1991	Canada
Office Depot	72	US	Office supplies	23 (3)	1993	Canada
Kesa Electricals [a]	92	UK	Electronics	6 (1)	1988	Belgium
H&M	93	Sweden	Clothing	20 (2)	1965	Norway
Inditex	102	Spain	Clothing	56 (4)	1988	Portugal
C&A	107	Belgium	Clothing	12 (1)	1911	Germany
Blockbuster	110	US	Video	25 (5)	1990	UK
Footlocker	118	US	Sporting	18 (3)	1980	UK
Decathlon	145	France	Sporting	12 (3)	1986	Germany
LVMH	150	France	Luxury	21 (4)	1885	UK
Sherwin-Williams	156	US	Hardware	5 (1)	1892	Canada
Borders	159	US	Books	6 (4)	1997	Singapore
HMV	173	UK	Music	7 (4)	1986	Ireland
Hachette	197	France	News media	17 (4)	1993	Belgium
Bauhaus	200	Germany	Hardware	10 (1)	1972	Austria
Luxottica [b]	208	Italy	Eyeware	17 (4)	1995	US
Payless Shoesource	222	US	Footwear	14 (2)	1997	Canada

Notes:
Only firms operating in at least five countries.

a. Kesa Electricals was spun off from the British firm Kingfisher in 2003. It includes a range of national retailers Kingfisher had acquired over the years. Of these French firm Darty was the earliest internationaliser with a Belgian entry in 1988.
b. Luxottica made numerous FDIs in non-retailing before 1995.

Sources: Deloitte (2006), company websites, Annual Reports and personal correspondence

Thus many of these firms expanded rapidly through the 1980s and 1990s. In an international environment of declining trade and investment barriers, lower transport and communication costs, and increasingly integrated global production processes, these firms did not face the barriers experienced by earlier generalist retailers.

The retailers with the greatest geographical spread are typically the specialist chains (Table 9.2). Many of these firms expanded quickly across several countries and continents, building upon sophisticated logistics systems that enable them to deliver products more cost effectively or more quickly. As we will see in the Australian context, further expansion by specialised retailers has sometimes been hampered by pre-emptive duplication of the concept in a specific market. This strategy can result in the incumbent firm developing location-bound FSAs that deter newcomers.

US firms tended to dominate the 'big box' format, fuelled by the CSAs of a more lax planning environment and greater domestic car usage. Many of these firms, again, chose to focus on the large North American market. The large-scale European examples such as Ikea had a greater need to internationalise because of small home markets. Clothing was more of a European success story (H&M, Inditex, Belgium's C&A, #107), with only Gap making a mark from the US. This may reflect the more vibrant fashion clusters in Europe and the capacity to utilise the free trade aspects of the EU.

Deloitte's list does not do justice to specialist success stories as the 'ultra-specialists' do not typically appear as their sales levels are lower than even solely domestic grocers. This also applies to franchised retailers. There are a range of focused spin-offs from the variety format, or completely new innovations, which have 'flown under the radar' in much of the discussion of retail internationalisation. Three examples help to make the point. Tie Rack, originally a UK-based retailer of ties and scarves, has expanded, principally via franchising to have stores in 30 countries across Europe, North America, Asia and the Middle East. They were acquired by Italian fashion group Frangi in 1999. Spanish fast-fashion specialist Mango claims to have over 800 stores in more than 80 countries – an extraordinary rate of growth for a firm that only ventured offshore in 1992. British cosmetics chain, The Body Shop, spread its environment-friendly stores across over 50 countries from the early 1980s.[12]

The Australian experience

The specialist portion of Australian retailing is a mixed bag of global players, local innovators, and opportunistic imitators. As summarised in Table 9.1, almost all of the inward FDI into Australia by large overseas players was by specialist retailers. Notable in their absence, however, were the office supplies and hardware superstores. Both of these formats were quickly and pre-emptively duplicated by local giants. Coles Myer introduced

Officeworks in 1994 after studying the US firms Office Depot, Staples Inc and OfficeMax (#103); by 2005 the brand had grown into a business of 87 stores and A$1.2b in sales (Shoebridge, 1996; Coles Myer, 2005). Rural conglomerate Wesfarmers built on a recent hardware retailing acquisition and introduced Bunnings Superstores in 1994. The Bunnings brand entered the Deloitte list in 2006 at #201, with a reported annual sales growth of 25.6 per cent over the previous five years. When Toys'R'Us entered the Australian market, Coles Myer unsuccessfully sought to ward them off with a duplicate competitor World 4 Kids, a strategic blunder reported to have cost the firm A$200million.

Nevertheless, Australia's has had limited exposure to specialist inward FDI. Of the 22 most internationalised retail specialists (Table 9.2), only eight had operations in Australia by late 2005. Ikea had a strong presence in its niche of the home furnishing market, and Blockbuster was the predominant video hire chain. Footlocker was locked in a battle with local sports superstore chain Rebel Sport, and Borders declared its first substantial profit in 2005 after seven years in the market. None of the major clothing chains had entered.

Outward FDI

As noted above, cases of outward FDI by the largest Australian retailers were few and typically only NZ-bound. Even Coles Myer's and Woolworths' specialist brands have not ventured much further afield, although Woolworths' electronics arm, Dick Smith Electronics, announced in late 2005 a joint venture project with Indian conglomerate Tata that could see them open 50 stores on the subcontinent.

Amongst the big players, Harvey Norman was an exception. From the mid-1980s the firm built a substantial chain of stand-alone homemaker centres across Australia. Each superstore was a series of independently managed in-store product franchises.[13] In 1999 Harvey Norman acquired a controlling interest in Pertama, a publicly listed company in Singapore, which had 11 retail shops in Singapore, as well as a wholesale business and one retail store in Malaysia. A single store was opened in Slovenia in 1999 with another due to open in 2006.[14] A more strategic move was an entry to Ireland: by late 2005 the firm had three stores with another six openings proposed for 2006. This was billed as an attempt to assess the viability of the British market. Founder Gerry Harvey, an idiosyncratic and very wealthy entrepreneur, has long flagged his interest in expanding into the UK, Italy, Croatia, Serbia, Hungary, Austria, India and China (Hannen, 2001). The internal franchising model may serve as a competitive advantage in new markets by tapping into local entrepreneurship. The firm will, however, need to overcome significant locational differences in tastes, property availability and supplier networks.

From the 1990s several smaller specialists took bolder steps. Five of these – Barbeques Galore, Flight Centre, Cash Converters, Cartridge World and OPSM – demonstrate different paths to growth (see boxes). Country selections varied, as did entry mode choices. Each firm leveraged FSAs in multiple countries. There are clear lessons about international opportunities for Australian retailers, and retailers from other small, isolated economies.

Barbeques Galore

Barbeques Galore opened its first store in Sydney in 1977, offering an unprecedented large range of outdoor dining equipment, some of which was firm-manufactured. The company expanded to the United States in 1980, opening a store in Sante Fe Springs, a suburb of Los Angeles. The firm concentrated initially on warm-weather US states such as California, Nevada, Arizona, Hawaii, Texas, Georgia and Florida. Later they ventured into more seasonal markets such as North Carolina, Virginia, Maryland and Washington DC. Over time the firm increased the percentage firm-manufactured stock by acquisitions and organic growth. In late 2005 the firm had similar store numbers in Australia (92: 44 company-owned and 48 licensed) and the US (75: 68 company-owned and seven franchised). More than half (54 per cent) of the group's revenue came from the US business (Barbeques Galore, 2005). After ten years as a listed company on the Australian Stock Exchange, Barbeques Galore delisted in 1996, and soon after listed on the US NASDAQ (Lambiris, 1999). In late 2005, the firm was delisted from the NASDAQ after a leveraged buy-out by an Australian venture capital firm.

Flight Centre

Flight Centre introduced the 'bucket shop' travel agent format – discounted airline ticketing through bulk purchasing – to Australia in 1981. The firm's founders had considerable experience running a very successful tour company in the UK. The firm quickly built a strong local network of stores which further boosted its economies of purchasing. They coupled innovative product offerings – very cheap international flights – with a distinct set of managerial practices built around employee empowerment and profit-sharing (Dunford and Palmer, 2002; Gottliebsen, 2003). By 1990 they had opened stores in New Zealand, the UK and US. The UK and US offices were closed in 1991 in the face of the Gulf War. Expansion began in earnest with a move to South Africa in 1994, Canada in early 1995, and the UK later that year. US operations recommenced in late 1999 (Johnson, 2005). By mid-2005, Flight Centre was operating 1063 retail outlets across Australia (657), Canada (118), New Zealand (108), the UK (92), South Africa (90) and the US (15). Just over a third (37.5 per cent) of the group's revenue came from the overseas subsidiaries (Flight Centre, 2006). The firm was recently listed as the ninth largest tourism firm in the world by foreign assets (UNCTAD, 2004: 324).

Cash Converters
Cash Converters emerged from Perth in 1983 with a modern, efficient version of an old retail form – pawnbroking – and in 2005 claimed to be the 'the world's largest franchised retailer of quality pre-owned household goods' (Anon., 2005b). The firm had 450 stores across 28 countries (including 16 in Europe, five in Asia, two each in North America, Africa and Australasia, and one in South America). Australia represented only 25 per cent of the store count. The first expansion was into the UK in 1992 – an operation that expanded to 105 stores by 2005. New Zealand (1993, now 27 stores), South Africa (1994, 57 stores), France (1994, 23 stores), Canada (1995, 24 stores), Spain (1995, 34 stores) and the US (1994, 10 stores) followed.

Cartridge World
Cartridge World emerged from Adelaide in 1997 as a specialist chain refilling, recycling and retailing printer cartridges. The firm expanded very quickly through franchising and by early 2006 had over 1100 stores worldwide in at least 25 countries (including 17 European countries, and two each in Asia, North America, South America and Australasia). Australia represented only 20 per cent of the store count, as the firm grew more quickly in larger markets. The first British store opened in early 2001. By late 2005, there were over 280 stores in Britain. The first US store opened in mid-2003. By late 2005 there were over 320 US stores and the firm was claimed to be awarding a new franchise every day.

Exploitation of FSAs by smaller specialists
Barbeques Galore was an early 'category killer' in Australia, achieving advantage from its large range of product in various price segments. The firm moved quickly to improve its profitability via backward integration. These FSAs of range and margin could be easily transferred, as long as there was a sufficiently large market for the product. Barbeques Galore judged the US retail market to be a viable one, due to some similarities in lifestyle together with countercyclical revenue streams in what is a highly seasonal market. CEO Stuart McDonald explained the firm's rationale for US entry as: 'We looked around and saw there was nothing like what we were doing in Australia' (quoted in Korporaal, 1986b: 15).

Flight Centre revolutionised the retailing of international air-travel in Australia by shifting to a model where profitability was driven by volume rather than margins. Initially they built a price advantage by bypassing ticketing wholesalers, seeking out less well-known airlines, and also by arbitraging price differentials across markets. They quickly built a large local network of stores and developed an innovative incentive package for staff that reinforced the high-volume model and encouraged employee entrepreneurialism. Employees initiated several of the international moves (Johnson, 2005), typically into markets that had sufficient independent travellers and were mainly reliant on air travel. The model proved profitable in each market over time, although the firm never had the significant bargaining power it possessed in Australia.[15]

Cash Converters' FSA lay in standardising and modernising pawnbroking. Pricing, stock control and financing tools were packaged up within a franchising model and supported by consistent brand management that aimed to remove the stigma from what was regarded as a disreputable retailing segment. The firm entered the market it deemed most like Australia (and large enough) – the UK – but the retail concept soon attracted franchisees in a wide range of countries.

Cartridge World also expanded by franchising. They offered franchisees innovative, but low-cost technology that targeted an expanding market niche. The firm built further FSAs by encouraging shop-owners to set up in suburbs and inner-city locations close to small businesses and consumers that would prize proximity and convenience. This approach contrasted with that of its major competitors – 'big box' office-suppliers – who sought wider spheres of attraction.

Why did these firms venture so far, while their larger domestic counterparts did not? There were aspects of the Australian retail scene – CSAs – which supported their growth and allowed them the opportunity to build the aforementioned FSAs. They faced modern consumers with high incomes and increasingly refined demands. A fellow international player – Westfield (Chapter 19) emerged, – offering world class, sprawling, suburban shopping centres. The Australian environment was increasingly standardised and non-idiosyncratic – much more like the US and the UK in its regulations and buyer preferences. This helped these firms to step out into the world.

As noted throughout this chapter, operating in the Australian environment might also be viewed as a disadvantage. Though modern, the market was geographically isolated. This led many retailers to build FSAs around their ability to establish and maintain local supply chain relationships. Such FSAs are inherently location-bound, and drove many Australian firms to seek internal expansion opportunities via diversification into related retail lines. The four firms discussed above overcame these potential country-specific disadvantages by developing retail models that had more transferable supply-chain characteristics.

Barbeques Galore built a vertically integrated operation that allowed the firm to offer a unique mix of products from its own manufacturing facilities. Flight Centre dealt with similar suppliers of international travel across its six national markets and sought to leverage any knowledge of national quirks into a competitive advantage relative to solely domestic competitors. Cash Converters was in the enviable position of having its customers as its suppliers. As such, their retail model could be easily replicated from country to country. In a similar fashion, Cartridge World was principally focused on technological advantage. This technology was universally applicable due to the global nature of the printer/computer hardware business: consumers tended to need the same brands of printer cartridges refilled in each market. The firm also sold printer accessories, sourced again from the same Original Equipment Manufacturers and branded giants. Any bargaining disadvantage the firm might have had in purchasing such accessories relative to the big office-supply giants was traded off against the firm's own proximity-to-consumer advantage, and diminished by the firm's speedy expansion. This is a lesson that other specialist retailers may heed as a more attractive long-term strategy for expansion than the alternative of domestic diversification.

Each of these firms had a good retailing 'idea' that they believed could be applied in multiple countries. Barbeques Galore took the big gamble of competing in what most view as the most competitive retail market in the world – the US – because that was the country with the most suitable customers for the product. Flight Centre's country choices were similarly motivated. The two franchisors – Cash Converters and Cartridge World – viewed their innovations as universally applicable and have chosen an entry mode and country mix that reflects this view. The firms have reduced the risk of FSA replication by moving swiftly. Again, other specialist retailers should view these firms as examples of targeting a 'gap' in the market aggressively and decisively.

There is one final example of an Australian specialist retailer expanding offshore. OPSM (see box) was an example of a strong chain that developed a profitable and large presence in Australia in a typically small-scale, non-entrepreneurial sector. The firm standardised store fronts within its three brands and pitched each at different price segments. OPSM saw the opportunity to enter less developed markets in the immediate region. They sought out existing chains and re-branded them. Their efforts attracted the attention of the world's largest optical specialist, Italian firm Luxottica, who has tapped into OPSM's FSAs through the region. As Lewis and Zalan (2005b) have argued, this might also be a viable strategic option for firms seeking to make the most of their domestic dominance and initial overseas efforts – luring cashed-up international suitors. Italy's Luxottica was an ideal candidate to acquire OPSM as it was a major supplier of quality optical wear globally and needed to secure a large retailer in Australasia and booming Southeast Asian markets.

OPSM
Founded in Sydney in 1932, and publicly listed in 1953, optical retailer OPSM was a slow mover into international markets, entering New Zealand in 1994. The firm entered Hong Kong and Singapore in 1998 via an acquisition of a local chain (Blake, 1998). The Singapore business was expanded in 2000 by another acquisition (Goodfellow, 2000). Later that year, they expanded further into the region by an acquisition of a 13-store optical business with headquarters in Kuala Lumpur (Anon., 2000b). By 2003, the Asian operations constituted just over 14 per cent of group activity (OPSM, 2003). The company operated 461 stores under three brands (OPSM, Laubman & Pank, Budget Eyewear) in Australia, 35 stores in New Zealand (where they were market leader), 75 stores in Hong Kong and 12 in Singapore (under the Optical Shop brand), and 12 in Malaysia. In May 2003, OPSM was taken over by the Italian spectacles manufacturer and retailer, Luxottica (#208).

CONCLUSION

Australia is a neat 'natural experiment' in retailing. The nation entered the twentieth century as a modern economy with GDP per capita levels comparable with, if not ahead, of North America and Western Europe. The country had further advantages for budding retailers. It was highly urbanised, but not hampered by pre-industrial infrastructure. Retailers had easy access to properties and consumers. As the nation was geographically distant and disconnected, and local suppliers were protected by high tariff walls, domestic retailers quickly built considerable location-bound advantages over any potential inward FDI. Entrepreneurial locals and later powerful incumbents were able to 'cherry pick' concepts from overseas and introduce them to Australian consumers confident of their likely success. The barriers to inward investment worked similarly in reverse, however. Successful retailers with location-bound supply-chain and real estate advantages focused on diversifying across retail niches and concepts rather than expanding into the nearby underdeveloped or inaccessible Asian markets.

Eventually as institutional and technological barriers fell, a trickle of overseas specialist players entered the Australian scene. Around the same time a number of Australian success stories ventured offshore, in a diverse range of niches and to a mix of locations. These firms were able to overcome any liability of distance, because they had firm-specific advantages in the form of good retail concepts that were not bound by location. In particular, each was unhampered by the local specificity of supply chain arrangements. In most instances, they sought out countries that bore some similarity to the Australian market and they all built up a significant overseas presence. Their experiences highlight the scope for Australian retailers to build upon the positive dimensions of the Australian market – affluent customers and first-world infrastructure – and thereby minimise the burden of isolation.

NOTES

1. Coles Myer and Woolworths earned approximately 0.05 per cent and 0.5 per cent respectively of their sales in New Zealand in 2005.
2. The concept of the 'good idea' in retailing is illustrated by the expansion mode of many firms – franchising. Here the firm attempts to bundle up and exchange its FSAs. Typically the value for franchisees exists in the *ex ante* reputation of the franchisor brand, and the *ex post* economies of scale advantages in ongoing research and development, purchasing, logistics and marketing.
3. These are: Mitsukoshi (Japan, #84), which operates department stores in eight nations across Asia, Europe and the US; Isetan (Japan, #113) in six Asian nations; Debenhams (UK, #178) in 14 nations across Europe, the Middle East and Asia; and S.A.C.I Falabella (Chile, #228) in three South American nations.
4. As Seth and Randall (2001: 190) note, in 1990 the market share of the top 20 firms was roughly the same as that of the top 50 in 1950, and few names had changed.
5. The exception was Safeway, which expanded into Canada in 1925, the UK in 1962, and Australia in 1963. Tellingly, the challenge of impending consolidations, amongst other competitive pressures, led Safeway to abandon both the UK and Australian operations by the mid-1980s.
6. There is still considerable debate around the performance of many of these overseas operations (Anon., 2005a; Seth and Randall, 2005).
7. In early 2006, Coles Myer announced the sale of the Myer department store chain.
8. This is contrast to their reported figures for 1964 of 17 per cent for Woolworths and 0 for Coles.
9. For example, under the banner of Project Refresh, Woolworths has achieved significant gains via the adoption of many of US giant Wal-Mart's supply chain processes (Gottliebsen, 2003).
10. Over the past decade Daimaru has closed all of its overseas stores: in Hong Kong, Thailand, France and Singapore, as well as in Australia.
11. Unless noted, all the firms mentioned here originate from the US.
12. Both Mango and The Body Shop grew principally via franchising. As they were also the principle manufacturers of the products in the franchised store, it could be argued they are not truly 'retailers' in the narrow definition adopted in this chapter.
13. For example, a given location might include a furniture franchisee, a whitegoods franchisee, an electrical goods franchisee and a computer products franchisee. In 2005, there were 162 stores in Australia and 527 franchisees (Harvey Norman, 2005).
14. This was an opportunistic entry based on the family background of a senior staff member (Kirby, 2003). The firm also ran an unsuccessful store in East Timor for a brief period in 2000-2001.
15. With the emergence of internet booking services, the firm started in the early 2000s to switch its focus away from B2C retailing towards non-retailing corporate travel services. The firm has expanded into less mature markets in this area, such as Hong Kong, India, China and Singapore.

10. The Wine Industry

Geoffrey Lewis and Tatiana Zalan

INTRODUCTION

Although classified as a primary industry, the wine industry is actually one of Australia's few triumphs of internationalisation in manufacturing. Its success in international markets throughout the 1990s and early 2000s has been described as nothing short of phenomenal (Porter and Bond, 2004; Porter and Solvell, 2003). Initial success was in the form of exports, but more recently firms have been undertaking outward foreign direct investment (FDI). According to Porter (1990), international competitiveness can be assessed by two measures: (1) the extent to which the share of industry exports exceeds the country's share of world exports, and (2) significant outbound foreign investment based on skills and assets created in the home country. By the first definition, Australia's share of global wine exports (7.1 per cent by volume) was significantly higher than Australia's share in world trade (1.1 per cent) (Table 10.1).

Table 10.1: Australia's share of world wine exports, percentage

	Volume share		**Value share**	
	1997	**2003**	**1997**	**2003**
France	24.6	21.1	40.8	38.8
Italy	23.8	18.9	17.8	17.8
Spain	15.4	15.6	9.9	10.0
Australia	**2.5**	**7.1**	**4.0**	**9.1**
Moldova	4.2	5.2	3.2	4.3
Chile	3.2	5.1	3.1	3.5
USA	3.0	4.5	3.6	3.2
Germany	3.8	3.7	1.5	2.4
South Africa	1.6	3.2	4.1	2.3
Argentina	2.1	2.0	2.0	1.2

Source: AWBC, www.awbc.com.au/winefacts/data

By the mid-2000s the Australian industry exported 27 per cent of its production (compared with 17 per cent by Old World producers such as France and Italy) and by value commanded 9.1 per cent of the world wine exports. Australia's success in the international wine industry was not unique. Over much the same period Argentina, Chile, South Africa and New Zealand have also overcome the friction of distance to become significant exporters, but the Australian experience was outstanding. Despite the inward-looking administrative heritage and institutional context of Australian firms (Chapter 3), this result was built on natural and created advantages and was achieved without government subsidies or trade protection, albeit with some tax incentives. Export orientation was a feature of the entire industry, not only the preserve of the largest companies – even small boutique wineries were pursuing export markets (Aylward, 2002). Tables 10.2 and 10.3 provide background information on the Australian wine industry as of 2004.

Table 10.2: The Australian wine industry at a glance, 2004

Wineries		1,899
Vineyard area (ha)		164,181
Tonnes crushed		1,860,352
Beverage wine production (ML)		1,401
Domestic sales (ML)		417
Exports	(ML)	643
	($M)	2,745
	($/L)	4.27
Imports	(ML)	19
	($M)	152
	($/L)	8

Note: All data are as of 31 December. Vineyard area includes non-bearing vines

Source: The Australian Wine Industry Directory (2005: 5)

Scholars who have analysed the Australian industry suggest that its international competitiveness is a recent phenomenon (Marsh and Shaw, 2000; Porter and Bond, 2004; Roberts and Enright, 2004). Nevertheless, the industry's success had a long gestation period before the export drive of the 1990s. Porter's (1990) theory of the national advantage and his complementary cluster theory (Porter, 1998) are useful frameworks for analysing the industry's international competitiveness. At the heart of a country's competitiveness is the capacity of its companies to innovate and upgrade, driven by demand conditions, factor (input) conditions, related and supporting industries (or clusters), and firm strategy, structure and rivalry.

Table 10.3: Australia's largest exporters of branded wines, 2004

Rank by volume		Rank by value	
Southcorp Wines	1	Southcorp Wines	1
Hardy Wine Company	2	Hardy Wine Company	2
Casella Wines	3	Orlando Wyndham Group	3
Orlando Wyndham Group	4	Casella Wines	4
McGuigan Simeon Wines	5	Beringer Blass/Foster's	5
Beringer Blass/Foster's	6	McGuigan Simeon Wines	6
Evans and Tate	7	Yalumba Wine Company	7
Kingston Estate Wines	8	Evans and Tate	8
Yalumba Wine Company	9	Peter Lehmann Wines	9
Angove's	10	Kingston Estate Wines	10

Source: The Australian Wine Industry Directory (2005: 18)

These four attributes, together with government policy and exogenous chance variables, individually and as a system, constitute the 'diamond of national advantage'. We use this framework to guide our discussion in the first part of the chapter. Our analysis builds on earlier research into the wine industry in the areas of economics (Anderson et al., 2004), marketing (Aurifeille et al., 2002), strategic management (Marsh and Shaw, 1999; Enright and Roberts, 2001; Aylward, 2004) and history (Halliday, 1994; Beeston, 2001; Rankine, 1996). In this chapter we seek to explain which factors led to the industry's outstanding international success – reaching Paradise, to use our metaphor. We argue that the Paradise which the industry strived to achieve in international markets was never actually gained and the industry is now at a critical juncture in its strategic evolution.

DEVELOPING INTERNATIONAL COMPETITIVENESS

Early Origins of the Australian Wine Industry

Australia's tradition of wine-making is as old as the history of European settlement. Vines were introduced to the continent in 1788 by the first white settlers. By the end of the first half century of settlement, wine was being produced in New South Wales, Victoria and South Australia. In those early days, wine was used for household consumption rather than commercial sale and as an alcoholic beverage was far less popular than either beer or spirits. Despite a decision that the penal colony should become the 'Vineyard of

Great Britain', Australian viticulture did not become firmly established until the 1830s and annual wine production was well under half a million litres up to the Gold Rushes of the early 1850s (Unwin, 1996). Over the next century, the industry experienced four cycles of boom and bust in domestic supply and demand and changing export orientations which are well described in Osmond and Anderson (1998). The fourth cycle, which occurred in the decades after World War II, was characterised by a series of structural changes that transformed the industry and marked the birth of the modern wine industry (Rankine, 1996; Halliday, 1994; WGCA and WFA, 1994). The competitive strengths of the modern industry provided the platform for the fifth, and current, cycle which is based on the dramatic growth of exports.

Demand Conditions

During the fourth cycle, the industry underwent a significant transition in demand from fortified to table wine. In 1950, for example, 86 per cent of output was fortified, made mostly from lower-quality, non-premium grapes (Rankine, 1996). Beer was the beverage of choice for the mass of consumers and per capita consumption increased until 1970 (Chapter 15). Even industry participants were unable to perceive a new market trend toward table wines, although they made table wines out of 'technical interest' for their own consumption (Croser, pers. comm.). In the two decades after World War II the consumption of table wine steadily increased and by 1969-1970 it was clear that the Australian consumer preferred table wines (Beeston, 2001; Rankine, 1996; Osmond and Anderson, 1998; Halliday, 1994). The per capita consumption of table wine accelerated during the next three decades and by the turn of the millennium the production of fortified wine had paled into insignificance.

This shift in demand can be attributed in large part to important cultural and economic events. Beer rationing during and immediately after World War II gave a short-term boost to the wine industry, but the major factor underlying the trend toward table wine was the shift in consumer preferences associated with the massive influx of wine-drinking migrants from Italy, Greece and Central Europe, the growing popularity of the Mediterranean diet and the emergence of the café and restaurant culture. The increased sophistication of Australians in food and drinking coincided with greater prosperity and increased exposure to international travel.

However, the influx of migrants and subsequent cultural changes do not explain why Australians became more demanding consumers of wine (an important factor in Porter's diamond of national competitiveness): European migrants were not necessarily discerning wine-drinkers for they were satisfied to drink the local equivalent of *vin ordinaire*. The explanation lies in a complex interaction of demand conditions with the other three dimensions of the diamond that led to the industry developing the capacity to offer mass consumers consistent, high quality wine at reasonable prices. More specifically, technological and marketing innovations, development of education and research institutions, the emergence of the wine judging system, extensive media coverage, and the rise in boutique wineries all resulted in Australian wine consumers becoming more informed and discerning. Controlled pressure fermentation, refrigeration and improvements in filtration, among others, marked the start of the technological revolution, initially in white wine-making (Halliday, 1994) and increased the ability of wineries to produce wine of consistent quality. Perhaps the most significant marketing innovation was 'bag-in-a-box' packaging – the wine cask as it is now more commonly known – commercialised by Wynns in 1971. Not only did the cask provide the thrust for the Wynns marketing slogan 'The luxury of wine at little expense' (Halliday, 1994: 17), but it also was, in the words of Orlando's managing director, 'the saviour of the industry' (Rankine, 1996: 83).[1] During the 1970s, per capita wine consumption doubled, and the cask component increased from 2 per cent in 1971 to 65 per cent in 1985, signalling the emergence of a new market (Rankine, 1996; Industry Commission, 1995).

Education and research have a long history in the Australian wine industry. Established in 1955, the Australian Wine Research Institute undertook innovative studies on wine chemistry and composition. In the 1970s and 1980s highly qualified wine-makers, formally trained for the demands of the modern industry, also played a significant role in raising the general quality of wine production (Halliday, 1994; Unwin, 1996). The wine judging system, which started as part of the Adelaide Agricultural Show in 1845, had a profound influence on wine quality, style and label promotion. Over the years, the show system provided a forum for winemakers to compete on technical grounds and became a training ground for judges of fine wines, who in turn assisted in educating producers and the Australian public about wine and wine-making (Rankine, 1996). Because success at shows could be converted into marketing advantages, the system attracted strong industry support and helped to raise technical standards throughout the industry.

Finally, the rise of boutique wineries, which were able to offer regionally differentiated premium wines, had a lasting impact on the quality and diversity of wine available to the discerning consumer. Boutique wineries began to proliferate in the 1960s, when members of more affluent professions (doctors, lawyers and bankers) took advantage of tax incentives for rural development to establish small-scale vineyards and cellars. Sometimes the appeal was simply 'lifestyle'. The 1980s saw the rise of the professional winemaker-proprietor (Beeston, 2001). Small independent wineries were encouraged by local authorities for their tourism potential, reinforcing the emerging wine-tourism cluster.

By the early 1990s, the Australian consumers' palate had matured, and table wine had become an essential part of Australian lifestyle. The growth in demand from 7.3 litres per capita in 1950 to 18.5 litres in the early 1990s was accompanied by a marked shift in the composition of demand – a shift toward premium bottled wine and away from non-premium cask wine and fortified wines (Rankine, 1996; Industry Commission, 1995). In 1993/94 over 20 per cent of wine production was exported (Osmond and Anderson, 1998).

Factor Conditions

By the early 1990s Australia had become a cost-competitive producer of high-quality wines. Australia was well endowed with natural resources and had a large choice of climate, land and adequate water availability. Its vineyards yielded at or above those in California, often cited by industry observers as its competitive benchmark. It was also free of regulatory rigidities and elaborate *appellation/denominazione* systems that stifled innovation and expansion in Old World countries. Although labour costs were higher than in California, land costs were significantly lower (Porter and Bond, 2004). Despite these advantages, according to a Rabobank survey cited in Marsh and Shaw (1999), Australia did not rank as 'outstanding' on any of the natural factors (geography, climate, land, raw materials and labour) relative to its Old World and New World competitors.

The industry's success could be better explained in terms of created as opposed to natural endowments. These included high-quality resources (human and capital) and infrastructure (physical, administrative, information, scientific and technological) that led to innovativeness and high productivity. The pace of technological change accelerated in the 1960s and the Australian wine industry has since been at the forefront of technological innovation in viticulture and wine-making (Rankine, 1996). The widespread use of irrigation, including drip irrigation – a technology that Australia adopted in 1969 from Israel – enabled the development of large vineyard planting schemes in warm dryland areas where irrigation was essential. A second major innovation was mechanisation. Until the 1950s vineyard operations were still carried out by hand with horses, small tractors and carts; by the 1970s machine harvesting, pruning and hedging became widely accepted, dramatically reducing labour costs along with demand for seasonal labour. Temperature-controlled cool fermentation of white wines allowed wine producers to make light, crisp dry wines, rather than the traditional heavy, oxidised wines (Unwin, 1996). All these innovations boosted the Australian industry's productivity relative to other countries' industries, particularly in the Old World. These technological developments ensured the production of wines of consistently good quality regardless of vintage and storage conditions (Unwin, 1996), which in turn helped to stimulate demand. These developments were the basis for Australia's later positioning in the commercial (popular premium) wine segment of the international market.

Much of the industry's success in terms of created advantages could be attributed to Australia's outstanding human capital – its wine-makers, scientists and managers – and the education and research institutions that nurtured and developed them. Australian wine-making methods and trained personnel were exported to most wine-producing countries. For example, affiliates of Australian enterprises such as Hardy's La Baume, James Herrick and Yalumba (in the south of France) showed that they could make better wines than the local producers on their own territory. The phenomenon of Australian 'flying winemakers' became widespread – a far cry from the earlier days of the modern industry when Australian winemakers were regarded as 'youngsters' in the field, with a long way to go (Rankine, 1996; Hooke, 1999). The industry did not rely on charismatic, 'natural' winemakers to magically produce successful wines: its viticulturists and winemakers were highly trained by local institutions (such as Roseworthy and later Charles Sturt) to international standards (WGCA and WFA, 1994: 10).

Overall, only France was ahead of Australia in relation to created and natural factor advantages. According to the Rabobank survey, France scored five outstanding and four good ratings; Australia scored four and five, respectively. The US wine industry scored the same overall result as Australia (Marsh and Shaw, 1999).

Related and supporting industries

The third broad determinant of the Australian wine industry international success was the presence of related and supported industries that were internationally competitive (Figure 10.1). Cluster effects were twofold: they delivered the most cost-efficient inputs and, more importantly, provided advantages in innovation, upgrading and knowledge diffusion based on close working relationships (see Porter, 1990; Hoen, 2001, Maskell, 2001). The most significant production costs for the industry were the cost of grapes (which as a percentage of total production cost varied from 24 per cent for ultra-premium to 10 per cent for non-premium grapes); packaging (glass products, paperboard and plastics) and labour (Industry Commission, 1995).

Although Porter (1998) stresses the presence of capable, internationally competitive *locally-based* suppliers, the Australian cluster in the early 1990s was in fact a combination of local and overseas suppliers. Glass products and paperboard, labour, capital, training and other specialised inputs (such as pump suppliers and tanks) were sourced locally, while cork, insurance services, plastic products, and oak barrels were imported (Marsh and Shaw, 2000). Grape growers were an integral part of the industry, rather than just a supplier: premium and boutique wine producers tended to be vertically integrated, while larger companies relied on a combination of their own vineyards, quasi-vertical integration (working closely with contracted growers over a long period of time to improve grape quality and efficiency), and grapes sourced on the spot market or by short-term contracts. Prices of locally sourced glass (manufactured by ACI) and cartons (manufactured by Amcor and Visy) were widely believed to be uncompetitive by world standards: industry participants indicated that glass packaging (which constituted approximately 16 per cent of the total cost) was up to 30 per cent more expensive in Australia than in Europe (Industry Commission, 1995).

Australia's research institutions and education providers were among the best in the world. Their collaboration, supported by the Wine Overseas Marketing Board, was instrumental in funding John Fornachon's 1934 groundbreaking research into bacterial spoilage of fortified wine, a problem that had plagued the industry's exports. Research and development was carried out by two major organisations – the Australian Wine Research Institute which had an international reputation for the quality and breadth of its wine research, and the CSIRO Division of Horticulture, with contributions to strategic research also made by government departments and the University of Adelaide (Industry Commission, 1995). In the early 1990s Australia produced 20 per cent of the world's research papers on wine while producing only two per cent of the world's wine (WGCA and WFA, 1994: 36). Tertiary institutions offered a full range of programs in viticulture and oenology from shorter competency-based training courses to bachelor courses and research supervision leading to doctoral degrees.

Two related clusters – the agricultural cluster and the tourism/ hospitality cluster – operated at world class standards. As a supplier to the industry, the agricultural cluster had always been an important area of strength for Australia due to a combination of sparsely populated and relatively unpolluted arable land, favourable climate and highly productive and innovative farming (Morkel and Osegowitsch, 1999). The cluster was also instrumental in developing viticulture skills and research based on a long tradition of agriculture research and innovation. For example, Roseworthy Agricultural College, established in 1883, had viticulture as a compulsory subject virtually from the outset, with a diploma in oenology established in 1936 (Halliday, 1994). The tourism/hospitality cluster experienced strong growth in the late 1980s to early 1990s, when visitor arrivals grew by eight

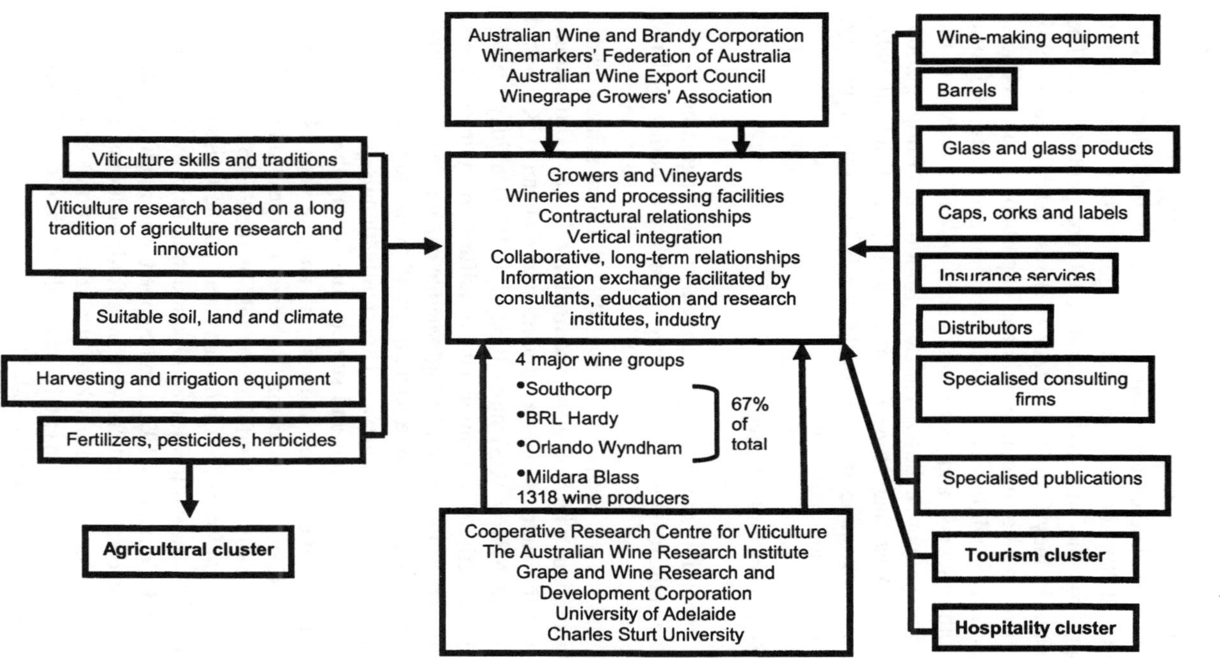

Figure 10.1: The Australian wine industry cluster, early 1990s

Source: Authors, based on Porter (1990)

per cent per annum driven by consumer preferences toward authentic experiences, cultural and eco-tourism (WGCA and WFA, 1994). Complementarities between tourism and wine started to be realised in the 1970s, with the growth of the boutique winery and cellar door trade, and wine tourism gaining momentum in the mid-1980s (Halliday, 1994).

The various industry bodies and their functions are well described in Marsh and Shaw (2000) and Roberts and Enright (2004), but two are particularly salient for the industry's international competitiveness. The Australian Wine and Brandy Corporation (AWBC) was established in 1981 to encourage and promote consumption, sale and exports of grape products, improve their production and provide research into their marketing. Because it represented both growers and wine producers, AWBC provided the catalyst for developing a more cohesive industry (Roberts and Enright, 2004; Halliday, 1994). The Australian Wine Export Council (established in 1992) further separated the promotion activities of the AWBC from its regulatory, information and certification activities.

Firm Strategy, Structure and Rivalry

The nature of competition dramatically changed at the beginning of the fourth cycle of the industry with the takeover of family wineries by large corporations (Osmond and Anderson, 1998). The first large wave of acquisitions and takeovers occurred in 1965-1976, when some smaller family-owned Australian wineries were acquired by larger corporations, including foreign multinationals such as Reckitt and Colman (UK), Allied Vintners (UK), Philip Morris (US) and Gilbeys' (UK) (Halliday, 1994). Most of this takeover activity was unrelated diversification by international conglomerates and part of the wave of conglomerate expansion of that time. These multinationals brought the American notion of rivalry to a closely knit industry of well-established families. The multinationals were keenly focused on price-based competition and started questioning the established practices of investments in education and research and the very existence of industry associations (Croser, pers. comm.). Several large producers went from family to corporate control: Penfolds was sold by the Penfolds family to the brewer Tooth and Co. in 1976; Lindemans was publicly listed in 1953 and taken over in 1971 by Philip Morris; Orlando was sold by the Gramp family to Reckitt and Colman in 1970; and Seppelt was publicly listed in 1970. The reasons for corporatisation were manifold, including dilution of ownership, intra-family tensions and lack of strong direction. But the most significant reason was insufficient capital to meet the technological needs of the rapidly changing industry (Beeston, 2001).

A new wave of consolidation occurred in 1989-1992. The main driver behind this wave was the capital intensity of the industry required for rapid expansion to accommodate surging exports. The capital intensity of grape growing was about 50 per cent more than of other agricultural crops, and that of wine-making was more than 20 per cent higher than in general manufacturing (Osmond and Anderson, 1998). However, the momentum of the rationalisation was accelerated by the most severe recession since the 1930s, which resulted in decreased domestic consumption (including of 'recession-proof' premium and super-premium wines) and price reductions for wine producers, distributors and retailers (Halliday, 1994). The recession made purely domestic wine producers vulnerable to takeover by the large corporate firms. Industry rationalisation culminated in the emergence, by the early 1990s, of four large players: Southcorp, BRL Hardy (Berri Renmano and Thomas Hardy merged in 1992), Orlando Wyndham (acquired by the French multinational Pernod Ricard in 1990) and Mildara Blass (which merged with Wolf Blass in 1991) (Halliday, 1994; Rankine, 1996).

Meanwhile, ongoing new entry into the industry by many small wineries created a new strategic group (McGee and Thomas, 1986; Beverland, 2002), which did not compete directly with the major players, and fed the process of innovation and added to the variety and heterogeneity of the industry (see also Swaminathan, 1995). Although not having the scale and resources of the larger firms, these new companies generated hundreds of new brands and wine styles each year to accommodate the increasingly sophisticated Australian palate and swings in drinking fashion (WGCA and WFA, 1994).

Industry consolidation created the platform for the industry's fifth boom cycle. By the mid-1990s, the four-firm concentration ratio of production had reached 69 per cent, and the export concentration ratio was even higher, at 87 per cent (Marsh and Shaw, 2000). Producer concentration led to economies of scale along the entire value chain – R&D, grape-growing, wine-making, distribution and brand promotion. These large firms had the capital, technical expertise, market power, economies of scale and the marketing skills to produce and market large volumes of consistent, popular premium wines that used grapes from several regions (Osmond and Anderson, 1998). Popular premium wines were well suited to the opportunities in the industry's two most important export markets – the UK and the US (Halliday, 1994). Industry exports would not, most likely, have taken off without the efforts of some of the industry's largest players, particularly Orlando Wyndham, Penfolds, Lindemans, BRL Hardy, Mildara Blass, Negociants International/Yalumba and Rosemount Estates (WGCA and WFA, 1994). As an outcome of consolidation, a few firms ended up with dominant market shares, scale and volume as sources of competitive advantage. By default, however, these dominant players adopted strategic positions, which left them straddling the super-premium/fine wine segment that came with the various acquisitions and the popular premium position built on economies of scale in domestic and export markets (Porter, 1996). This straddling would have consequences in the early 2000s when the fifth boom cycle became the fifth 'bust', particularly in international markets.

The Role of Government

Porter (1990) sees government's proper role in the development of an internationally competitive industry as that of catalyst and challenger, succeeding only when working in tandem with favourable underlying conditions of the diamond. In the 1980s government played the role of catalyst by providing incentives to mobilise industry groups to work together on product development and marketing (Roberts and Enright, 2004). It supported the development of industry associations, such as the Australian Wine and Brandy Corporation (established in 1981) and the Wine Makers' Federation (established in 1989), and was instrumental in the development of high-quality educational and research institutions and R&D funding. The Government also insured regulatory stability (which was critical for the wine industry because of its long production cycles) and facilitated exports through various market development grants.

Throughout the history of the Australian wine industry government policies contributed to the boom-bust cycles through taxation, excise, export bounties and similar measures (Osmond and Anderson, 1998). For example, tax incentives to expand plantings via the accelerated depreciation allowance for vineyard establishment costs eventually led to the government financing a vine-pull scheme in the mid-1980s. Similar tax benefits led to a doubling of vineyard area in the late 1990s, which supported the export-driven fifth boom cycle and contributed to the fifth bust cycle.

Export success

Exporting has always been part of the industry, with the first export shipment from Australia to England in 1822. However, despite some early successes at wine shows in Vienna (1873) and Bordeaux (1882), the industry had no significant impact on the British market until the interwar years of 1918-1939 (Unwin, 1996), largely because of the inconsistent quality of dry red table wines, significant freight costs and travel times, combined with lack of effective marketing and distribution in the face of long-established exports from France. In the 1920s table wines were overtaken by fortified wines with the introduction of the Wine Export Bounty Act (1924), which offered an export subsidy to producers of sweet fortified wines. The subsidy was intended to make Australia better able to compete in the UK market with

Portugal and Spain. Because of lack of maturation and bad storage on arrival, these early shipments of fortified wines proved to be of very low quality, creating a poor reputation for Australia as a new supplier. Despite the problems (later ameliorated by Fornachon's research into bacterial spoilage), exports reached its peak in 1936-37, representing nearly 23 per cent of Britain's imports, still behind Portugal and Spain, but well ahead of France and Italy (WGCA and WFA, 1994). The export market, with its sole dependence on Britain, collapsed in the late 1940s when imperial preference (introduced in 1925) was abolished (WGCA and WFA, 1994). From then until the 1980s, the industry enjoyed little international success (AWF, 1995). The approach to exporting was opportunistic, geared toward getting rid of surplus, low-quality grapes not absorbed by domestic demand – exactly the same rationale applied to steel exports (Chapter 14).

During the mid-1980s exports started rapidly to increase. Their value doubled from $20.5 million in 1985-86 to $44.6 million in 1986-87 and then doubled again in the following year (Osmond and Anderson, 1998). Ten years later exports had reached over $60 million. The surge in the volume and value of exports was attributable to several factors (Industry Commission, 1995). In the early stages of the boom (1985-88), export growth was stimulated by a surplus of premium grape varieties due to over-planting in the early 1970s and the devaluation of the Australian dollar.

By the late 1980s Australia's 'diamond of national advantage' had developed to the stage where the industry could sustain competition in international markets. The *ad hoc* advantages associated with government export bounties and preferential tariffs had been replaced by beneficial specialised highly developed clusters, sophisticated demand conditions, and large-scale, competitive firms. Driven by the demands of corporate growth, these firms had begun strategically to exploit the opportunities presented by international markets. An important element of this strategic approach to internationalisation was a focus on premium table wines and creating a credible presence in overseas markets by building brands and own distribution networks rather than relying on an agency system. Australian wine producers started to develop wines specifically targeted to the overseas markets (Beeston, 2001). Because their industry had developed as a technologically-driven, innovative industry responsive to changing consumer preferences, Australian producers had become more flexible than Old World producers in adapting traditional winemaking processes to cater to market preferences for new wine styles (Hooke, 1999). By the mid-1990s the industry had established itself as a major exporter among the highly competitive New World Wine producers (Table 10.1).

LOSING THE WAY

'Strategy 2025'

In 1995/96 the industry adopted a long-term industry strategic plan entitled *Strategy 2025*, championed by two industry bodies, the Australian Wine Makers Federation and the Australian Wine Foundation. The plan stated that by 2025 the Australian wine industry would be 'the world's most influential and profitable supplier of branded wines, pioneering wine as a universal first-choice lifestyle beverage' (AWF, 1995). The plan anticipated a threefold increase in real value of wine production, with a 30-year industry objective of more than 50 per cent exports, generated by stipulating specific practical requirements for plantings, water and skilled personnel. In terms of export growth, the plan outlined three stages:

- *Volume growth* (1996-2002) during which rapid vineyard expansion would overcome product shortages thereby enabling expansion in existing markets and penetration of new markets;
- *Value growth* (2002-2015) which would place increased emphasis on building brand strength, sector share and margins;
- *Pre-eminence* (2015-2025) when Australia would have established brand leadership in specific market segments. By 2025 the industry planned to achieve $4.5 billion in annual sales.

Strategy 2025 has often been credited with changing the industry mindset from a production to a marketing focus thereby reorientating it to global markets (Australian Business Foundation, 2005). Throughout the late 1990s Australian wine exports grew more than three times faster than the global average. At annual rates of more than 16 per cent in volume terms and 21 per cent in value terms, the industry reached its export target of $1 billion in 1999, a year ahead of schedule. *Strategy 2025* was also believed to have been fundamental in strengthening both related and supporting industries domestically and producer, grower and supplier integration (Marsh and Shaw, 2000). Other industry observers were less positive about the role of the industry plan, arguing that the wine industry was already on the way to becoming an export success. All *Strategy 2025* did, they argued, was to document the nascent success *ex post* and extrapolate trends into the future (Croser, pers. comm.).

The strategic intent implicit in *Strategy 2025* was first to leverage Australia's low-cost position to increase volume, then in Stage 2 to enhance value as the industry increased differentiation to finally reach Pre-eminence, which would combine a high consumer willingness-to-pay and low cost. Similar strategies had been pursued by Japanese car manufacturers to establish dominant shares in major international markets. *Strategy 2025* represented one of the more strategically informed approaches to internationalisation in Australian business, contrasting sharply with the industry strategies adopted – or not adopted – in other industries (Griffiths and Zammuto, 2005).

By the early 2000s the wine industry had become Australia's best-known example of an internationally successful, non-random, knowledge-based and market-led cluster (Maskell, 2001). Yet despite the industry's export success throughout the 1980s and 1990s and the ambitious goals of *Strategy 2025*, by the mid-2000s the industry's competitiveness was being eroded, reflected in a decline in the average export price. In 2003-04 overseas export volumes of Australian wine increased 13 per cent over 2002-03, but the average price fell nine per cent to $4.27/L (ABS, 2005b). Moreover, its export performance, measured as growth in the average export price, was now being matched by other producers.

How did the Australian wine industry reach the point where Paradise appeared lost before it was actually gained? We propose three factors: major wine firms executives' global aspirations; the 'race to the bottom' response to growing retailer power; and firms' lack of insight about their strategic positioning.

Global aspirations

So far we have explained the industry's export success in terms of the diamond of national advantage. An important factor behind the success was industry consolidation resulting in significant economies of scale in manufacturing and depth of management and marketing skills in the domestic market, supported by committed investments in brand-building and distribution in overseas markets. Nevertheless, the largest industry players (Foster's Group/BBWE and, on a much smaller scale, Southcorp) attempted to switch from export competitiveness based on a strong national diamond to foreign direct investment (FDI). Foster's acquisition of California-based Beringer Wine Estates (US$1.47 billion) in 2000 and cross-border acquisitions in wine clubs and wine services (Chapter 15) marked a transition from exporting combined with some export-supporting FDI (for example, foreign sales and distribution activities) to foreign investments in operating businesses (strategic FDI).

The general view of analysts was that these investments were not profitable (IBISWorld, 2006; also Chapter 15), raising concerns about whether such investments enhanced shareholder value. The common rationale for cross-border mergers and acquisitions given by senior executives of large beverage producers was the intention to build global brands and buy access to distribution in foreign markets to leverage these brands. As pointed out by Roberto (2003), however, firms embarked on cross-border acquisition for reasons other than the rational, profit-maximising pursuit of scale, scope and learning economies and agency problems played a role in some cases. Examples below show that FDI in productive assets was not necessary to succeed in foreign markets – Casella Wines achieved US market success without making major acquisitions. Indeed, global aspirations may contribute to misallocation of resources and distract management of wine companies from the two most pressing issues facing the Australian wine industry, that is maintaining short-term domestic profitability and ensuring a viable competitive position domestically and internationally.

The race to the bottom

The second factor threatening the industry's international competitiveness was a 'race to the bottom' as a result of overproduction and the increasingly higher concentration of the Australian liquor retailing industry (Chapter 9). In the early 2000s, two retailers, Woolworths and Coles Myer, already controlled more than 50 per cent of the liquor market, with independents controlling a further 30 per cent. To offset the growing market power of retailers, Australian wine producers pursued further consolidation (Table 10.4). The industry was further consolidated by the $1.5 billion merger of Southcorp and Rosemount in early 2001 and the $3.7 billion acquisition of the merged Southcorp by Foster's Group in 2005.

With the encouragement of retailers, the popular premium segment of the industry quickly became commoditised, intensifying price rivalry between producers. This forced producers to pass lower prices back to grape growers, who had enjoyed good profits throughout the 1990s as export volumes grew. Record vintages, as a result of new production from tax-driven vineyard plantings in cool climate regions, combined with better than average seasons, led to a build up of wine stocks over a period of several years, which aggravated year-on-year grape oversupply of between $0.5 and $1 billion in the mid 2000s (Croser, pers. comm.). To compound the problem, the stronger Australian dollar effectively raised export prices and further depressed grape prices. The growing antagonism between producers and growers undermined industry collaboration, jeopardising investments in R&D and human capital and, ultimately, the capacity of the industry to innovate.

The 'race to the bottom' in the domestic market also undermined the international reputation of Australian wine producers, who took the opportunity of low grape prices to produce millions of wine bottles which by the mid-2000s had come to dominate the very bottom end of the popular premium segment in the US market.

Table 10.4: Company shares of still light grape wine, Australia, 2002

Company	Markets share (%)
Southcorp Limited	25.0
Foster's Group	23.0
BRL Hardy	15.0
Orlando-Wyndham Group	12.5
McGuigan Simeon Wines	3.3
McWilliams Wines	2.3
Others	18.9

Note: Still wines exclude sparkling wines and fortifieds

Sources: Euromonitor, based on trade press (Australian Liquor Retailer, Liquor Week, National Liquor Retailer), company research, trade interviews, Euromonitor estimates. premium segment in the US market (Grossman, 2006). In addition, the Southcorp/Rosemount merger led to a discounting war against supermarkets and retailers in the UK, which destroyed margins for everyone (Grigg, 2006: 70)

Lack of strategic insight

Although a strategic approach to internationalisation was implicit in *Strategy 2025*, it failed to recognise that Stage 2 – value growth through increasing consumers' willingness to pay – depended on establishing clear strategic positions, which could only be done at the firm level. Strategic positioning involves choices about which segments to serve and, because positions are usually mutually exclusive, a willingness to sacrifice certain segments (Kim and Mauborgne, 2005; Porter, 1996). A truism of business strategy is that universal positions are not sustainable – a firm can do anything, but not everything. The two broad segments in which the Australian wine industry competed in international markets in the early 2000s – popular premium (commercial/industrial) wines and super-premium (fine) wines – were, in effect, two separate industries with different underlying technological characteristics (different viticultural and wine-making processes), economics, consumer behaviour and marketing techniques.[2]

The popular premium (commercial wine) segment was based on the identification of the country of origin in support of varietal branding, and economies of scale in production and distribution. These wines, exported at a value of less than \$5/litre f.o.b., were consistent, standardised and homogenised, recently described by industry observers as 'all tastes the same', 'boring', and likened to 'commodities' and Coca-Cola. Consumers of these wines valued a consistently pleasing taste experience commensurate with the money expended and treated wine as another alcoholic beverage along with beer and mixers (Croser, 2004). By the later 1990s, this segment had become intensely competitive as New World countries, including the US Chile, Argentina, South Africa, Australia and even France aggressively competed for market share.

Super-premium wines ('fine wines') were better quality, differentiated, site identified and supported by the artisan winemaker's individual skills and techniques. The vast majority of fine-wine producers were small and not viable as commercial wine suppliers because viticultural technologies (such as hand picking and low yields per hectare) and wine-making technologies (such as small batch processing and French oak barriques) substantially raised costs. Marketing to this highly profitable segment was heavily reliant on maintaining an image of authenticity and channel promotion (Beverland, 2005). Super-premium wines were sold in specialist stores, restaurants and by mail order. This segment was highly fragmented on both the production and distribution side but, because of its ability to sustain superior profits, was 'a segment of the market into the future' (Croser, 2004: 14). French wine producers dominated this segment. Australian fine wines were consumed mostly by Australians and did not enjoy the same degree of success as Australian commercial wines in the global market (Croser, 2005).

Industry experts questioned whether it was possible for a producer of popular premium brands also to earn credibility for the production of super-premium wines, and that these incompatibilities were increasing with consumer awareness (Croser, 2004). This had two strategic implications. First, significant mobility barriers deterred movements between segments (Caves and Porter, 1977; McGee and Thomas, 1986; Mascarehnas and Aaker, 1989). It was very difficult for fine-wine producers to succeed in entering the commercial wine segment because of lack of scale. Second, large firms that attempted to compete in both segments would find it hard to 'straddle' two very different businesses against more focused competitors.

The examples of Casella Wines and Torbreck show two different focused approaches to strategic positioning in overseas markets. Based in the irrigated Riverina district of New South Wales, Casella Wines, which exported almost 97 per cent of its production, was highly successful and profitable in the US with its popular premium yellow tail brand. Casella Wines made clear choices about which customer segments to pursue and, even more importantly, which segments to sacrifice. yellow tail was initially available only as a white (Chardonnay) and a red (Shiraz), had an uncomplicated soft palate with strong primary flavours and carried no technical jargon on the non-traditional bright label. The brand leapfrogged competitors with no promotional campaign, mass media or consumer advertising. In the short space of two years, yellow tail emerged as the fastest growing brand in the history of the Australian and US wine industries, the number one imported wine in the US, surpassing the wines of France and Italy, and commanded over 36 per cent of the Australian category in the US (Kim and Mauborgne, 2005). Casella Wines had entered the highly competitive US wine industry with a value proposition carefully tailored to the selected segment, based on the market insights of Casella's US distributor, and constructed a focused supply chain to deliver this value proposition at minimum cost. Its yellow tail brand had been built on the back of its value proposition with almost no advertising, while the majority of Australian commercial wine producers were doing exactly the opposite (large brand advertising but a poorly defined value proposition). Casella Wines' strategy is, in principle, the same as the positioning strategies of firms such as Wal-Mart, McDonald's, Dell Computers and Southwest Airlines. These highly successful firms established sustainable competitive advantage by using a clear value proposition as the point of departure and then tailoring activities to deliver the value proposition at minimum cost.

In contrast, Torbreck from the Barossa Valley, a premium wine producing region, positioned itself as a producer of 'icon' wines that attracted a very high willingness to pay and commensurate margins (its wines ranged from $25 to $245) and very low volumes (the first crush of the winery in 1995 was only three tonnes) and high costs (fruit from old shiraz vines and small batch processing). Its founder, David Powell, described this as a 'room at the top' strategy (Schreiner, 2005). Alongside other small producers from premium wine-growing regions of Australia, Torbreck built on the reputation Grange had established for Australia with international palates and critics as a producer of fine wines. When Powell made the decision to double prices at the risk of slowing down the rate of sales, the winery actually started to sell the wines twice as fast, a classic example on an upward-sloping demand curve. In short, unlike the major Australian wine producers, Casella Wines and Torbreck did not attempt to straddle the two market segments. It should be noted that it would be just as foolhardy for Casella Wines to attempt to straddle the fine wine segment as it would be for Torbreck to attempt to compete in the popular premium wine segment.

CAN PARADISE BE GAINED?

At least until the early 2000s, the wine industry represented one of Australia's few successful cases of internationalisation in manufacturing. Much of this outstanding performance can be explained after Porter (1990) in terms of the industry's capacity continuously to innovate and upgrade. The sustainability of its competitiveness, however, is now in jeopardy because of the aspirations of major companies to become global wine firms, a 'race to the bottom' in response to the increasing market power of retailers, and a lack of strategic insight with regard to the way firms should position themselves.

One of the key conclusions from our analysis is that the time for industry strategies and the generic 'Brand Australia' has passed. Unfortunately, a well-grounded strategic analysis of Australia's future international competitiveness is still lacking. Recent 'visions' of the industry's future tend either dangerously to extrapolate past trends, to offer unrealistic solutions such as exporting significantly greater quantities into already crowded markets, or simply to confuse industry strategy with the strategies of individual companies (Gladstone, 2005; Scott, 2006).

Australia's diamond of national advantage is robust, but the industry needs to recognise that future success depends on firm-level strategies. The industry will be able to sustain a wide range of strategic positions internationally only through individual companies crafting unique strategic positions. This will involve making choices about what value proposition to offer to which segments and then systematically tailoring activity sets to deliver these value propositions at minimum cost (Porter, 1996). This will happen only if industry participants accept the fact that the Australian wine industry has evolved into two discrete industries: the popular premium (commercial) wine industry and the fine-wine industry. Rather than simply being a 'false dichotomy' between wine styles, as some industry participants have claimed (Gladstone, 2005), the distinction between these industries rests on different economics. As strategically focused competitors emerge in Australia and other New World markets, and as the Old World producers refocus, the major Australian wine producers' strategy of straddling is bound to fail. If the Australian wine industry is to enjoy a sixth boom, the industry must be restructured around firms which have adopted clear strategic positions.

NOTES

1. Orlando (with Coolabah) and Lindemans (with Cellarpack) were early adopters of the wine cask.
2. The basic segment (*vin ordinaire* or value brands) was the third segment in the industry. The profitability of this segment was driven by economies of scale in production and distribution. These wines were consumed locally. Pricing was key, willingness to pay was low, consumer loyalty was non-existent, and wines (often cask wines) were sold in supermarkets and liquor stores.

11. Engineering Services

Thomas Osegowitsch

INTRODUCTION

The provision of engineering and construction services in overseas markets is no recent phenomenon. In fact, the engineering and construction companies of the major colonial powers were at the forefront of internationalisation in the service sector. However, international engineering and construction – by then split into two separate industries – really came of age after World War II. The internationalisation of 'consulting engineers' and 'contractors', as they are known today, accelerated in the 1960s, driven by the expanding oil industry and strong demand for import-substituting manufacturing plants (Strassman and Wells, 1988: 2).

Australian consulting engineers were not in this vanguard. In the years after World War II there was plenty of work to be had at home, especially on resource and infrastructure projects. Nevertheless, the industry has since evolved into one of the bright spots in the country's business landscape. While it has enjoyed an enviable growth record at home, its success in international markets, as measured by exports and outward FDI, has been even more spectacular. This chapter advances some tentative explanations for this Australian success story.

It is perhaps not surprising that Australia should have produced internationally competitive firms in what many would regard as a niche industry. Specialisation helps to evade the cut-throat competition of other, more significant industries, but Australia also boasts a set of unique locational advantages that have facilitated the emergence of a number of home-grown consulting engineering firms with sizeable international operations. The same advantages also explain the 'centre of excellence' roles assumed by the Australian subsidiaries of many foreign-owned MNCs.

This chapter begins with a brief overview of consulting engineering before detailing the Australian industry and its international engagement. After summarising the motives for international expansion, we review the locational advantages that helped locally based firms to hone their competitive advantages and the favourable circumstances aiding their exploitation in foreign markets.

THE INDUSTRY

Until the mid-nineteenth century, engineering and construction were united within the 'master builder'. They gradually separated as engineering was elevated to the status of a profession in response to the greater technical complexity introduced by new construction methods and materials (Kluenker, 2001). Consulting engineers, as they eventually became known, were charged with finding technical solutions to engineering problems, aiding in and supervising their implementation and representing the client's interests vis-à-vis contractors. Consulting engineering was provided on a fee basis and bore all the hallmarks of a proper profession.

The role of the traditional contractor, by contrast, was to carry out the designs provided by the consulting engineer as cost-effectively as possible. Contractors were chiefly constructors, although all of them held *some* engineering expertise. With virtually all of the traditional contractor's work secured through competitive bidding, it was a tough business preoccupied with efficiency.

Not surprisingly, the two sectors have been characterised as irreconcilably different in mindset and culture. Some professional engineering associations went so far as to discourage their members from becoming employees of contractors (Casson, 1987: 170). A number of recent trends, however, have blurred the boundaries, with companies from both sides encroaching on the other's territory. For reasons such as client demands for 'integrated solutions' and the putative synergies of so-called 'design-build' project delivery, contractors are electing to broaden their skills in the areas of design and planning. Many of these firms have acquired engineering consultants in a bid to boost their technical capabilities. At the same time, traditional consulting engineers have added skills in the areas of project management, risk assessment and finance and have begun touting for business as prime contractors, sometimes referred to as 'design-led, design-build'. As a corollary, many of these firms are today assuming a greater share of project risk, so that fee-based income accounts only for a small portion of their total income.

This chapter concerns itself solely with *dedicated* consulting engineering firms. We acknowledge that professional engineering and related services are not the sole domain of dedicated firms but are also offered by competitors associated with other industries. Besides construction companies, which provide engineering skills as part of their services, more recent competitors include accounting firms as well as management and real estate consultancies that offer services such as construction risk analysis, selection of the most appropriate delivery method and project management (Silver, 1999: 5-6).

Unfortunately there is no entirely satisfactory definition of what constitutes consulting engineering. Along with others, we use the term loosely to encompass all companies performing primarily civil, structural and related engineering services on major capital assets such as buildings, manufacturing plants, power stations and waste water treatment facilities.[1] Consulting engineering firms do two things: they provide planning and design services and they manage the various organisations participating in the completion of a project.

As a type of professional service, consulting engineers share a number of traits with law firms, management consultants and advertisers, which set them apart from other industries (Lowendahl, 2000: 145). Firstly, value creation centres on the delivery of highly knowledge-intensive services, delivered by highly educated employees. Secondly, services tend to be highly customised to each client's needs. Thirdly, there are considerable information asymmetries between client and service provider, primarily owing to the high degree of credence quality (Darby and Karni, 1973). Due to the inherent complexity and deferred benefits it may be difficult (or even impossible) to gauge quality prior to, as well as *after,* service delivery.[2] Fourthly, delivery entails a significant degree of interaction with the client and, finally, delivery entails a high degree of discretion and professional judgement on the part of the individuals providing the service.

Competitive advantage in consulting engineering is derived overwhelmingly from two elements, technical capabilities and reputation, both of which derive from 'the accumulated experience of the firm' (OTA, 1987: 138). Capabilities related to the planning, designing and managing of projects are honed over many years of performing projects and solving client problems.

Because clients cannot readily identify the consultant with the best technical expertise, a firm's reputation in the market place is an important way of signalling the desired capabilities (Aharoni, 2000). The main route to establishing a reputation is, of course, experience, that is, taking advantage of opportunities to build the firm's capabilities and to establish rapport with clients. This leaves newcomers in a tricky situation. Lack of reputation prevents them from being considered by project owners, thus precluding them from building the required technical capabilities; in turn, their lack of experience and the corresponding capabilities means they do not enjoy the reputation they crave. The only way to overcome this dilemma is a gradual process of successfully completing minor projects, possibly as sub-consultants, before moving on to more challenging projects. Not surprisingly, there are no 'born globals' in this industry (Knight and

Cavusgil, 2005), although a reputation in one country can sometimes be successfully leveraged into another country by piggy-backing on domestic clients with international operations.

Given the somewhat vague definition of the industry, it is no surprise that it is difficult to accurately account for its size. According to the most recent estimate, the annual world market for services provided by dedicated consulting engineering firms stood at US$224 billion in 1999 (Tulacz, 1999: 12-13). However, this figure is based on industry gross revenues and double counting – due to the outsourcing of services to sub-consultants – is likely to account for a significant portion of that figure. We offer US$150 billion as a conservative estimate of current worldwide client spending on professional engineering services.

By the standards of other industries, consulting engineering is highly fragmented. For instance, 2004 revenues for the world's 200 'most international' firms as ranked by the trade journal, *Engineering News Record*, stood at US$58.6 billion (ENR, 2005), not even half of our estimated total of the world market.[3] Among those 200 MNCs, the top four firms accounted for US$7.8 billion or a mere 13 per cent of total billings. A lack of concentration is also evident in the 'international market', with the top four firms collectively claiming US$5.8 billion or 17 per cent of total *foreign* revenues received by the 200 ranked MNCs (author's calculation, based on ENR, 2005).[4]

THE AUSTRALIAN CONSULTING ENGINEERING INDUSTRY AND ITS INTERNATIONAL ENGAGEMENT

Total revenues of the Australian consulting engineering industry – encompassing both locally owned firms and subsidiaries of foreign-based MNCs – were recently estimated by the Australian of Consulting Engineers Australia at $9.3 billion (ACEA, 2004a), although concerns regarding double counting again apply. The same organisation identified some 11,000 consulting engineering firms in the country. Their numbers had grown by more than 12 per cent per annum over the preceding decade. The typical firm today has annual revenues of $1.5 and 12 staff members. In total, the industry employs nearly 80,000 persons, roughly 40 per cent of which work as engineers (ACEA, 2004a).

The Australian industry is as fragmented as its worldwide equivalent, with 96 per cent of firms employing fewer than 20 persons and a significant number consisting of a single engineering professional. The smaller firms in the industry invariably concentrate on serving local clients, providing cost-effective solutions to comparatively simple engineering problems, for example in residential housing. Bigger and technically more complex projects are the domain of the more substantial firms.[5]

The latest ACEA (2004a) census identified only 20 'large' firms, defined as having 300 or more staff.[6] Most foreign MNCs which established subsidiaries in Australia – lured by massive mining and hydrocarbon projects as well as large infrastructure programs – refrained from taking over local first-tier companies. As a result, Australia's large firms represent a balanced mix of locally- and foreign-owned entities. The fact that most home-grown firms have remained in Australian hands is partly due to the fact that they are, overwhelmingly, privately-owned – typically by senior (and other) employees. As such, any takeover attempts require the consent of staff. Hostile takeovers (by foreign or local companies) are also precluded by a keen appreciation of the mobility of firms' most valuable assets, their staff.

The large firms as defined by ACEA account for the overwhelming majority of the industry's international revenues. Invariably they date back several decades and almost all of them are experienced international operators. According to ACEA, the main market segments they serve (in descending order of importance) are buildings (mostly non-residential), infrastructure, industrial plants, energy and mining. The disciplines of civil and structural engineering account for roughly 60 per cent of the business generated, with the remainder consisting of electrical and mechanical engineering, project management, environmental and geotechnical services as well as miscellaneous 'other'. In terms of clients, the private and public sector in the domestic market account for roughly 40 per cent and 30 per cent, respectively, of large firms' total income, with the rest coming from overseas clients (ACEA, 2004b).

While the large firms account for 92 per cent of the sector's overseas income (ACEA, 2004a: 3), the size threshold for international engagement in this industry is decidedly low. Exporting, in particular, is facilitated by the project nature of consulting engineering and the mobility of its professionals. ACEA confirms that a full one third of its approximately 300 members undertake some overseas work, overwhelmingly in the form of exports. The majority of overseas income, however, is earned through wholly- or part-owned subsidiaries.[7] Subsidiary sales are the sole province of the industry's large firms, as defined by ACEA. There are no other significant forms of international market entry apart from exports and wholly- or part-owned FDI.[8]

At an aggregate level, Australian exports of 'architectural, engineering and other technical services' (such as surveying, geological or scientific services) have grown at almost 12 per cent per annum, from $141 million in 1992/93 to $519 million in 2004/05 (CSES, 2002; ABS, 2005). While this category also contains the export activities of dedicated architects, surveyors, geologists and environmental scientists, the resulting bias is likely to be small since consulting engineering traditionally accounts for roughly three quarters of those exports and has recently enjoyed a higher growth rate than the other services (CSES, 2002: ABS, 2005a).

Imports in the same category amounted to $398 million in 2004/05, resulting in a positive trade balance of some $121 million for the year. With the exception of three aberrant years – due to the Asian Crisis and the surge in domestic demand leading up to the Sydney Olympics – the industry has consistently shown a positive trade balance for the past fifteen years (CSES, 2002; ABS, 200a). While total export revenues of $519 million may not seem a particularly impressive figure, these were generated by relatively few and comparatively small firms. In 2002/03 the industry's exports represented 1.4 per cent of Australia's total service exports of $32.5 billion (ACEA, 2005: 2).

Separate data on foreign income derived from subsidiary sales are currently not available because firms typically only report an aggregate 'international sales' figure. The Australian representative body will only confirm that subsidiary sales, virtually all of which are collected by the industry's large firms, 'are known to be substantial' (ACEA, 2005: 3). A quick extrapolation can shed light on the magnitudes involved. In 2002/03, overseas income accounted for some 23 per cent of total industry income, which in turn amounted to roughly $9.5 billion, thus allowing us to calculate total foreign income at roughly $2.2 billion. Since export income stood at approximately $350 million in that year (assuming three quarters of $450 million of export income from 'architectural, engineering and other technical services' are attributable to consulting engineers), subsidiary sales can be estimated at roughly $1.85 billion or more than five times export income.

Overall, the portion of revenue earned abroad (from exports and subsidiary sales) has soared from seven per cent of total billings in 1993/94 to 23 per cent in 2002/03 (ACEA, 2004a: 4). Since 'large' firms as defined by ACEA account for 92 per cent of the industry's international revenues, much of our subsequent discussion pertains to them. Virtually all of these firms are involved in overseas business and, for the average firm, projects on foreign soil have contributed roughly 30 per cent of total income in recent years. For some of them, such as the Meinhardt Group, they accounted for up to three quarters of total revenues in the recent past (Way, 2004b).[9]

Australia's 'large' firms figure prominently among global rankings of the largest engineering consultancies. The 'World's Top 200 Consulting Engineering and Architectural Groups' as compiled by the Swedish Federation of Consulting Engineers and Architects (SFOCEA, 2004) shows four Australian-owned companies among the Top 100 (SKM, GHD, Connell Wagner, Meinhardt Group), with SMEC sitting just outside in position 105 –

brief profiles of these five firms can be found in the Appendix. Since SFOCEA rankings are biased by the inclusion of a small number of 'industrial consultants' (such as software engineers), Australia can credibly claim to have five companies among the Top 100 engineering consultancies worldwide. By comparison, in the same year Australia claimed only six firms among the world's 500 largest companies across all industries (Fortune, 2004).

The disproportionate representation of Australian-owned consulting engineering firms would seem to confirm the country's competitiveness in this industry, although its must be taken into account that consulting engineering MNCs overwhelmingly are domiciled in the developed world.[10] On the other hand, it could be argued that any rankings on the basis of *home country* firms neglect the significance and contribution of *foreign-owned* subsidiaries in Australia, especially where their responsibilities extend beyond the country's borders.

Qualitative research by Osegowitsch (2003) revealed that a majority of foreign-owned engineering consultancies with a significant presence in Australia make extensive use of 'mandates' (see also Chapters 5 and 6). In other words, their Australian subsidiaries have responsibilities beyond the domestic market. Occasionally they may serve as the Asia-Pacific headquarters of the group, but more commonly they act as the company's 'centre of excellence' (CoE) in designated areas such as mining engineering (see Box 11.1). CoE status may be officially accorded by corporate headquarters, or may be informal and hence only recognisable from extensive transfers of specialist expertise to sister units in other countries. Such transfers may take the form of staff secondments or remote support from Australia, such as specialists in an Australian office conducting design reviews for a project carried out by an overseas unit. Most often these CoE roles are regional in scope although outstanding specialist capabilities are also leveraged globally.

MOTIVES FOR INTERNATIONAL ENGAGEMENT

The motives for international engagement in the industry are varied. In the past, much of the FDI originating from Australia and, by default, all Australian exports, were 'market seeking' (Dunning, 1993). In other words, local companies sought to capitalise on their existing capabilities by selling them in foreign markets. Market-seeking motives are still dominant, but others are beginning to complement them.

Box 11.1: Arup Australasia and its Façade Engineering Centre-of-Excellence

Arup Australasia is the Australian-based subsidiary of the global Arup Group. The subsidiary was established more than 40 years ago and has been exporting its services for some 35 years. Arup Australasia's main focus is the Asian region but the specialist expertise and experience it has developed in areas such as façade design have taken it to other regions, including the Middle East, the United States and the United Kingdom.

John Ryder, principal at Arup Australasia, emphasises the delicate touch that is required when working with other Arup units: 'Being part of a global network, we have to be mindful of remaining focused on serving our primary market – Australasia – and allow other offices to manage other regions. This can be constraining at times. However, there are still opportunities to work with other offices and to take on projects on a stand-alone basis. This provides us with the opportunities to create our own place in markets outside our primary target market'.

Arup Facade Engineering (AFE) is a centre of excellence set up within Arup Australasia. It provides consultancy services for all aspects of building façades. According to John Ryder, Australia is well-known for its sophisticated approach and technical prowess in façade design and engineering. The Australian offices' achievements in this regard prompted some of Arup's other subsidiaries to form façade engineering groups of their own. The role of Arup Australasia in this process was to help establish these groups and to help them grow their business, which in turn would generate opportunities for the Australian offices.

Arup Australasia first noticed strong demand for its expertise when servicing a number of façade projects in Singapore on a fly-in basis during the late 1990s. In early 2000, John Ryder and two colleagues (all based in Sydney at the time) committed to spend significant time in Singapore to demonstrate a commitment to the market and to generate the workload that would warrant the establishment of a permanent presence. Once that was achieved, by early 2001, one of Ryder's colleagues agreed to transfer to Singapore and to manage the façade business unit on a full-time basis. A similar process was followed in creating a façade engineering group in Malaysia. Both units are now well established in their respective markets but continue to be an important source of work for the Australian unit, which provides its specialist expertise on an as-needed basis.

Source: Based on ACIF (2002b)

Increasingly, 'resource seeking' motives (Dunning, 1993a) – entering foreign markets in search of cheap labour – are taking hold. While contractors have for some time utilised low-cost engineering centres in countries such as India or China, consulting engineers have traditionally shunned such practices and have only recently begun to adopt them. With staff costs typically accounting for more than 50 per cent of total expenses, there is broad agreement in the industry today that the use of foreign low-cost design centres – typically for commodity services such as detailed design – will continue to increase. For instance, the Australian firm SMEC, which until little more than a decade ago was still a government-owned entity, recently established an Indian unit employing some 300 engineering staff, many of whom provide low-cost engineering services to the rest of the group (Way, 2004a). The arbitrage of labour cost differentials, however, is not restricted to countries such as India and China. Australia boasts a highly educated engineering workforce coupled with salaries that are, as a rough guide, one third below US and European standards. Interviews by Osegowitsch (2003) revealed that the Australian subsidiaries of foreign MNCs are also sometimes tapped to take advantage of their lower cost (and spare capacity).

Some companies also cite 'knowledge seeking' motives for their international engagement. In an industry where the generation of new knowledge is 'a 'by-product' of operations' (Lowendahl, 2000: 151), the most challenging projects offer the greatest prospects for acquiring unique capabilities which subsequently may be utilised in other countries. As a result, multinational engineering consultancies may have a decisive advantage over domestic operators in that they have access to a larger set of learning opportunities (Ghoshal, 1987). A corollary of international expansion for knowledge-seeking reasons may be economies of scale in back-office operations, such as the codification of methodologies and project solutions acquired from around the world (Lowendahl, 2000: 151).

A final and increasingly powerful motive for international expansion are advantages in attracting and retaining staff. Engineering consultancies compete fiercely for the best employees and access to diverse and challenging projects in different countries is highly attractive to professionals. According to Robin Povey, GHD's Director for Global Development:

> Having offices all over the world helps us to achieve one of our other goals: to become an employer of first choice for graduates. We want graduates to look at us and say, 'I want to work for them. They have offices or projects in Asia, South America and the Middle East.' Having those international offices gives us a bigger range of top-quality graduates (ACIF, 2002a: 8).

Many of the companies interviewed by Osegowitsch (2003) voiced similar sentiments and noted that overseas offices also allowed for the possibility of international transfers as a career development tool. Through secondments, junior staff can be exposed to various different working environments, thereby producing more experienced and adaptable individuals.

EXPLAINING AUSTRALIA'S COMPETITIVENESS

The Australian diamond

The evidence presented earlier would suggest that Australian consulting engineering is an example of an internationally competitive industry. With most of the country's larger firms engaged in overseas markets, for a variety of motives, it is apt to ask what explains the industry's success.

The question why a nation may give rise to internationally successful competitors in a particular industry was also asked by Michael Porter. He proposed that the magnitude of an industry's (net) exports and/or (net) outward FDI is a reflection of its companies' ability to exploit strengths nurtured by the home-country environment (Porter, 1990: 18). Four elements, which collectively form a country's 'diamond', provide the pressures and incentives for firms to create the innovations required to succeed in international competition. These elements are: (1) related and support industries; (2) demand conditions; (3) competitive rivalry;[11] and (4) factor conditions (see also Chapter 10). Individually, and as a system, these four elements represent the context within which a nation's firms are created and compete. A critical mass of favourable diamond elements is needed to hone the capabilities of a nation's firms and, in turn, to help them succeed internationally. The role of government in Porter's model is limited to that of catalyst and challenger and more direct forms of government influence are rejected.

While Porter's framework has been criticised (Grant, 1991; Cartwright, 1993), it is generally accepted that firms' competitive advantages tend to reflect the particular *locational* advantages of their country of origin. While, historically, locational advantages were narrowly defined in terms of abundant raw materials or cheap labour and capital, Porter's work drew attention to more subtle advantages, such as 'demanding customers' and the systemic relationships among the various advantages.

Consulting engineering firms typically work in conjunction with prime contractors. The presence of strong, internationally competitive contractors in Australia such as Leighton, Multiplex, Bovis Lend Lease, Barclay Mowlem and Clough may be seen as one component of a favourable

Australian 'diamond', namely the existence of *strong support industries*. The same may be said about a number of specialist service firms, such as geotechnical consultants and environmental scientists, which frequently cooperate with consulting engineers.

Inasmuch as prime contractors not only work with engineering consultancies, but also hire them, these firms also act as *demanding clients*. The same role is frequently played by Australia's large mining houses. In certain niches of the economy, Australia boasts large-scale and highly sophisticated demand – such as enormous mining projects in remote and trying locations or the challenging deep-water conditions of the North-West Shelf oil and gas fields – that requires engineering consultants to come up with new solutions.

The same effect has been ascribed to the *fierce rivalry* that exists in the domestic market, including foreign-owned operators, many of whom have become insiders owing to their long-term presence in Australia.

Finally, Australia has provided favourable *factors* in the form of highly competent (and comparatively low-cost) professional engineers produced by the nation's universities. The same institutions, with special funding from the Commonwealth Government and private sponsors, have also provided world-class research in select areas, such as the Pyrometallurgy Research Centre and the Julius Kruttschnitt Mineral Research Centre (both within The University of Queensland) and the A.J. Parker Cooperative Research Centre for Hydrometallurgy. Generally, the Australian mining sector – which accounts for more than one third of the world's minerals R&D (Roberts, 2006) – has spawned significant engineering-related knowledge.

At a broader level, the industry may have also benefited from its distinct policy framework, or rather the lack thereof. By virtue of its niche status, it has escaped government attention and may have thrived at home and abroad by avoiding the protectionist policies that tended to shape the 'administrative heritage' of so many other industries in Australia (Chapter 3).

While the favourable conditions of the Australian national diamond helped spur the development of competitive advantages in local (and foreign-owned) companies, the leveraging of these advantages in foreign markets was also assisted by a set of facilitating conditions.

Facilitating Conditions

Transferability

The most generic enabler of internationalisation is the industry's knowledge-intensity. Contrary to tangible resources, knowledge can be reused, which allows for economies of scope from the international transfer of expertise in planning, design and project management. Competitive advantages of such a nature are transferable in codified form, such as design blueprints or proprietary methodologies, or through staff secondments.

By virtue of being an intermediate service, delivered to businesses rather than individual consumers, consulting engineering also faces fewer pressures for responsiveness to country-specific characteristics.[12] In industries such as retailing, competitors need to be very mindful of cultural differences among consumers as well as differences in retail legislation, distribution systems, etc. By contrast, an intermediate service such as consulting engineering is relatively unencumbered by cultural and institutional differences across countries that need to be accommodated and thus stymie the transferability of existing knowledge (Roberts, 2001).

Owing to the technical nature of consulting engineering, there is also a lesser need to respond to country-specific idiosyncrasies compared to other professional services. For instance, engineering lacks the strong creative element, with its ties to local culture and tradition, that renders advertising skills partly immobile. It also lacks the strong institutional roots of professions such as law or auditing (Nachum, 1999: 137). As a result, engineering capabilities built up in one country tend to be applicable elsewhere. The comments by Robert Hopton, director of Woodhead International, are instructive:

> Our skill base and what we have to offer is eminently transferable and sellable... I think the key to our overseas marketing has been building on what we've already done... Like many other Australian companies, the 2000 Olympics in Sydney attracted a lot of attention for us. We were involved in the design of the refurbishment and extensions to the Sydney International Airport and several luxury hotels. We're currently working on a number of Olympic-related sites. The Chinese were very impressed with what we, as Australians, did with the Olympics, and this exposure has led to opportunities... [Moreover,] our local work on the Sydney International Airport and, for Ansett, Cairns Airport and Coolangatta was very successful. That's now led to projects like the three we are currently working on: Quingdao Luiting Airport in China, Changi Terminal Three in Singapore, and the Hong Kong Airport. (ACIF, 2002c: 3)

The innate transferability of consulting engineering capabilities is also evident in the breadth and diversity of countries serviced by engineering MNCs. For instance, in the financial year 2004/05, GHD carried out work for clients in some 40 countries.

Historically, consulting engineering firms have expanded into culturally and psychologically very distant countries without hesitation, given sufficient demand. For instance, it is well documented that, during the 1970s and 1980s, many Western engineering firms opened their *first* international office in the Middle East, where the flood of petrodollars in the wake of the oil crises sparked ambitious engineering projects. Sharma's (1991) doctoral dissertation highlights the fact that for 64 per cent of all Swedish consulting engineering firms, the first foreign market entered was a developing country, attesting to the nonlocation-bound nature of their competitive advantages.

Secondary Internationalisation

The role of Australia's contractors and mining houses as demanding customers and/or support industries has already been canvassed. These firms also played a more direct role in the internationalisation of the country's engineering consultants, by helping to pave their way into overseas markets. Along with other Australian suppliers and service providers, many engineering consultancies were allowed to piggy-back their initial overseas forays on the international activities of these 'flagship firms' (DFAT, 2002: 79; Rugman and D'Cruz, 2000). For instance, GHD established an office in Chile because 'several Australian mining companies were already there that we thought we could work with'. (ACIF, 2002a: 3)

Niche Industry

Consulting engineering clearly is a niche industry. As a result, (foreign) markets are typically less protected since they do not command the same political attention as mainstream sectors of the economy. In some countries, a lack of local engineering capability even meant that foreign companies were actively encouraged to undertake projects and to establish a local presence.

Limited Risk

Internationalisation was also facilitated by the industry's low capital intensity and the feasibility of exports as an initial market entry mode. Both meant that barriers to foreign market entry and the attendant risks were limited, allowing firms to try their luck and to gradually increase their financial commitments if their initial forays met with success.

In the academic literature, the process of international expansion is typically conceptualised in stages, from arms-length transactions to the establishment of full-scale operations in foreign markets (Johanson and Vahlne, 1977). While the phenomenon has been studied almost exclusively in the context of manufacturing industries, the model appears to fit the experiences of consulting engineers in the early stages of internationalisation (Roberts, 1999).

The project-nature of engineering and the mobility of engineering professionals lend themselves to opportunistic exports to new markets, although that ability is decreasing because of client and host government pressures to provide services locally. Exports are carried out through temporary project offices, typically staffed by expatriates from the home country (or third countries) who may work in conjunction with some locally-employed personnel. A project office may also receive extensive remote support from sister units in other countries.

By undertaking minor export projects in a new country, a firm has the opportunity to familiarise itself with the market and its competition. This helps to arrive at an informed decision as to whether to build a more permanent presence by investing in (wholly- or part-owned) subsidiaries. The internationalisation of Melbourne-based Meinhardt Group mirrors such a gradual, risk-reducing approach. The firm's strategy has been to secure export contracts in targeted countries, thereby accumulating local knowledge with the long-term aim of establishing permanent offices (Way, 2004b).

Aid Projects

While the industry appears to have thrived from government neglect, the Commonwealth Government's foreign aid program, a significant portion of which goes towards infrastructure projects, has had a direct and significant impact on the internationalisation of Australian firms. Much of that assistance is tied to products and services provided by Australian-based companies. As a result, local consulting engineers face only limited competition when bidding for government aid contracts, which has led some critics to describe the aid segment as an 'artificial market' (Reina and Tulacz, 2001: 67). For some Australian companies, aid projects still account for a sizeable portion of international work, financed not only by the Australian government but also multilateral institutions such as the World Bank and the Asian Development Bank, whose projects are open to firms from donor countries only.

A number of countries have significant aid programs that favour their consulting engineering firms. In particular, the Japanese government has been a generous donor for decades and a significant portion of the country's assistance consists of (tied) construction aid (Raftery et al., 1998). Unlike their Australian counterparts, however, Japanese engineering consultants have failed to use aid-funded projects as a springboard to establish a *bona fide* presence in international markets. According to Japan's main consulting engineering body, the overseas activities of its members still consist overwhelmingly of development projects funded by the government and aid organisations, with only five per cent of firms' international revenues being derived from non-aid clients (Engineering Consulting Firms Association, Japan 2003).

CONCLUSION

The consulting engineering industry is unquestionably one of the bright spots in Australia's industry portfolio. Apart from its impressive growth at home, the industry has also very successfully internationalised. Income from overseas business has grown from seven per cent of total income in 1993/94 to some 23 per cent in 2002/03 (ACEA, 2004a: 4). Much of this international success is due to the industry's large firms, which collectively account for more than 90 per cent of overseas income, most of it through subsidiary sales. The disproportionate number of Australian-owned entries among the world's largest engineering consultancies provides further evidence that the country is 'punching above her weight' in this industry.

The industry's success is founded on a fortuitous convergence of factors that favoured the building of competitive advantages in the domestic market, and subsequently facilitated the exploitation of these advantages in overseas markets. Porter-style locational advantages – in the form of capable support industries, demanding customers, auspicious factor conditions and strong industry rivalry – provided pressures and opportunities for the building of competitive advantage in the form of proprietary knowledge.

While the Porter 'diamond' provides insight into industry dynamics, a fundamental criticism of the model is its lack of appreciation of the role of MNCs. Locally-owned MNCs are likely to compensate for local deficiencies by harnessing foreign advantages, while the local subsidiaries of foreign-owned firms may help to create the favourable conditions that give rise to home-grown MNCs (Rugman and Verbeke, 1993; Myles Shaver and Flyer, 2000). Our analysis of the Australian consulting engineering industry seems to support such criticism. Australia's locational advantages attracted significant foreign investment, with numerous overseas MNCs establishing subsidiaries 'down under'. Many of these subsidiaries later assumed 'centre of excellence' responsibilities within their group and now regularly transfer their specialist capabilities to sister units throughout the region and beyond. These foreign-owned subsidiaries contribute to Australia's balance of payments by way of exports but their presence also strengthens the local 'diamond' by enhancing competition, serving as capable suppliers and acting as demanding customers to Australian second-tier consultants, as well as helping to finance advanced factors such as research institutions and industry associations.

While locational advantages allowed Australian and foreign operators to hone their capabilities in the local market, another set of enabling conditions helped them to exploit these capabilities in overseas markets. Most importantly, existing capabilities were eminently transferable for they required only negligible adaptation to overseas host markets. Firms internationalised by harnessing their existing relationships with Australian flagship MNCs, and by taking advantage of comparatively open foreign markets, the feasibility of relatively low-risk entry modes, and the Commonwealth Government's aid program. The last item would seem to vindicate Porter's critics (Cartwright, 1993; Yetton et al., 1992). His view of the role of government allows little scope for direct intervention. In the case of the Australian consulting engineering industry, the government's aid program was instrumental in many firms' initial entry into foreign markets.

In conclusion, locational advantages and facilitating conditions were important but did not guarantee success. They merely provided pressures and incentives for the entrepreneurial acts of Australian consulting engineers. Unencumbered by the dominant administrative heritage that weighed on more established industries, these companies rose to the challenge and took full advantage of the opportunities they encountered.

Appendix 11.1: Profiles of the five largest (Australian-owned) consulting engineering MNCs

SKM (Sinclair Knight Merz)	
Founded:	Early 1950s (Merz) and 1964 (Sinclair & Knight). Companies merged in 1996 to form SKM.
International Offices:	Chile, Fiji, Hong Kong (China,) Indonesia, Malaysia, New Zealand, Philippines, Singapore, Thailand, United Arab Emirates, UK
Total Staff:	4,700
GHD (Gutteridge Haskins Davey)	
Founded:	1928
International Offices:	Chile, China, Egypt, Indonesia, Malaysia, New Zealand, Philippines, Qatar, United Arab Emirates, USA, Vietnam
Total Staff:	4,000
Connell Wagner	
Founded:	1956 (John Connell & Associates), earlier origins in the 1930s.
International Offices:	China, Hong Kong (China), Indonesia, Malaysia, New Zealand, Singapore, Thailand, UK
Total Staff:	2,200
Meinhardt Group	
Founded:	1955
International Offices:	China, Hong Kong (China), India, Indonesia, Malaysia, New Zealand, Pakistan, Philippines, Singapore, Thailand, United Arab Emirates, UK, USA, Vietnam,
Total Staff:	1,800
SMEC (Snowy Mountains Engineering Corporation)	
Founded:	1970 established by the Australian Government to preserve the technical skills (hydro-power, roads, bridges and other infrastructure) assembled for the Snowy Mountains Scheme (1949 to 1974). Corporatised in 1989 and privatised in 1993 by sale to staff.
International Offices:	Bangladesh, Cambodia, China, Hong Kong (China), India, Indonesia, Kazakhstan, Malaysia, Mongolia, Pakistan, Papua New Guinea, Philippines, Tanzania, Tonga, United Arab Emirates, Vietnam
Total Staff:	1,400

Source: Company websites

NOTES

1. Most engineering consultants, like other professional service providers, also offer a wide range of 'non-core' services.
2. For instance, the quality of financial advice may only be assessable years after the service was purchased. The quality of a bridge designed to withstand a '100-year flood' may never be tested during its lifetime.
3. Conclusions based on ENR rankings are indicative only since they include contractors who participate on the basis of their consulting engineering revenues as opposed to their construction revenues.
4. The 'international market' as quoted by ENR is a somewhat arbitrary concept. For instance, when a US consulting engineering firm wins a contract in Germany, the international market increases by the corresponding value; had that contract been secured by a German firm, the international market would have remained unchanged.
5. This division of labour resembles that of other professional services such as accounting, management consulting or law (Davis et al., 1993; Lowendahl, 1997).
6. These were: Sinclair Knight Merz, GHD, *Maunsell Australia*, Connell Wagner, *Hatch Associates*, *Kellogg Brown & Root, Parsons Brinckerhoff Australia, URS Australia*, Cardno, *Arup Australasia, Hyder Consulting*, Coffey Geosciences, Norman Disney & Young, *Golder Associates*, Snowy Mountains Engineering Corporation, *MWH Australia*, Brown Consulting, Robert Bird Group, Douglas Partners and Wood & Grieve Engineers (subsidiaries of *foreign-owned* MNCs in italics).
7. The distinction between subsidiary sales and exports is fraught with difficulty since many subsidiary sales contain a significant element of intra-firm exports in the form of personnel transfers or remote support from the parent or subsidiaries in other countries.
8. In view of information asymmetries and the difficulties in ensuring service quality and protecting proprietary knowledge, contractual forms of market entry, such as licensing, are generally not feasible in this industry (Dunning, 1989).
9. Inexplicably, the Meinhardt Group does not feature among the 'largest' consulting engineering firms in ACEA's list.
10. SFOCEA's Top 100 consultancies contain only 11 entries from industrialising (Taiwan, Brazil, Korea) or developing countries (India, China, Egypt, Lebanon), the largest of which is ranked 52nd.
11. This element of Porter's 'diamond' was originally entitled 'firm strategy, structure and rivalry'. It represents a catch-all category comprising a nation's industry structure, predominant firm strategies, social norms and business practices. The issue of firm rivalry in an industry is typically accorded pre-eminence among these numerous variables (Grant, 1991).
12. We stress that whereas there is a lesser need for *country-specific* responsiveness, engineering services are extensively customised to individual clients' demands and/or (logical, geological, ecological, climatic) site conditions.

PART III

Firm Cases

Part III: Firm Cases

Firm cases are the weft to the warp of the surveys and industry studies discussed in Parts I and II. Only at the firm level do we see strategy in process. Management has to assess the competitive environment and decide how best to allocate the firm's resources. These are matters of judgement. The future cannot be known, information on the present is imperfect, and all the fallibilities of group decision-making come into play. As we have already seen, firms cannot escape the organisational constraints of their administrative heritage. Those firms which against the odds consistently make good decisions or learn quickly from their mistakes survive and prosper; those which fail to do so sooner or later lose their identity. Globalisation raises the stakes. Firms which take on this challenge and internationalise may put everything at risk. Yet those which seek to defend a domestic market position are likely to be outflanked by more battle-hardened rivals. The Australian economy is no longer a safe place to hide.

For all their richness, the firm cases are also idiosyncratic and intractable to simple generalisation. Especially in the case of large organisations, one needs to understand each one in detail and observe it over a long time before the pattern of decision-making and the interaction of personalities and interests can be identified with any confidence. This requires patience and dedication to read beyond the sanitised information contained in annual reports and media releases. If firm studies and cases are no longer the bedrock of management research, they do at least serve as an antidote to excessive quantification.

As in the case of industry studies, however, there arises the problem of selectivity. Hundreds of cases are worthy of study. Space restricts us to nine. One criterion of choice was that cases relate in more depth to one of the industry studies of Part II. Thus Foster's (Chapter 15) is a leading firm in the wine industry (Chapter 10), TNT (Chapter 18) (was) a leader in shipping and logistics (Chapter 8), Westfield (Chapter 19) in retailing (Chapter 9) and Macquarie (Chapter 20) in banking (Chapter 7). However, overall the firm cases are more representative of the manufacturing sector: Aspro-Kiwi in consumer goods and pharmaceuticals (Chapter 13), BHP Billiton in resources and steel (Chapter 14), Foster's in beer and wine (Chapter 15),

Coca-Cola Amatil (CCA) in beverages (Chapter 16) and conglomerate Pacific Dunlop (Chapter 17) in almost everything.

There is some bias towards older firms. Burns Philp (Chapter 12), Aspro-Kiwi, BHP, Foster's (formerly Carlton and United Breweries), CCA (formerly British Tobacco) and Pacific Dunlop (formerly Dunlop) were all well-established businesses before the 1950s. Nevertheless, their trajectories of internationalisation were very different. Whereas Burns Philp, Aspro and Kiwi were Australian pioneers of foreign direct investment, BHP, Foster's, CCA and Pacific Dunlop remained profitably sheltered behind the tariff wall until the policy reforms of the 1970s (Chapter 2). Ironically the firms which had long established their international beachheads were unable to consolidate their competitiveness, while the newcomers went through some painful learning experiences. BHP emerged as an international leader in resources and mining; Pacific Dunlop and TNT both enjoyed early success and then disintegrated; CCA has struggled with the constraints of being a franchisee and Foster's is still learning. It is a very mixed bag. More impressive is the performance of two relative newcomers. Westfield first ventured into offshore shopping centres in 1977 but not until the 1990s did it begin to establish itself as an international player; Macquarie Bank's internationalisation has been a phenomenon of the twenty-first century. Both illustrate the logic of being very competitive in niche markets.

12. Burns Philp

Howard Dick and Paul Evans

Burns Philip & Co. Ltd (BP) stands out as one of the pioneer firms to incorporate in Australia and do most of its business offshore. By the early 1920s it had extensive shipping, trading, agency, insurance, copra and pearling interests throughout the mainly British colonies of the South Pacific and as far west as Java and Singapore, a subsidiary in San Francisco and a London office. BP was Australia's one great colonial company with a solid reputation as a 'blue chip' firm. By the mid-1960s, however, it had clearly lost its way. The old businesses were contracting but new businesses were not being identified. A belated quest for new directions delivered mixed results and did not offset declining earnings. In 1984 a new CEO was appointed who sought to transform the company from a 'South Seas trader' to a global food and yeast group focused in the United States. BP built turnover but in the face of a ruthless price war with incumbent McCormick & Co. failed to achieve profitability. Nevertheless, in 1997 BP still ranked as Australia's 59th largest listed company with a valuation of $1.4 billion (Wood, 1997). It soon turned out that this valuation was wildly unrealistic. By the end of the year the company was valued at around just $100 million. As one journalist asked, 'So how did Burns Philip, the old South Seas trading House with its colourful history, its impeccably conservative credentials and painstakingly built global operations, go completely and hopelessly off the rails?' (Wood, 1997)

In fact BP survived this near-death experience. New main shareholder Graeme Hart, who had lost a fortune on his investment, put more funds into the business to keep it solvent. Although already heavily geared, he audaciously raised the funds for a $2.3 billion takeover in April 2003 of struggling food conglomerate Goodman-Fielder, making BP a major player in the Australasian food industry. After floating off most of this stake, he then took control of New Zealand pulp and paper producer, Carter Holt Harvey. Burns Philp thereby re-emerged as a force in Australasian business, albeit no longer a multinational.

ORIGINS

BP traces back to 1876 when James Burns, a young Scot who operated a trading store in the North Queensland port of Townsville, took into partnership Robert Philp (Buckley and Klugman, 1981). Burns then moved to Sydney and rapidly developed their shipping and trading interests in North Queensland and Torres Strait to the point where the partners were soon predominant. Burns, Philp & Co. Ltd was incorporated in 1883. During the 1880s the firm built up a substantial interest in the pearling industry based on Thursday Island and began its expansion into Papua. In 1896 BP acquired its first steamer to trade to Papua and New Guinea and quickly extended its shipping and trading interests to the New Hebrides, Fiji and Tonga. A London office was opened in 1901 and in the following year a steamship line was inaugurated to Java and Singapore with a particular interest in the refrigerated meat trade. Towards the end of that decade, copra plantations were developed in the Solomon Islands. By 1920 when the subsidiary Burns Philp (South Sea) Co. Ltd was floated off with a capital of £750,000, BP had built a vast commercial empire in which its original merchandise business had grown into a network of trade stores throughout the South Pacific from Papua New Guinea via the Solomons, Gilbert & Ellice Islands and New Hebrides to Fiji, Samoa and Tonga. These were integrated with deepsea and inter-island shipping, lucrative agencies, insurance, and extensive interests in copra and marine products, the staple exports of the South Pacific (Buckley and Klugman, 1983). James Burns himself evolved from merchant-adventurer to establishment figure. He was also long-serving chairman of the Bank of North Queensland, the North Queensland Insurance Company and the New South Wales Mortgage, Land and Agency Company and director of various other firms; he was appointed for life to the Legislative Council of New South Wales in 1908 and was knighted in 1917 (NSW, 2006).

The death of founder and entrepreneur James Burns in 1923 at the age of about 77 brought to an end several decades of relentless expansion and diversification. Insurance was the last significant line of business to be expanded before his death (Buckley and Klugman, 1983: 152). Facing limited opportunities for expansion in familiar territory, in the 1920s BP consolidated its existing lines of business, harvested the profits and began to invest more of those profits in a portfolio of government bonds and equities. These strong reserves enabled the company to ride out the depression of the 1930s and the enormous disruption of the Pacific War (1941-45). The trend towards 'passive investments' became even more apparent in the two decades after 1942 when the ultra-conservative autocrat 'Joe' Mitchell took over as General Manager (Buckley and Klugman, 1983: 106, 359). The company had no adequate response to postwar pressures of rising costs in company had no adequate response to postwar pressures of rising costs in shipping, falling copra prices and increasing competition in both wholesale and retail trades. Management ossified. By the mid-1960s the company was being chaired and managed by octogenarians clinging to the last remnants of a colonial world.

Change began cautiously in 1967 when 70-year-old P.T.W. Black took over as general manager from 83-year-old Joe Mitchell and David Burns took over the chairmanship from his father (Sykes, 1992). Black sold off the last deepsea ships in 1970, the year of Fijian independence. There followed the independence of Papua New Guinea in 1975 and Vanuatu (formerly New Hebrides) in 1980. Meanwhile BP had embarked on a diversification spree that led it into new fields such as hardware, building materials, automotive, food and beverage, cables, toys, lighting, packaging, electrical goods and iron ore mines. Sykes (1992: 86) depicted it as 'one of Australia's messiest conglomerates'.

NEW HORIZONS

By the early 1980s BP was still a 'blue chip' company but its jumble of subsidiaries and activities had no core business and no obvious future. In 1981 net profit was $20 million on $700 million in assets by book value; two years later earnings had fallen to $5 million while the share price slumped accordingly (Sykes, 1992). Merger with rival island trading firm W.R. Carpenter Holdings, founded by a former BP ship's master, was explored on and off as a means of consolidating the offshore interests but the controlling families could not agree on a mutually acceptable structure (AFR, 2/8/83). Carpenters were taken over in 1983 but BP's share register was better defended with more than 40 per cent of holdings controlled by Chairman David Burns through family, friends and cross-shareholdings (Sykes, 1992: 86). For example, Burns Philp held almost half of QBE Insurance, of which David Burns was also chairman, and QBE in turn held 11 per cent of BP.

Outside directors cut the Gordian knot by insisting on new blood and new ideas at the top (Sykes, 1992). In 1984, Andrew Turnbull, the dynamic Scottish engineer who since 1981 had been BP's Australian manager, was elevated to CEO. Having come out of General Electric (Australia), Turnbull had a grasp of strategy and quickly decided that BP had no future in the South Pacific and that residual assets there should be sold off as part of a ten-year restructure. Instead he sought to build up a core local business in retail hardware distribution through BBC Hardware, which through acquisition had begun to build up a profitable Australia-wide network. He also identified a core competency in yeast-making through the now wholly owned food subsidiary Mauri Bros. and bought into yeast-makers in the United States.

Then in 1988 BP ventured more recklessly into the spices, herbs and seasonings business by taking over two minor US firms, followed in 1992 by acquisition of Durkee French from Reckitt and Colman (Sykes, 1992). German yeast maker Karl Ostmann GmbH was added in 1994. The aim was by 1990 to increase BP's share of the global herbs and spices market from two to ten per cent and of yeast from 14 to 30 per cent, primarily by acquisition (Wood, 1997).

Turnbull's strategy was to look for niche markets in which BP could be market leader without competing directly with 'global giants' (Sykes, 1992: 88). In fact BP's aggressive price-cutting to gain shelf space in United States supermarkets in herbs, spices and seasonings provoked just the sort of competition that it had sought to avoid from global market leader, McCormick & Company Inc. (McCormick, 2006). In the face of tough competition in the United States, BP's efforts to transform itself into a global specialist in herbs, spices and yeast absorbed much more capital than expected, necessitating disposal of all 'non-core assets' (SMH, 5/5/94; Wood, 1997). In 1995 even the profitable BBC Hardware chain, which accounted for a quarter of earnings, was sold off for $446 million.[1] This was a serious mistake. Under management of Howard Smith (Chapter 8), BBC turned into a bonanza, whereas BP's spices and yeast divisions failed to return a profit.

Meanwhile a nasty distraction had emerged over BP's trustee business. In 1983, without carrying out proper due diligence, Burns Philp Trustee Co. became trustee for Estate Mortgage, whose six trusts were frozen in 1990. Several months later Burns Philp Trustee Co. itself was placed in liquidation, triggering a claim on behalf of the 52,000 unit-holders against the parent company for $1 billion (Sykes, 1994: ch. 11). Reuben Lew, manager of Estate Mortgage, was later convicted and jailed. Chairman David Burns, grandson of the founder and main shareholder, believed that BP had a moral obligation to make an *ex gratia* payment but the board refused to accept legal liability for the collapse, obliging him to step aside. There ensued seven years of unpleasant litigation that badly tarnished BP's once eminent reputation and undermined its share price.

In 1997 matters came quickly to a head. In May the loss-making spice business was put up for sale with an estimated book value of $850 million, leaving BP to focus on the better yeast business. This was accompanied by the retirement of managing director Ian Clack, who took responsibility for the debacle (Age, 20/5/97). In the following month New Zealand entrepreneur, Graeme Hart, bought 19.9 per cent of BP at $2.50 a share, believing it to be a sound long-term investment. In July, BP finally agreed to settle the messy Estate Mortgage claim for $116 million, and Tom Degnan took over as Managing Director. On 22 September, Graeme Hart joined the board. Two days later BP wrote off $700 million from the book value of its herbs and spices division, breaching its borrowing covenants. BP shares went into free fall and by November were worth just 20 cents (Age, 8/11/97). By late 1998 the share price was as low as 3.5 cents. The company teetered on the verge of liquidation as assets were sold off, including the palatial Bridge Street headquarters (Australian, 10/10/97). Graeme Hart suffered an enormous financial loss and became the target of media ridicule.

LAZARUS

BP's new majority shareholder and chairman, Graeme Hart (born 1955), was a self-made billionaire from New Zealand. His business career had begun humbly as a tow truck driver, then panel beater. In 1976 with modest capital he established Hart's Printing Company located in Auckland and ran the firm successfully for several years before divesting (BRW, 17/7/03). He then pulled off a series of risky and increasingly large takeovers, beginning with privatisation of the New Zealand Government Printing Office in 1989 and followed by book and stationery chain, Whitcoulls, in 1991. The former deal marked his emergence from the ranks of successful small businessmen onto the national business scene. The printing office had a book value of NZ$38 million, but Hart secured it for $20 million and managed to save $1 million in interest when a dispute over contracts allowed payment to be deferred for several months (BRW, 17/7/03). Deferred payment thereafter became a regular feature in Graeme Hart deals. At the time of the printing office purchase, his holding company Rank Group had total assets of just NZ$8.5 million, yet he managed to secure loans of about NZ$25 million to back his first leveraged buyout (BRW, 17/7/03). With this acquisition, the Rank Group had swallowed a company three times its size.

Hart's move in mid-1997 to become the leading shareholder in BP was his first significant venture outside the small New Zealand economy with its very limited growth potential. Almost immediately he seemed to have destroyed the fortune accumulated over the previous 20 years. Nevertheless, Hart saw BP as a vehicle and showed himself determined to persevere with restructuring and divestures until it turned into a profitable company. By May 2002 the share price had gradually risen back to 74 cents, still well below his entry price of around $2.50. Nevertheless, Hart took advantage of the low share price to further increase his stake to a 54 per cent majority interest (AFR, 17/2/06).

In 2003 BP astounded the market by a $2.3 billion hostile takeover of food brands conglomerate Goodman Fielder (GF). GF was more than twice the size of Burns Philp in terms of sales revenue (Table 12.1). Moreover, at its heavily discounted share price BP was already highly geared with a debt/

equity ratio of 400 per cent. GF's weakness was that its enormous portfolio of brands was heavily concentrated in the Australasian market and under-performing: GF's ratio of net profit to sales was only 4.7 per cent compared with 11 per cent for BP. In a 2002 briefing paper BP stated that the rationale for acquiring GF was to acquire businesses that would expand its international food ingredients interests, in particular yeast, because GF was a major force in the Australasian bread industry. Nevertheless, bread and baking was only a minor part of the GF portfolio. Most GF brands had no synergies whatsoever with any BP business. Analysts were sceptical. Rowan Wilke from Goodman Sachs JBWere commented that 'nothing in the data released to date has changed our initial view that we struggle to see major value creation from the proposed deal (SMH, 28/10/05).

Table 12.1: Comparison of financial indicators, BP and GF, 2002

Indicator	Burns Philp	Goodman Fielder
	$m	$m
Sales Revenue	1,361	2,958.0
Cost of Goods Sold	731	1,891.0
Gross Profit	631	1,066.0
Net Profit	146	140.0
Net profit/sales rev. (%)	11	4.7
Earnings Per Share	17.3	12.8
Total Assets	2,365	2,409.0
Total Liabilities	1,885	1,314.0
Debt/equity ratio (%)	398	119.0

Source: BP (2002), GF (2003)

Nevertheless, Hart was astute enough to see that he could buy a significant part of the Australasian food industry at a modest price with enormous scope for restructuring both GF and BP. There was also the consideration that revenues from food are fairly stable and can therefore carry more debt than other industries, allowing a longer period of time for creating value. What astounded the market was not GF's vulnerability but BP's ability to finance the deal. By rights a struggling company having a 400 per cent debt/equity ratio was not a good credit risk for a $2.3 billion takeover. Early in 2003 Hart had launched a NZ$212 million corporate bond, in effect a junk bond note of sub-investment grade (BRW, 17/7/03). Perpetual Investments sold out of the stock when the GF takeover was announced because of concern at the extremely high gearing. Yet Credit Suisse First Boston extended a loan of

$1.3 billion to supplement a series of smaller bond issues in the US and New Zealand. Their willingness to do so had more to do with Graeme Hart than Burns Philp. Hart had a track record of hostile takeovers and of turning around poorly performing firms. This had been shown by his acquisition of the New Zealand Printing Office (1989) and then Whitcoulls (bought in 1991 for NZ$71 million and resold to United States Office Products in 1996 for NZ$316 million) (BRW, 17/7/03). Institutional investors at least did not underestimate Hart, noting his reputation for meticulous planning, risk-taking, tenacity and sometimes extraordinary luck.

BP moved on GF at the right time, when debt was still cheap, and then improved its value through cost reductions. GF headquarters staff of 500 was slashed and dozens of mills were sold (BRW, 26/6/03). The next step was to re-bundle the mature baking, spreads and oils businesses of the combined BP-GF portfolio and float them off with assets of Rank Group's New Zealand Dairy Foods and about $1.1 billion of debt as a new Goodman Fielder entity (AFR, 27/10/05). BP sold 80 per cent of the new firm and recouped $2.1 million from the public offering, not much less than the purchase price 30 months previously (AFR, 20/12/05). The Uncle Tobys snackfood division was kept out of the float and at a higher price-earnings ratio sold to Nestlé in May 2006 for $890 million (SMH, 24/5/06).

In 2004 BP argued that it is not geographically constrained: 'we're not just focused on New Zealand and Australia… we have demonstrated to our satisfaction, and to the world, that we are well capable of running a global business' (SMH, 9/8/04). Nevertheless, in July 2004 Hart sold Burns Philp's global yeast and herbs and spices business to Associated British Foods for A$1.9 billion (BRW, 29/7/04). This finally realised the decision taken in 1997 to cut away former CEO Andrew Turnbull's ill-starred international ventures. The subsequent play with Goodman Fielder was confined to Australasia. With the funds released back to Hart through the GF float, his Rank Group moved to acquire a controlling stake in the New Zealand forestry, paper and building products group Carter Holt Harvey for NZ$1.7 billion, subsequently building its stake to 90 per cent with entitlement to compulsory acquisition of minority shareholdings (AFR, 18-19/3/06). This move also suggested that internationalisation was more aspiration than reality and raised the question as to whether the new BP retained international capabilities, although certainly having the funds to make a substantial international investment. On completion of the sale of the Uncle Tobys division and the intended sale of the New Zealand snack business Bluebird, BP expected to have cash funds of between $2.5 and 3 billion (SMH, 24/5/06). The group had a demonstrated ability to borrow a multiple of this and, according to CEO Tom Degnan, was looking at target companies in Australasia, North America and the UK.

CONCLUSION

As a case of internationalisation, Burns Philp goes against the grain. It embarked on internationalisation – or at least regionalisation – at a very early stage in its life cycle. By the 1880s it was already a force in northern Australia and by the early twentieth century throughout the South Pacific and as far away as Southeast Asia and California. By the 1920s it was a leading 'blue-chip' firm. If any firm had the capabilities to become Australia's first real multinational, BP was the one. Yet it did not do so. After the 1920s its businesses did not extend their geographic reach and by the 1960s could be seen to be in gradual retreat. The momentum was lost. After 1984 new management sought to reinvent the company, joining in the outflow of hopeful Australian FDI, but the strategy was ill-conceived and all but destroyed a proud company within little more than a decade. Today, under an aggressive new majority owner-chairman, BP has been restored to viability, even if its footprint scarcely extends beyond Australasia.

What can be learned from BP's vicissitudes? First, that its periods of success have coincided with the dominance of two entrepreneurs, first (Sir) James Burns from foundation to 1923, then Graeme Hart since 1997. Both men displayed remarkable business acumen, cautious yet aggressive at the same time. During the intervening period the company lacked either the drive or the strategic flair to consolidate its firm-specific advantages. In short, as management literature has come back to recognising, entrepreneurship matters.

The second lesson is an insight in to strategy. Between the 1920s and 1980s BP was unable to identify its very considerable international capabilities and to leverage from them to create new businesses with a broader and less vulnerable geographic base. To the extent that BP was successful in establishing or developing new businesses over this period, it was back in the home market of Australasia, most notably in insurance through QBE (Chapter 7). When Andrew Turnbull as the new broom of the mid-1980s sought to re-internationalise BP, he made the serious strategic error of selling a very good domestic business in BBC Hardware to fund international businesses that were still speculative and hungry for cash. This ignored the basic strategic wisdom of ensuring that there is a sound domestic base to fund international expansion (Menzer, 2004). Graeme Hart's reconstruction of BP's domestic base therefore looks to be sound strategy.

Finally, BP illustrates the tenacity of the firm as a legal entity, independent of personnel, business activities and strategy. The connection with the venerable 'blue-chip' firm extends not much further than the name. Graeme Hart's new BP is less a business manager than an investment vehicle. Its current market capitalisation of around $2 billion depends less on vehicle. Its current market capitalisation of around $2 billion depends less on earnings than on expectations of the next entrepreneurial play (AFR, 28/4/06). The disadvantage of this structure was the reporting obligations of the public company. In August 2006 the parent Rank Group offered $1.3 billion to buy out the 42 per cent minority interest and then delist the 123-year-old public company (Age, 23/8/06; AFR, 7/9/06).

NOTES

1. This was the second time that BP had sold out of Australian retailing. The Penney's Ltd chain of retail stores in Queensland and rural NSW had been sold to G.J. Coles in 1956 (Fleming, et al. 2004: 89-90).

13. 'Aspro' and 'Kiwi'

David Merrett

Although Australia's industrialisation occurred behind a tariff wall, two manufacturing firms, Nicholas 'Aspro' and 'Kiwi' Polish,[1] were precocious in being 'born global'. Within a decade of their beginnings in the early twentieth century, both did more business outside Australia than within. Each began exporting but quickly moved to establish production facilities in their major markets in the northern hemisphere. Both entered emerging and related industries, Nicholas in pharmaceuticals and Kiwi in home care products, at a time when a cornucopia of new, cheap, mass-produced, branded products poured onto world markets, the result of developments in the chemical industry. Even before World War II both firms had developed global brands by selling their products in more than a hundred countries.

For decades each firm was able successfully to challenge the brands of their international competitors in pain relievers and shoe care products. They challenged them in extended product lines that included other medical and veterinary products, packaged food, disinfectants and cleaning products and so on. However, their competitive advantages waned over time. Neither firm was able to produce another product that enjoyed the success of its original brand. They lacked the resources to undertake the necessary R&D and to advertise on the scale required to launch new products nationally or internationally. Increasingly they struggled to maintain market share and the brand value of their existing products in competition with the likes of the American pharmaceutical firms such as Merck, Sharpe & Dohme, American Home Products, Sterling Drugs, Proctor & Gamble, Colgate-Palmolive, and Britain's Unilever and Reckitt & Colman.[2] Nicholas and Kiwi sought respite by merging in 1981. However, this move provided only short-term protection. In 1984 a leading US competitor in the fast-moving packaged goods business, Consolidated Foods (beneficial owner Sara Lee Corporation), paid a handsome premium to acquire the brands that had been the lifeblood of the two companies.

The experience of Nicholas Kiwi and its forebears tell us that it was possible to become a successful multinational based in Australia. These two firms both did so for 80 years. Was the end inevitable? Nicholas Kiwi's fate in the 1980s was similar to that of dozens of small- to medium-sized firms around the world in similar types of industries that relied on increasingly expensive science and marketing. Nicholas Kiwi was swallowed up in a decade of massive consolidation in the pharmaceutical and home products industries by merger and acquisition (Nohria et al., 2002: 266-70; Wasserstein, 1998: 513-18; Woodhead, 2003; Hast, 1991; Derdak, 1988).

COUNTRY-BASED ADVANTAGE

At birth being Australian was a crucial advantage to both firms. The country's involvement in World War I provided the circumstances for a critical breakthrough by each firm. 'Kiwi', whose founder pioneered the combination of shoe polish and a restorative colour stain, was introduced to the Australian market in 1906. Its sales rose steadily to become a leading brand by 1912. It was introduced into Britain in that year with immediate success. Sales of 6,000 gross tins of polish in 1913 equalled all previous Australian sales. However, unexpected demand from Australian and British forces during World War I made it a truly international business (Kiwi, 1951). From 1917 it found another significant market with the United States military. Sales to the armed forces remained an important market throughout.

World War I also provided opportunities to Nicholas. The German chemical firm Bayer, the leading supplier of aspirin, had its trademark suspended by the Australian government. It was there for the taking for any local producer able to meet the required standards of purity. By September 1915 George Nicholas, having synthesised acetylsalicylic acid in a makeshift home laboratory, was deemed to have met the requirements of the British Pharmacopoéia (Kolm, 1988: 656-7; Smith and Barrie, 1976). The trademark propelled the Nicholas family on its way to fame and fortune.[3]

Being an Australian firm, with head offices in Melbourne, eventually consigned both firms to second-tier status within their globalising industries. From a resource-based view of the firm, sustainable competitive advantage is derived from the firm's accumulation of resources whose unique characteristics generate competencies and capabilities that competitors cannot match. These combinations of valuable and scarce inputs provide the basis for efficiency and innovation, allowing firms to constantly reshape industry boundaries and being first to market. In comparative terms, the Australian economy lacked the specialist resources that both firms required, particularly in science and marketing skills. The gap between the industry-specific resources available in Australia and the home countries of their principal competitors, Germany, Britain and the USA, widened over time. Throughout the twentieth century Australia was part of the first world in terms of discretionary consumption but not on the cutting edge in R&D or marketing. Moreover, it lagged behind in the introduction of new media for mass marketing, particularly through radio and television.

OWNERSHIP AND CONTROL

Timing played as important a role as location in the two firms' eventual demise. Both were late starters into their respective industries and lagged behind their international competitors in the race to transform start-up family businesses into modern corporations. They remained controlled by their founding families throughout their existence with successive generations serving as chairmen of directors and holding key executive positions. The organisational architecture necessary to manage a complex multinational was never put in place.

The Nicholas brothers, Alfred and George, dominated the business from its inception until the death of Alfred in 1937 and the retirement of George in 1947. Maurice, son of Alfred, became a director at the time of father's death, and his cousin Hilton, a younger son of George, joined the board in 1947. They were chairman and deputy chairman of Nicholas Australia respectively as late as 1970. Other family members, Arthur and Pat Lightfoot, cousins of Maurice, played important roles in the organisation from the 1930s. Maurice's eldest son, Anthony, also joined the board in 1971. Both he and his uncle Hilton were directors, the latter deputy chairman, of Nicholas Kiwi International (Wall, 1988: 18-20; Smith and Barrie, 1976).

The Kiwi Polish Company was led by four generations of the Ramsay family after the dissolution of the original partnership with Hamilton McKellan in 1912. The founder, William Ramsay, died in 1914. His father, John, who returned to Australia in 1916 after managing the British side of the business, and uncle, James, acted as joint managing directors until John's death in 1924. He was succeeded in this post by his daughter-in-law, Annie. Another William Ramsay of Motherwell in Scotland and a cousin of the Australian William took over management of the British branch from 1916 until 1946. William and Annie's sons, John and (Sir) Thomas, joined the business in 1921 and 1926 respectively. John became managing director in 1928, a position he held until his retirement in 1976. Thomas who had held the post of general manager, joint managing director and managing director, succeeded his brother as chairman. Upon his retirement in 1980 at age 72, Thomas was succeeded by a cousin-in-law, J.O. Wicking (Kiwi, 1951; Langmore, 1988: 328-9; Iverson, 1963: 291; Were: Box 767).

The combination of family ownership and managerial control was not necessarily a source of weakness. What really mattered was the quality of the human capital that the family could provide. The founding Nicholas brothers, the chemist George and administrator Alfred, provided enormous energy and drive through the firm's formative years. However, that impetus had run its course well before Alfred's death in 1937. The brothers, now distant from one another, had become very conservative. Moreover, both were more interested in activities outside the business. Money was siphoned out of the firm, at the cost of foregoing strategic investments, to fund local philanthropic causes and large bequests. Maurice became the next driving force in the organisation, providing leadership and strategic vision of a high order. He drove a more coordinated marketing campaign, including standardising 'Aspro' packaging in 1950, and instigated the policy of diversification. However, he was hamstrung by the legacy of a largely autonomous subsidiary in the UK, the most important source of sales, which the family owned but could not fully control once it had been listed as a public company in 1935. The once trusting relationship between Alfred and George and the UK chairman from 1927 to 1943, George Garcia, had soured badly. Garcia's immediate successors had engaged in highly questionable activities, resulting in their resignation and dismissal. Melbourne continued to struggle, dealing with a subsidiary roughly twice its size.

John and Thomas Ramsay played a similar role in Kiwi Polish that Maurice Nicholas had in his organisation. By the 1930s the brothers had made a positive response to the many challenges facing the firm. They were builders who travelled constantly in search of new opportunities. New factories were opened in France and New Zealand in 1934 and Poland in 1937, the USA in 1948 and Canada soon after. The products of the Australian plant and the five overseas factories were sold in 116 countries (Kiwi, 1951; Were: Box 346). Like Nicholas, Kiwi diversified into many other lines of business through the 1950s and 1960s (Potter, 1972: 117).

STRATEGY AND INTERNATIONAL COMPETITVENESS

The rate at which the two firms could accumulate resources was limited by the nature of their ownership. Kiwi remained a private company until 1967, Nicholas until 1968, obliging them to rely on retained earnings as a source of funds. Their many acquisitions were actually paid for in cash rather than equities.[4] After they were listed on the stock exchange, neither sought large injections of new cash from the public. An authoritative source claimed that the two million new shares offered by Kiwi in 1967 were to provide cash for the vendors of Kiwi Polish. No additional cash was raised until its acquisition by Nicholas International in 1981 (Jobson's, 1969: 273). When Nicholas went public in 1968, it offered only 1.5 million new shares to the public out of a total of 14.4 million (Jobson's, 1969: 357). In 1970 a further 25 million shares were issued to purchase the UK side of the business, half of which were owned by the public (Smith and Barrie, 1976). Thereafter, no further cash was raised from the public (Jobson's, various). These capital raisings had diluted the families' share but did not undermine their ability to determine the fate of the firms. At the time of the acquisition in 1984, the Nicholas family still held 24 per cent and the Ramsay family 19 per cent of the stock (Were: Box 767), with the balance held by other directors, a nominee company representing the staff and the public who had had shares in Aspro-Nicholas.

By the third quarter of the twentieth century, both businesses had evolved from small family concerns to large modern organisations. This transformation resonates with Chandler's (1990) discussion of the creation of organisational capabilities. By the 1950s the multiple activities of production, sales, R&D and administration were located in up-to-date buildings designed for the task. For instance, in the 1950s Nicholas made large investments in research laboratories at Slough in the UK and Burnham Beeches in Melbourne together with a new headquarters in the Melbourne suburb of Chadstone. Both firms had become multi-unit businesses whose operations spanned a large number of countries. The size and complexity of the operations had outgrown the capacity of family members to manage both the day-to-day operations and to make the strategic decisions. Increasingly outside managers were hired with the specialist skills to undertake particular tasks, such as R&D. Both firms evolved into multi-divisional organisations that were organised around geography rather than product. In making these organisational transformations, building up human capital and fine-tuning their management information systems, Nicholas and Kiwi were doing as well as any other firm in Australia at the time (Fleming et al., 2004). The issue is whether their businesses were managed as well as those of their major international rivals. It is difficult to believe that either matched the organisation skills of firms such as Unilever or Proctor & Gamble (Jones, 2005b; Dyer et al., 2004).

To continue to grow and to survive in the longer term, the firms looked to find new markets overseas. Their geographic scope increased after World War II. By the early 1960s Kiwi had increased the number of countries in which it had factories from the five in 1945 to 16, the newcomers including branches and subsidiaries in Singapore/Malaya and East Africa, associated companies in Pakistan and Ireland, packaging operations in Italy and Peru, and licensees and contract manufacturers in Japan, South Africa and Ceylon (Iverson, 1963: 290; Kiwi, 1962: 1). In another 93 countries where it did not own a distribution network, ranging from Iceland to the Falklands, it employed agents (Kiwi, 1962: 52-6). Nicholas also added to its presence outside Australia with factories in Indonesia, the Netherlands, Austria, Spain, India and Pakistan and a number of African countries (Nicholas Australia, 1970).

The ultimate test facing both firms was to generate new products that were as successful as the original brands. They failed. The life of 'Aspro' was extended by changes in packaging and product improvements, culminating with the introduction of a soluble 'Aspro Clear' in 1974. However, the brand was losing market share domestically and internationally even before a new generation of non-aspirin drugs and superior analgesics were released in the 1970s (Derdak, 1988: 623, 700, 708; Mann and Plummer, 1991). By the 1960s 'Aspro' was outsold three to one in the Australian market by 'Vincent APC' (Smith and Barrie, 1976: 143). In the early 1990s, 'Aspro' had only 12 per cent of the analgesic sales through Australian grocery outlets compared to 62 per cent for 'Panadol' produced by Sterling Winthrop (Retail World, 1993: 56, 219). Kiwi fared better with its premium brand, 'Kiwi' shoe care products. It maintained its market share domestically, sharing the Australian market with Reckitt & Colman's 'Nugget' (Edwards, 1982: 43). It claimed to hold second spot in the US market in the early 1960s and a third share of the British market (Were: Box 346). Kiwi pursued a policy of brand extension introducing a wide range of shoe-care products (Kiwi, 1962; Potter, 1972: 117). However, in the early 1960s two-thirds of its revenues came from its polish brands (Were: Box 346), falling just short of the 70 per cent of a single product or 'dominant business' as defined by Rumelt (1974: ch. 1).

Both firms embarked on major diversification programs with only moderate success. Kiwi invested heavily in the food industry in Australia and Britain in the 1950s through acquisition (Kiwi, 1962). In that decade it also acquired 'Bon Ami', a cleaning brand and manufacturer of aerosol sprays (Were: Box 346). Nicholas's diversification strategy was on a far grander and more ambitious scale. The growing ability of drug companies to produce a growing array of medicines targeted at specific medical conditions tapped a new market for healthcare products. Expenditure on prescription or ethical drugs quickly outstripped the sales of over-the-counter products such as 'Aspro' (Balance et al., 1992; Taggart, 1993). Nicholas attempted to transform itself into a pharmaceutical company by developing a pipeline of prescription drugs for humans and animals.[5] A joint venture with Monsanto in the late 1920s produced salicylates, a principal ingredient for 'Aspro' that offered the possibility of further development. Despite considerable investments in R&D both in Australia and in Britain (Morgan, 1959; Kolm, 1988: 656-7), it was 'on a scale far too small by the standards of the international pharmaceutical business' (Kolm, 1988: 656-7). The firm showed great enterprise in this endeavour by acquiring chemical manufacturing companies in Britain, attempting to forge alliances with major pharmaceutical firms, and collaborating with Australian universities and its premier government-owned research organisation, CSIRO. The quest to go it alone ended when it ceased basic R&D activity at Slough in 1974. The writing had been on the wall for some years because the firm had no presence in the domestic market for drugs listed on the Pharmaceutical Benefits Scheme (PBS),[6] being eclipsed even in the analgesics group (Industries Assistance Commission, 1974: Appendix 4, Table A4.6) and having only 0.2 per cent of prescription drug sales in Australia (Ralph, 1979: Appendix IV, 154-5).

Kiwi attempted a bold stroke to break into the pharmaceutical business on a large scale in 1979, when it bid to acquire F.H. Faulding, one of Australia's few domestic drug manufacturers. One of Faulding's new products 'Eryc', an antibiotic with a modified release, had recently been approved by the Food & Drug Administration in the United States (Donovan and Tweddell, 1995). Kiwi's bid was bitterly contested by Faulding and failed. Faulding went on to become a successful multinational pharmaceutical firm through an alliance with Parke-Davis to manufacture and distribute its drugs overseas (Donovan and Tweddell, 1995; Minchev, 1999).

The alternative field of 'home products', cleaning agents, antiseptics, toiletries, personal care items and so on proved to be equally daunting for both Nicholas and Kiwi. Once again, they faced competition in their product lines from global giants in their domestic market. Leading British firms, Unilever and Reckitt & Colman, had begun trading in Australia in the 1880s, long before Kiwi and Nicholas were established (Fieldhouse, 1978: 64-96; Edwards, 1982). Glaxo's 'first concentrated attempt to enter the Australian market' was made in 1912 (Davenport-Hines and Slinn, 1992: 111). Parke, Davis & Co. and Sterling Pharmaceuticals were operating in Australia before World War I. In the 20s and 30s they were joined by a host of others, including Johnson & Johnson, Bristol-Myers Co. and Proctor & Gamble. Thus prominent multinationals in pharmaceuticals, toilet preparations and cosmetics were introducing their established brands into the Australian market while Kiwi and Aspro were building their own brands at home and abroad.

The invasion gathered pace after World War II (Brash, 1966: 316-20). By the mid-1960s foreign companies controlled three-quarters of the Australian market for pharmaceutical and toilet preparations (Department of Trade and Industry, 1966: Table 2, viii-ix). US firms owned about 70 per cent of the assets of these foreign firms with the British coming a distant second at 23 per cent – although the list did not include the giant British firm Unilever which was classified in the food, drink and tobacco group. The disparity between Kiwi and Nicholas and their foreign competitors is starkly revealed by a comparison of the size of their respective assets. At 30 June 1970, Nicholas's Australian assets were $15.5 million and its global assets $48.7 million; Kiwi International had assets of $15 million in 1971. Unilever's and Reckitt & Colman's Australian assets alone were comparable to Nicholas's global assets. Many of the other foreign firms, including Glaxo, Merck Sharpe & Dohme, Pfizer, Roche Products, Sterling Pharmaceuticals, Avon Products, Colgate-Palmolive, and Johnson & Johnson, had Australian assets that matched those of Nicholas's local operation and Kiwi's global balance sheet.

The overseas companies, particularly the American firms, enjoyed a number of competitive advantages in the Australian market (Chapters 5, 6). They operated on a scale that matched those of the Australian firms. More importantly, they possessed superior capabilities. These came from prior experience forged in their larger and more sophisticated home markets. Mass retailing and modern marketing had come earlier and advanced further in the USA and Britain compared to Australia (Laird, 1998; Strasser, 1989; Fraser, 1981; Jefferys, 1954). Managers of foreign firms in these non-durable consumer goods industries could draw on organisational knowledge in dealing with the emergent supermarkets chains. American firms especially had experience of new marketing techniques, particularly through the use of radio and television. Before World War II, Australian firms did not use radio as a way to advertise to the same extent as American firms (McNair, 1937: 189); television came to Australia only in 1956. Moreover, foreign manufacturers tended to use their home-country advertising agencies in Australia. Both Nicholas and Kiwi relied on local agencies to do battle against the international experience of agencies such as J. Walter Thompson, Lintas or McCann-Erickson (Frost, 1965; Sinclair, 1987: 132-45).

In the longer term neither Nicholas nor Kiwi could produce enough new brands to hold their market share. The number of products on the market rose significantly over the years. For instance, the European division of Nicholas International sold 'about 200 products in 1,000 different packets' (Nicholas Australia 1970: 22). Both firms tried brand extension for 'Aspro' and 'Kiwi', respectively. Neither enjoyed much success in generating new products in-house, relying instead on a series of acquisitions to capture important new brands such as 'Vincents', 'Rennies', 'Radox' and 'Bon Ami' (Smith & Barrie, 1976; Kiwi, 1962). They simply lacked the resources and skills to match the innovations of the larger firms in products as diverse as detergents, deodorants, feminine hygiene products, non-abrasive cleaning products and over-the-counter pharmaceuticals. The cost of launching a new product nationally in Australia, estimated around 1970 as a quarter of a million dollars, was becoming too expensive (Were: Box 746). By the early 1990s, 'Radox' bath salts was the only brand of the dismembered Nicholas-Kiwi business that held its place in a list of 100 products dominated by a single brand in Australian supermarkets. The other two dozen comparable health related categories were held by the likes of Unilever, Johnson & Johnson, Colgate Palmolive and Sterling Winthrop (Retail World, 1993: 64-5).

The merger of Nicholas and Kiwi had attractions for both. Nicholas gained access to the US market, where Kiwi had a strong position; Nicholas offered Kiwi an entrée into the pharmaceutical and over-the-counter business it had sought through its bid for Faulding a few years earlier. Before the merger, Nicholas drew three-quarters of its sales from pharmaceuticals and toiletries (Table 13.1): its markets were spread around the world, a mix of first- and third-world countries, the latter having been a particularly lucrative market for 'Aspro'. By 1984, after the merger, the contribution of the medical and cosmetics business fell sharply as 'shoe care' and 'household products' brought in more than 40 per cent of revenues (Table 13.2). The geographic composition also shifted significantly, with a pronounced movement towards the Americas and Europe.

Table 13.1: Nicholas sales by region and product, 1976

Product	%	Brands	Regions	%
Home medicines	37	Aspro, Vincents, Rennies	Pacific	36
Prescription	15	Genticin	UK & USA	24
Toiletries	23	Radox, Ambi	Africa & central Asia	23
Equipment	17		Continental Europe	16
Fine chemicals	4			
Confectionery	3	James Chocolate		

Note: Pacific includes Australia

Source: Nicholas International, Annual Report 1976

In the event, the merger was too little, too late. The new firm emerged when Australia's corporate landscape was being transformed by a wave of debt-fuelled takeovers, creating what proved to be a number of large and unsustainable conglomerates (Sykes, 1994). In 1984 the firm was subject to the unwelcome attention of three suitors. The first came from Castlemaine Toohey's Brewery, which next year fell into the clutches of raider Alan Bond. This bid aroused the interest of Britain's Reckitt & Colman and the US firm Consolidated Foods, with the latter prevailing. Its parent, Sara Lee, allowed the management of Nicholas Kiwi Australasia considerable autonomy in many of its overseas markets under a management contract. The arrangement ended in 1986 when the Australian-based operations were absorbed into the parent organisation. Sara Lee was more interested in building the personal care and home products and sold the iconic 'Aspro' brand to the Swiss pharmaceutical company, Roche, in 1991 (Roche, 2003).

Table 13.2: Nicholas Kiwi sales by region and product, 1984

Region	%	Products	%
Americas	24	Shoe Care	27
Pacific	21	OTC medicines	25
UK	18	Household products	16
France	11	Toiletries & cosmetics	15
Africa & Asia	10	Prescription drugs	7
Europe	9	Other Kiwi	6
East Asia	7	Other Nicholas	4

Note: Pacific includes Australia

Source: Nicholas Kiwi International, Annual Report 1984

CONCLUSION

In the 1920s local entrepreneur Helena Rubinstein transplanted her cosmetics business from Melbourne to New York and never looked back.[7] Could Nicholas Kiwi have survived and prospered if it had relocated from Australia back to Britain? Both firms were born global in that operations were conducted almost simultaneously in Australian and Britain from the outset. Control was transferred to Australia, swiftly in the case of Kiwi and much later in the case of Nicholas. A strong case can be made that from the 1920s onwards they would have done better trading as public companies located in Britain. There they would have had access to a larger capital market, better scientific skills and all of those things that are captured by Michael Porter's phrase 'supporting and related industries' (Porter, 1990). Locating in larger and more dynamic markets might have strengthened their capabilities. It might also have hastened their demise in an industry characterised by consolidation, where the biggest soon gobbled up the small fry. In the end they would have suffered the same fate as Helena Rubinstein, whose business was purchased after her death first by Colgate-Palmolive before eventually ending up as part of L'Oreal. Size mattered more than location. Other larger firms were better placed to extract value from the portfolio of brands these pioneers had created and nurtured.

Faulding's success in the 1980s and 1990s was the exception that proves the rule: Australia has not been fallow ground for local pharmaceutical companies (Department of Trade, 1960; Industries Assistance Commission, 1974b). It was a small market, generating just one per cent of global sales of ethical drugs in 1989 (BIE, 1991: Fig.2.3). Moreover, subsidiaries of foreign pharmaceuticals have long dominated the prescription drug market. In 1994-

pharmaceuticals have long dominated the prescription drug market. In 1994-95 the two largest Australian companies had only five per cent of the domestic market and their sales were eclipsed in dollar terms by each of the nine largest foreign firms (Industry Commission, 1996a: Table 2.7, 28). The dilemma for local firms is that the local market is too small to recoup the high costs of the necessary R&D and the subsequent approvals process, besides which government health policy puts a cap on the price of many prescription drugs (BIE, 1991). It is now even less likely that an Australian firm will be able to emulate the success of kitchen chemist George Nicholas in going international. The only viable strategies for holders of Australian patents are either to sell out or go into alliance with an established foreign multinational.

NOTES

1. Both companies changed names on several occasions as they shifted from partnerships to proprietary limited to public companies and also because of mergers and acquisitions. Nicholas began as Smith Nicholas & Co. in 1915, becoming G.R. Nicholas in 1916 and Nicholas Pty Ltd in 1921. The UK business was registered as Aspro Limited in 1927 and floated there as a public company in 1935. The Australian company became a public company in 1968 as Nicholas Australia Limited. The Australian firm acquired the UK firm in 1970 with the merged entity named Nicholas International (Smith and Barrie, 1976). Kiwi began life in 1901 as a partnership of McKellan and Ramsay. It became Kiwi Polish Company in 1911 and remained in family hands until becoming a public company, Kiwi International, in 1967. The two firms merged in 1981 to become Nicholas Kiwi, which was acquired in 1984 by Consolidated Foods (beneficial owner Sara Lee) and renamed Nicholas Aspro Australasia. It was delisted from the Australia Stock Exchange on 3 December 1986 (ASX, 1997).
2. Brief histories of these companies appear in Derdak (1988), and Hast (1991). Chandler (2005), provides a study of the industry's evolution from an American and European perspective.
3. The US government also confiscated Bayer's assets and patents. In 1917 they were sold at auction to Sterling Drug Incorporated for US$5.3 million (Derdak, 1988: 698).
4. The exception was the purchase of the UK Aspro-Nicholas by Nicholas Australia in 1969, a transaction that kept most of the shares in family hands.
5. In 1960 its product range consisted of 'proprietary medicines (principally "Aspro"), ethicals (27 products, of which 12 are associated with nutrition) and veterinary preparations (14 products)' (Department of Trade, 1960: 75).
6. Since 1948 the Australian government has made a range of drugs, prescribed by doctors, available free of charge until 1960 and with large subsidy thereafter. The number of drugs available under the PBS has risen steadily over the years.

7. Helena Rubinstein, born in Krakow in Poland, arrived in Australia in 1896. She began manufacturing and selling her 'Valaze' face cream in Melbourne in 1903 (Woodhead, 2003: ch. 2).

14. BHP Billiton

Robin Stewardson*

BHP Billiton, an Australian-headquartered, dual-listed multinational, is the world's largest diversified resources company. It is a leading supplier of raw materials for steelmaking, the world's second largest copper producer, the second largest exporter of energy coal, the third largest producer of nickel metal, the fourth largest producer of uranium, the fifth largest producer of aluminium, and has a significant oil and gas business and substantial interests in diamonds, silver and titanium metals. Worldwide BHP Billiton operates in 25 countries (BHP Billiton, 2005).

BHP Billiton was formed in 2001 by the merger of BHP, an Australian company, and Billiton, originally a South African company but latterly listed and headquartered in London. Both were already large companies. For many years BHP had been Australia's largest company and in the 1980s and 1990s it had been known as 'The Big Australian'.

This chapter is concerned primarily with BHP. The first part of the chapter briefly describes the course of BHP's globalisation, culminating so far in its merger with Billiton. The second part addresses the strategic issues behind BHP's globalisation. By way of comparison, some mention is also made of BHP Billiton's main rival, Rio Tinto, another dual-listed firm that also has strong Australian connections.

TOWARDS GLOBALISATION

BHP was founded in 1885 as a miner of silver, lead and zinc at the remote site of Broken Hill in western New South Wales, hence its original name of The Broken Hill Proprietary Company Ltd (BHP, 1960). The company's next step was to move downstream into smelting, at Port Pirie in South Australia. For this it required iron ore as a flux and also coke, leading the

---

* Robin Stewardson was Principal Economist of BHP from 1974 to 1990 and Chief Economist from 1990 to 1997. The views expressed here are those of the author and not necessarily those of BHP Billiton.

company to develop iron ore deposits at Whyalla in South Australia and coal deposits at Newcastle in New South Wales. The resultant silver, lead and zinc were exported in large quantities to Europe and Asia.

When the company's silver, lead and zinc deposits at Broken Hill began to run out, BHP moved into steel-making, for which it already possessed the two main raw materials in iron ore and coking coal. The Newcastle steelworks opened in 1915. In 1935 BHP made a major horizontal integration move by purchasing the other Australian steel producer, Australian Iron & Steel Ltd, based just south of Sydney at Port Kembla. BHP thereby became a monopolist in a protected domestic market.

During the 1950s and 1960s new mines were developed, at least partly to supply ingredients for the steel works. This involved iron ore quarries in Western Australia, limestone sands in South Australia and a manganese ore mine in the Northern Territory, together with a ferro-alloy plant in Tasmania.

In the early 1960s BHP re-established its overseas representative offices to facilitate its exports of steel and minerals. According to annual reports, over the next three decades BHP exported varying quantities of steel, ranging from nine per cent to 42 per cent of its total steel sales annually and averaging more than 20 per cent over that period. Those export sales did not reflect a more permanent international outlook but rather the need to find a market for output which from time to time was unable to be sold domestically, especially when Australia went through a low point in economic cycles.

In the 1990s BHP's Steel Division adopted a very different philosophy. It now sought to establish a permanent and continuous presence in the export market for steel with only marginal quantities fluctuating inversely with Australian domestic demand. The Steel Division's attitude to capital investment also changed to reflect the philosophy of a 'long term exporter'.

In the field of minerals, an export orientation was manifest much sooner. From the mid-1960s to the mid-1980s BHP opened a number of large mines in Australia whose output was destined largely for export. The Groote Eylandt manganese mine in the Northern Territory was commissioned in 1966 and the huge iron ore mine at Mount Newman in the Pilbara opened in 1969 – BHP was manager but only 30 per cent owner at that time. BHP also moved into the export of coal. In 1976 it acquired 58 per cent of the Moura and Kianga export coal mines in Queensland, then in 1980 opened the Gregory mine and in 1983 the Riverside mine, both also in Queensland (BHP, 1997).

The third main leg of BHP's activities – oil and gas production – also started in the 1960s. As joint-venture partners, Esso and BHP discovered commercial quantities of natural gas in 1965 and crude oil in 1967 under Bass Strait, the wide channel that divides the island of Tasmania from the southeastern mainland. The first deliveries of natural gas onshore to the state of Victoria were made in 1969. By 1971 the Bass Strait oil and natural gas fields were in full production.

In retrospect BHP's globalisation, in the sense of overseas-based production as distinct from export sales from Australia, can be thought of as occurring in three leaps. Each of these leaps was associated with a takeover or merger: John Lysaght in the 1970s, Utah and other companies in the mid-1980s, and the merger with Billiton in 2001.

The first leap seems small in terms of BHP Billiton's current global activities, but it was significant at the time in initiating BHP's experience of overseas operations. In 1970 BHP acquired 50 per cent of John Lysaght Australia, which in 1979 became a wholly owned subsidiary. For BHP the motive was a forward vertical integration in the domestic steel industry through acquisition of John Lysaght's substantial cold-rolling and coating operations in Australia. However, with the acquisition came a number of small roll-forming mills in Asia.[1] These small plants represented BHP's first overseas operations and indeed, throughout the 1970s and early 1980s, were virtually its only overseas operations.[2] In the late 1980s and early 1990s many more of these roll-forming mills were constructed in various countries, building upon the network established by John Lysaght.

The second leap, and a major transformation, occurred with the acquisition in 1984 of US mining company Utah International Inc.. Utah had dual attractions for BHP. One was its large part-owned and managed export-oriented coal mines in Queensland, which were very profitable and fitted well with BHP's own expanding coal operations there. The other attraction was its operations outside Australia: significant domestic steaming coal mines in the US, a medium-sized copper mine in Canada, and a 49 per cent share in a large iron ore mine in Brazil. Apart from the copper, these were commodities with which BHP was already familiar and comfortable. Utah also brought with it various exploration properties, the most significant of which was the Escondida copper deposit in Chile, which BHP subsequently brought into production in 1990. Escondida was BHP's big new mineral development of the 1990s and became the jewel in its portfolio, though there were also a number of other significant mineral developments in Asia, Africa and Canada in that decade. Utah was a very big mouthful for BHP and in order to be able to manage it BHP sold off part interests in Utah's Queensland coal mines, keeping intact the activities which represented the step into globalisation.

The second half of the 1980s also saw a number of petroleum acquisitions overseas. In 1985 BHP bought two medium-sized US companies with petroleum reserves and production capacity, Energy Reserves Group (in January) and Monsanto Oil Company (in December). In 1987 BHP acquired

51 per cent of Hamilton Oil with production and very significant reserves in the North Sea. The remaining 49 per cent of Hamilton was acquired in 1991. BHP acquired an oil refinery, gas utility and petrol retailing business in Hawaii, Pacific Resources Inc., in 1989. In the early 90s BHP developed oil and gas fields in the Irish Sea and brought the Dai Hung oil field off Vietnam into production. BHP also produced oil and gas offshore from Western Australia, part owned the large North West Shelf natural gas project, produced oil and gas in the Timor Sea and explored and produced both oil and gas in the Gulf of Mexico.

The third major step in BHP's globalisation was its aforementioned merger with Billiton in July 2001. The UK-listed Billiton's original home base was South Africa and it had a number of operations there as well as elsewhere overseas. Almost by definition, the dual-listed merged company, BHP Billiton, had a wider global spread of activities than BHP alone. However, BHP's motive in going into the merger was almost certainly more to diversify in minerals than to obtain a greater geographical spread of operations *per se*. BHP brought to the merger primarily its businesses in iron ore, metallurgical coal, oil, gas, LNG and copper; Billiton brought businesses in aluminium, alumina, export steaming coal, titanium minerals, copper and ferro-alloys.

About the same time, BHP's steel-making operations were spun off into separate companies. In October 2000 the long products business was spun off as OneSteel Ltd, and in July 2002 the flat products business was spun off as BHP Steel Ltd, with a subsequent change of name to BlueScope Steel Ltd. BlueScope Steel has continued the pattern of downstream development overseas which prevailed when it was part of BHP. The company has established additional coating, painting and roll-forming plants, mainly in Asia, and has recently announced an expansion of this process into India, in conjunction with Tata Steel. BlueScope Steel has also taken a significant step further downstream by acquiring Butler Manufacturing, an American company producing pre-engineered building systems in North America and China. By 2005, three years after its separation from BHP Billiton, BlueScope Steel had increased the value of its total assets by 73 per cent, and the proportion of its assets outside Australia had risen from 27 to 41 per cent (BlueScope Steel, 2005).

The purpose of these steel spin-offs was to divest BHP Billiton of the manufacturing activity of steel-making so that it would become, and be seen by investors as having become, a focused resources company specialising in minerals (albeit a wide range of minerals) and petroleum.

A side-effect of these spin-offs was to make the company more globally oriented. In regards to both production and sales, the steel group had always been much more Australian-oriented than the minerals and petroleum groups.

A statistical comparison of the proportion of BHP Billiton's current assets, production and sales overseas compared with that before the steel spin-offs is therefore somewhat misleading because the company has changed its composition in a way which automatically biases these figures.

Given that the union of BHP and Billiton was a merger rather than a takeover, one could define the South African, as well as the Australian, assets, production and sales as 'domestic', and only those outside both those countries as international. Nevertheless, this paper takes the approach of looking at globalisation from the point of view of BHP. Moreover, the head office for the merged entity is still based in Australia, making Australia legitimately the domestic country.

Table 14.1: Percentage of BHP's gross assets by region (Years ending 31 May or 30 June)

	1980[a]	1985[b]	1998	2000	2002[c] including BHP Steel	2002[c] excluding BHP Steel	2004
Australia	99	78	57	59	38	34	32
North America	-	20	14	9	12	13	14
Europe	-	-	8	8	6	7	12
South America	-	-	9	14	23	25	21
Southern Africa	-	-	-	-	17	19	18
Rest of World	1	2	12	10	4	2	3

Notes:

a. Figures for 1980 are the author's estimate.

b. After acquisition of Utah and ERG.

c. After merger with Billiton, BHP Steel was spun off in July 2002.

Source: BHP and BHP Billiton, annual reports

BHP's path towards globalisation is summarised by Table 14.1, which shows the proportion of BHP's gross assets by region for selected years from 1980. In 1980 virtually all of BHP's assets were in Australia, with the Asian roll-formers representing only a tiny proportion of total assets. By May 1985, after the acquisition of Utah and ERG (the first of the overseas petroleum acquisitions), the proportion of assets in Australia had fallen to 78 per cent. By 2000 the proportion of Australian assets had been further diluted to 59 per cent. The merger with Billiton brought the proportion of Australian assets down to 38 per cent and then 34 per cent after the spin-off of BHP Steel in July 2002. The latest available figure, for the year 2004, is 32 per cent (BHP Billiton, 2004). Thus, despite BHP's long history as a major exporter from Australia, it is only in the last 20 years or so that the company has invested in production overseas.

Rio Tinto

Some other major Australian mining companies have followed a broadly similar globalisation path to BHP, of which Rio Tinto is the outstanding case and also now BHP Billiton's main rival. Like BHP Billiton, dual-listed Rio Tinto is one of the world's largest mining and resource companies. It has 61 per cent of its assets in Australia and New Zealand and 39 per cent elsewhere, predominantly in North America (Rio Tinto, 2005).

Like BHP, Rio Tinto traces the Australian part of its origins back to Broken Hill. The three sister companies, Broken Hill South, North Broken Hill and Zinc Corporation, commenced their existence mining silver, lead and zinc at Broken Hill–Zinc Corporation actually started out by treating the tailings dumps (Blainey, 1963: 265). They began operations later than BHP with rights to deeper parts of the ore body, so that production did not peak until the early 1900s but was sustained over a longer period. Like BHP, the firms smelted lead at Port Pirie – indeed they bought BHP's lead smelter to do so – and also refined zinc electrolytically in Tasmania. They were very substantial exporters of lead and zinc for many years.

Over time the three companies worked more closely together and became known as the 'Collins House' group after their shared headquarters in Collins Street, Melbourne. Just as BHP turned from lead-zinc mining to domestic steel production, so the 'Collins House' group companies invested a good part of their profits from lead and zinc into domestic manufacturing industries – metals, paper and even aircraft.

One company of the group, Zinc Corporation, gradually moved away from the others. In 1949 Zinc Corporation merged with the UK company, Imperial Smelting Corporation, to form Consolidated Zinc Corporation. In 1962 Conzinc in turn merged with another UK company, Rio Tinto, to form Rio Tinto-Zinc Corporation (RTZ). At the same time the Australian interests of those two companies were merged to form Conzinc Riotinto of Australia (CRA). In this new guise, CRA, like BHP, took advantage of Japan's economic resurgence and the abolition in 1961 of the ban on iron ore exports to develop big new mines, mainly in Australia.

Buoyed by Rio Tinto's injection of capital, CRA undertook substantial exploration and developed three large new export mines: the Hamersley iron ore mine in the Pilbara region of Western Australia, the Bougainville copper mine in Papua New Guinea and the Comalco bauxite mine at Weipa in far north Queensland. It refined the bauxite at Gladstone in central Queensland and smelted some of it at Bell Bay in Tasmania, while also undertaking a small amount of manufacturing of aluminium products. The Bougainville copper mine in Papua New Guinea, which was discovered in 1964 and received the go ahead to mine in 1969, was CRA's first major mining activity overseas. At about the same time the CRA group established a zinc refinery at Budel in The Netherlands. These were the first two overseas production operations developed by the group, although it had operated a smelter at Avonmouth in the UK since the merger with Imperial Smelting Corporation.

In the 1970s CRA found that it was constrained in Australia by the Australian Government's legislation regulating investment by foreign-owned companies. However, it did manage to develop the Argyle diamond mine in the Kimberley region of Western Australia and the Blair Athol and Tarong coal mines in central Queensland. It took further steps overseas with the establishment of an aluminium smelter at Bluff in New Zealand, and later the very large Kaltim Prima coal mine and the Kelian gold mine, both in the Indonesian province of East Kalimantan.

Meanwhile, the parent company RTZ had developed a wide range of activities in many parts of the world. From 1988, it concentrated on developing a worldwide mining and resources profile. This included taking a 30 per cent share in the Escondida copper project, majority owned and operated by BHP.

In 1995 RTZ and CRA opted for a dual-listed company structure and in 1997 merged under the common name of Rio Tinto. Thus from similar origins but along a very different path, CRA has ended up with the same legal structure and a similar profile as BHP although, unlike BHP, Rio Tinto now has its headquarters in London.

In the case of both BHP and CRA, there was a long history of exporting from Australia before moves towards globalisation. In both cases investment in mining activities overseas is comparatively recent, albeit CRA's moves predated BHP's by about a decade.

STRATEGY

As already noted, BHP's initial offshore investments occurred almost unintentionally when acquisition of John Lysaght's Australian flat-products operations brought with it, as an incidental part, several roll-forming plants in Asia. The next move was more strategic: Utah International had the dual attractions for BHP of overseas operations to diversify risk geographically and its Queensland coal mines to reinforce BHP's existing operations there. Thereafter, in minerals, petroleum and steel, BHP pursued a course which would almost inevitably result in becoming a globalised company. Globalisation was not an end in itself, but it was the likely outcome of the company's growth policy.

The rationale for BHP's globalisation can be summarised in a few simple propositions. BHP had been pursuing growth as part of its drive to increase shareholder value. Having outgrown the Australian market in many of its business activities, BHP had to sell outside Australia as well as within it. Selling internationally often involves producing internationally to be competitive, for two main reasons. First, some markets, particularly those for standard, basic raw materials, are supplied most competitively from the lowest-cost ore deposits, irrespective of where they may be located. Second, other markets, particularly those for finished goods that are costly to transport, easily damaged and/or highly customised, are often most efficiently served by producing close to the market to enable quick and flexible response to shifts in demand. Moreover, the larger the company the greater the need to spread risk by diversifying markets in respect of both product and country, thereby avoiding having too many eggs in the one basket or, in the case of BHP in the 1980s, two baskets, namely Australia and Japan.

These simple propositions can be elaborated by taking each of BHP's main activities separately. The case of minerals is perhaps the most obvious one for globalisation. From the viewpoint of BHP Billiton's current market positioning, it seems obvious to look for the best resources to develop wherever in the world they can be found. BHP arrived at that position in the following way. Its production in Australia of iron ore and manganese ore had for a long time exceeded total Australian consumption of those minerals, so clearly the balance had to be sold overseas. In the case of coal and natural gas, Australia's total production exceeded its total consumption, so that BHP, as a substantial producer within that Australian total, would have to gain a large share of the domestic market to avoid selling overseas. So again it was clear that BHP has to sell many of its mineral products in the international market.

It was also obvious that to compete in the international market BHP needed to produce as competitively as possible. Principally that meant operating low-cost mines, which in turn meant mines with high grade ore and low extraction costs. Australia happens to be well endowed with good mineral deposits but so also are a number of other countries. When selling on the world market, it is simply common-sense to look worldwide for the best deposits to develop.

The case of petroleum is very similar to minerals. Domestic demand for natural gas was inadequate to absorb total domestic production, thus necessitating involvement in overseas markets. However, for oil as well as for natural gas, the greatest motivating force for overseas exploration, and subsequently operations, was very much the relative prospectivity of various areas of the world for oil and gas development, spurred on perhaps initially by recognition of the eventual exhaustion of oil resources in Bass Strait.

Finally there is the case of steel which, although now spun off, is in many ways BHP's most innovative example of globalisation. Australian demand for steel had grown very little, if at all, over the last few decades and, being a mature economy, at best slow growth was expected in the future. BHP already held some 75 per cent of this market, so clearly there were limits to the growth potential of its sales in Australia. That potential hinged on marketing initiatives supported by a significant technology and research effort to develop new products and new product applications through technological change. However, while BHP was working on that front, the immediate gains were unlikely to be dramatic. The company therefore saw the need and the opportunity to develop its business outside Australia.

The form of overseas investment was closely related to the technology of steel processing. Crude steel is first hot rolled, then flat steel products are cold rolled before in many cases being coated, painted, and finally roll formed into final shape for use in roofing, light construction, cladding and so on. Because steel products assume so many different shapes and sizes, there are good reasons for producing the finished product close to the market where production and delivery can respond quickly to market demand. For this reason BHP had constructed numerous roll-forming plants throughout Asia, the Pacific and the west coast of the United States, supplying these subsidiaries from Australia.

The critical question was therefore the point in the production chain at which processing needed to be established in the country of final market. Economies of scale are more important in the earlier stages of the production process than in the later stages, thus pushing the desirable point of export from the home country down the production chain.[3] On the other hand, the developing countries of Asia are keen to have basic industries like steel located in their own country. The steel company wants to provide the most competitively priced feed to its roll forming plants overseas and it wants to have a secure source of supply to those plants. Security of supply tends to favour locating some of the prior stages of production in the same country as the roll former. Moreover, tariffs in many Asian countries escalate with value added, thus providing an incentive to perform more of the later processes such as cold rolling, coating and painting in those countries.

BHP's response was to establish operations upstream from roll forming (coating and painting) in a number of overseas countries (and in the US even a mini-mill producing crude steel), thus increasing its degree of globalisation.

Not all of BHP's globalisation initiatives succeeded. One unhappy experience concerned the Ok Tedi copper/gold mine in Papua New Guinea, in which BHP held a minority interest. BHP was sued on behalf of local landowners for allowing material from tailings dams to silt up the river, and the publicity from this case damaged BHP's international reputation. A more substantive example was the acquisition in 1996 of Magma Copper Company, which operated copper mines, a smelter and a refinery in the United States. It appears that BHP did not do sufficiently rigorous due diligence and problems with the operations were subsequently exposed, the negative effects of which were magnified by an untimely fall in the price of copper. The then managing director bore the consequences. His successor, appointed from outside the company, was an American.

The Magma debacle, therefore, had the unintended consequence of speeding up the internationalisation of the top executive level of the company. Until 1998 BHP's board and top management had been almost wholly Australian. The appointment of American Paul Anderson, as managing director in December 1998 heralded a wave of appointments of Americans to senior positions (including that of chief financial officer Chip Goodyear, who was later himself to become chief executive officer). Similarly, the merger with Billiton brought a wave of South Africans into senior positions in the merged company.

An interesting counterfactual question is why BHP did not start operating overseas much sooner, particularly in the case of minerals. There is probably some minimum size at which a minerals company can support overseas exploration and operations, but BHP would have surpassed that size well before it undertook significant overseas operations. BHP's high-quality Australian mineral deposits and the strength of Japanese demand allowed it to sustain growth from its Australian production base for many years. The eventual timing of its globalisation in minerals was attributable to the acquisition of Utah, whose worldwide operations and exploration areas gave BHP a big impetus to invest more overseas. Moreover, that acquisition coincided with a general opening up of the Australian economy and many aspects of its business life to the international economy (Chapter 2). In the 1990s, the increasing difficulties of getting approval for mineral developments in Australia also tended to make overseas developments a more attractive proposition.

Another intriguing counterfactual question is whether BHP was slower to globalise under its Australian bosses than it would have been if the Americans and South Africans had come in before 1998. Table 14.1 shows that BHP had already substantially globalised under Australian management. From 1985 to 1998 (the last full year prior to Anderson's appointment) BHP increased its proportion of gross assets held overseas from 22 to 43 per cent. There has been continued, but not radically more rapid, organic globalisation since then, but the big change in the figures in recent years was caused by the merger with Billiton and the spin-off of BHP Steel. It seems that the timing and extent of BHP's globalisation has had much more to do with the company's stage of development than with the nationality of its leaders.

CONCLUSION

BHP has been a major exporter from Australia for many decades but has undertaken significant foreign direct investment in offshore production only in the last 20 years. The same is broadly true of rival CRA, now Rio Tinto.

The case of BHP illustrates the point that as a company outgrows its domestic market and comes to export a significant proportion of its output, the economics of the industry or industries may eventually lead to production, as well as selling, overseas. From the company's point of view, globalisation is not so much an end in itself as an outcome of irresistible competitive forces.

In short, globalising is just a natural process of expanding an international business, and is remarkable only because it crosses the artificial boundaries that delineate countries. Successful globalisation primarily depends on developing sound and efficient businesses overseas in just the same way as any domestic business expansion, though it also brings with it additional elements such as a more extended line of management control, the need for country risk analysis and initially unfamiliar business environments. BHP was fortunate that it learned quickly and that its mistakes, though not inconsequential, did not prove fatal. Where some Australian companies were discouraged and pulled back, BHP pressed on all the harder to become a leading global firm.

NOTES

1. Roll forming is a finishing process in flat steel production in which coated and painted steel sheet is rolled into shapes such as corrugated profiles for roofing.
2. There was also an unsuccessful tin mine in Indonesia from 1970 to 1981 and a small investment in a steel rope manufacturing plant in Malaysia.
3. Nevertheless, changing technology including electric-arc technology is allowing more steel products to be produced on a small scale, thus making it economically viable to operate small plants in developing countries.

15. Foster's Group

Tatiana Zalan and Geoffrey Lewis

INTRODUCTION

With sales in excess of US$3 billion, Foster's Group is the largest wine and beer producer in Australia and distributes in more than 150 countries. After the disposal of its leisure and hospitality business in 2003-04, Foster's Group is now a focused multi-beverage company producing and marketing a portfolio of premium beer, wine, spirits, cider and non-alcoholic beverages (Foster's, 2005). Around 44 per cent of group assets and 36 per cent of sales are in overseas markets.

Foster's Group had all the prerequisites for becoming a formidable multinational brewer: proprietary brewing technology, superb marketing capabilities honed in an intensely competitive domestic market, the ability to produce low-cost beer of consistent quality and a pool of high-calibre managers. These firm-specific advantages should have been sufficient for Foster's to become an international market leader. In fact Foster's story provides an extraordinary example of a highly successful domestic firm with a long international record of a mixture of early promise, false starts, and clear failures. Export success led to significant FDI that eventually failed in its core beer business. The jury is still out on whether its foreign ventures will be more successful in the wine industry. In this chapter we describe the evolution of Foster's as a multinational firm with specific focus on its administrative heritage in the domestic market and the gradual internationalisation of the beer and the wine businesses. In conclusion we assess Foster's global strategy, present possible explanations for its lack of success, and draw out lessons for other internationalising firms.

FOSTER'S ADMINISTRATIVE HERITAGE[1]

Foster's Group has a long and successful heritage in the Australian beer industry. The diversified alcoholic beverages company began in 1888 with the establishment of the first commercially successful lager brewery in the gold rush city of Melbourne, Victoria. In 1907, Foster's and five other

Melbourne brewers amalgamated to form Carlton and United Breweries (CUB) to resolve a crisis of overcapacity in the local Victorian market. CUB's market position was consolidated by the acquisition of major competitors, whose brands and distribution channels were used to leverage economies of scale in production. Underpinning CUB's success was its ability to produce consistently high-quality but low-cost lager beer with a long shelf life, a key factor as it expanded its geographic reach. Process innovation played an important role: in the 1950s, researchers at CUB revolutionised the industry by developing a hardier variety of locally grown hops and in the 1960s a research team developed an extract to replace the less scientific process of boiling the hops.

In the 1960s in response to the entry of British brewer, Courage, to the Victorian market, CUB aggressively built its brands through massive media advertising. Given that the marketing skills of other Australian brewers were only just beginning to develop, the threat from Courage (later acquired by Sydney brewer, Tooth) made CUB an even more formidable competitor. The threat from Courage was fundamental in establishing a marketing approach built around national brands and becoming an export success with 'Foster's Lager'. This period in CUB's history as an independent, focused beer company shaped much of Foster's administrative heritage, manifested in the development of business-specific capabilities which eventually translated into strategic assets – brands, proprietary process technology, scale economies, control of distribution channels through tied-up arrangements with hotels, and a dominant share in the Victorian market.

1983-84 signalled a new phase in the evolution of Foster's administrative heritage. In 1983 CUB acquired the business of Tooth and Company, a leading brewer in the main state of New South Wales, which gave CUB about 50 per cent of the total Australian beer market, well ahead of competitors. Then in 1984 CUB itself was taken over by Elders IXL, a conglomerate, which had been rapidly assembled by the young and brash Australian entrepreneur, John Elliott.[2] Before the takeover, CUB had been a conservatively run company with virtually no debt. Many of the assets were underperforming and passive investments – including substantial stakes in Elders and Henry Jones (IXL) – were not generating adequate returns. John Elliot and CUB's incoming CEO, Peter Bartels, restructured CUB by selling poorly performing assets, significantly lifting its return on capital and changing management structures and performance management systems.

By the mid-1980s, the oligopolistic Australian beer industry had become dominated by just two competitors. CUB dominated the Victorian market, Bond Corporation dominated the Western Australian markets and the two brewers shared the large, fiercely competitive New South Wales market. In 1985, there began a fight for national market dominance as both companies made a strong marketing push outside their traditional state markets. The marketing battle between the national brewers quickly escalated into what was described as 'the most costly single marketing duel ever staged in this country' (Kiely, 1986: 10). After several years of intense competition, détente was reached and both players redirected their aggressive growth ambitions towards international markets.

All the constituents of Foster's Group administrative heritage were now in place. CUB was highly profitable in a duopolistic national market, relying on positional advantages that had accumulated over time as it brought its superior capabilities to bear in the market and through acquisitions. CUB had played a central role in the consolidation and restructuring of a local industry into a national one. However, these industry restructuring opportunities were exhausted by the mid-1980s. After the takeover by Elders, CUB's domestic and international strategies were heavily influenced by its corporate parent, which itself had grown to be one of Australia's largest and most successful conglomerates. John Elliott, the role model of the Australian big business and the epitome of the smart, hard-working and successful executive, vowed to 'Fosterise the world' (Fleming et al., 2004: 123) and encouraged CUB to build up a significant position in the global beer market. Acquisition became the key mechanism of CUB's foreign market entry strategy.

'FOSTERISING THE WORLD'

CUB's approach to internationalising the beer business was consistent with the internationalisation process model, which predicts overseas expansion by an individual firm as a function of its gradual acquisition, integration and use of knowledge about foreign markets and successively increasing commitment to overseas operations (Johanson and Vahlne, 1977). CUB's exports to the UK began in the late 1950s and early 1960s, when CEO Reginald Fogarty, in anticipation of a business trip to London, shipped Foster's lager so that he could entertain with his own product. The presence of Australia-born expatriates in London, a growing number of in-bound tourists, free advertising in a cult magazine, and a new group of consumers (West Indians) who developed a tremendous thirst for Foster's Lager during the 1975 Test series cricket assisted the brand in penetrating the market without any concerted promotional effort. By the early 1970s, CUB had become a hugely successful exporter to the UK, representing 80 per cent of the Australian beer consumed in that market, though only about 0.5 per cent of total UK beer consumption (Merrett and Whitwell, 1994). In 1977, CUB employed an export manager for the first time. A licensing agreement with Watney, Mann & Truman signed in 1981 to brew Foster's Draught and then

Lager ensured much wider distribution of CUB's brands. By the mid-1980s the two brands, imported and locally produced, had captured six per cent of the UK lager market and 12 per cent of the London trade (Merrett and Whitwell, 1994). CUB became a major sponsor of the Formula 1 Grand Prix, which attracted a worldwide television audience in the hundreds of millions.

CUB's penetration of the North American market followed a similar pattern from exporting in the 1960s to brewing under licence. Elders IXL accelerated the strategy of exporting Australian-brewed beer to the US and, despite the difficulties of launching and maintaining Foster's Lager, by the late 1980s Foster's was ranked as the 11th ranking imported beer and sold in all 50 American states. In 1986, Elders IXL entered into a licensing agreement with Canadian brewer, Carling O'Keefe, to brew Foster's for the Canadian market.

By 1985 Foster's had become the best-known Australian beer and one of the most recognisable Australian products in the UK, the US and Canada. Having gained knowledge about the UK and North American market, CUB then shifted to a more aggressive strategy involving acquisitions and joint ventures and hence much more investment in production. The strategic rationale for the acquisition in the UK was to use the investment as a platform for building a pan-European brand. After an unsuccessful attempt to bid for Allied-Lyons, a major British food and beverage company, in 1986 Elders IXL acquired Britain's sixth largest brewer, its old foe, Courage, for £1.4 billion from Hanson Trust. Canadian licensee Carling O'Keefe was acquired in 1987. CUB then sought to strengthen its position in the North American market by entering into a joint venture agreement with Molson, the second largest Canadian brewer.

CUB's internationalisation strategy came under serious threat after the stock market collapse of 1987. The high gearing of the parent Elders IXL eventually led to the breakup and disposal of all its businesses except for the brewing interest, which in 1990 was renamed Foster's Brewing Group. The rival Bond empire also collapsed under the burden of debt and its brewing interests were acquired by Lion Nathan, a New Zealand company. During the near-death experience of the early 1990s, Foster's laboured under more than $2 billion in debt and gearing above 300 per cent, much of it incurred in leveraging the extensive diversification of parent company, Elders IXL. When Peter Bartels became Elders' and then Foster's CEO in 1989, he announced a massive sale of Elders' non-brewing assets. Throughout the early 1990s, Foster's concentrated on upgrading its brewing facilities, improving industrial relations, investing in new technology and reducing costs. Under Ted Kunkel, who succeeded Bartels in 1993, Foster's refocused from being a sprawling conglomerate with $15.4 billion of assets in finance, brewing, agribusiness and entrepreneurial investment businesses, to a predominantly brewing group with assets of $7.4 billion.

Foster's next step to 'Fosterise the world' included a three-stage entry into China in 1993 via joint ventures and a greenfield investment. The goal was to establish a national brand and to develop a national brewing presence and distribution capabilities in the premium and sub-premium markets. China turned out to be a case of 'third time (un)lucky' (Chapter 3). Foster's over-estimated the size of the Chinese market for premium beer, faced intense competition with other global brewers as a result of excessive investment and overcapacity, and struggled to build a national brand in the absence of any national distribution infrastructure. Foster's quit the two joint ventures in the late 1990s after several years of losses and write-downs. Not until 2001 did Foster's Asian operations – now extending beyond China to breweries in India and Vietnam – break even for the first time. In mid-2006 all Foster's Asian breweries were put up for sale, though Foster's intended to retain the rights to the Foster's brand in Asia. In June 2006 the Shanghai brewery was sold to the Japanese group Suntory for $15 million. According to industry observers, Foster's had suffered combined losses of up to $150 million from its China operations and overall wrote down $167 million worth of assets (Evans, 2006a).

From the mid-1990s Foster's gradually reduced its level of FDI in Europe, North America and Asia. Foster's decision to divest the UK beer operations was motivated by the fact that their returns had never exceeded their cost of capital (Ferguson, 1999b). Between 1995 and 1997 it divested all its UK assets but retained licensing rights: Courage was divested in 1995 at a loss, and the pub ownership rights were sold in 1998. The North American market also proved extremely tough. CUB's strategy focused on making Foster's a national brand in Canada, but Canadian legislation prohibited the selling of beer across provincial borders, which effectively prevented the development of national brands – each province had to have its own breweries and brands. In addition, CUB had to spend $400 million on turning Molson's breweries into world-class facilities capable of competing in the North American market. In the late 1990s, after five consecutive years of declining market share and competitive battles with entrenched local brewers, the North American operations were restructured, the Canadian interests sold, and Foster's presence confined to exporting and licensing.

In the mid-2000s the international beer business continued to struggle, delivering a margin of only seven per cent compared with 28 per cent on domestic sales and a return on assets of only eight per cent compared with 31 per cent domestically (Foster's, 2005). In early 2006 Foster's trademark in Western Europe, Russia and Turkey was sold to its distribution partners, Scottish & Newcastle, for $750 million. The retreat was almost complete.

INTERNATIONALISING THE WINE BUSINESS

Faced with declining beer volumes in the domestic market and lacking success in its international beer strategy, in the mid-1990s Foster's sought new vehicles for growth via industry diversification. In 1996 Foster's entered the wine industry by acquisition of Mildara Blass, a premium Australian wine producer, for $482 million, and expanded its investments in leisure and hospitality activities. Mildara Blass commanded nine per cent of the Australian bottled wine market, 25-20 per cent of the premium bottled wine market, 55 per cent of the sparkling wine market and about six per cent of the Australian export market. Despite being one of the most profitable wine companies in Australia, Mildara's returns were only half the corporate hurdle, which triggered Foster's further diversification into less capital-intensive wine clubs and wine services. This was followed by a period of rapid expansion through acquisition of traditional wine producers, wine clubs and contract services businesses in Europe, Japan and the US and investments in vineyards and joint ventures in California and Chile. In the mid-2000s the wine clubs and wine services businesses were underperformers in Foster's corporate portfolio, leading to speculations about their possible divestment (Evans, 2006b; Ferguson, 2005).

Foster's most important international acquisition, the first one of such magnitude made by an Australian company, was the purchase of Beringer Wines Estates, a premium Californian producer, for $2.9 billion. This acquisition marked Mildara's transition from a strategy of exports to one of strategic FDI. The integration of the two businesses (renamed Beringer Blass Wine Estates, or BBWE) created one of the largest premium wine-makers in the world. Beringer was a better performing business than Mildara Blass, with its profitability enhanced by outsourcing production. The acquisition of Beringer shifted the balance of Foster's assets from beer to wine and increased the foreign-assets to total assets ratio from 21 per cent to 51 per cent. The initial motivation for the acquisition seemed to be risk diversification across products, geographies and varietal types (Reuters, 2000). Only later did Foster's management express the intention of developing Beringer Vineyards and Wolf Blass Wines into premium global brands in the adult beverages segment (Odell, 2005).

Foster's takeover of Southcorp, the largest but struggling Australian premium wine producer (Chapter 10), for $3.7 billion in May 2005, made Foster's the custodian of the quintessential Australian wine labels Penfolds, Lindemans and Rosemount. The acquisition created the largest premium wine company in the world with estimated combined revenues of US$2.8 billion, leapfrogging US firms Constellation (US$1.4 billion), and Gallo (US$1 billion) and France's Pernod Ricard (US$0.7 billion) (Odell, 2005).

This acquisition was controversial in terms of both the strategic logic, the expected synergies and alleged 'Pepsi-fication' of Southcorp's super-premium brands (Ferguson, 2005; Einstein, 2005). The acquisition further blurred Foster's competitive positioning and value proposition in the domestic and international markets.

EXPLAINING THE LACK OF INTERNATIONAL SUCCESS

The beer division of Foster's, still named CUB, continued to generate superior returns in the domestic market, as it had done throughout the period of internationalisation. There was little doubt that Australian beer was the cash generator that had underpinned the internationalisation and diversification into wine. Despite the declining volumes, the business continued to deliver earnings growth, while developing a successful export business. By contrast, Foster's FDI-based international beer strategy failed to meet expectations: over the period 1992-2000 Foster's lost over $400 million in its overseas operations in the UK, Canada and Asia while earning almost $2.7 billion in Australia. Similarly, the wine division's domestic operations were profitable and returning their cost of capital, while the US wine trade operations had some way to go to earn economic profit (Gluyas, 2001). Market analysts believed that the wine returns after the Beringer acquisition were not meeting expectations (Evans, 2006b, 2006c).

Foster's lack of international success and the poor return on international assets seems to have no single cause. Rather, it appears to be a combination of flaws in decision-making and rational choices gone wrong. One of the strategic errors was to assume homogeneity of markets in North America, Europe and China, which can be traced back to Foster's experience in building national beer brands in the domestic market. This strategic assumption was embedded in the mindset of Foster's senior managers. Foster's also under-estimated the strength and competitiveness of incumbent firms. The US is a notoriously competitive market, and good beer is not difficult to make even in China, where most consumers prefer local beers. Such misunderstanding was exacerbated by institutional and competitive barriers that existed in Canada, China and Europe to creating national or pan-European brands.

The key error, however, was that of not properly understanding the sources of competitive advantage in the domestic market and their transferability to international markets. These competitive advantages, as we have argued above (Chapter 3), had evolved from being dynamic capabilities to being strategic assets. The underlying causes of these strategic errors can be categorised under the labels of: over-optimism; agency problems and resulting cross-subsidisation; conglomerate mentality; and the changing nature of commitments.

Foster's executives could have been overly optimistic in their assessment of international opportunities. Behavioural economics suggests executive over-optimism can be traced both to cognitive biases in the way the mind processes information and organisational pressures (Lovallo and Kahneman, 2003). In Foster's case, over-optimism may have stemmed from the firm's administrative heritage, particularly its record of dominance in the domestic market. Foster's was an outstanding domestic brewing business, but dominance in an oligopolistic market can lead executives to confuse market power with strategic capabilities. Over-optimism was reinforced by the export success of Foster's Lager. Because growth opportunities in the domestic market had been exhausted, it was tempting to adopt an overly optimistic view of international opportunities in response to financial market pressures for growth.

A less benign, but equally plausible explanation is agency problems whereby managers made foreign investments to satisfy their own objectives (growth in assets under managerial control) rather than maximising returns to shareholders. International expansion of the beer business, followed by diversification into wine, proved to be, in essence, a portfolio management strategy aimed at using the free cash flow from the domestic beer business. Foster's was quite explicit in the 2001 annual report, which stated 'Beer=Returns, Wine=Growth', leaving little doubt that the cash flow from beer was used to underwrite the growth strategy in wine and posing the question whether cross-subsidiations enhanced shareholder value (Roberto, 2003). Some analysts were openly critical of this approach, claiming that the company had done 'the wrong thing by its shareholders by taking a very good business in beer, and diluting its returns with wine' (Evans, 2006b: 44). Analysis would suggest that synergies between beer and wine are likely to be limited (Roberto, 2003). Notwithstanding the claims of CEO Trevor O'Hoy in mid-2005 that the beer and wine were totally integrated (Beveridge, 2005), capturing synergies would require merging the very different structures and cultures of the two businesses.

Related to the agency problem is what we term a 'conglomerate mentality', or what Porter has recently described as the strategy of 'get big fast' (Hammonds, 2001: 150). Foster's CEO Ted Kunkel (2001) provided the rationale for the company's growth strategy:

> While we lead the alcoholic beverage market domestically in terms of market capitalisation, we are just mid-sized on an international scale... We need to get closer to where the main players are – that means doubling our current market

> capitalisation – for two important reasons: to be recognised by global financial institutions, and because large companies attract higher share price to earnings ratios – and thus a higher share price. So in three to five years, we want to be one of the best companies in the world, inspiring global enjoyment and be at about $20 billion market capitalisation. That's our vision.

This vision of bigness appears simplistic and more suggestive of agency problems than concern with shareholder returns. These statements also assume inefficiencies in capital markets, which are unlikely to remain in developed economies like Australia (Chapter 7).

The cognitive and behavioural biases described above were compounded by the changing nature of resource commitments to foreign markets, as Foster's progressed from being an opportunistic exporter, strategic exporter/ licensor to making investments in overseas sales subsidiaries and, finally, investing in operating beer and wine businesses in foreign markets. The decisions that Foster's managers faced at advanced stages of internationalisation involved lumpy, irreversible commitments to what Ghemawat (1991) describes as specialised 'sticky' assets, particularly when acquisitions are used to enter the market. These investments became a constraint on Foster's international strategy and undermined the return on the firm's international assets.

CONCLUSION

The story of Foster's internationalisation reinforces the notion that domestic market dominance is not of itself a strong base for internationalisation. The associated problems of over-confidence, unconscious reliance on strategic assets and free cash flow from monopoly and oligopoly rents often tempt executives into extravagant overseas investments. Dominance and scale in a modest domestic market such as Australia does not give the depth of resources (including capital) to gain sufficient market share and achieve the minimum efficient scale necessary to sustain low cost in the main markets for beer. Much larger brewers than Foster's struggled to internationalise – even Miller (US) and South African Breweries, both large successful brewers, opted for a merger.

In consumer products like beer and wine, market share can be gained initially on the basis of novelty, as was the case of Foster's Lager in the UK. However, early success can give rise to the illusion that competitive advantage in foreign markets is readily gained – this simply reinforces the problem of over-optimism. Market share becomes much harder to sustain when the next novelty brand comes onto the market if it is not based on any underlying competitive advantage.

Internationalisation involves much more than building brands via extensive marketing campaigns and acquiring production and distribution assets in foreign locations. Unless the internationalising firm can add value to these assets by enhancing their competitive advantage, shareholder value will be destroyed. The next challenge is to build managerial and organisational capabilities (Bartlett and Ghoshal, 1989) to support value-creating international strategies. This becomes particularly pressing when firms shift from the stage of export supporting FDI to strategic FDI.

NOTES

1. This case draws on Minchev and Lebed (1999) and Langfield-Smith and Lewis (1993).
2. A McKinsey consultant at the time, Elliott had acquired control of jam and fruit canner Henry Jones IXL in 1972; merger in 1981 with pastoral, trading and finance company Elder Smith Goldsborough Mort formed Elders IXL.

16. Coca-Cola Amatil

Thomas Osegowitsch

INTRODUCTION

Australian companies are regularly advised to insert themselves into the value chains of leading MNCs (Box, 2004; James, 1999). Becoming a preferred supplier or manufacturer/distributor to these leading firms is seen as a promising means of internationalisation for firms from a geographically isolated 'latecomer' country. Such an arrangement is said to facilitate rapid international expansion and to minimise the accompanying risks.

One Australian company which has followed this advice is Coca-Cola Amatil (CCA) Ltd. For more than 15 years the company has been a strategic partner to the US-based Coca-Cola Company (CCC). While the latter provides its marketing muscle and the proprietary blends that form the base of its soft drinks, CCA runs the bottling plants that manufacture the product and is responsible for distribution. Its 'anchor bottler' status with CCC facilitated the company's entry into numerous international markets in Europe and Asia within a few short years.

In this chapter we chart CCA's evolution from an Australian tobacco company to a focused multinational bottler. We document the company's rapid expansion into Europe and Asia during the 1990s with the imprimatur of its partner, and its subsequent contraction as its European operations and then its Philippines business were hived off. We also explore the relationship between CCC and its bottlers to test whether CCA's internationalisation might serve as a model for other Australian companies.

ORIGINS

The origins of Coca-Cola Amatil (CCA) Ltd date back to the beginning of the century when its predecessor, British Tobacco Company (Australia) Ltd, emerged from the acquisition of four Australian tobacco firms. The company remained focused on tobacco products until 1959, when it diversified into manufacturing light machinery and, of all things, tenpin bowling. Following the prevailing trends of the time and seeking profitable investments for the healthy cash flows generated from its tobacco business, the company extensively diversified during the 1960s and 1970s, leading it to change its name to Allied Manufacturing and Trading Industries (later shortened to AMATIL).

The company expanded into printing, packaging, a raft of tenuously related food businesses (from ice cream to frozen foods, meat processing, snack foods, a salt mine, cattle properties and fast food outlets) as well as beverage interests (from beer brewing to soft drinks). Among the latter was the Coca-Cola bottling franchise in Perth, which the company acquired in 1965 and which was followed by franchises in other Australian cities and regions (Morkel, 1996).

By the early 1970s several of the company's businesses were losing money and a new strategy called for consolidation into a few key product lines. Non-core businesses were gradually sold off, with the proceeds going towards consolidation and further expansion of the identified core businesses in tobacco, printing and packaging, snack foods and beverages.

In beverages, AMATIL continued to expand its domestic operations. In 1982 it made its first overseas investment with the acquisition of two Coca-Cola bottling franchises in Austria. By 1988 the company held more than 80 per cent of Coca-Cola sales in Australia and its respective shares in New Zealand and Austria stood at over 50 per cent (Morkel, 1996: 247). At the time, Coca-Cola accounted for the overwhelming majority of cola sales in all three markets.

In 1989/90, AMATIL was divided into three separate parts. Printing and packaging was sold off to a leveraged buyout consortium. The remainder of the group was then split into two listed companies, one assuming control of the tobacco operation and the other taking charge of the beverage and snack food interests (Morkel, 1996). Analysts interpreted the transaction as an attempt by the Amatil CEO to 'get closer to Coca-Cola and acquire more Coke franchises around the world' (Shoebridge, 1989: 35). These sentiments seemed to be confirmed when the US-based Coca-Cola Company (CCC) of Atlanta, Georgia, acquired a 60 per cent stake in the newly-created beverage and snack food venture, which was renamed Coca-Cola Amatil (CCA) to reflect its new focus. The snack food business was disposed of in January 1993.

COCA-COLA COMPANY AND ITS BOTTLERS

Coca-Cola was first formulated in 1886 by Dr John Pemberton and was sold at the counter of his pharmacy in Atlanta, Georgia. 'Soft drinks' had existed since the early 1800s when US druggists concocted blends of fruit syrups and carbonated water which they sold at their soda fountains. Pemberton's was merely one of many such drinks and, like others, contained an infusion of coca leaf (Pendergrast, 1996).

The success of Coca-Cola was such that the newly formed company soon sold the syrup to other pharmacies and began to advertise the drink to the masses. In a bid to place the beverage 'in arm's reach of desire' for everyone, the company established a network of franchised bottlers. It granted its first bottling franchise in 1899 (Wayland, 1994: 5). From the outset, CCC saw the brand as its most valuable asset. The company vigilantly guarded its trademark and relentlessly prosecuted imitators (Giebelhaus, 1994: 194).

Although CCC had recorded limited exports of syrup to countries such as Mexico and Canada as early as the turn of the century, its international business took off during World War II. Following the Pearl Harbour attack, CEO Robert Woodruff pledged, at the request of General Eisenhower, to make Coca-Cola available at five cents to every GI in the armed forces, wherever he or she might be stationed. Bottling plants soon followed advancing US soldiers into every theatre of war. This powerful first mover advantage helped the company to establish a dominant position in world markets that remains to this day. In 2004, international sales accounted for 78 per cent of Coca-Cola soft drink volume (CCC, 2005: 5).

Relationship with Bottlers

The relationship between CCC and its domestic and international bottlers is predicated on a strict separation of roles. CCC manufactures the concentrate – a 'secret' blend of various raw materials – and ships it to the bottlers. Under its franchise agreements, CCC grants franchisees the right to manufacture and sell the company's products in defined territories (CCC, 2005). Typically the company insists on an exclusive relationship, although bottlers can sometimes bottle the non-competing lines of competitors. Bottlers purchase concentrate from CCC and add carbonated water (and sometimes sweetener) before bottling or canning the soft drinks (Wayland, 1994: 2). The process is highly automated and requires massive investments in large-scale, dedicated plants. In addition, bottlers are responsible for distribution and developing local sales by cultivating strong relationships with the various customer groups. To that end they invest in extensive distributional infrastructure such as delivery vehicles, vending machines and in-store coolers. CCC is in charge of marketing to end consumers but it relies on its bottlers to finetune and manage promotional campaigns in each country.

CCC views full control of the value chain as essential and reaches into every aspect of its partners' operations. Beyond the formal influence derived from its ownership stakes – nearly three-quarters of bottled soft drink volume comes from bottlers in which the company has an equity stake (CCC, 2005) – numerous CCC managers and technicians are seconded to bottlers. CCC also negotiates with suppliers of sweeteners and containers on behalf of its bottlers (Wayland, 1994: 3).

To a point, the relationship between CCC and its partners is symbiotic: the bottlers' success in generating local sales growth also drives demand for CCC's concentrate. Nevertheless, CCC is primarily concerned with the performance of the parent corporation. It measures the performance of its (part-owned) anchor bottlers in terms of increases in *per capita* consumption of Coke products but remains mostly unconcerned with conventional performance criteria such as ROE dividend yields (Ferguson, 1999a). CCC's main interest is in increasing consumption and achieving high concentrate prices. The latter conflicts directly with bottlers' objectives because concentrate accounts for roughly 20 per cent of bottlers' costs of good sold (Wayland, 1994: 3). Concentrate prices are renegotiated annually between CCC and each of its bottlers, taking into account volume growth, input costs such as sugar and packaging as well as CCC's marketing expenditure for each country (Ferguson, 2000a). Clearly CCC has the upper hand in these 'negotiations'. Reductions in concentrate prices are virtually unheard of (Ferguson, 2000a). In its annual report CCC boasts that it 'generally has complete flexibility to determine the price and other terms of sale of the concentrates' (CCC, 2005: 6). As a result, bottlers around the world post, at best, moderate returns while CCC has enjoyed extraordinary returns over many decades.

Changes to the relationship between CCC and its bottlers invariably originate in the US. For instance, the 1980s saw a serious competitive challenge by rival Pepsi in the US market, which sent advertising ratios soaring. At the same time, higher-priced ingredients such as aspartame were introduced and concentrating retailers increasingly flexed their bargaining muscle in negotiations. Much of the resulting pressure on margins was passed on to bottlers, whose financial performance deteriorated as a result (Wayland, 1994: 13). In a quest to cut costs, Roberto Goizueta, the legendary CEO of CCC, imposed rationalisation upon its ailing US bottling network. Production was increasingly concentrated in 'mega plants' and concentration in franchise ownership saw the ten largest of CCC's US bottlers emerge with 78 per cent of volume sold by 1988 (Pendergrast, 1996: 382).

CCC itself bought out many of the poorly performing franchisees. These acquisitions were only a temporary step though, since the company had already decided to sell-down its existing majority- or wholly-owned bottlers. Conceived by Doug Ivester, who was to succeed Goizueta as CEO, the '49 per cent solution' transferred the company's bottling interests in the US into a single entity, Coca-Cola Enterprises (CCE), 51 per cent of which was floated to the public. CCE was a means of maintaining a tight grip on these bottling operations while allowing CCC to hive significant assets (and matching debt) off its consolidated balance sheet, thus boosting reported returns on assets and on equity (Pendergrast, 1996: 377-9).

The consolidation process and 49 per cent solution that had allowed CCC to streamline its US bottling network was subsequently used as a blueprint for international markets. 'Anchor bottlers', as they came to be known, began to dominate international bottling. These large partners typically were responsible for bottling operations in multiple countries and were effectively controlled by CCC through a minority stake (Pendergrast, 1996: 378).[1] CCA was one of these chosen few and the company's anchor bottler status facilitated its rapid overseas expansion. CCC's initial majority stake in CCA had been diluted to 40 per cent by 1995 (Pringle, 1996).

CCA's INTERNATIONAL ENGAGEMENT

Throughout the 1990s, CCA shadowed CCC's expansion in Eastern Europe and parts of Asia. The company acquired and successfully developed bottling franchises in these regions. Within a few years, it had transformed itself from a diversified, Australian-oriented group to a highly focused partner of CCC with significant international exposure. By 1998, CCA had accumulated businesses in 19 countries in the Asia Pacific (Australia, Fiji, Indonesia, New Zealand, the Philippines and Papua New Guinea) and Europe (Austria, Belarus, Bosnia Herzegovina, Croatia, Czech Republic, Hungary, Italy, Poland, Romania, Slovakia, Slovenia, Switzerland and Ukraine). In all of these markets it had become the major or sole Coca-Cola bottler (Coca-Cola Beverages, 1998).

CCA was then brimming with confidence, as reflected in Chairman Dean Wills's comment that 'We believe our growth is limited only by our imagination, skills and the energies which we bring to our tasks' (Pringle, 1996: 328). Following the acquisition of the Philippines franchise in 1997 from San Miguel, the country's dominant beverage, food and packaging firm, CCA became the biggest anchor bottler outside the US. However, San Miguel thereby acquired a 25 per cent holding in CCA, which had consequences later on (Lopez, 1998).

By 1997, CCA had grown so large that the then CEO of CCC, Doug Ivester, decided 'to break it in two' (Hayes, 2004: 183). In the following year, CCA announced its intention to focus on developing the Asia-Pacific businesses and spun off its European operations to create a new, publicly-listed company, Coca-Cola Beverages. Despite the acquisition of the South Korean franchise, which CCC sold to CCA as part of the de-merger, the company ended up with only half of its previous sales volume.

On the whole, market sentiment towards the de-merger was favourable at the time. Analysts believed that:

> ...dividing CCA into two businesses, one focused on Europe and one on the Asia-Pacific region, makes more sense than trying to run an increasingly global and capital-hungry operation from Sydney. It will be easier to manage, and the management should be more focused. (Bartholomeusz, 1998: 4)

Only a few pundits voiced criticism, complaining that it was difficult to assess the deal since the Korean entity had only recently been created by consolidating four separate bottling businesses (Bartholomeusz, 1998). Valuation of the Korean business was further complicated because the country was still in the grip of the Asian crisis and, like other regional currencies, the Korean *won* had depreciated drastically. Chairman Wills was forced to defend the transaction, stating that 'we are not a dumping ground. We have sought to grow the business in the Asia-Pacific region and Korea is now available to us' (Cummins, 1998: 25).

Sale of the Philippines Business

The Asian crisis made for difficult trading conditions in the aftermath of the de-merger. By December 2000, an investment of $1000 in CCA three years earlier was worth a mere $433 (Ferguson, 2000a). Not only shareholders were unhappy with CCA's performance, with CCC rumoured to be rethinking the company's anchor bottler status. In the event, CCA would not only lose its existing Asian businesses (Indonesia, Philippines and South Korea) but also be denied opportunities for buying additional territories in the region (Todd, 2000). Such speculations were given credence when CCC and San Miguel, which together held more than 50 per cent of CCA stock, offered $2.9 billion for CCA's Asian assets, well below what the company had paid for these businesses. The offer was rejected by CCA's board (Ferguson, 2000a).

CCC had previously reclaimed an Asian bottling franchise without offering it to CCA, the designated regional anchor bottler. Since the purported rationale for CCA's floating of its European assets was to concentrate on developing Asian markets, pundits interpreted this as further evidence of CCC's dissatisfaction (Ferguson, 1999).

In April 2001, CCA finally succumbed to pressures from San Miguel and CCC and sold back the Philippines franchise for $2.3 billion. Only four years earlier, the same assets had been valued at $3.4 billion when they were acquired from San Miguel in exchange for a 25 per cent stake in CCA

(Lopez, 1998). San Miguel had originally been intent on selling its interest to retire debt but the decision was reversed when the CCA share price fell sharply. By selling the Philippines business back to the original owner, CCA rid itself of the share overhang caused by San Miguel's inability to sell its stake at an acceptable price. At the same time, CCA disposed of a business whose mismanagement had caused frictions with Atlanta. CCA stood accused of failing to understand the nuances of distribution and marketing in the Philippines and endangering the relationship with local retailers (Ferguson 2000b).

Michael Clarke, president of CCC's regional company, strenuously denied that CCA's surrender of the Philippines franchise was a harbinger for the loss of its anchor bottler status. He also insisted that the sale 'was a decision by the CCA board' (James, 2001: 68). Despite such assurances, concerns that it was 'only a matter of time before CCC comes back for its remaining businesses in Asia' persisted for some time (Ferguson, 2001). The rumours were fuelled by the fact that CCA had failed to get a guarantee from CCC that it would not be trying to buy back its Indonesian and South Korean assets in the future (Ferguson, 2001: 21).

Recent Events

In light of persistent criticism of CCA's relationship with CCC, the company has in recent years been at pains to appoint to the board of directors more locals without ties to Atlanta (Hannen, 2002). In 2001, Terry Davis, an Australian with a wine industry background, was appointed CEO. He followed David Kennedy and his predecessor Norb Cole, both senior CCC managers before their appointments. An identical change was effected when, in the same year, the role of CCA chairman was passed to Australian David Gonski, a solicitor and former law firm partner. He succeeded Joe Gladden, whose main role had been as general counsel for CCC (Bartholomeusz, 1999). As of 2005, only two out of eight directors on the board were CCC appointees.

The new CEO set out to quash 'the view held by many that Amatil is merely a puppet of Coca-Cola' (Hannen, 2002: 36). Under his leadership, the company diversified further into water and juices. Exactly those same businesses, however, are targeted by CCC at a global level, prompting a new round of questions about the independence of CCA's decision-making. These questions were validated by the fact that with every significant acquisition of water and juice interests, a minority stake was sold on to CCC (Ferguson, 2003).

CCA's improved performance under Davis was attributed to diversification and product line extensions. Most of the company's growth in recent years has come from non-carbonated beverages, chiefly water and sports drinks, which by 2005 accounted for 20 per cent of CCA's sales (CCA, 2006a). These developments had also contributed to a modest increase in the company's bottom line. Even more important in the recovery was a change in CCC's formula for setting concentrate prices, which began taking into account bottlers' gross profit margin (Ferguson, 2004).[2]

Recently, the solid performance in Australia and Oceania (New Zealand, PNG and Fiji) and, to a lesser extent, in Indonesia, was marred by a persistent failure to turn around the troubled South Korean franchise (Rochfort, 2005). After seven years under CCA ownership, the Korean operation still was 'a long way from earning its cost of capital' (Mitchell, 2006: 15). Analysts pondered whether the Korean business should be offloaded and the company restrict itself to territories closer to home. That same decision has been under constant review by CCA top management and board for several years (Knight, 2004).

THE RELATIONSHIP BETWEEN CCC AND CCA

Undeniably, 'by being part of the Coca-Cola system [as one of its nominated anchor bottlers], CCA has access to the world's most popular branded beverages supported by strong advertising and unique marketing properties' (CCA, 2005: 82). The unique pull of CCC's brands facilitated CCA's entry in international markets. In turn, CCA helped expand local demand and ensured availability of CCC's products.

There are, however, strong indications that the successful partnership between the two is one-sided, with CCC calling all the shots. Like other bottlers, CCA is a virtual price-taker with regard to CCC's proprietary concentrates. Moreover, CCC's volume growth targets for CCA regularly interfered with the bottler's objectives, such as capital management, with a number of its markets plagued by surplus assets (Hannen, 2002). Atlanta also stands accused of vetoing CCA's plans for diversification into areas such as premium alcoholic beverages that could be bundled with the existing soft drink lines (Ferguson, 2003). Not surprisingly, it has become a ritual for incoming CCA executives to proclaim the company's independence from CCC.

The best benchmark for judging the one-sidedness of the arrangement is a comparison of the partners' respective long-term profitability. Return on shareholders equity (ROE) for CCA averaged less than five per cent over the period 1997 to 2001 and the company was castigated as one of Australia's 'perennial underperformers' (CCA, 2002; Hannen, 2002). While it has posted modest improvements in ROE in recent years, realising 8.9 per cent in 2004, the last time it exceeded ten per cent was in 1993 (CCA, 2005; CCA,

1998: 34). By contrast, CCC is regularly lauded for its stellar profitability. Between 1992 and 2004, the company's ROE averaged more than 40 per cent (CCC, 2003, 2005).

From a strategic management perspective, the differential profitability of buyer and seller may be explained with reference to their differences in competitive advantage and thus bargaining power. In the case of CCC, their indisputable competitive advantage lies primarily in their brand management capabilities.[3] By contrast, CCA is in the business of exploiting a local (manufacturing, distribution and sales) monopoly granted by CCC. It is unclear whether CCA can claim an independent competitive advantage and, if so, of which type.

CCC executives answer any questions concerning CCA's competitive advantage in the affirmative. For instance, Michael Clarke, president of CCC's regional company, claims that:

> We need that bottler, because sometimes the bottler has business systems in its market that are competitive in their own right... [For example, in Indonesia] CCA has invested in small trucks that can go down tiny lanes to get products into kiosks in Jakarta. It gives our products a competitive advantage. Coca-Cola doesn't have that. (James, 2001)

Comments such as these suggest that there is little in the form of *intangible* resources to set CCA apart. Earlier in its history, when the company was expanding in former Eastern Bloc countries and parts of Asia, it may have had manufacturing, distribution and promotional skills superior to lacklustre local operators. In the meantime, it seems that most of CCA's skills have become commoditised as local operators have caught up. The company's experiences in the Philippines and South Korea further suggests that differences across markets may limit the transferability across countries of any existing capabilities, especially in promotions and customer relations. As a result, CCA's disappointing returns in some foreign markets may be seen as the inevitable result of a company that lacks significant non-location-bound competitive advantages.

CONCLUSION

A key question for Australian business is whether local 'companies participate effectively in the integrated international chains being established by the world's global corporations' (James, 1999: 68). While some Australian firms have thrived as suppliers or distributors of leading MNCs, the case of CCA gives some cause to reflect. Being a strategic partner to the dominant soft drink company in the world has provided CCA with many opportunities for international expansion. The strength of the Coca-Cola brands and other CCC resources facilitated CCA's entry into overseas markets and significantly reduced the attendant risks. Yet it is clear that being a partner with such a powerful corporation is a double-edged sword. Effectively, CCA is a licensed agent that is granted the right to exploit CCC's strengths on its behalf. Because CCA lacks strong competitive advantages of its own to balance the relationship, CCC as the dominant entity is likely to extract most of the value. If CCA pays 'full price' for its franchises, it can expect only lacklustre returns.

Moreover, the enforced de-merger in 1998 suggests that CCC is prepared to constrain the international expansion of its partner in order to protect its own bargaining powers. As of 2006, CCA employs only about half the 34,000 people who had worked for the company prior to the de-merger (CCA, 2006a). In the search for growth, CCA has recently embarked on domestic diversification. In February 2005, the company acquired SPC Ardmona, an Australian maker of ready-to-eat fruit and vegetable products. The latest annual report shows the non-beverage division accounting for nine per cent of company revenue (CCA, 2006b: 6). Only time will tell whether this move, on which analysts are divided, will enhance the company's profitability and share price.

The case of CCA reinforces the importance of competitive advantage in internationalisation. If a company's growth and profitability are forever at the mercy of a dominant foreign partner, the merit of such internationalisation is open to question. Unless expansion into international markets holds the potential for adequate returns and/or affords the company opportunities to expand its own competitive advantage, what is the point? In the final analysis, internationalisation is worthwhile only if the company has an existing (and extendible) competitive advantage that will allow it to extract a sizeable share of the value created in conjunction with its partners. The experience of CCA should remind Australian companies not to accept orthodox advice about international expansion without due reflection. In particular, it should remind them not to lose sight of the issue of competitive advantage as they strive to enter overseas markets.

NOTES

1. CCC's bottling network at present includes independently-owned bottlers, bottlers in which the company has a minority (unconsolidated) stake, and bottlers in which it holds a majority (or 100 per cent) stake. Minority-owned bottlers predominate, accounting for nearly two-thirds of the company's bottled soft drink volume in 2004 (CCC, 2005: 7).

2. Not only CCA, but the other three big anchor bottlers, all of which had been struggling financially, managed to increase their financial returns significantly in the wake of the policy change (Ferguson, 2004).
3. In 2005, Coca-Cola was rated the most valuable brand in the world, estimated at a worth of US$67.5 billion (Berner and Kiley, 2005).

17. Pacific Dunlop

Geoffrey Lewis and Tatiana Zalan

Pacific Dunlop Ltd was one of Australia's oldest, most successful and innovative conglomerates.[1] It was also an Australian leader in internationalisation, covering the entire gamut of strategies from exporting and offshoring to FDI via acquisition. Ironically, Pacific Dunlop ended where it had begun, as an overseas-based rubber company: in 2002, Pacific Dunlop became Ansell Ltd, a protective gloves and condom manufacturer, with nearly 60 per cent of assets located in the US and Europe. Like all firms, Pacific Dunlop developed within a specific historic, geographic and institutional context. The strategic assets and capabilities on which Pacific Dunlop's success was built were developed within this context (Markides and Williamson, 1996; Teece et al., 1997; Chapter 3). As the competitive environment changed, Pacific Dunlop's strategic assets were eroded and the corporate strategy became a constraint rather than a driver of change. The firm became imprisoned in its administrative heritage (Bartlett and Ghoshal, 1995; Chapter 3), failing to respond to the changing environment or understand the sources of its competitive advantage in a globalising world. Pacific Dunlop demonstrates the power of administrative heritage to constrain strategic thinking and action, even in good firms managed by committed, experienced and talented managers. This chapter seeks to explain the group's success and eventual failure in terms of the concepts of corporate and international strategy.

FROM DOMESTIC CONGLOMERATE TO GLOBAL SPECIALIST[2]

Building a Conglomerate

In 1893, Dunlop of England established a small factory in Melbourne to produce a revolutionary type of bicycle tyre. In 1899 the parent company experienced financial troubles and sold the Australian business to a company floated under the name of the Dunlop Pneumatic Tyre Company of Australasia. In the early part of the twentieth century, while bicycle tyres remained the mainstay, the company manufactured an astounding range of products – cycle and car tyres, hot water bottles, weatherproof coats, rubber boots, tennis and golf balls, garden hoses – at a new factory in Port Melbourne, using formulas that were a tightly guarded secret. The viability of the Australian rubber industry was sustained during this period, as it was for the next six decades, by tariff protection.

From this base, Dunlop's strategic evolution followed a pattern typical of other large Australian corporations (Fleming et al., 2004, Chapters 3, 16). In an attempt to decrease reliance on rubber products (many of which were losing money), Dunlop pursued related linked diversification (Rumelt, 1974; Wrigley, 1970), diversifying into such products as latex foam, sporting goods, and surgical rubber. The progression from rubber tyres to rubber products made obvious sense because of Dunlop's preferential access to the strategic assets of rubber manufacturing technology and access to inputs. The 1950s was Dunlop's most prosperous decade as Australia industrialised behind the tariff wall. The company continued to develop into the mid-1960s as a manufacturer and distributor of rubber and synthetic-rubber products, supplemented by unrelated diversification via acquisition into footwear, bedding and innerspring mattresses. This diversification pattern was typical of Australian companies as they responded to emerging opportunities and technologies. At that time external capital markets were poorly developed, and such opportunities were unavailable to foreign companies because of foreign investment policies and tariff barriers. By the mid-1960s Dunlop had become one of the five biggest manufacturing companies in Australia and boasted a sound financial performance.

The next step in Dunlop's strategic evolution – growth through unrelated diversification by acquisition of public and private companies – was led by CEO Eric Dunshea. In line with management trends overseas, his intention seems to have been to transform the company into an American-style conglomerate. General Electric was arguably Dunlop's role model. Dunlop was perhaps the first example of the conglomerate strategy in Australia, but other domestic companies quickly followed suit (Fleming et al., 2004; Chapter 3). Dunlop was an early adopter of decentralisation, another US management innovation led by GE.

Nevertheless, the Dunlop conglomerate eventually became unmanageable. Dunshea then let the subsidiaries go their own way, fearing that interference from the corporate centre would destroy the entrepreneurial initiative and efficiency that was driving the growth of earnings and return on capital. Dunlop's performance remained impressive but, as the economy slowed and credit tightened, proved fragile and was further threatened by tariff reductions. Most of the companies acquired during that time were fairly small and still run by their original owner-entrepreneurs, so that the group's leadership was in no position to impose the structural changes and financial discipline that were essential to the efficiency of the conglomerate form. Having neither the financial nor the managerial strength to deal with the control crisis effectively, Dunlop became a holding company rather than a tightly controlled conglomerate and any strategic logic that might have justified the acquisitions was lost. By the early 1970s all Dunlop's financial indicators were pointing in the wrong direction against a background of economic downturn, rising wages and a 25 per cent across-the-board tariff cut.

A turnaround was achieved by a disciplined approach to restructuring the businesses aimed at maximising the value of the asset portfolio and selling the under-performing assets, efficiency improvements, layoffs and liquidation of more than one hundred companies. Financial restructuring to return capital to shareholders changed Dunlop's standing in the capital markets and enabled the long-term repositioning of Dunlop's businesses. The late 1970s were also a turning point in Dunlop's internationalisation strategy.

The final stage in the evolution of the domestic conglomerate was under the leadership of the new CEO, John Gough. Dunlop's corporate strategy crystallised around a complicated blend of targeted acquisitions, organic growth, capital injection and restructuring of industries and businesses. The tyre and the footwear/clothing and sporting goods industries were rationalised in the face of falling tariffs and increasing global competition – in effect, Dunlop was learning how to compete against international competitors. Dunlop's strategic priority in the 1980s was to achieve a low-cost position through scale, process technology and productivity, which required high-volume, low-cost products with strong brand names. Diversification moves typically started by capturing a significant domestic market share through the acquisition of companies with well-recognised brand names and was supplemented by 'clip-on acquisitions' to increase the penetration of existing market segments and the development of new ones. These acquisitions were supported by strong restructuring skills, as management was able to improve the price-earnings ratio through stripping out under-performing assets and investing capital to improve productivity. Gough, a highly skilled executive and strong leader, drew on preferential access to acquisitions based on superior information, networks (business and government), reputation and access to capital markets.

Company structures, systems and processes were consistent with this strategy. In the mid-1980s Pacific Dunlop was decentralised into 'strategic business units' which were run as autonomous businesses, often competing with each other. Strict measures of performance applied to all businesses units such as market share, return on investment and return on equity.

Financial control was tight and centralised with foreign exchange, insurance and leasing all undertaken by the corporate centre, which also played the role of investment banker, advising the board on which businesses Pacific Dunlop should move into, or out of. Board members represented a wide range of experience across different industries, both in Australia and internationally.

By the late 1980s, Pacific Dunlop Limited – renamed to distinguish it from the British Dunlop company that had been acquired by BTR Nylex in 1985 – had emerged as a major Australian-based company with a growing position in world markets. Its market capitalisation of $2.4 billion made it the fourteenth-largest company in Australia. It was considered a glamorous, high-growth stock and a solid, recession-proof diversified company – $1,000 in shares bought in 1980 would have been worth $15,000 by 1988 (assuming all dividends had been reinvested). Dunlop was spectacularly successful, not only in terms of growth and earnings, but also in the convincing articulation of the strategy it was pursuing. This clarity was communicated to the investment community, whose high regard for Dunlop was reflected in its share price. Pacific Dunlop continued its acquisition strategy, buying businesses at an average rate of one every six weeks, making it one of the most acquisitive firms in Australian corporate history (Webb, 1988).

Nevertheless, the company was clearly approaching its growth limits in the mature traditional businesses built around strong brands and high-quality manufacturing of low-value products. Although Pacific Dunlop had a dominant market position in Australia – most of its businesses held at least 40 per cent market share (Menzies, 1988) – it was wrestling with the challenge of maintaining economic scale in the manufacture and marketing of low-value products in globalising markets. The scale logic did not apply with some products (such as shoes) and where it did (sport shoes, cables and clothes), Pacific Dunlop could not compete with emerging major brands that were sourcing from low-cost Asia suppliers.

In response to maturation of its core businesses and stock market pressures, Pacific Dunlop under the leadership of Philip Brass undertook two major diversifying acquisitions – of Nucleus and Petersville Sleigh – which significantly changed the nature of the conglomerate. In 1987-88, Pacific Dunlop ventured into high technology with the friendly and opportunistic acquisition of Nucleus Limited, a Sydney-based entrepreneurial developer and manufacturer of heart pacemakers. In 1984, Nucleus had formed Cochlear to commercialise the bionic ear developed at The University of Melbourne. Nucleus also owned 53 per cent of Telectronics Holdings, a world leader in another form of pacemaker. Technological development was critical to sustaining a competitive advantage in this business and Telectronics was spending $25 million a year on R&D. Nucleus was the world leader in the manufacture of cochlear bionic ear implants with 50 per cent of the world market, and ranked third in terms of sales for heart pacemakers with about 15 per cent of the market (Webb, 1988; Lecky, 1988).

Petersville Sleigh Limited, a leading Australian food products company, was acquired in 1991 from Adsteam, another Australian conglomerate which had collapsed under the burden of debt. Food was expected to represent a significant proportion of Pacific Dunlop's long-term sales growth, both in the domestic and Asian markets, and Petersville was assessed as having a strong stable of brands operating in predictable, rationalised, recession-proof markets. With this acquisition, followed by the purchase of Plumrose and Pasta House and additional capital expenditure, more than $1 billion had been invested in the business.

An Australian Multinational

Pacific Dunlop's international expansion was a gradual, incremental process, more often linked to the firm's domestic market objectives (Bartlett and Ghoshal, 1995). From its establishment in 1893 until the late 1970s it operated exclusively in Australasia and was predominantly an importer of goods and raw materials (Blainey, 1993). The 1899 agreement between the Australian Dunlop and the British Dunlop effectively barred it from becoming a strong exporter or engaging in FDI. The two companies pegged out their respective territories and were careful not to poach. This division broke down in the late 1960s. The fast-growing Australian population in most decades, a social trend toward using cars as a major means of transportation and high tariff protection of domestic manufacturing which ensured profits for even moderately efficient plants together provided further strong incentives for Pacific Dunlop to focus on the home market. By contrast, Ansell, a manufacturer of condoms and surgical rubber acquired by Pacific Dunlop in 1969, had become a significant exporter since the 1960s, taking advantage of the high demand for its products overseas and export incentives devised in 1961 by the Australian government. Sixty nations were buying Ansell products, the chief among them being the UK, the US, Canada, Germany and Norway.

The turning point in Pacific Dunlop's internationalisation strategy came in 1977. In response to the oil crisis, which had significantly increased the cost of local inputs, and the Whitlam Labor government (1972-75), which had lowered tariffs and abandoned the export incentive scheme, Pacific Dunlop decided to shift offshore the manufacture of low-value products which were no longer profitable in Australia. It built factories for latex gloves and condoms in Malaysia (followed by plants in Thailand and Sri Lanka), and acquired the shoe manufacturer, Grosby-Rubberworld, in the Philippines.

Design, machinery and manufacturing technology were supplied from Australia and combined with offshore labour and raw materials (such as latex in Malaysia) while taking advantage of the host governments' tax incentives. Pacific Dunlop devised what appeared to be an innovative scheme to further arbitrage labour costs in its glove business: the gloves were shipped through Californian ports to a packing facility in Mexico, where costs were low and taxes waived. According to Pacific Dunlop's senior executive, '[t]he incredible thing was that no one else was taking advantage of this approach' (Menzies, 1988: 3). In the late 1980s, Ansell's products were sold predominantly in North America (51 per cent) and Europe (12 per cent), with Australia and Asia far behind (12 per cent and 9 per cent, respectively) (Gottliebsen, 1988). Dunlop had also built up a significant presence in China in its shoe and textiles businesses well before the Chinese explosion in manufacturing.

Unlike the previous stage of internationalisation, which was essentially focused on securing key inputs and accessing low-cost factors of production, the third stage in Pacific Dunlop's internationalisation strategy was triggered by market-seeking behaviour. Starting in the early 1980s, the company expanded overseas not only to cope with obstacles in the domestic market, but to access much larger markets in the US and Europe. For example, in the late 1980s Pacific Dunlop was the largest purchaser of leather footwear in China, which it distributed through numerous sales outlets, including 81 footwear shops in New York and New Jersey acquired during that period. The battery business (the Pulsar Battery was an invention of Dunlop staff in Australia) was expanded with the 1985 acquisition of Chloride Group's UK assets with international interests (some of them in the US). The business pursued further FDI in the US with the purchase of GNB Holdings Inc. in 1987. A joint venture in the US with the Japan Storage Battery Company, the leading Japanese producer, gave Pacific Dunlop access to the Japanese manufacturing technology and created a new manufacturing and sales subsidiary to supply batteries to the growing Japanese segment of the US automotive industry. The tyre business in 1986-87 entered into partnership with Goodyear to sell tyres in Australia and New Zealand. The joint venture company, South Pacific Tyres, gave the Goodyear group a stronger base in the Asia region, while Pacific Dunlop had gained access to the world-class technology essential to competing in the tyre industry. Tapping into overseas technology underpinned much of Pacific Dunlop's success throughout its long history – the business was formed on the basis of the pneumatic tyre licence, Olympic Cables relied on a technology licence with Pirelli of Italy, and Ansell, most likely, also started with a technology licence (Blainey, 1993).

As a result of geographical diversification and acquisitions in the domestic market, by the mid-1990s Pacific Dunlop had world-wide sales of $7 billion, assets of $6.8 billion, employed more than 49,000 employees worldwide, with 12,000 employees, 38 factories and over $700 million invested in Asia. It sold in more than 80 countries, had become the biggest foreign buyer of shoes from China, the largest manufacturer of surgical gloves and condoms in the world, and had developed global procurement and distribution capabilities. Pacific Dunlop believed that its competitive advantages had grown from a combination of 'innovative products, creative marketing and cost competitive sourcing' and in nurturing 'world class technology' (Upton and Seet, 1996: 3).

Unravelling a conglomerate

Pacific Dunlop's strategy started to unravel at the time of the acquisition of the food business. The company's intention in moving into food had been to build a strong domestic business, with perhaps some export potential for value-added food products. There was a view that Pacific Dunlop's food strategy had begun to drift under the pressure of external expectations. The federal government started to promote the idea of 'value-added' industries at that time. Given Australia's advantages in terms of quality and natural resources, the food industry became caught up in the rhetoric. The media perception was that the Asian market was the Food Group's strategy priority. Major multinationals, including Unilever and Nestlé, were making large-scale investments in China, and the investor sentiments were that if Pacific Dunlop did not act, they would be locked out of the Asian markets, particularly China, where they had good networks based on extensive experience with other businesses. The firm's own analysis showed, however, that the cost of building brands in Asia would be prohibitive: the segments of the food market in which Pacific Dunlop competed were essentially multi-domestic and the cost of building a strong brand in each market could be as high as $25 million. In order to generate expected shareholder returns, the Food Group had not only to succeed with expansion in Asia, and sustain competitive advantages relative to the much larger multinationals, but also to commit to restructuring the domestic food industry. Restructuring involved rebuilding value for the consumer, cutting rebates to retailers, introducing innovation, and building brands. Although Pacific Dunlop had the skills, in the end it ran out of time: the Food Group's profits did not grow as fast as market analysts expected and never earned its cost of capital. Under the pressure from institutional shareholders, the food assets were eventually sold in 1996 to major multinationals such as J.R. Simplot, Nestlé and Pillsbury.

In addition to the problems in the Food Group, in early 1995 Pacific

Dunlop was faced with product liability litigation against its US subsidiary Telectronics Pacing Systems as a result of faulty leads in implanted pacemakers (defibrillators), causing deaths and injuries. The Australian financial market was unsure of the financial impact of the litigation and lost confidence in Pacific Dunlop. Further pressure on the business came as it announced $971 million write-offs for the Telectronics subsidiary and the GNB battery division, both international, technology-associated businesses. In 1995 around 85 per cent of GNB's sales and 80 per cent of its profits were coming from the US, where it was being squeezed by price competition in the automotive battery market – GNB eventually turned out to be a major destroyer of value in Pacific Dunlop's portfolio (Kohler, 1997). Media coverage shifted from concerns about the problems with Telectronics and the performance of the Food Group, to the more general issue of appropriateness of Pacific Dunlop's overall strategy.

These events triggered a major corporate re-organisation under the theme 'The Power of One' to capture the strategic objective of maximising performance by leveraging resources across the company, through cross-functional teams representing all groups. Once again Pacific Dunlop (along with many other Australian businesses) was taking its lead from US corporations such as GE. As had been the case with Dunshea's attempts to mimic the US conglomerate model, the underlying concepts of the new integrated model were not well understood, which compromised its implementation. The new strategy was reflected in a series of moves aimed at sorting out the portfolio of businesses and facilitating internal alignment. Many of these moves, such as the acquisition of the Perry medical gloves in the US and the new lead smelter commissioned in the US for US$50 million, involved significant amounts of FDI.

By 1996 all Pacific Dunlop's divisions were under pressure, and speculation was rife that Pacific Dunlop could become an acquisition target for a foreign buyer. However, unwinding the international conglomerate proved to be more difficult than building it – not until December 2005 was the last of the old assets, South Pacific Tyres, sold back to its US partner, Goodyear. Many of the company's assets were sold to Pacific Dunlop's joint venture partners or foreign multinationals. The textiles and footwear business was restyled as Pacific Brands Ltd, sold off to a private equity firm and then floated in 2004. Cochlear had already been listed in 1995. Unwinding the conglomerate was accompanied by massive destruction of shareholder value. Pacific Dunlop's market capitalisation in May 1996 was only $2.7 billion compared with $6.4 billion in 1994; its share price fell from the $6 high in 1994 to under $1 in 2001 (Ries, 1996; Price, 2001). The last remaining asset, Ansell, became a US-based rubber company after relocating its headquarters to Atlanta in April 1996 (now back in Melbourne).

INSIGHTS AND LESSONS

The underlying theme of Pacific Dunlop's strategic evolution is that of transformation from a domestic conglomerate with strong international links to a multinational enterprise. The firm's administrative heritage was typical of many other large Australian firms (Chapter 3), being based on a portfolio management approach to corporate strategy with a heavy overlay of business and industry restructuring (Porter, 1987). This strategy was supported by organisational arrangements consistent with this approach: highly independent SBUs competing for capital, strict financial performance measures, and centralised corporate controls. As a result of related and unrelated diversification, Pacific Dunlop came to dominate the domestic market and relied on strategic assets – such as dominant market positions, brands, proprietary technology and control of distribution – in each of its businesses. However, Pacific Dunlop's administrative heritage constrained what they could do internationally. Transformation into a multinational entailed the challenge of building a new heritage encompassing new managerial mindsets and new configurations of strategic assets and capabilities.

Pacific Dunlop's story lends support to the proposition that the value of a firm's product and geographical scope changes over time (Peng et al., 2005). Matsusaka (1993: 358) documents investor sentiment toward conglomeration as 'positive in the 1960s, neutral in the 1970s, and negative in the 1980s'. Australian conglomerates such as Pacific Dunlop, Elders IXL, BTR Nylex and Southcorp used to be perceived by external capital markets as being efficient allocators of capital. Internal capital markets operated by larger firms with access to capital and management skills had significant advantages over small firms or new ventures. However, as external capital markets developed in Australia in the 1980s, this advantage became less valuable. Conglomerate strategies were right for their time, but in the long-term it would be unrealistic to expect an Australian conglomerate to build and maintain a competitive advantage in its businesses as they experienced globalisation pressures. In its cable business, for example, Pacific Dunlop was competing with Alcatel, BICC and Sumitomo in an increasingly consolidating and global industry in which scale economies and product technology were the keys to survival. The same was true of the battery and the tyre businesses. Pacific Dunlop was left with only two options: either to become globally competitive or to sell the businesses.

Pacific Dunlop's evolution into Ansell is a good illustration of strategies pursued by some diversified MNCs in more recent times. These firms either increase the extent of international diversification while decreasing product diversification, or abandon product diversification strategies altogether to become specialists in global niche markets. For example, Swedish firms such as Electrolux, Atlas Corpco, Skanska and SKF pursued higher geographical scope while reducing the level of product diversification between 1985 and 1998, and this shift in strategy was associated with a strong increase in financial performance (Bengtsson, 2000). Likewise, diversified Danish firms such as GN Great Nordic and Danisco accelerated internationalisation to become global MNCs with strong market positions in each of the triad markets at the expense of a sharp reduction in product diversification. These strategic responses seem to be driven by shifts in the relative importance of country-specific and business-specific resources and capabilities due to changes in internal and external environments, particularly the globalisation of markets and supply chains (Meyer, forthcoming). It appears that Pacific Dunlop came under so much pressure from the market analysts in the 1990s because they were aware of these latest trends and were arguing that Pacific Dunlop should follow the fashion of global expansion in a single 'core' business. The rise of profitable global specialists may well be the next stage in corporate evolution in Australian business, following the period of excessive product diversification and disastrous forays in foreign markets. Nevertheless, the emergence of Ansell and Cochlear as global specialists might well have been impossible without Pacific Dunlop's prior corporate ownership and its conglomerate strategy.

NOTES

1. The case draws heavily on Blainey (1993) and also an earlier case developed by Melbourne Business School MBA students under the supervision of Geoffrey Lewis.
2. We borrow this title from Meyer (forthcoming).

18. The TNT Group

Howard Dick*

The transportation group TNT Ltd was a pioneer in global logistics. Beginning its overseas expansion in the mid-1970s from a strong domestic base, within a decade it had assembled a global network by investment and acquisition. In 1985 the managing director boasted that TNT was operating 'the most diverse range of transport services to be found in a single group anywhere in the world' (TNT, 1985). TNT was in every mode (road, rail, sea and air), in break-bulk, bulk and express freight, security delivery and waste disposal, in freight forwarding, customs clearance, warehousing and equipment hire. In short, TNT did almost everything. Its best, though still vague, attempt to formulate a cohesive overview was 'a comprehensive range of transport services with door-to-door delivery of goods under the control of a single organisation and with all forwarding formalities covered by a single consignment note' (TNT, 1986). By 1987 the group employed 60,000 people and generated revenues of A$3 billion: 35 per cent in Australasia and Southeast Asia, 39 per cent in North America, 23 per cent in Europe and three per cent elsewhere (TNT, 1987). Yet by 1991 the group was in financial crisis. In 1996 the core business was sold to the Dutch Post Office (Koninklijke PTT Nederland, KPG). This takeover rescued the business and restored its global competitiveness. In 1998 TNT Post Group (TPG) listed separately from the telecommunications business and in 2005 the mail, express and logistics divisions were consolidated under the brand name as TNT (TNT, 2006).

FROM TRUCKS TO MULTI-MODAL EMPIRE

The driving force behind TNT was (Sir) Peter Abeles (b. 1924), who arrived in Australia in 1949 as a young Austro-Hungarian immigrant. He set up a trucking firm, Alltrans P/L, which in 1967 merged into listed venture partner

---

* I am grateful to Ian Farquhar, Peter Morris and Tom Stevens for comments on previous drafts but am solely responsible for the judgements made.

Thomas Nationwide Transport Ltd, invariably known as TNT and from December 1985 officially as TNT Ltd. Abeles then became managing director and deputy chairman of the new merged firm, five years later displacing its founder, Ken Thomas. Having become the leading Australian road transport operator, in 1968 TNT made its first move into coastal (bulk) shipping (R.W. Miller & Co. Ltd). This led in 1970 to two dramatic initiatives that quickly transformed the shipping industry in Australia and New Zealand. In mid-1970 TNT traded its 25 per cent interest in Millers for a one-third interest in Bulkships Ltd, which in 1968 had become the parent of the main private coastal general cargo operator, Associated Steamships. The attraction for the acquisition was that in 1969 Bulkship had upgraded its pioneer coastal container service from one to three ships operating between Brisbane, Sydney, Melbourne, Adelaide and Fremantle. A few months later it was announced that TNT was negotiating with the British owner P&O to buy the former Union Steam Ship Company of New Zealand Ltd. As of January 1972, TNT and Bulkships gained control of Union Company, giving access to the vehicular ferries running across Bass Strait between the Mainland and Tasmania and across the Tasman to New Zealand. Subsequently in 1974 TNT increased its holding in Bulkships to 50 per cent, thereby giving it full control over the combined Australasian fleet as Union Bulkships. Also in 1972 TNT made a bold attempt to gain control of the second domestic airline and freight operator, Ansett Transport Industries, but after political intervention by the Premier of Victoria had to be content with a passive stake of 23.4 per cent.

In 1968 TNT had already flagged its international ambitions and made its first international moves while still consolidating its Australasian base (Bugler, 1968).[1] In 1969 through Alltrans it expanded into trucking in Canada and the US, then in 1970 into UK/Europe. In 1973 Acme Fast Freight Inc. was acquired with US rail licences; in 1974 Kwikasair was established in Brazil. In mid-1976 through the Alltrans Group International Inc. TNT moved to connect its North American and European interests by means of a weekly, non-conference, trans-Atlantic container freight line, Trans Freight Lines (TFL), between northern Europe and the UK to east coast ports of the United States. Astute negotiations secured the early withdrawal of two rival non-conference lines, some of whose principals became agents for TFL, ensuring that the ships secured good loadings almost from the outset (Cheslin, 1976). The original two ships were containerships redeployed by Bulkships from the Australian coast, where profitability had been undermined by rising costs and intensifying competition from transcontinental rail. Transferred to the Singaporean subsidiary Timur Carriers (Pte) Ltd, they were re-flagged with Scandinavian officers and Singaporean crews. In 1977 six new and larger container ships were ordered through Timur Carriers and in 1980 TFL acquired another six ships from US operator Seatrain Ltd (Log, 1980: 124). By 1982 TFL had captured 17 per cent of the trans-Atlantic liner trade and by the following year ranked by tonnage as the second largest carrier (TNT; 1982, 1983). By 1980/81 TNT had also built up to a 50 per cent share in the non-conference, round-the-world operator ABC Containerline, whose principal, Tsvi Rosenfeld, was a long-time friend of Sir Peter (Farquhar, 2002b). Thus by 1985 TNT was active around the world in non-conference container shipping, also in bulk shipping and offshore supply ships. Its total fleet – owned, operated and managed – comprised 68 ships of 1.4 million tonnes capacity (TNT, 1985).

The American land transport market nevertheless proved particularly difficult. The Acme Fast Freight venture quickly turned into a financial disaster, when it became apparent that its rail freight licences could not be matched by the necessary state-regulated road freight licences to provide door-to-door transport. There was also the need to negotiate with the separate state-based branches of the powerful Teamsters' Union. Acme was sold in 1976 but TNT learned from the experience. The revised strategy was to create a 'land bridge' from the west to the east coast of the United States by means of Canadian rail. This required TNT to negotiate only with the west coast Teamsters' Union and the east coast Longshoremen's Union, both controlled by the Mafia, with whom Sir Peter dealt very discreetly (Lipson and Walters, 2006: 168-9). In due course TNT did build up a national land bridge across the US by acquiring a series of regional operators: Alaska Freight Forwarders (Washington, 1977), Pilot (Carolinas, 1982), Schuster Express (New England, 1983), Holland Motor Express (Michigan, 1984), Best-Way Transportation (Arizona, 1985), and so on. These separate entities, which in 1987 were co-branded as TNT, delivered volume, but not profits.

Similar difficulties plagued the trans-Atlantic liner trade. Notwithstanding a respectable market share concentrated in high-rated cargoes, in the 1980s TFL suffered from over-capacity and falling rates across the trade. In 1983 it tried to stem the losses by joining the conference, but thereby ceded the freedom to 'cherry pick' the more profitable cargoes. In 1984 TFL accounted for $30 million of TNT's $48 million losses in the US (TNT, 1984). In March 1986 a 50 per cent share in the line was sold to the British consortium OCL (P&O), which in mid-1987 became sole proprietor. The venture had lasted barely a decade and probably lost as much as it had earned.

In January 1980 the TNT group was reconfigured by achievement of Abeles' long-cherished ambition to win control of Ansett Transport Industries. Ansett was Australia's second domestic airline and enjoyed a privileged position in a duopoly underwritten by protective legislation known as the 'two airline policy'. It was also a rival national trucking firm and freight forwarder with diverse other investments. In a hostile takeover jointly with Rupert Murdoch's News Corporation – whose aim was to take over Ansett's national television station Channel 0 – TNT thereby became fully multi-modal. Ansett seemed to be a golden goose. With the benefit of the government-backed franchise, Ansett generated a large cash flow to fund the internationalisation of both TNT and News Corporation. Ansett was also strongly backed by realisable non-core assets. In 1984, for example, when TNT found itself in a cash squeeze, it was able to sell off Ansett's stake in gas producer, Santos.

Abeles nevertheless squandered this huge opportunity. The 1981 Annual Report featured him posed behind a large model of an Ansett plane and it does seem that he allowed a boyish enthusiasm for aeroplanes to overcome his better judgement. In 1985 TNT and News Corp. jointly established Ansett Worldwide Aviation Services (AWAS) to buy and lease commercial aircraft. By the beginning of 1991 it ranked third in the worldwide business with 55 aircraft on lease, 26 for delivery in 1991 and another 90 over the following six years to a value of US$3.5 million, almost none of this noted in TNT's accounts (Parker, 1991) – by 1996 it was valued at A$350 million (Ferguson, 1996: 25). Other sources refer to Abeles' penchant to attend the Paris airshow and there buy whatever aircraft took his fancy (Easdown and Wilms, 2002: ch. 6). In 1989 as the protected two-airline arrangement approached termination, a month's-long pilots' dispute resulted in heavy short-term losses. When new competition did emerge, earnings suffered. In the long run Ansett therefore probably detracted from the group in terms of strategy and executive time and attention. Nor did it help that Murdoch's 50 per cent of the profits was continually bled out of Ansett, whose eventual collapse in 2001 was attributable primarily to starvation of new investment, resulting in an old, ill-assorted and high-cost fleet (Ballantyne, 2002).

THE PERSONAL FACTOR

The key to TNT's extraordinarily rapid rise and fall was the charming, ruthless and idiosyncratic character of Sir Peter Abeles. Like other high-flying but ill-fated Australian entrepreneurs of the 1980s, Abeles was what is colloquially referred to as a 'deal junkie'. If an asset was for sale and he had money to buy, he bought; if there were funds to launch a new venture, it was launched. Ideas were not subjected to rigorous scrutiny. Due diligence was not performed. The action was wherever he was at the time. When he travelled to London, for example, he would summon his European managers to his hotel – he rarely bothered to visit the offices themselves or to concern himself with the lesser minions (Stevens, pers. comm.). Every week country managers had to provide Sydney head office with a detailed report of performance, which Abeles went through himself (Morris, pers. comm.). The rest of the time he networked. An observer noted perspicaciously that Sir Peter did not waste time with bureaucracy or middle management: he 'target[ed] the commercial and political elite' (Leser, 1990: 30).

Abeles' first political patron was (Sir) Robert Askin, Premier of New South Wales, whose gambling debts Abeles allegedly paid and who in 1972 conferred upon him a knighthood (Goot, n.d.; Wilkinson, 1987; Lipson and Walters, 2006). In 1976, a few months into retirement, Sir Robert was made a director of TNT and given a suite of offices in the new head office. The Askin connection gave Abeles great influence in Sydney, though not in Melbourne, where in 1972 Premier Bolte blocked his attempted takeover of Ansett Transport Industries. When the Labor Party came to power in the state of New South Wales in 1975, Abeles forged a close relationship with Premier Neville Wran: on retirement his company Allcorp Cleaning Services won a large contract to clean Ansett's Sydney airport terminal (Leser, 1990: 29).

Abeles' greatest patron, however, was Bob Hawke, prime minister of Australia from 1983 to 1991. The friendship was forged in the early 1970s when Hawke led the peak trade union, the ACTU, and Abeles found a good ally in maintaining industrial harmony in TNT's extensive and potentially restive work force. Within a year of Hawke becoming prime minister, Abeles was appointed to the board of the Reserve Bank. Sir Peter used his connection ruthlessly to defend the duopolistic two-airline policy, to the extent of undermining the Minister for Transport and Aviation, Peter Morris, who was determined to terminate the protected regime. Abeles was even Hawke's witness of the Kirribilli House agreement with Paul Keating in November 1988 to regulate the prime ministerial succession. Hawke was at Sir Peter's bedside when he died in June 1999, delivered the eulogy at his funeral and wrote the obituary in the national newspaper — other obituaries were less complimentary, some scurrilous.

The business was deal-driven and dependent on cash flow. Important decisions were therefore often made 'on the run' by Abeles, as opportunity offered, and ratified by the board after the event. Thus in the mid-1970s TNT made the bold but potentially justifiable decision to venture into the trans-Atlantic trade, as well as a reckless and shortlived adventure into the Nigerian trade. There were no obvious boundaries as to what might be attempted, or where it might be done, except perhaps that TNT was wary of Asia, where despite various shell companies in Singapore and Hong Kong it had no expertise. Cash flow was also fundamental. From the time of the buy into Bulkships, Abeles displayed great skill in leveraging off other people's money and stripping out the other party's assets to suit his balance sheet. Sir Ian Potter was well rewarded for his cooperation, but Union-Bulkships, both on the Australian and the New Zealand side, were eventually left as empty shells. The same fate befell Ansett after TNT sold out in November 1996 to Air New Zealand (Easdown and Wilms, 2002). The huge sums that were transferred into ill-planned ventures like TFL, ABC Containerlines and AWAS were frittered away to no long-run advantage. Abeles was ingenious, if not always wise, in his foreign exchange transactions, and shared the view of many entrepreneurs that payment of tax was an impediment to business development. It was therefore helpful if the flow of funds was not easily traced. Despite allegations of financial manipulation through offshore tax havens, charges were either not tested or dropped when they came to court (Toohey, 1989; Hansard, 1991). He was not perhaps the most fit and proper of persons to be appointed to the Reserve Bank, although his business insights would no doubt have been refreshing. There is, perhaps, a certain irony that he met his demise, as did the group, at the hands of his trusted finance director.

The downfall of the empire was sudden and relentless. In January 1991 in the midst of recession in Australia, the share price halved, raising doubts about the group's ability to re-finance its $3 billion debt on equity of $1.1 billion (Parker, 1991). No further dividends were paid. Abeles' recommendation that the European operations be hived off was rejected and he was ousted in a boardroom coup (Ferguson, 1996). The new CEO was former finance director David Mortimer, who headed a drastic restructure but in the process destroyed the organisational strengths that had allowed such a ramshackle group to work (Ferguson, 1996).

In the end only the express courier-logistics business proved sound enough to maintain competitive advantage, albeit under new management, in the face of tough international competition. The pioneer firm of United Parcel Service (UPS) and newcomer DHL (1969), both US-based, were also both specialist firms that were more focused and systematic in developing their networks in the 1980s. In 1983 TNT took over rival and pioneer Australian courier firm, IPEC (Skypak), but at this time Abeles was still too distracted by development of Ansett and AWAS to concentrate upon the core business of international courier services and fast freight. TNT had the network – in fact multiple and overlapping networks – but it was losing market share and profitability. This included failure to grasp the importance of rising Asia and reconfiguring Asian networks to take advantage of that booming traffic. For the group as whole, this was fatal, even if the business survived by takeover in 1996.

CONCLUSION

TNT's hastily assembled multi-modal and global empire was impressive in scope but never properly organised as a corporation. Its establishment was visionary, but there was no integrated corporate strategy to build on first-mover advantage and sustain competitive advantage. 'TNT was a hotchpotch of small and medium-sized companies mostly run by middle managers as little fiefdoms' (Ferguson, 1996: 23). Sir Peter himself exercised a highly personal, 'autocratic' and at times capricious style of management without long-term strategic direction. He had the ability to appoint and promote very good financial officers and operating personnel but such resources and capabilities were scattered around the world without any proper coordination or integration. TNT personnel offshore not infrequently discovered what other parts of the company were doing in the same country only by chance encounter (Stevens, pers. comm). As Ferguson (1996) wryly observed of Australian operations, personnel liaised better with their competitors than with other firms in the TNT group. Not until 1987 was a common TNT brand applied throughout the group, and this was only the first step towards integration.

TNT displayed most of the strengths and weaknesses of a business dominated by a single, founding entrepreneur. Abeles was not a self-made man. On the contrary, he came from a family well-established in the business world of pre-war Vienna and he had an instinctive grasp of both business and politics. He started out in the fiercely competitive world of domestic trucking but was fortunate in that his timing coincided with rapid growth of the Australian economy and a massive shift in interstate freight from sea to road. He also had the vision to see that the future of the business was not in trucks but in the new industry of freight forwarding, in which he emerged as one of the four leading firms (Rimmer, 1970). From there it was a logical development to go both multi-modal and international, a path to which his own background seems to have drawn him. His vision of seamless global logistics emerged from his Australian experience and it was by no means accidental that the global pioneer emerged from a vast country confronting 'the tyranny of distance'. Moreover, unlike the United States or Europe, Australia's logistics were not hampered by regulatory and/or national barriers. This being the case, Abeles clearly underestimated the extent to which US regulations would be intractable to his vision, especially in road transport.

The fundamental weaknesses, however, were organisational and strategic. Abeles had around him a stable core of loyal lieutenants but they were subordinate to his will and, until the very end, proved unable to stand up to him in the mapping out and implementation of strategy. As major shareholder and CEO he stacked the board with his cronies, ignored any distinction between board and management, and absolutely dominated both until his sudden downfall.[2] Corporate strategy was a global chess game, a game of wits, not a well-conceived template for the long-term development of the company. Creative chaos could be sustained as long as there was growing cash flow, but the group convulsed whenever there was a constriction. Eventually it was the combined squeeze of competitive pressure on the core businesses and reckless wagers on non-core ventures such as AWAS that caused the group to collapse like a house of cards. The TNT vision, brilliant as it was, never translated into a proper group business model. TNT's supremacy in Australasia and Abeles, top-level political alliances may well have led him to think that international logistics were easier than they were. After the halcyon years of the 1980s, TNT's global competitors mastered and re-configured their new industry faster than TNT could re-configure and organise itself. The pioneer became prey for others. Now under Dutch control, the TNT brand and business is thriving but under Australian ownership it must be regarded as a glorious pioneering failure.

NOTES

1. New Zealand is not counted here as international. Alltrans had established trucking interests in New Zealand before the merger with TNT, so that acquisition of Union Company was a logical means of connecting the Australasian network rather than a completely new initiative.
2. TNT annual reports show at the board was remarkably stable. Apart from Abeles and co-founder of Alltrans George Rockey (1969, d. ca 1980), Kenneth Smith (1961), William Martin (1966), Peter Thomson (1968) and Chief General Manager Ross Cribb (1969) were all TNT personnel from before the merger; financier Sir Ian Potter (1971-87) had been instrumental in giving TNT control of Bulkships; Chairman Fred Millar (1967) and Sir Arthur George (1973) were professional outside directors; lawyer John Horrocks (1970) represented the New Zealand interests, Allsebrook (1973) the UK interests, TNT stalwart Thomson (1973) the USA and QC Morley Koffman (1976) the Canadian interests. Sir Robert Askin (1976, died 1981) is mentioned above. Some new blood was injected in 1985, two bankers and a lawyer, but it was hardly a distinguished board for such a complex global operation.

19. The Westfield Group

André Sammartino and Frances Van Ruth

The shopping mall has been championed as 'an American cultural phenomenon', symbolic of US consumers' relentless pursuit of happiness (Farrell, 2003: xi). Yet the firm anointed in 2002 by *The Economist* as the shopping centre industry's 'only global predator' did not hail from the US (Anon, 2002: 82). Australian Frank Lowy, through his firm Westfield, had taken an American icon, recast the concept for the Antipodean environment, honed its execution, and subsequently taken on the originators on their home turf. In doing so Westfield has become the largest retail property group in the world, with a portfolio of around 120 shopping centres housing almost 22,000 retail outlets across Australia, New Zealand, the US and UK. This chapter examines the firm's rise within Australia, its expansion into the US and beyond.

Westfield's Australian roots have not been a significant impediment to international growth and success. Indeed, the similarities between suburban, postwar, baby-boom Australia and the US might be viewed as a country-specific advantage (CSA), particularly in light of Westfield's quick adoption and propagation of the shopping centre concept (Rugman and Verbeke, 1992).[1] We argue that Westfield developed firm-specific advantages (FSAs) across the shopping centre value chain. As one of the few integrated players in the industry, they made construction and redevelopment innovations and pioneered the branding of centres. They built considerable location economies via clustering of centres and used their size in given markets to squeeze greater margins out of their property assets. They utilised sophisticated financial instruments and corporate structures to attract investors. They also selected a country, the US, where the industry was highly 'fragmented' and followed an appropriate consolidation strategy (Porter, 1980).

This chapter opens with a brief summary of the emergence of the shopping centre and the resources and capabilities needed to survive and prosper in this business. The following sections chart the rise of Westfield in Australia and their move into the US. Consideration is given to how they developed and leveraged firm-specific advantages.

THE SHOPPING CENTRE INDUSTRY

Undercover shopping environments with multiple vendors have operated for three millennia, dating back to the bazaars of the Middle East. The spacious and luxurious arcades of nineteenth-century London, Paris and Milan were precursors to the post-World War II retailing innovation of the suburban mall (Jackson, 1996). Planned community shopping spaces as designated retail squares on new housing estates emerged from the 1920s in various middle-American towns. The first open-air parallel strip mall (Northgate) opened in Seattle in 1950, and the first enclosed centrally heated and air-conditioned shopping centre (Southdale) was opened in Detroit in 1954 (Farrell, 2003). The latter, designed by the highly influential commercial architect Victor Gruen, offered 'a fully enclosed, introverted, multitiered, double-anchor-tenant shopping complex with a garden court under a skylight' – the model which has dominated the shopping centre world ever since (Gladwell, 2004: 120). Changes in US tax laws regarding depreciation, along with suburbanisation, increased consumerism and an uptake of automobile usage, fuelled a tremendous boom in shopping centre building over the next few decades. Similar countries like Canada and Australia quickly followed suit. Constrained by existing infrastructure and strict planning laws, Europe was much slower to respond (Jackson, 1996).

Shopping centres differ from the typical street-based retailing environment as the centre is privately-owned space. An economic agent – typically a firm – designs and builds the centre, determines the mix and location of retailers and secures a rent from the retailers' presence. This rent often includes some percentage of retailers' sales. Shopping centre managers and proprietors are required to develop considerable competencies across a wide variety of tasks. Some have chosen to specialise in selection, construction and/or redevelopment of sites; others in management of the day-to-day operation of centres. A small number have been successful in managing the complete value chain. Westfield has been one of them.

WESTFIELD'S RISE IN AUSTRALIA

Westfield was the brainchild of two East European survivors of the Holocaust, Frank Lowy and John Saunders, who arrived in Australia as young men in the early 1950s (Kune, 1999; Margo, 2000). The two met when Lowy delivered smallgoods to Saunders' small Sydney delicatessen. They quickly became business partners in a coffee shop in the outer suburbs, then seized an opportunity to buy and subdivide re-zoned farmland in a newly suburbanised part of western Sydney. Their new business – Westfield – progressed through housing subdivisions into small, kerb-side shopping strips and, in 1959, their first shopping centre. Westfield Place centre in Blacktown in Sydney consisted of twelve stores, a supermarket and a small local department store, set around an open square, with 50 car-parking spots (Westfield Holdings, 2000). This was not the first such venture in Australia, but it set the ball rolling for Lowy and Saunders.[2]

From the outset, Lowy and Saunders took turns travelling annually to the United States to learn more about the burgeoning industry (Korporaal, 1986). They toured centres, particularly in California, and became active participants in the conferences of the International Council of Shopping Centres (Margo, 2000). Saunders became a devotee of Gruen's philosophy of building new social spaces (Kune, 1999). They brought this knowledge back to Australia and used it to build more centres. The company floated on the Australian Stock Exchange in 1960 and built another five centres throughout New South Wales before expanding into Victoria and Queensland in 1966-67. Shopping centres were not at this time their sole business. The firm also built supermarkets in New South Wales for retail giant Coles. Westfield leveraged this relationship to secure the land and an anchor tenant for its first Victorian site (Doncaster, opened in 1969). Centres were built on land secured through the purchase and demolition of residential properties (Burwood, Sydney opened in 1966), and via development of previously unused and fringe land (Toombul, Brisbane opened in 1967). Westfield made its first acquisition in 1969 when it was called in to revitalise an ailing centre owned by Myer (Miranda, in southern Sydney).

By the late 1960s the firm had become skilled along the industry's value chain. Westfield kept architects, engineers and financial specialists on staff. The firm developed considerable project management capabilities. 'Critical paths method' was utilised to complete the large Burwood development six months ahead of schedule. Lowy and Saunders honed their negotiation skills with residential property owners, retail leaseholders, and also joint-venture partners such as the large department store and supermarket chains. Westfield did not just build a centre and then sit back and watch the rents roll in. Usually they refurbished and extended the site to retain tenants, attract more customers and stores, and tap into the growing suburban populations around the centres. Centres were extended as often as every five years, with these extensions often doubling the available lettable space. Kune (1999: 127) suggests that Lowy and Saunders did not view shopping centres as 'static structures': 'Each had a life of its own, and each needed expansion and regular upgrading, as well as changes to what was sold there and how it was sold, in harmony with the changing needs of shoppers'. These refurbishments were often innovative. The firm experimented with car-parking arrangements, such as underground and rooftop parking, and utilisation of shared spaces, such as food courts.

By 1977, Westfield had 15 centres in Australia, and had secured the major retailers such as Myer, Coles and Woolworths as major clients/partners. Westfield has become the predominant centre developer and operator in the country. The options for continued domestic expansion lay outside their core business. Westfield had built up local interests in office buildings and motels. In the mid-1980s they took ownership of one of Australia's national television networks, Channel Ten. This venture, which lasted little more than four years, was a disaster, resulting in losses of more than $500 million, including more than $100 million directly from Lowy's pockets (Margo, 2000: 236-8). Diversification was eschewed from then on. Lowy focused his attentions offshore (John Saunders had severed his day-to-day relationship with Westfield in 1986). In doing so Westfield left behind their more timid retail partners (see Chapter 9).

WESTFIELD'S EXPANSION INTO THE US

Westfield first went international in 1977, when it purchased Trumbull Shopping Centre in Connecticut, US (Korporaal, 1986). This was followed in 1980 with the purchase of three centres in California, Michigan and Connecticut and three centres in California, New Jersey and Long Island, New York in 1986.[3] Each acquired centre was revamped and redeveloped considerably. It was to be eight years before Westfield expanded their US portfolio of seven centres. Westfield's involvement in the US market increased dramatically in 1994 when together with General Growth and Whitehall Real Estate they purchased 19 centres for US$1 billion. Westfield later bought out General Growth and Whitehall and established itself in the top five owner/managers of shopping centres in the world (Westfield Holdings, 2000: 141). Acquisitions continued over the next seven years, such that by December 2005, Westfield's US portfolio included 67 centres with 9,400 retail outlets and assets valued at US$16.9 billion (see Table 19.1).

The US shopping centre industry of the 1980s was enormous but struggling with some substantial issues. Shopping centre construction had exploded in the late 1950s and through the 1960s. In 1955 there were 21 large regional shopping centres in the US. By 1960, there were 98 completed or under construction. By 1967, there were 397 (Hanchett, 1996: 1098).[4] The 1970s saw construction of at least another 400 large centres (Veatch, 2001: 2). Yet, by the early 1980s, construction numbers had fallen considerably, big-box category killers were usurping the department store-anchored centres (see Chapter 9), and questions were being asked about the vitality and relevance of many malls.

Table 19.1: Westfield's empire (December 2005)

	Australia	US	UK	NZ
No. of centres	43	67	7	11
Retail outlets	10,900	9,400	800	1,400
Gross lettable area (million sq. metres)	3.4	6.6	0.3	0.3m
Asset value (billion)	A$20.4	US$16.9	£3	NZ$2.2

Source: Westfield (2006)

Hanchett (1996) argues that the postwar boom can be attributed to the introduction in 1954 of accelerated depreciation into federal tax laws. Legislation, intended to encourage capital investment in manufacturing and stimulate a slowed economy, allowed considerable deductions for the costs of developing business properties. The new shopping centre concept proved suddenly attractive to developers who had previously subdivided land into housing estates with quicker returns. Investors rushed into these new tax-shelter vehicles, writing down the immense up-front construction costs against other income sources, and on-selling the centres to other parties (for a capital gain) once the depreciation benefits had disappeared, usually within six to seven years. There was no deduction for redevelopment, so the incentive was to find new sites, ideally on the cheapest land. Land itself was also not depreciable. The outcome of these institutional idiosyncrasies was a complex mix of ownership structures. Often investors owned only part of the shopping centre complex, such as the land or the buildings, and typically through tailored, and restrictive, financial and legal entities such as property trusts. These ownership and governance decisions were regularly driven by income and taxation preferences rather than competitive considerations.

The outcome was a highly fragmented environment with few businesses genuinely focused on developing and managing any large numbers of centres for any considerable length of time. There were very limited levels of vertical integration and many 'hands off' asset managers. Over time, many centres ended up as either single, forgotten, run-down assets in wealthy family's portfolios, or as a bundle of low-risk, steady-income-streams on the books of institutional investors.

THE WESTFIELD ADVANTAGE

Frank Lowy summarised his motivations for entered the US as follows:

> Australia at that time was a relatively small market, and expansion opportunities were limited. We wanted to extend our business. The

> United States, although it was far, had all the other components: We understood the business, we knew the conditions, we spoke the language. And it was a relatively simple matter to do except for the distance. (as quoted in Hazel, 2001)

Westfield had developed considerable firm-specific advantages (FSAs) through its Australian expansion (Rugman and Verbeke, 1992). It now had strong competencies along the value chain, in the areas of (i) property selection; (ii) redevelopment; (iii) branding and marketing; (iv) retailer relations; and (v) financing. Each of these proved highly transferable and valuable in the US.

Westfield selected its property targets very judiciously. As noted above, by the mid-1970s the US market was overflowing with investment options. The seven centres bought between 1977 and 1986 were selected because each was 'in a prime location, fed by densely populated areas with community incomes well above average and backed by healthy employment and growth prospects' (Margo, 2000: 269). Westfield sought to form clusters of centres around particular cities or within a small number of states. They built considerable holdings on the east coast and in California before expanding in the Mid-West (Table 19.2). By 2000, Westfield was the largest mall owner in Connecticut, in California (specifically in San Diego, LA County and in Silicon Valley at San Jose), in St Louis, Missouri and in Maryland/Washington DC (Westfield Holdings, 2000: 137). Such clustering allowed Westfield to build up location-specific knowledge and relationships and to leverage bargaining power, with sub-contractors, suppliers, planning officials, media and retailers. In this way the firm did not tackle the whole of the US at once, just pockets of attractive locations. Extensive due diligence was also undertaken on any potential acquisitions utilising the firm's own data management systems (Margo, 2000: 280).

As Frank Lowy boasts, Westfield is 'the only company in the global mall business with a focus on the redevelopment and expansion of existing assets to maximise value' (Catalano, 2006). Unlike its competitors, Westfield has been involved in both the construction and management of shopping malls from their inception. This combination gave them the unique expertise that enabled them to capitalise on redevelopment opportunities both at home and abroad. In Australia Westfield learnt to use space wisely in order to extract maximum returns. With less reliance on cars, greater public transport usage and more concentrated populations, shopping centres in Australia were typically situated in metropolitan areas where the land was more expensive. In the US, by contrast, centres were often built on farmland on the outskirts of town, fed by highways, and surrounded by sprawling car parks (Korporaal, 1986). Westfield's strategy was to reduce land usage by building rooftop and underground parking and squeeze in smaller retail outlets. Even today, Westfield's Australian centres have a ratio of retail outlets to gross lettable space more than twice that of their US centres (Table 19.1).

Table 19.2: Westfield's US portfolio of shopping centres (by state) in select years

	Year	1986	1994	1999	2005
East Coast	CT	2	4	4	4
	NJ	1	-	-	1
	NY	1	1	1	1
	NC	-	-	1	2
	FL	-	-	-	5
West	CA	2	9	20	26
	WA	-	1	2	4
	CO	-	1	1	1
Mid-West	MI	1	-	-	-
	MO	-	4	6	6
	MD	-	2	3	3
	OH	-	-	-	6
	IN	-	-	-	1
	IL	-	-	-	6
	NE	-	-	-	1

Notes: CT = Connecticut; NJ = New Jersey; NY = New York; FL = Florida; CA = California; WA = Washington state; CO = Colorado; MI = Michigan; MO = Missouri; MD = Maryland; OH = Ohio; IN = Indiana; IL = Illinois; NE = New England

Source: Harvard Business School (1999); Hewett (2005); Westfield (2006)

Westfield has been well placed to respond not only to changes in consumer spending habits, such as the desire for one-stop shopping, but also to evolving business practices and their effect on the demand for certain kinds of spaces, such as the effect of just-in-time delivery on the amount of storage space retailers required (Harvard Business School, 1999). The expansion and redevelopment of centres is not limited to existing assets, however, as Peter Lowy explains: 'Our philosophy is that we buy malls from other companies and then bring our skills to bear reinvesting capital, expanding and redeveloping' (Papps, 2004). Westfield succeeded in the US by buying run-down malls that no one visited anymore and turning them around when the tendency of others in the industry was to go and build a new mall. Development is integral to the group's competitive advantage such that it has become the group's 'primary source of earnings and growth' (Steven Lowy cited in Harley, 2005: 54). In 2004 Westfield announced a five year plan to redevelop their US portfolio at an estimated cost of $8 billion (Papps, 2004); in 2005 Steven Lowy predicted that the group would start $1.5 to $2 billion of projects every year worldwide (Harley, 2005a).

The International Council of Shopping Centres acknowledged that Westfield was the only global shopping centre developer to establish its name and centres as a brand (Westfield Holdings, 2000). Being referred to as the mall equivalent of McDonald's is certainly a tribute (Anon. 2002). Westfield views its branding campaign as a major point of differentiation from its competitors but as the story goes it was the customer rather than company that first used the Westfield brand. Lowy apparently overheard a conversation on a Sydney street in mid-1960s in which one woman said to another 'Let's go to Westfield's'. Soon the Westfield Shoppingtown brand was born (Harvard Business School, 1999). Westfield's branding efforts such as common signage, promotions and customer services programs were designed to increase shopper recognition and loyalty. This branding worked particularly well because of the aforementioned clustering of centres.

From the outset Westfield nurtured its relationships with retailers. It saw the value of 'anchor tenants', coupled with branding, as magnets for consumer traffic and, thus, other tenants.[5] Westfield always prided itself on designing and redeveloping centres that maximise the number of retail spaces. Lowy claims he and Saunders never forgot their own retail roots, and that this made them the exception: '...the developers in America at the time, and probably even now, don't have the retail flair, consumer flair that we had' (as quoted in Hazel, 2001). The firm was renowned for being ruthless with its tenants, however; for squeezing them hard on lease arrangements so as to extract maximum returns from its assets.[6] The firm's data management systems allowed them to closely monitor customer traffic and tenant performance. Tenants expressed satisfaction at the increased performance of redeveloped sites (Margo, 2000: 143).

Acquisition and redevelopment of centres is a capital-intensive activity, with considerable up-front financial burdens and deferred and somewhat risky income streams. As Westfield developed in both Australia and then the US, the firm has attracted investors via innovative means. Concerned by the vast amounts of capital tied up in the firm's property assets and the additional loan commitments for ongoing acquisitions and developments, in 1978 Lowy split Westfield's public company in two. A property trust now owned most of the centres. A separate listed holding company managed the centres and undertook development activities. At that time, property trusts had enormous tax advantages and many investors benefited considerably. Swift changes in the tax laws reduced many of these benefits, so the trust itself was itself floated. Westfield subsequently floated parts of its international operations in both holding and property trust forms, listing one in the US. The aim and outcome was to free up funds and attract a mix of investors who could now choose the vehicle that best suited their income needs (Pollard, 1988). The property trusts earn rental income and share in any capital gain on resale of properties. These are low risk, stable incomes and attractive to investors such as pension funds. Managing centres and redeveloping is a more volatile business and attracts different investors (Anon., 2002). The strategy proved highly successful. It has been calculated that an investor purchasing $1,000 worth of Westfield Holdings shares upon float in 1960, and reinvesting every subsequent dividend and bonus paid, would by 2005 have had a $167 million investment (Buffett, 2005).

One other important aspect of the Westfield expansion story was Frank Lowy's willingness to commit his own time to the US venture. He spent almost six months in the US overseeing the Trumbull project. He used the venture as a training ground for his son David, and soon David and a US recruit, Richard Green, were heading up the US business from a Los Angeles base. David eventually departed, and the late 1980s saw another son, Peter, take on a leadership role in the US arm of the business. Peter Lowy and Richard Green remained at the helm in 2006. This continuity represented considerable institutional memory for the firm and reflects the enormous commitment made by Westfield to establishing themselves as a legitimate player in the US. It also pointed to the firm's commitment to continue its expansion beyond the eventual exit of the founding father.

WESTFIELD IN NZ, UK AND ASIA

Westfield's internationalisation was never a story of extreme risk-taking. Frank Lowy saw little value in acting as the pioneer in environments where the payoffs were too low. As long as there were opportunities to be had in the US, then Europe, Asia and New Zealand could wait. Eventually in 1997 the group took over the management of ten St Luke shopping centres in New Zealand. In 2000 Westfield Trust and St Lukes Group merged and the New Zealand centres were re-branded as Westfield centres. Attempts to enter the UK market in the 1970s and 1980s were unsuccessful. Lowy expressed considerable frustration with the lack of dynamism in the UK investment houses and lack of planning enthusiasm (Margo, 2000). Not until early 2000 did Westfield finally obtain access with a 75 per cent stake in a centre at Broadmarsh, Nottingham. The firm has made considerable headway since, with seven centres on the books, and is set to open the largest centre in Greater London in early 2008. Westfield briefly entered Asia in 1998 with a ten per cent share of Suria Kuala Lumpur City Centre in Malaysia. This investment was short-lived, however, with the company withdrawing in 2000 after the Asian currency crisis. Today Westfield's focus continues to be further expansion in the US and Europe. Frank Lowy claims Asia '...is on the radar screen – but it is too early' (as quoted in Hewett, 2005: 1).

CONCLUSION

Through Westfield, Frank Lowy became a multi-billionaire. In early 2006 his personal wealth was calculated at A$5.4 billion (BRW, 2006). In less than half a century he had transformed from a poor migrant to not only a business success story, but a prominent philanthropist and sports administrator.[7] The path to riches came from a carefully executed internationalisation strategy, grounded in an immigrant's world view. Along with John Saunders, he saw the similarities between 1950s Australia and the US and systematically adopted, adapted and transplanted a US idea to Australia. Once successful in Australia, and unsatisfied with resting on his laurels, Lowy felt no qualms in 'migrating' once more. Judiciously, rather than audaciously, Westfield ventured to the birthplace of the 'mall'. Lowy looked at the US not as one, enormous, market to be conquered, but rather as many small Australia-like opportunities. In these worlds, Westfield was a big fish, with finely honed advantages. Westfield had taken a leaf from Porter's 'competitive strategies' (Porter, 1980: ch. 9). They had found an incredibly fragmented industry where few players envisaged economies of scale, with diverse market needs and high exit costs. Westfield utilised their firm-specific advantages to better serve customer needs and achieve localised scale economies. Over time, they consolidated their operations across the US, and embarked upon further internationalisation, again in a judicious and tempered fashion.

In 2004, the US had almost 2 square metres of retail space per capita. Australia had 0.6 metres. The rest of the world had typically less than 0.3 metres (Baker, 2004). There remain enormous global opportunities for an experienced, competitive, innovative and ambitious shopping centre developer. If Westfield could sell shopping centres back to the US – the proverbial instance of selling ice to Eskimos – then further expansion may be much easier.

NOTES

1. This is in direct contrast to the effect geographic isolation and small, unconnected markets had on the broader retail sector (see Chapter 9).
2. The first Australian shopping centre opened in 1957 at Chernside Park in Brisbane. It was a considerably larger centre than Westfield's, with 700

carparks. There are claims that this was the first such centre outside the US (Westfield, 2000), but it is more likely it was the first outside North America.

3. This purchase was, at the time, the largest real estate transaction in the history of the mall business. Westfield paid the owners, Macy's, US$364 million.
4. A large regional shopping centre is defined as anything with over 300,000 square feet (27,871 square metres) of retail space.
5. Anchor tenants are large stores that take a significant portion of a centre's 'footprint'. Typically in the US, these have been department stores, with the store chain often owning that portion of the centre. In Australia, Westfield applied a slightly different model, with greater use of supermarkets and variety stores as anchors, and little co-ownership.
6. In 2001, Australia's competition regulator, the Australian Competition and Consumer Commission (ACCC), began proceedings against Westfield for restrictive and unconscionable tenancy contract clauses regarded as tantamount to 'bullying'. The resultant hearings saw Westfield 'undertaking not to abuse its substantial power when settling retail tenancy disputes' (Hughes, 2004: 21).
7. Under his stewardship, the Australian national soccer league was rejuvenated and in 2005 the national men's soccer team qualified for the World Cup for the first time in 32 years.

20. Macquarie Bank

David Merrett and Shey Newitt

In contrast to the uneven internationalisation experiences of the major trading banks (Chapter 7), Macquarie, one of the more than one hundred investment banks[1] operating in Australia since the mid-1980s, has gone from strength to strength. In the 1980s the dismantling of government controls of the finance sector radically altered the environment in which merchant banks operated. In response to this government deregulation, many foreign operations elected to withdraw from the Australian market. One of these foreign banks, Hill Samuel,[2] the UK parent of Hill Samuel Associates, was prepared to exit the Australian scene in 1985 by allowing a management buy-out. The resulting entity, now named Macquarie Bank, was one of the new banks to receive a banking licence in 1985. Further major changes in government policy permitted the privatisation of infrastructure in the mid-1990s by which time Macquarie had listed on the Australian Stock Exchange.

These broad environmental changes provided the same challenges and opportunities for a large number of investment banks in Australia. Deregulation and privatisation altered what Rugman and Verbeke (1990) would describe as the country-specific advantages (CSAs) available to firms in the financial services industry. The closer integration between Australian financial markets and those of the world placed greater pressures on local firms to meet international standards in terms of the range of products on offer and their cost. This was particularly the case for those firms servicing the needs of corporate clients. Macquarie's predecessor, Hill Samuel, did provide the traditional fare of investment bankers such as advisory services, treasury products, debt origination and placement through the 1970s and 1980s. However, from the mid-1990s, Macquarie, taking advantage of being in the right place at the right time, chose to strike out in a different direction. The bank developed a set of firm-specific advantages (FSAs) that enabled it to identify and exploit niche markets first in Australia and almost simultaneously overseas. Within a decade 40 per cent of its assets were located overseas and 40 per cent of its revenues originated outside Australia (Macquarie, 2005: 84).

HILL SAMUEL TO MACQUARIE BANK

Merchant banks flourished in Australia because they were able to offer a range of new products to businesses which were unavailable from the trading banks because of government regulation. However, Australian trading banks responded to the challenge posed by these new institutions by taking minority positions in merchant banks from the late 1960s, although they were prevented from 100 per cent ownership until 1984 (Skully, 1987: Table 4.3, 22, 59-62). Merchant bank numbers rose more quickly after the emergence of a local short-term money market in the late 1950s and the beginning of the mining boom of the 1960s (Skully, 1987: 18-20). Foreign firms held sway in numbers and influence with British merchant banks being first off the mark (Skully, 1987: Table 4.4, 24). American and Japanese banks, whose clients had significant investments in the manufacturing and the emerging resources industries, also set up merchant banks as a way of circumventing the fact that they were prohibited from securing a banking licence. The influx of foreign firms was checked in the 1970s by a combination of a deteriorating economic environment and, more importantly, by government regulations (Skully, 1987: 24-6).

Hill Samuel, a long-established British merchant bank, entered the Australian market in 1970. The venture was a very modest affair, with five staff and a capital of $250,000 (Thomas, 1991). Nevertheless, Hill Samuel prospered over the next 15 years to become one of the biggest operators in a crowded market. By the mid-1980s it had the largest number of staff (300) and was one of the few merchant banks to have nation-wide representation (Skully, 1987: Tables 18.9, 221-2 and 6.4, 48-9). After 1985, the newly formed Macquarie Bank offered a similar range of products to its rivals but did not hold a leadership position in any of them, with one exception (Skully, 1987). It was a clear leader in the field of cash management trusts, which it had pioneered in 1980 (Skully, 1987: Table 13.8, 168), but that product became less attractive after deregulation which then allowed banks to offer market rates of interest.

Deregulation posed strategic challenges for merchant banks. As Wallace (1993: 231) argued, it ‘widened the scope for the merchant banks’. However, the issue was whether a merchant bank was the best vehicle for providing the range of services on offer. Many of the foreign parents of merchant banks took over those services within their newly licensed banks. A number of foreign merchant banks, including Hill Samuel, received banking licences enabling them to combine deposit taking and merchanting banking activities. Local banks which had set up merchant bank subsidiaries also took them back in-house. Many of the complex partnerships between foreign and local partners, some a product of government regulations, were unwound. The orgy of lending that accompanied deregulation and the inevitable crash that followed wiped out the non-bank owned local merchant banks. Thus the industry was restructured by the early 1990s with 90 per cent of assets owned by banks licensed locally (Wallace, 1993: 228-39).

Like the rest of the industry up to the 1980s, Macquarie's activities were focused on serving the domestic market. The high degree of foreign participation had, of course, dampened potential outward FDI. Local subsidiaries had a mandate to operate in Australia and to leave overseas markets to their parents or subsidiaries already established in key markets around the world. Local companies lacked the scale and skill to be of interest to major international corporations. Macquarie had offices in New Zealand and Hong Kong, the most common destination for those firms which ventured offshore (Skully, 1987: Table 16.2, 203). There was nothing then to suggest that over the next 20 years that Macquarie would emerge as the powerhouse of Australian merchant banking.

Since achieving its banking licence in 1985, Macquarie's balance sheet and market share has expanded rapidly. Its share of total banking assets within Australia is one measure of its expansion. In 1991, Macquarie held 0.6 per cent of total banking assets behind 25 larger institutions. The Bank's share rose to 1.1 per cent in 1996 and to 2.2 per cent in 2006. It rose in the rankings from twenty-sixth place in 1991 to sixteenth in 1996 and eighth in 2006 (RBA, various; APRA, various). Macquarie quickly emerged as a leading second-tier deposit-taking institution in a market where the big four trading banks' combined share rose from 55 per cent in 1991 to around 66 per cent over the next 15 years.

These impressive data do not capture all of Macquarie's growth. First, investment banks rely heavily on fees for advisory services for example, which are largely independent of assets. Moreover, the bank has a large number of managed funds with a value significantly exceeding its banking assets. The assets under management in these funds rose from $13.8 billion in 1996 to $88.9 billion in 2005 (Macquarie, 2005: 92). An unequivocal measure of its success is its rate of return on shareholder's funds. Its share price rose twelve-fold from its listing in 1996 to end September 2005 compared to a rise of 113 per cent in the S&P/ASX 200 Index over the same period (Mellor, 2006).

International expansion has been the driving force behind Macquarie's success over the past decade, now accounting for around 40 per cent of revenues. Macquarie's overseas expansion since the mid-1990s needs to be put in the context of a radical re-ordering of global investment banking over recent decades. The reduction in barriers within national financial markets, for example the ending of the separation of investment and deposit-taking banking in the United States, and greater freedoms to move money across national boundaries since the 1980s, have permitted large banks to offer services globally. Leading Wall Street investment banks and large commercial banks from the US, Europe and Japan now compete to provide a comprehensive set of banking services to governments and very large corporations (Grosse, 2005; Durisin and von Krogh, 2005). Many of these banks have a presence in the Australian market (APRA, various). The premier firms are able to raise funds and deliver services in a wide range of countries. Durisin and von Krogh (2005: Table 2.2, 50; 61-3) divide their list of the more than 40 firms active in global investment banking in the 1990s into four groups, three of which are already global, full-service firms or aspiring to become so, and a fourth sub-set that have a regional or special focus. Macquarie, although not listed, would fall into the last category by virtue of its strength in 'specific product categories, sometimes on a worldwide level' (Durisin and von Krogh, 2005: 63).

MACQUARIE BANK'S BUSINESS MODEL

Macquarie's unique business model applies the traditional skills of an investment bank to new markets. It acts as financier, operator and fund manager of a growing list of assets around the world. Macquarie led the way in identifying and securing niche markets where the assets in question have an element of natural monopoly, such as toll roads, airports or water supply.

Macquarie's growth has been driven by a new set of products and a new business model that would increasingly take it abroad. In 1994 Macquarie and Leighton Holdings put in a bid to finance the construction of the Eastern Distributor toll road in Sydney. They won the tender for an extended project in 1996 (Walker and Walker, 2000: 211) and raised the finance through an IPO. This highly lucrative venture was the first step in 'buy[ing] monopoly assets such as roads, bridges and water companies and then take them public, usually bundling them into funds that are listed on various stock exchanges. Macquarie manages the funds and retains a stake [in the asset], earning fees at every stage' (Mellor, 2006). Acquisitions of infrastructure have taken Macquarie into many countries around the world and have given rise to 27 associated funds, Macquarie Infrastructure Group being the largest, listed on the Australian, New York, Singapore, Seoul and Toronto stock exchanges (Mellor, 2006).

First-mover advantage has been an important element of Macquarie's success. To minimise the threat of competition from the top-tier investment banks it has sought out under-developed markets, second-tier transactions, and less attractive geographical regions or industries (Oldfield, 2005a; Economist, 2004). The infrastructure management sector, in which Macquarie has a commanding presence, generates lower margins than other major corporate finance projects. As a result, the sector attracted little interest from US-based banks. Similarly, Macquarie entered Asia when most investment banks were concentrating on European and American markets.

Once the bank had a presence in the new market, time and resources were invested to augment Macquarie's expertise and knowledge to build competitive advantage and provide a platform to diversify into 'adjacent' markets offering similar potential (Harley, 2005b). This model has been used often to enter new geographical locations, industries and product markets. For example, Macquarie's expertise in funding and managing toll roads, which was developed in Australia during the 1990s, has been successfully exported to destinations in Europe, Asia, Africa and the Americas (Table 20.1).

Table 20.1: Macquarie Bank toll road projects worldwide as at 2004

Location	Project	
North America	US:	Detroit-Windsor tunnel; SR125 South road Michigan
	Canada	407 ETR toll road
South America	Chile	Talca-Chillan road, Temuco-Rio Bueno road, Collipulli-Temuco road, Santiago-Talca road
Europe	Britain	M6 toll road; Yorkshire Link road; Bristol airport
	Portugal	Tagus Crossings road; Algarve tollroad; Norte Litoral toll road
	Germany	Warnow tunnel
	Spain	Autema road; Ausol I road; Ausol II road; Europistas road; M45 road; Artxanda road; Radial 4 road
Asia	South Korea	Soojungsan tunnel; Kwangju toll road; Daegu-Busan expressway; Baekyang tunnel; Machang bridge
	Japan	Hakone turnpike
Africa	South Africa	N3 toll road; N4 toll road

Source: Boyd and Murray (2004)

Macquarie has become the biggest toll road operator in the world (Clegg, 1999), with toll roads representing almost half of its entire investment worldwide (Economist, 2004).

Macquarie has applied its expertise in financing projects with a high cost of capital to enter horizontally adjacent markets. It owns airports in Australia, Britain and Italy, and electricity generators in Chicago. Cross-border leasing of aircraft was exported into cross-border leasing of shipping containers in the US, and communications equipment in Ireland, France and the United States (Shand, 2002).

This strategy of entering adjacent markets produced a unique pattern of foreign expansion. Macquarie distinguishes itself from the global, full-service investment banks mentioned above in that its international presence is highly focused. The Bank's operating divisions employ a diverse range of exposures in the conduct of their international business. For instance, the Investment Banking Group, which includes all aspects of infrastructure funding and management, is most heavily involved. The bulk of the business in leasing and infrastructure matters takes place through offices in Canada, the US and UK. The Banking and Property Group finds customers in a wider range of countries, including the US, Hong Kong, Italy, UK, Japan and Korea. In contrast, the Treasury and Commodities Group is involved in advisory, funding and trading activities in Canada, Brazil and the US. The Equity Markets Group provides a wide range of advisory services and sophisticated products in a number of Asian countries. Each of the Group's offshore businesses offers a wide range of products, which are targeted to those locations where Macquarie has identified an opportunity.

Macquarie attempts to minimise risks by entering those markets in which it perceives itself to have a competitive edge. This tactic requires a cautious, focused strategy of expansion underpinned by rigorous analysis and a willingness to reject the idea if not supported by the data and modelling. Macquarie's growth has been organic and incremental. While operations in the UK and New Zealand pre-dated Macquarie being awarded its banking licence in 1985, there was a short delay before moves offshore began in the early 1990s. Canada became the first new host, followed by Malaysia (1993), Hong Kong (1994), the US (mid-1990s), Korea (1996), Singapore (1997), Brazil (1999) and the Philippines (2004). In 2006 it has offices in 22 countries outside Australia whose staff numbers range from several hundreds in the UK, Hong Kong and Korea to 30 or less in China, Malaysia, Brazil and the Philippines (Macquarie, 2006).

FIRM-SPECIFIC ADVANTAGES

How was Macquarie able to achieve such success as a new bank operating out of the small Australian market? The Bank's competitive advantage lies in its ability and experience in sourcing, distributing and handling financial assets which it applies in particular markets, such as infrastructure projects, property, and cross-border leasing (Korporaal, 2002). This expertise adds value in projects that incur most of their costs as a result of debt financing:

> Typically, 97 per cent of the expense [of toll-roads] is paying the debt on the asset, so the key determination of its value is financing and our organisation has become expert in sourcing the transactions and doing the deal – which is usually highly tricky. (Nicholas Moore, in Greenblat, 2004)

Macquarie has generated a sustained competitive advantage through the accumulation and exploitation of superior intangible assets, especially the knowledge of its employees, embedded within the organisation (Durisin and von Krogh, 2005: 37-9). Macquarie has been able to do this with superior recruitment and retention policies. Merchant banking is characterised by high levels of staff turnover. The growth of the industry in Australia up to the mid-1980s gave rise to poaching of individuals and specialist teams as banks scrambled to find and retain talent. Firms offered higher salaries and fringe benefits to attract and retain staff at all levels of seniority and experience, making merchant bankers amongst the highest paid executives in Australia (Skully, 1987: ch.18).

Macquarie trod a different path. Like the rest of the industry it recognised that its people were its most valuable asset. However, rather than headhunting experience, Macquarie paid particular attention to the hiring of raw recruits whom it would train in its systems and induct into its deal-making culture (Shand and Ryan, 2005). The Bank recruited large numbers of new staff, its personnel numbers rising from 1,732 in 1996 to 6,556 by 2005 (Macquarie, 2005: 92).[3] One of its competitors regretted that it had not followed suit in the early 1990s noting that 'what we should have been doing at the time was investing in people. Macquarie went the other way, they staffed up big and eventually they benefited from it' (Haigh, 1999: 415). Macquarie recruits the brightest people it can find, looking to graduates from business schools but also recruiting those without tertiary training (Kavanagh, 2001).[4] All applicants undergo a rigorous selection process including numerous interviews and comprehensive psychometric testing designed, in part, to 'weed out misfits' (Hewett, 1993; Oldfield, 2005b). The tests include questions to ascertain a candidate's level of comfort with risk-taking and gambling. The testing is aimed at identifying innovative and often unconventional thinkers who have an innate ability to recognise opportunities. Those who are selected have their first taste of the Macquarie culture and ethics at induction sessions at what is known as 'Camp Macquarie' (Boyd, 1994).

Macquarie has had little trouble attracting the brightest and best. The pay is fabulous, so much so that it draws adverse comment from shareholders' associations, the press and politicians. CEO Allan Moss is the highest paid executive in Australia, taking home $18.6 million in 2005 (Mellor, 2006).

Those lower down the ranks earn so much that Macquarie has been dubbed 'the millionaires factory' (Bartholomeusz, 2000). However, there are other inducements for staff to stay. While the hours are long and the work demanding, employees are given high levels of responsibility and are able to exercise discretion. For instance, Mellor (2006) has described Macquarie as '...an unusual amalgam. While it contains elements of a conventional investment bank, it also acts like a private equity operator, venture capitalist, hedge fund, mutual fund and exchange-traded fund.' A competitor says 'they are like an incubator; wheelers and dealers go look for projects, they then take them on the balance sheet. They then consolidate all those assets and try and lift them off into a vehicle on the market' (Teh quoted in Mellor, 2006).

In targeting and developing new niche markets, the Bank encourages entrepreneurship and innovation in its staff. Such initiatives are promoted at one level through team and individual financial rewards. It also requires an organisation design that allowed entrepreneurship to flourish within the 45 business units. To this end Macquarie has adopted a 'loose-tight' control structure which encourages executives to act in an entrepreneurial manner, propose ideas, and take ownership of new ventures but be subject to independent assessment of the associated credit, market and reputational risks of each venture (Kavanagh, 2001; Ross, 2005). Moreover, any new proposal must be shown to leverage an existing competitive advantage. The primacy of the risk management function is clearly demonstrated in the figure describing Macquarie's organisational structure in the Annual Report (Macquarie, 2005): it is close to the centre of a circle with the operating groups ringed around it. Risk management systems apply to the Bank as a whole as well as to each of its divisions on a daily basis (Myer and Moncrief, 2005). These policies have stood the Bank in good stead over the years, allowing it to avoid the losses and adverse publicity suffered by many of its peers, particularly in the 1980s and 1990s.

Macquarie's success rests in large part on its reputation. The Bank has provided a bonanza for its shareholders and investors in its listed funds. More importantly, it has built very strong relationships with its customers, the owners of the assets which are purchased, managed and sold on their behalf to the public by the Bank. Developing market-specific skills and experience is a slow process, involving not only learning how to conduct business in a specific market, but also allowing time to build a solid reputation and business networks that are critical to the conduct of a viable business (Oldfield, 2005a). Macquarie's commitment to sustaining these relationships permits it to be 'in the deal stream' so acquiring new business (Durisin and von Krogh, 2005: 45). A further niche advantage, as explained by Allan Moss, has been Macquarie's strategy of putting its 'A' team into Asian markets while its competitors from Wall Street and Europe sent their

'C' teams (Hyland, 2001). This strategy of commitment enabled the Bank to break into markets in China, Taiwan (Seeder, 2001) and Korea (Korporaal, 2002), largely unopposed (Macfarlane, 1999). Although competition in infrastructure is increasing, a head start of almost a decade provides Macquarie with superior skills and expertise in this area, a position that its rivals have not as yet been able to replicate (Boyd and Murray, 2004).

CONCLUSION

Macquarie has been one of a number of Australian success stories in recent years. In a globalising market for financial services that has provided limited openings to Australia's small- to medium-sized banks, Macquarie has distinguished itself as a small and nimble niche player. Entrepreneurship, innovation and focused discipline have mattered more than the size of its balance sheet. Operating from Australia has not been a disadvantage. Its staff comb the world looking to structure new deals, connected to head office by the internet. The spread of offices around the world and listing on multiple stock exchanges give them access to the world's money markets. Distance is no longer a tyrant. Hill Samuel's departure in 1985 was perfectly timed in terms of positioning its offspring, Macquarie, to capitalise on the newly deregulated market. Government policies of reforming the financial system and privatising infrastructure tilted the CSAs for financiers in ways that provided opportunities for any firm with the insight and capacity to seize them. In response, Macquarie quickly developed a set of FSAs that set it apart from its domestic and later international rivals.

Success or failure in investment banking rests in large part on the quality of the human capital assembled by each firm. In this respect Macquarie has been outstanding. The stability and longevity of its senior team, all of whom are Australian, is in marked contrast with the musical chairs played by the big trading banks. Investment banking is a knowledge industry where 'what you do' is visible to competitors but 'how you do it' is hidden from view. In the language of the strategic management literature, sustainable competitive advantage rests on possessing a stock of resources that are scarce, valuable and immobile, resulting in capabilities that rivals cannot easily match (Durisin and von Krogh, 2005: 36-9). Macquarie is currently ahead of the pack as an investment bank with a buoyant infrastructure business added on. However, it is about to face competition from the global, full-service giants in its niche markets and investors in its funds who are starting to question the very high fees being charged and the excessive remuneration packages of its principals (Mellor, 2006). A new or modified business model may be required to maintain market leadership.

NOTES

1. In Australia the terms merchant bank and investment bank are interchangeable.
2. Hill Samuel Bank was acquired by TSB in 1986 and is now part of Lloyds TSB Group plc.
3. These numbers include full-time and part-time staff plus contractors.
4. Macquarie's first joint-managing directors, David Clarke and Mark Johnson, and current CEO, Allan Moss, all have MBAs from Harvard (Mellor, 2006).

21. Conclusion

Howard Dick, David Merrett and Tatiana Zalan

When we embarked on this project we were confident that we could identify and explain a specific Australian experience of internationalisation. In the course of researching, writing, reviewing and revising the 20 chapters, we have come to a broader and more subtle view. What appeared from the 1990s to be a rather disheartening experience of internationalisation looks in restrospect to be more nuanced than we had thought. As explained in Chapters 1 and 2, until the 1980s the horizons of the overwhelming majority of Australian firms had been limited either to the domestic market or to intermittent exporting. Good profits were to be made within the domestic market, so there was little pressure upon managers from either shareholders or banks to seek higher returns in international markets. In most industries strategy was a matter of establishing or defending a domestic market position. What dynamism did exist, tended to come from outside through inwards foreign direct investment, although there was also some borrowing of American concepts of business strategy.

One of the most important changes in the early 1980s was the deregulation of the banking system. Suddenly banks were willing and able to lend for ventures which hitherto would have been regarded as speculative. There emerged a cast of corporate cowboys, aptly named by business columnist, Trevor Sykes, as 'the bold riders', some educated in American management concepts, others self-made men, who borrowed to the hilt to fund takeovers across the spectrum of the Australian economy. The outcome was a set of rapidly assembled conglomerates. Most of these crashed during the severe domestic recession of the early 1990s, leaving vast corporate wreckage and badly wounded and sorely chastened banks.

The other significant change was the abolition of foreign exchange restrictions and the floating of the Australian dollar in 1983. These came on top of phased reductions in tariff protection, especially of the manufacturing sector. From the 1990s in a program of 'microeconomic reform', governments sold off their business enterprises in banking, insurance, water and electricity, railways and airports. As a result, further large segments of the economy were introduced to the pressures of the market. Moreover, a powerful regulatory body, the Australian Competition and Consumer Commission (ACCC), enforced a tough competition policy regime. Australian firms now had unimpeded access to the world economy and powerful incentives to seek growth opportunities beyond the domestic market.

During the heady years of the 1980s there was a marked acceleration of outward FDI, albeit from a low very base. The motives for this were mixed. In some cases there was a genuine desire to expand beyond the constraints of the domestic market (the major banks, Pacific Dunlop in manufacturing and Southcorp in wine), and sometimes it was outright empire-building (Foster's and TNT). Whatever the motives, a good deal of investment was poorly conceived and executed. Some CEOs simply did not have the experience to appreciate the pitfalls of international business and were too over-confident to want to find out what they did not know. Nevertheless, most played it safe, looking predominantly to what seemed to be the culturally familiar markets of Britain and the United States rather than to unfamiliar and apparently daunting markets closer to home in Asia. For all these reasons it is hardly surprising that so many of these early ventures, as with Burns Philp's herbs and spices (Chapter 12), Foster's beer (Chapter 15) and TNT's logistics (Chapter 18), ended in tears. In some other cases, such as Bond Corporation's ill-advised purchase of Canadian breweries, they hastened corporate collapse. This was the simple story that we imagined that we would tell.

Nevertheless, it is now apparent from aggregate figures from industry studies and from firm cases, that these initial chastening experiences were an early stage in a learning process. What makes the subsequent history so interesting is the wide range of different outcomes. Banks and resource companies represent the two extremes. Australia's four main banks expanded offshore in the 1980s, then pulled back in the 1990s when results did not live up to expectations (Chapter 7). The sale of foreign assets for conversion back to a weak Australian dollar looked to be a ready means to restore unhealthy balance sheets. Profitability has been restored but the Australian government's 'four pillars' policy, which prevents mergers or takeovers by the domestic banks of one another, limits expansion within the local market. Once again the banks have begun to venture to find new markets offshore. However, they are doing so more cautiously than before. Their incrementalist expansion has meant that they are falling further behind their international peers in terms of balance sheet size. The merchant bank, Macquarie (Chapter 20), has followed a different path relying far more heavily on international markets.

In marked contrast with the four main banks, the aggressive internationalisation of BHP (now BHP Billiton) and CRA (now Rio Tinto) has taken both enterprises to become leaders in the global resources industry. BHP's internationalisation occurred only over the past two decades (Chapters 8 and 14). In the 1990s it was badly compromised by an unwise and ill-timed acquisition of US-based Magma Copper, and environmental and public relations problems with its minority stake in the Ok Tedi copper project. However, BHP did not pull back but consolidated, restructuring both senior management and the company itself. The outcome has been not one but two very successful international firms, first the merged resources giant, BHP Billiton, and secondly, flat steel products manufacturer, BlueScope Steel, both pursuing focused strategies in what they do best. BHP and BlueScope both achieved that transformation within five years. They now have as many assets outside Australia as within.

Our study therefore allows no clear finding as to the success or failure of Australian firms in international markets. Pioneers such as Burns Philp, Aspro and Kiwi were unable to capitalise on decades of advantage as early movers. Firms such as Pacific Dunlop and TNT which appeared to be faring extremely well in the 1980s have since disappeared. Other firms, such as BHP, Foster's and Newscorp, have survived serious overseas business failures but have since restructured and are becoming stronger multinationals from the experience. Newcomers such as mall developer, Westfield (Chapter 19), and merchant bank, Macquarie (Chapter 20), as well as smaller retailers, winemakers and services firms in architecture and engineering, accounting, consulting and legal services, have thrived.

Such mixed outcomes strongly suggest that what matters in the long-run is not so much general country-specific advantages and disadvantages as the quality of firm strategy. Business failures often reflect misunderstanding of firm-specific advantages. In particular, strength in the domestic market based on location-bound strategic assets is a weak basis for sustainable competitive advantage in global markets, which requires internationally transferable capabilities (Chapter 3). Westfield's ability to innovate in mall design and redevelopment (Chapter 19) and Macquarie Bank's skills in financing infrastructure (Chapter 20) are both very good examples of getting it right by applying a focused strategy. By contrast, Foster's global beer strategy (Chapter 15) and TNT's global logistics (Chapter 18) reveal the pitfalls of blithely seeking to translate domestic market dominance into the international arena. Coca-Cola Amatil (CCA) hedged its bets by internationalising very successfully as a franchisee in the Coca-Cola value chain, then in the late 1990s discovered that what the parent gives it can also take away (Chapter 16). This last case provides evidence that preferred suppliers to foreign multinationals face both opportunities and constraints (Chapters 5, 6).

A subsidiary consideration is capital market pressures. Since the 1980s Australian firms have benefited from capital market liberalisation, but at the same time, as public companies, they have become more vulnerable to the market's fairly short-term expectations. Pacific Dunlop was battered by the market in the mid-1990s. Newscorp, by contrast, enjoyed the bulwark of a largely family-controlled share register and with its large reserves was not so severely punished for its misadventures. Westfield, like some smaller retailers, has also enjoyed the insulation of closely held shareholdings, as have engineering consultancy firms organised on a partnership basis (Chapters 11, 19). At the same time, Westfield also epitomises the benefit of defining and explaining international strategy to the market (Chapter 19).

For boards and managers of Australian firms the big question is therefore not whether to internationalise, because in many cases they have few other growth options. Even if they confine themselves to the domestic market, firms can expect to face intensifying competition from more aggressive global players on their own turf. Supply chains run both ways. If they allow some firms such as Coca-Cola Amatil (Chapter 16) to move offshore, they also assist foreign multinationals to enter the domestic market. Foreign multinationals have a long history in Australia. An unintended consequence of twentieth-century protection was to encourage foreign investment, especially in domestic manufacturing. This inflow continues, bringing on the one hand competition and on the other opportunities for collaboration and knowledge spillovers (Chapters 5, 6).

The key questions are therefore *how* to internationalise and *whether* such a strategy improves financial performance in the long-run. Recent empirical evidence on the performance of large MNCs suggests that being more global is not necessarily more profitable. International diversification can bring substantial benefits, including access to new markets and learning opportunities, but it can also be associated with very high costs. Nevertheless, internationalisation can be a profitable strategy, provided managers understand which capabilities add most value and so position themselves strategically in foreign markets.

Competing successfully in international markets will remain a challenge for managers of Australian MNCs, because it involves breaking away from the constraints imposed by the firms' administrative heritage (Chapter 3). Historically the Australian business environment has been more insular and culturally homogeneous than that in North America or Europe and company structures and systems further narrow the scope and ways of creative thinking. If managers and investors of Australian MNCs believe that international success can be achieved 'on the cheap', empirical evidence strongly suggests that they are deluding themselves. The right decisions about internationalisation will not be made, and shareholders will keep on losing money as long as managers pursue ill-conceived international ventures. Making right decisions will require substantial investment, a strategic, long-term perspective by management and investors, and much more sophistication in the way managers conceive and carry out their international strategy.

A critical issue here is company structure and organisation. Because most companies have internationalised by increments, overseas operations have often been poorly integrated with internal labour markets. Decision-making hierarchies have also been attuned to domestic operations. Thus even when firms appointed good international managers, information on international markets and operations was not necessarily well assimilated and managers with successful international experience did not necessarily enjoy commensurate reward as manifested in career promotion. Within the organisation, achieving recognition became a matter of politics. Managers who had secured their positions in more inward-looking times often resisted the intrusion of more worldly newcomers. Those with international experience could become restless and impatient of established routines, thereby generating antagonism. The four banks illustrate the phenomenon very well (Chapter 7). They dabbled in international ventures but did not adapt their cumbersome organisations to meet the challenge of becoming regional or global players.

Such issues have to be resolved from the top down, which in turn points to the importance of boards and CEOs with sufficient international experience to identify and diagnose the problem. BHP Billiton is one company which has restructured its management to befit a genuine multinational, albeit with the loss of some Australian identity. Other Australian multinationals are still wrestling with this challenge. It may help that there is now a growing pool of Australian senior managers with extensive international experience gained from working offshore or with foreign multinationals in Australia (Chapters 5, 6). Increasingly boards are displaying willingness to headhunt such people from outside the firm, or indeed take a geocentric view by appointing well-qualified foreign nationals.

LESSONS FOR OTHER SMALL COUNTRIES

In Chapters 1 and 2 we established that Australia shared characteristics with several groups of countries but is typical of none. It is a medium-sized OECD economy with high income per capita but, because of its remote location, is still heavily dependent upon primary exports and only just emerging from a transition in regulatory regime. Because the internationalisation experiences of Australian firms have been so varied, it turns out to be even more difficult than we had expected to distil the lessons for other small to medium countries. Indeed, the first lesson is that firms have the capability to transcend nationality and country-specific disadvantages. This is intrinsic to the firm's Schumpeterian ability to innovate and to develop firm-specific advantages.

Nevertheless, the smaller and the more remote the country, the more difficult it tends to be for its firms to achieve the minimum efficient scale necessary to sustain competitive advantage. In Australia's case this problem is compounded because, although the economy as a whole is by no means small, economic activity is dispersed across eight capital cities and a vast continent. This has been a factor in the steady contraction of the domestic manufacturing sector since the 1960s, and along with relatively high real wages helps to explain why Australian manufacturers have been less successful than resource-based and services firms in penetrating global markets.

One respect in which scale has clearly changed is that of organisational size and structure. Even behind the twentieth-century tariff wall, diversified and conglomerate firms were common because the modest size of the domestic market encouraged firms to diversify, which seemed much less risky than internationalisation via FDI. There was little incentive to internationalise beyond exporting or licensing. Then in the 1980s financial deregulation gave rise to a mania of takeovers that resulted in a new set of domestic conglomerates with international ambitions. Few of these have survived into the twenty-first century. Pacific Dunlop stood out as one of the few conglomerates to internationalise quite early in its history, but it could not sustain competitive advantage in the face of more focused competitors in rapidly globalising industries. Wesfarmers stands out as a conglomerate which continues to prosper, but its businesses are almost entirely confined to the domestic market. The conglomerate is not a viable way to sustain competitive advantage as a multinational firm because quite different strategic and organisational capabilities are required (Chapter 3).

At the other extreme and upsetting the standard paradigm of international business is the newly recognised phenomenon of 'born globals'. Here a set of trends may be working to Australia's advantage. Advances in production technology and information and communications technology (ICT) are lessening economies of scale in manufacturing industries. Meanwhile the unbundling of goods and services and the trend towards contracting out is increasing the opportunities for smaller firms to enter and be competitive in international niche markets. There are also around half a million Australians working overseas and thereby acquiring first-hand experience of the international economy. This is not a large diaspora by world standards but these offshore Australians are by and large tertiary educated and younger than the home population. The outflow of Australians abroad is countered by large inflows of foreign students studying at Australian universities. As business people and bureaucrats, the returnees will ease the way for Australian firms to operate in their countries. Together these two cohorts of migrants will be a promising seedbed for future managers of 'born globals'.

An important issue is the extent to which government policy may facilitate or impede internationalisation. Australian government policy has lacked coordination, which reflects the complications of a federal system with powers divided between a Commonwealth Government and eight self-governing states and territories. Since the mid-1970s there has been a general trend towards liberalisation and deregulation which has facilitated inward FDI and created an environment more conducive to outward FDI. However, except for Closer Economic Relations (CER) with New Zealand, Australia has had no opportunity for the kind of close regional economic integration experienced in Europe or, to a lesser extent, in North America. Through the Asia-Pacific Economic Cooperation (APEC) forum and other regional and bilateral agreements, the Australian government has had some success in liberalisation of trade and investment but these are as yet early steps towards regional economic integration, of which many Asian governments remain wary. Within Australia's own domestic market, governments have thus been slow, reactive and often quarrelsome in pursuing the fine detail of economic integration that is of such commercial consequence. Isolation combined with federalism has been a significant impediment.

In terms of industry policy, there have been marked policy shifts. Until the 1970s, there was a bipartisan policy of 'protection all round', which was an updated variant of what Butlin (1982) referred to as 'colonial socialism'. The Hawke–Keating Labor governments of the period 1983 to 1996 adopted explicit industry policies to restructure the problem industries of steel, automobiles, textiles and shipping. The mixed success of these policies combined with an ideological shift led succeeding conservative governments to disown industry policy altogether. Despite this neoclassical rhetoric, government has nevertheless pursued some *de facto* industry policies with mixed results. In the airline industry, for example, Qantas has been consistently privileged as a national airline, to the advantage of its private shareholders and the disadvantage of consumers. In telecommunications, however, the former monopolist, Telstra, still 51 per cent owned by the government, has seen its market capitalisation steadily eroded by a combination of under-investment and regulatory controls. Qantas is one of the world's most profitable airlines; Telstra's foreign ventures have been debacles. Nevertheless, the annual Council of Australian Governments (COAG) has been instrumental in the achievement of a national competition policy as part of a broader and evolving national and bi-partisan reform agenda.

There are also signs of more outward-looking and business-friendly policies. Increasingly state and federal government agencies are promoting awareness of international opportunities and benchmarking standards. Learning from the European experience and a substantial literature, individual state governments are focusing on industry clusters and networks that incorporate synergies with local universities and other tertiary institutions and research institutes. Such initiatives would have been more productive 25 years ago but their emergence now is still an advance towards establishing cities as platforms for international competitiveness. Here the main problem has been the under-funding of public infrastructure because of an obsession with paying off public debt. Perth (Western Australia) and Brisbane (Queensland) have invested in urban infrastructure; Melbourne (Victoria) has maintained it and Sydney (NSW) has seen it deteriorate. There are few positive lessons to be found here for international best practice.

IMPLICATIONS FOR RESEARCH

If Australian firms have been 'late internationalisers', Australian universities have lagged even further behind in terms of research and the transfer of knowledge back to the business community. This book has mapped out the state of knowledge by bringing together a theoretically informed matrix of surveys, industry studies and firm cases. In doing so it has revealed how much research still remains to be done. In concluding it may be helpful to suggest important lines of inquiry that researchers of Australian firms – hopefully including international researchers – may wish to pursue.

A key conceptual issue is how to measure the success or failure of internationalisation. The strategy literature emphasises 'sustainable competitive advantage'. In the first instance this seems to be a fairly straightforward matter of selecting appropriate financial indicators and collecting and analysing the data (Chapter 4). Sustainability should be measurable by superior financial performance (Chapter 4). Implicit is the tricky issue of life expectancy or turnover. Even well-established and successful companies cannot realistically expect to survive more than a generation of 30 or so years without either suffering failure or becoming prey to acquisition. Statistically this outcome would result from a turnover rate of little over two per cent per annum, which is about the historical rate calculated by Fleming et al. (2004) for Australia's top 100 firms. In any case, competitive advantage for any given business model is hard to sustain much beyond five years. Unless they can sustain innovation, the performance of even the best-performing firms tends to regress to the industry mean over a period of about three to seven years. Success may therefore be quite fleeting. Moreover, even very good financial returns may not protect firms from takeover, whether by foreign or domestic firms. If acquisition leaves shareholders better off, does this count as success or failure? And does it matter beyond appearances if Australian nationality is thereby ceded?

Such entropy analysis has particular relevance for small-country multinationals. How do international business specialists answer the common critique that globalisation is concentrating wealth in fewer and fewer corporate hands? Rugman (2005) has argued that triad country multinationals predominate, with the United States and Japan being pre-eminent. Our findings suggest that relative to the country's economic size, Australian firms have played a significant role in international business, at least in some industries. There are grounds for believing that this will continue as Australians gain more experience of international business. If this is true also of other smaller economies, triad dominance may in time be somewhat eroded. A counter argument, however, would be that as Australian MNEs become successful there will be pressures either to move domicile, like Newscorp and CRA/Rio Tinto, or be taken over by a foreign MNC. It therefore becomes a question of whether the rate of emergence of new MNCs is sufficient to offset the attrition of existing ones. A steady state would be a fortuitous outcome. Of course it may well be that what will make the biggest difference is the continued emergence of Brazil, Russia, China and India, so that the triad will in time enlarge.

More comparative research into small-country multinationals is therefore much needed. One desirable line of research is a more comprehensive longitudinal study of the internationalisation of Australian MNCs against a benchmark of firms from other small open economies. Furthermore, the observed regionalisation and home-region orientations of managers of Australian MNCs are yet to be confirmed and further explored, based on a detailed investigation of mechanisms and means of value adding, attention to the upstream and downstream ends of the value chain, and more sophisticated measures of globalisation at the firm level. Above all, we still seem to know very little about where and how Australian firms can best compete internationally, which relates to the ongoing tension for Australian multinationals between markets perceived as culturally alike in Britain and the US and culturally less familiar markets closer to home in Asia. Research on such governance issues as board diversity, the orientations of top management teams and their impact on internationalisation should therefore be a high priority. A cross-national comparison of board composition and practices, with Australian MNCs as a sub-sample, constitutes a related line of inquiry. Researching these issues will help to answer the intriguing question of whether the current bias of Australian MNCs toward the home region is a reflection of an ethnocentric mindset of managers and boards or a realistic assessment that firms' competitive advantages do not translate well into more distant markets (Chapter 4).

The disadvantage of location has been a strong theme throughout the book. We may conclude on a more optimistic note concerning the prospects for Australian multinationals. The new information and communications technologies and much reduced costs of sea and air transport have reduced the 'tyranny of distance' suffered by Australian firms. There are new opportunities for Australian-based firms to connect with the rest of the world, whether on their own account or as part of wider supply networks. Moreover, as Geoffrey Jones' seminal studies of the evolution of multinationals (Jones, 1996, 2005a) reminds us, the first generation of multinationals before 1914 were dominated by resource-exploiting and service firms. Few Australian firms apart from the banks made enduring FDI in this era. From World War I onwards, manufacturing became the leading industry sector attracting inwards FDI. With the notable exceptions of Nicholas 'Aspro' and Kiwi, Australian firms lacked the scale and efficiency in their small, protected markets that might have facilitated ventures abroad. The resurgence of global FDI in resources and services industries from the late twentieth century therefore plays to Australia's strengths rather than its weaknesses. Its country-specific advantages have been enhanced by the reforms of the 1980s and 1990s. Individually, Australia firms have developed their own capabilities which now enable them to move offshore into mining and energy and a range of service industries. At the turn of the twenty-first century, time and opportunity may at last be on the side of Australian firms with global aspirations.

Bibliography

ABS (Australian Bureau of Statistics) (1999), Australia's international banking statistics [www.abs.gov.au/Ausstats@.nsf/0/E3E3C43A724D3BFoCA256F2A000 73473].

ABS (2002), Foreign Ownership Characteristics of Businesses Undertaking Research and Experimental Development Activity in Australia, published in Australian Economic Indicators, August (cat. no. 1350.0).

ABS (2002/03), Australian Outward Foreign Affiliates Trade (cat. no. 5495.0).

ABS (2003), Foreign Ownership Characteristics of Information Technology Businesses, published in Australian Economic Indicators, March (cat. no. 1350.0).

ABS (2004a), Foreign Ownership of Australian Exporters and Importers, 2002/03, June (cat. no. 5496.0.55.001).

ABS (2004b), Economic Activity of Foreign Owned Businesses in Australia, 2000-01, January 2004 (cat. no. 5494.0).

ABS (2005a), Australia's Balance of Payments and International Investment position (cat. no. 5302.0).

ABS (2005b), Media release 27/1/05 [www.abs.gov.au.mate.lib.unimelb.edu.au], 26 March 2006.

ABS (various), Foreign Investment, Australia (cat. no. 5305.0).

ACEA (Association of Consulting Engineers Australia) (2004a), 'ACEA Benchmarking Survey 1993–2003', Internal Document, ACEA, Sydney.

ACEA (2004b), ACEA Benchmarking Survey 1993–2003, Powerpoint Presentation, ACEA Internal Document, Sydney.

ACEA (2005), Submission to Australian Government Department of Foreign Affairs and Trade, China Free Trade Agreement, October [www.acea.com.au], 15 January 2006.

ACEA (2006), Internal Document, provided by John Ridgway, ACEA Senior Policy Consultant, Sydney.

ACIF (Australian Construction Industry Forum) (2002a), 'GHD', Export Case Study Series No.5 [www.acif.com.au/publications.asp?sid=700], 14 January 2006.

ACIF (2002b), 'Arup Australasia', Export Case Study Series No.17 [www.acif.com.au/publications.asp?sid=700], 14 January 2006.

ACIF (2002c), 'Woodhead International', Export Case Study Series No.18 [www.acif.com.au/publications.asp?sid=700], 14 January 2006.
Adsteam (2006a), [www.adsteam.com.au].
Adsteam (2006b), Interim result for six months ended 31 December 2005 [www.adsteam.com.au/announcements/pdf/060223_m.pdf], 27 March 2006.
AFR, *The Australian Financial Review,* daily, Sydney.
Age, *The Age*, daily, Melbourne.
Aharoni, Y. (2000), 'The role of reputation in global professional business services', in Y. Aharoni & L. Nachum (eds), *Globalization of Services: Some Implications for Theory and Practice*, New York: Routledge. Chapter 7.
Alexander, J. & R. Hattersley (1981), *Australian Mining, Minerals and Oil,* Sydney: David Ell Press.
Alexander, N. (1997), *International Retailing*, Oxford: Blackwell.
Alexander, N. & H. Myers (2000), 'The retail internationalisation process', *International Marketing Review*, **17** (4/5), 334–53.
American–Australian Free Trade Agreement Coalition (2003), *Partnership for a Stronger Future: U.S.– Australia Free Trade Agreement*, prepared by The Trade Partnership, Washington, DC, July.
AMP (2005) [www.amp.com.au/group/2column/], 26 September 2005.
AMSA (Australian Maritime Safety Authority) (2006), Australian Register of Ships [www.amsa.gov.au/Shipping_Registration/Guides/Australian_Register_of_Ships.asp], 29 April 2006.
Anderson L.C., J.A. Narus & W.V. Rossum (2004), 'Customer value propositions in business markets', *Harvard Business Review,* **84** (3), 90–100.
Andreff, W. (2003), 'The newly emerging TNCs from economies in transition: a comparison with Third world outward FDI', *Transnational Corporations*, **12** (2), 73–118.
ANL (2006), Company History [www.anl.com.au/about/index.php3], 1 May 2006.
ANMA (Australian National Maritime Association) (1989), *Australian Shipping: Structure, History and Future*, Melbourne: ANMA.
Annavarjula, M. & S. Beldona (2000), 'Multinationality–performance relationship: A review and reconceptualization', *International Journal of Organizational Analysis*, **8** (1), 48–67.
Anon. (1998), *Building Professionals of Australia,* Melbourne: Images Australia.
Anon. (2000a), *The Westfield Story: The First 40 Years,* Sydney: Westfield Holdings Ltd.
Anon. (2000b), 'OPSM's eyes on Asia', *The Australian*, 31 August.
Anon. (2002), 'Mall content', *The Economist,* 30 May, 82.
Anon. (2005a), 'Growing pains', *The Economist*, 15 April, 58–9.

Anon. (2005b), 'Cash Converters extends into Africa', *Biz Community,* 1 September, 2005.

Ansell (2005), [www.ansell.com/company/detailed_history.shtml], 7 December 2005.

APRA (Australian Prudential Regulation Authority) (various), Australian Banking Statistics [www.apra.gov.au/statistics], 15 March 2006.

APRA (Australian Prudential Regulation Authority) (2004), *Life Industry at a Glance*, Sydney: APRA.

Aristocrat (2005), 'History' [www.aristocrat.comau/AUS/Who/History.asp], 7 December 2005.

Arndt, H.W. (1988), 'Comparative advantage in trade in financial services', *Banca Nazionale del Lavoro Quarterly Review*, **164** (March), 61–78.

ASIC (Australian Securities and Investment Commission) (various). *Financial Bulletin*, Melbourne: ASIC.

Aston, H. (2005), 'Discounter Aldi no king hit on big rivals', *Daily Telegraph*, 2 May.

ASX (1997), *ASX Delisted Companies as at 30 June 1997*, Brisbane: Australian Stock Exchange Ltd.

Aurifeille, J–M., P. Quester, L. Lockshin & T. Spawton (2002), 'Global vs international involvement-based segmentation: A cross-national exploratory study', *International Marketing Review*, **19** (4/5), 369–86.

AUSTA Business Group (2004a), 'Australian Business Reviews the FTA' [www.austa.net/reaction.html], 5 April 2005.

AUSTA Business Group (2004b), Senate Select Committee on the Free Trade Agreement between Australia and the United States of America, 30 April 2004, Submission No. 398 [www.aph.gov.au/Senate/committee/freetrade_ctte/index.htm], 5 April 2005.

Australia (annual), *Year Book of the Commonwealth of Australia,* Canberra: Government Printer.

Australian Insurance and Superannuation Commission (various), *Financial Bulletin* (1988–2005).

Australia–Japan Economic Institute (1992), *A Directory of Japanese Business Activity in Australia 1992,* Sydney: AJEI.

Australian, *The Australian*, daily, Sydney.

Australian British Chamber of Commerce (1997), *British Australian Business Directory,* Sydney: ABCC.

Australian Business Foundation (2005), 'The Australian Wine Industry: Collaboration and Learning as Causes of Competitive Success' [www.abfoundation.com.au], 23 October 2005.

Australian Financial System Inquiry (1981), *Final Report of the Committee of Inquiry into the Australian Financial System*, Canberra: AGPS.

AWF (1995), *Strategy 2025: The Australian Wine Industry*, Adelaide: Winemakers' Federation of Australia for the Australian Wine Foundation.

Aylward, D.K. (2002), 'Diffusion of R and D within the Australian wine industry', *Prometheus*, **20** (4), 351–66.

Aylward, D.K. (2004), 'Innovation–export linkages within different cluster models: A case study from the Australian wine industry', *Prometheus*, **22** (4), 423–37.

Bach, J. (1982), *A Maritime History of Australia*, Sydney: Pan Books.

Baker, M. (2004), 'Shopping center industry benchmarks: An international perspective on the collection, analysis and dissemination of operating statistics', *Working Paper Series,* International Council of Shopping Centers [www.icsc.org/srch/rsrch/wp/globalwhitepaper.pdf], 18 May 2006.

Balance, R., J. Pogány & H. Forstner (1992), *The World's Pharmaceutical Industries: An International Perspective on Innovation, Competition and Policy*, Camberley, UK and Brookfield, US: Edward Elgar.

Ballantyne, T. (2002), 'What really went wrong at Ansett', *Airports and Aviation Outlook Conference,* Adelaide, 11-12 November [www.spiritofansett.com/history/ballantyne.htm], 22 October 2004.

Barbeques Galore (2005), 'Barbeques Galore Announces Financial Results', 10 August [www.bbqgalore.com/about/pressReleaseLibrary.bbq], 3 May 2006.

Barney, J.B. (1991), 'Firm resources and sustained competitive advantage', *Journal of Management,* **17** (1), 99–120.

Barney, J.B. (1995), 'Looking inside for competitive advantage', *The Academy of Management Executive*, **9** (4), 49–61.

Bartholomeusz, S. (1998), 'On Balance, Coca-Cola Amatil's De-merger Adds Up', *The Age*, 29 May.

Bartholomeusz, S. (1999), 'Coke, Amatil: A Mutual Reliance', *The Age*, 13 February.

Bartholomeusz, S. (2000), 'Real wealth for Macquarie chiefs a matter of options', *The Age*, 28 November.

Bartlett, C.A. (2000), 'BRL Hardy: Globalizing an Australian wine company', *Harvard Business School case 9-300-018.*

Bartlett, C.A. & S. Ghoshal (1989), *Managing across Borders: The Transnational Solution,* Boston: Harvard Business School Press.

Bartlett, C.A. & S. Ghoshal (1995), *Transnational Management: Text, Cases and Readings in Cross-Border Management*, Boston: Irwin McGraw–Hill.

Bartlett, C.A. & S. Ghoshal (2000), 'Going global: Lessons from late movers', *Harvard Business Review,* March–April, 133–42.

Beeston, J. (2001), *A Concise History of Australian Wine*, Crows Nest, NSW: Allen & Unwin.

Bellak, C. & J. Cantwell (1997), 'Small latecomer economies in a globalising environment: Constraints and opportunities for catching up', *Development and International Cooperation*, XIII (24–5), 139–79.

Bengtsson, L. (1999), 'The diversification trend in the largest Swedish industrial firms 1965–1994 and comparisons with the situation in the U.S. and the U.K', *Working Paper,* Department of Business Administration/School of Economics and Management, Lund University, Lund.

Bengtsson, L. (2000), 'Corporate strategy in a small open economy: Reducing product diversification while increasing international diversification', *European Management Journal*, **18** (4), 444–53.

Benito, G.R.G., J. Larimo, R. Narula & T. Petersen (2002), 'Multinational enterprises from small economies', *International Studies of Management & Organization*, **32** (1), 57–78.

Benjamin, R. (1988), *Paths to Professionalism: A History of Insurance Broking in Australia*, Melbourne: Craftsman Publishing.

Benjamin, R. (2004), 'Eliezer Montefiore (1820–94): artist, gallery director and insurance pioneer', *Australian Jewish Historical Society Journal*, **xvii**, 3.

Berghe, D.A.F. van den (2003), *Working across Borders: Multinational Enterprises and the Internationalization of Employment*, Rotterdam: Erasmus Research Institute of Management.

Berner, R. & D. Kiley (2005), 'Global Brands' [www.interbrand.com/surveys.asp], April 2006.

Betancourt, R.R. (2004), *The Economics of Retailing and Distribution*, Cheltenham, UK and Northhampton, US: Edward Elgar.

Beveridge, J. (2005), 'Foster's dares to mix its drinks', *Herald Sun,* 22 September.

Beverland, M.B. (2002), 'A Grounded Model of Organisational Development and Change: Evolution in the Australian and New Zealand Wine Industries', *Unpublished doctoral dissertation*, School of Marketing, Faculty of Business and Management, University of South Australia, Adelaide.

Beverland, M.B. (2005), 'Crafting brand authenticity: The case of luxury wines', *Journal of Management Studies*, **42** (5), 1003–29.

BHP (1960), *The Broken Hill Proprietary Company Ltd: Seventy-Five Years of B.H.P. Development in Industry*, Melbourne: BHP.

BHP (1997), *The BHP Pocketbook*, Melbourne: BHP.

BHP (annual), *Annual Report* (1970 to 2001).

BHP Billiton (2005), [www.bhpbilliton.com].

BHP Billiton (annual), *Annual Report* (2002 to 2005).

BIE (Bureau of Industry Economics) (1984), *Australian Direct Investment Abroad,* Canberra: AGPS.

BIE (1991), *The Pharmaceutical Industry: Impediments and Opportunities*, Bureau of Industry Economics, Canberra: AGPS.

BIE (1995a), *Australian Direct Investment Abroad*, Canberra: AGPS.

BIE (1995b), *Investment Abroad by Australian Companies: Issues and Implications,* Canberra: AGPS.

Birkinshaw, J. (1996), 'How multinational subsidiary mandates are gained and lost', *Journal of International Business Studies*, **27** (3), 467–95.

Birkinshaw, J. & N. Hood (1997), 'An empirical study of development processes in foreign-owned subsidiaries in Canada and Scotland', *Management International Review*, **47** (4), 339–64.

Blainey, G. (1963), *The Rush That Never Ended*, Melbourne: Melbourne University Press.

Blainey, G. (1968), *The Tyranny of Distance: How Distance Shaped Australia's History,* Melbourne: Macmillan.

Blainey, G. (1993), *Jumping Over the Wheel.* St Leonards, NSW: Allen & Unwin.

Blainey, G. (1999), *A History of the AMP, 1848–1998*, St Leonards, NSW: Allen & Unwin.

Blake, E. (1998), 'OPSM moves into Asia', *Daily Telegraph*, 18 May.

Block, R.O. (1967), *Delfin Digest 1967: The Top Companies in Australia, New Zealand and South East Asia,* Sydney: Development Finance Corporation.

Blomström, M., A. Kokko & M. Zejan (2000), *Foreign Direct Investment: Firm and Host Country Strategies*, Basingstoke, UK: Macmillan.

Bluescope Steel (2005), *Annual Report* [www.bluescope.com/], 7 December 2005.

Bora, B. (1998), 'Characteristics and behaviour of multinationals in Australia', *Flinders University Working Paper*, School of Economics, Flinders University of South Australia, Adelaide.

Box, J.E. (2004), 'Global Supply Chains – Trends and Issues for Australian Business' [www.icnqld.org.au], 7 March 2006.

Boyd, T. & L. Murray (2004), 'MacBank: the pressures', *Australian Financial Review*, 30 July.

Boyd, T. (1994), 'World's highest-rated little bank', *Australian Financial Review*, 22 June.

BP (Burns Philp & Co. Ltd) (2002), Briefing Paper, 17 December [www.burnsphilp.com/pages/asx_fr.htm], 10 November 2005.

Braithwaite, A. (2003), *The Supply Chain Risks of Global Sourcing* [www.som.cranfield.ac.uk/som/conferences/online/], 12 November 2004.

Brash, D. (1966), *American Investment in Australian Industry*, Canberra: Australian National University Press.

Brewer, T.L. & S. Young (1998), *The Multinational Investment System and Multinational Enterprises,* Oxford: Oxford University Press.

Broomham, R. (1996), *On the Road: The NRMA's First Seventy-Five Years*, St Leonards, NSW: Allen & Unwin.

Brown, B. (1991), *I EXCEL! The Life and Times of Sir Henry Jones*, Hobart: Libra Books.

Brown, W.F. (1948), 'Mass merchandising in Latin America: Sears, Roebuck & Co.', *Journal of Marketing,* **13** (1), 73–7.

BRW, *Business Review Weekly,* weekly, Sydney.

BRW (2004), 'The Top 200 Foreign Owned Companies', *Business Review Weekly*, 12 February.

BRW (2006), 'BRW 2006 Rich 200', 18 May.

Buckley, K. & K. Klugman (1981), *The History of Burns Philp: An Australian Company in the South Pacific*, Sydney: Burns Philp & Co. Ltd.

Buckley, K. & K. Klugman (1983), *The Australian Presence in the Pacific, 1914–46*, Sydney: Allen & Unwin.

Buffett, W. (2005), 'History hints at future market performance', *The Australian*, 23 November.

Bugler, P. (1968), 'Making friends with Millers: It's hard sometimes', *The Australian*, 16 August.

Bulcke, D. van den & A. Verbeke (eds) (2001), *Globalization and the Small Open Economy*, Cheltenham, UK and Northampton, US: Edward Elgar.

Bushnell, J.A. (1961), *Australian Company Mergers 1946–1959*, Melbourne: Melbourne University Press.

Business Council of Australia (2004a), 'Submission on Australia US Free Trade Agreement (AUSFTA) to Joint Standing Committee on Treaties', 19 April [www.bca.com.au/upload/JSCOT_BCA_Final_Submission_190404.pdf], 5 April 2005.

Business Council of Australia (2004b), 'Business Council Hails US Free Trade Agreement', News Release, 9 February [www.bca.com.au], 5 April 2005.

Butlin, N.G., A. Barnard & J.J. Pincus (1982), *Government and Capitalism: Public and Private Choice in Twentieth Century Australia*, Sydney: Allen & Unwin.

Butlin, S. J., A.R. Hall & R.C. White (1971), *Australian Banking and Monetary Statistics 1817–1945*, Sydney: Reserve Bank of Australia.

Calori, R., M. Lubatkin, P. Very & J.F. Veiga (1997), 'Modelling the origins of nationally-bound administrative heritages: A historical institutional analysis of French and British firms', *Organization Science*, **8** (6), 681–96.

Capling, A. & B. Galligan (1992), *Beyond the Protective State: The Political Economy of Australia's Manufacturing Industry Policy*, Melbourne: Cambridge University Press.

Capon, N., C. Christodoulou, J.U. Farley & J.M. Hulbert, (1987), 'A comparative analysis of the strategy and structure of United States and Australian corporations', *Journal of International Business Studies*, **18** (1), 51–75.

Carew, E. (1997), *Westpac: The Bank that Broke the Bank*. Sydney: Doubleday.

Carew, W.R. & J.B. Wilson (1971), *A Practical Guide for Australian Exporters*, Sydney: Rydge Publications.

Carney, M. & E. Gedajlovic (2003), 'Strategic innovation and the administrative heritage of East Asian family business groups', *Asia Pacific Journal of Management*, **20** (1), 5–26.

Carter, R. (1990), 'Obstacles to international trade in insurance', in E.P.M. Gardener (ed.), *The Future of Financial Systems and Services. Essays in Honour of Jack Revell*, London: Macmillan, 205–21.

Cartwright, W.R. (1993), 'Multiple linked "diamonds" and the international competitiveness of export-dependent industries: The New Zealand experience', *Management International Review*, **33** (2), 55–70.

Cassis, Y. (2002), 'Before the storm: European banks in the 1950s', in S. Battilossi & Y. Cassis (eds), *European Banks and the American Challenge. Competition and Cooperation in International Banking Under Bretton Woods*, Oxford: Oxford University Press, 36–52.

Casson, M. (1987), 'The scope of the firm in the construction industry', in M. Casson, *The Firm and the Market,* Oxford: Blackwell.

Catalano, A. (2006), 'Real estate: Property investors seek out global opportunities', *Financial News*, 12 February.

Caves, R.E. & M.E. Porter (1977), 'From entry barriers to mobility barriers: conjectural decisions and contrived deterrence to new competition', *Quarterly Journal of Economics*, **91** (2), 241–61.

CCA (Coca-Cola Amatil Ltd) (1998), *1997 Annual Report*, Sydney.

CCA (2002), *2001 Annual Report* [www.ccamatil.com].

CCA (2005), *2004 Annual Report* [www.ccamatil.com].

CCA (2006a), *Company Profile* [www.ccamatil.com].

CCA (2006b), *2005 Annual Report* [www.ccamatil.com].

CCC (Coca-Cola Company) (2003), *2002 Annual Report* [www2.coca-cola.com].

CCC (2005), *2004 Annual Report* [www2.coca-cola.com].

CCH Australia Ltd (1982+), *Australian International Tax Agreements*, with periodic updates, North Ryde, NSW: CCH Australia Ltd.

CEDA (Committee for Economic Development of Australia) (2004), *Innovating Australia*, CEDA Policy Statement, Melbourne.

Centre for International Economics (2004), *Economic Analysis of AUSFTA: Impact of the Bilateral Free Trade Agreement with the United States*, Report prepared for the Department of Foreign Affairs and Trade, Canberra and Sydney.

Chandler, A. (1977), *The Visible Hand: The Managerial Revolution in American Business,* Cambridge, MA & London: The Belknap Press.

Chandler, A. (1990), *Scale and Scope: The Dynamics of Industrial Capitalism*, Cambridge, MA & London: The Belknap Press.

Chandler, A. (2005), *Shaping the Industrial Century: The Remarkable Story of the Evolution of the Modern Chemical and Pharmaceutical Industries*, Cambridge, MA & London: Harvard University Press.

Chandler, A., F. Amatori & T. Hikino (eds) (1997), *Big Business and the Wealth of Nations*, Cambridge: Cambridge University Press.

Chatterjee, S. (1999), 'Australian management at the crossroads: Developing regiocentric competencies', in S. Neelemegham, D. Midgley & C. Sen (eds), *Enterprise Management: New Horizons in Indo-Australian Collaboration*, New Delhi: Tata McGraw-Hill, 415–28.

Chenhall, R.H. (1979), 'Some elements of organizational control in Australian divisionalised firms', *Australian Journal of Management,* **4** (1), Supplement, 1–36.

Chenoweth, N. (2001), *Virtual Murdoch: Reality Wars on the Information Highway,* London: Secker & Warburg.

Cheslin, D. (1976), 'TNT arrives with a bang', *Containerisation International*, October, 19.

Clark, R., L. Rex & D. Robertson (1982), *The Australian National Line, 1956–81: History and Fleet List*, Kendal, UK: World Ship Society.

Clarke, A.C. (1992), *How the World was One: The Turbulent History of Global Communications*, London: Victor Gollancz.

Clarke, I. & P. Rimmer (1997), 'The anatomy of retail internationalisation: Daimaru's decision to invest in Melbourne', *Service Industries Journal*, **17** (3), 361–82.

Clarke, J., R. Tamaschke & P. Liesch (2003), 'The degree of firm internationalisation, international experience and performance', *Academy of International Business 2003 Annual Meeting,* Monterey, CA.

Clegg, B. (1999), 'Infrastructure group tightens its grip on tolls for Macquarie', *Australian Financial Review*, 30 July.

Click, R.W. & P. Harrison (2000), 'Does multinationality matter? Evidence of value destruction in US multinational corporations', *Working Paper,* Federal Reserve Board, Washington, DC.

Coalition of Service Industries (2004), 'US–Australia FTA to Open New Opportunities for US Service Sector', Press release, 18 May [www.uscsi.org/press/], 5 April 2005.

Coca-Cola Beverages (1998), *Information Booklet* (distributed to CCA shareholders), London.

Cochlear (2005), [www.cochlear.com/Corporate/Investor/780.asp], 7 December 2005.

Coles Myer (2005), *Annual Report* [www.colesmyer.com/AboutUs], 3 May 2006.

Collins, J.C. & J.I. Porras (2000), *Built to Last: Successful Habits of Visionary Companies,* 3rd edn, London: Random House Business Books.

Collis, D.J. (1991), 'A resource-based analysis of global competition: The case of the bearings industry', *Strategic Management Journal*, **12** (6), 49–68.

Collis, D.J. (1997), 'Managing the multibusiness corporation', *Conceptual note 9-391-286*, Harvard Business School, Boston.

Collis, D.J. & C.A. Montgomery (2005), *Corporate Strategy: A Resource-Based Approach,* 2nd edn, Boston: McGraw-Hill Irwin.

Computershare (2005), Corporate profile: Company history [www._au.computershare.com?CorporateProfile/CompanyHistory.asp?cc] 7 December 2005.

Conan Doyle, A. (1892), 'The Silver Blaze', *The Strand Magazine*, London.

Crawford, J.B. (1968), *Australian Trade Policy 1942–1966,* Canberra: Australian National University Press.

Croser, B. (2004), 'Brand or authenticity?', *Wine Industry Journal*, **19** (2), 12–21.

Croser, B. (2005), 'The idea of quality: Creating sustainable competitive advantage' [www.finewinepress.com/modules.php?op=modloadandname =PagEdandfile=indexandtopic_id=32andpage_id=161], 12 January 2006.

CSES (Centre for Strategic Economic Studies, Victoria University) (2002), 'Engineering and Professional Services', Supporting Paper No. 7 provided to the Western Australian Technology and Industry Advisory Council, February.

CSL (2005), [www.csl.com.au].

Cummins, C. (1998), 'CC Amatil "Not A Dumping Ground" for US', *Sydney Morning Herald*, 2 April.

Darby, M.R. & E. Karni (1973), 'Free competition and the optimal amount of fraud', *Journal of Law & Economics*, **16** (1), 67–86.

Davenport-Hines, R. & J. Slinn (1992), *Glaxo: A History to 1962*, Cambridge: Cambridge University Press.

Davidson, L.S. & S. Salsbury (2005), *Australia's First Bank: Fifty Years from the Wales to Westpac*, Sydney: University of New South Wales Press.

Davis, E., G. Hanlon & J. Kay (1993), 'What internationalisation in services means: The case of accountancy in the UK and Ireland,' in H. Cox, J. Clegg & G. Letto-Gillies (eds), *The Growth of Global Business*, London: Routledge, 105–18.

Dawson, J. (2003), 'Towards a model of the impacts on retail internationalization,' in Dawson, J., M. Mukoyama, S. Chul Choi & R. Larke (eds), *The Internationalisation of Retailing in Asia*, London: Routledge-Curzon, 189–209.

Deane, R.P. (1963), *The Establishment of the Department of Trade,* Canberra: Australian National University.

Deborah Wilson Consulting Services Pty Ltd (2002), 'What buyers say they expect from suppliers to major projects', in *Market Analysis of Mining and Heavy Engineering Demand for Structural and Ferrous Metal Products and Machinery and Equipment*, Report prepared for the Department of State Development, Queensland, Brisbane.

Deloitte (2006), 2006 Global Powers of Retailing [www.deloitte.com/dtt/cda/doc/content/dtt_ConsumerBusiness_GlobalPowers_021006.pdf], 3 May 2006.

Denis, D.J., D.K. Denis & K. Yost (2002), 'Global diversification, industrial diversification, and firm value', *The Journal of Finance*, LVII (5), 1951–79.

Department of Industry, Tourism and Resources (2001), *The Internet's Impact on Global Supply Chains*, Report prepared by Ernst & Young.

Department of Industry, Tourism and Resources (2002), *Multinational Enterprises 2001: Positive Contributors to Australia's National Innovation System*, Canberra: AGPS.

Department of Industry, Tourism and Resources (2004), *Heavy Engineering and Infrastructure Action Agenda Evaluation Report*, Canberra; AGPS.

Department of Trade (1960), *The Australian Pharmaceutical Products Industry*, Melbourne: Industries Division Department of Trade.

Department of Trade and Industry (1966), *Directory of Overseas Investment in Australian Manufacturing Industry*, Canberra: DTI.

Department of Trade and Industry (1971), *Directory of Overseas Investment in Australian Manufacturing Industry 1971,* Canberra: DTI.

Department of Treasury (1972), *Overseas Investment in Australia*, Canberra: AGPS.

Derdak, T. (ed.) (1988), *International Directory of Company Histories,* Chicago and London: St James Press, Volume 1, 'Drugs'.

Deveson, I. (1997), *Evolution of an Australian Management Style*, Warriewood, NSW: Business & Professional Publishing.

DFAT (Department of Foreign Affairs and Trade) (1994), *Changing Tack: Australian Investment in South East Asia*, Canberra: DFAT.

DFAT (2002), *The Big End of Town and Australia's Trading Interests*, Canberra: DFAT.

DHL (2004), *DHL Export Barometer*, Issue 3 (November).

DHL (2005), *DHL Export Barometer*, Issue 4 (May).

Dick, H.W. (1992), 'Progress and frustration: Restructuring of coastal shipping and ports', in P. Forsyth (ed.), *Microeconomic Reform in Australia*, St Leonards, NSW: Allen & Unwin, 204–21.

Dick, H.W. & S. Kentwell (1988), *Beancaker to Boxboat: Steamship Companies in Chinese Waters*, Canberra: Nautical Association of Australia.

Donovan, P. & E. Tweddell (1995), *The Faulding Formula: A History of F. H. Faulding & Co. Ltd*, Kent Town: F.H. Faulding & Co. Ltd.

Doz, Y., J. Santos & P. Williamson (2001), *From Global to Metanational: How Companies Win in the Knowledge Economy*, Boston: Harvard Business School Press.

Drtina, T. (1995), 'The internationalisation of retailing in the Czech and Slovak Republics', in G. Akehurst, & N. Alexander (eds), *The Internationalisation of Retailing*, London: Frank Cass, 191–203.

DST (1970), *Australian Shipping and Shipbuilding, June 1970*, 23rd edn, Canberra: Department of Shipping & Transport, December.

Dun & Bradstreet (n.d.), *Jobson's Mining Year Book 1980,* Melbourne: Dun & Bradstreet.

Dunford, R. & I. Palmer (2002), 'Managing for high performance? People management practices in Flight Centre', *Journal of Industrial Relations*, **44** (3), 376–96.

Dunning, J. (1977), 'Trade, location of economic activity and the MNE: A search for an eclectic approach', in B. Ohlin, P.O. Hesselborn & P.M. Wijkman (eds), *The International Allocation of Economic Activity*, London: Macmillan, 395–418.

Dunning, J. (1981), 'Explaining outward direct investment of developing countries: In support of the eclectic theory of international production', in K. Kumar and M.G. McLeod (eds), *Multinationals from Developing Countries,* Lexington: Lexington Books.

Dunning, J. (1989), *Transnational Corporations and the Growth of Services: Some Conceptual and Theoretical Issues,* New York: UN Centre on Transnational Corporations.

Dunning, J. (1993a), 'The globalization of service activities', in J. Dunning (ed.), *The Globalization of Business: The Challenge of the 1990s*, London: Routledge, 242–84.

Dunning, J. (1993b), *Multinational Enterprises and the Global Economy,* Wokingham: Addison-Wesley.

Dunning, J. (1995), 'Reappraising the eclectic paradigm in the age of alliance capitalism', *Journal of International Business Studies*, **26** (3), 461–91.

Dunphy, D. & D. Stace (1990), *Under New Management: Australian Organizations in Transition,* Sydney: McGraw-Hill.

Durisin, B. & G. von Krogh (2005), 'Competitive advantage, knowledge assets and group-level effects: An empirical study of global investment banking', in R.A. Bettis (ed.), *Strategy in Transition*, Malden, MA: Blackwell, 35–80.

Dyer, D., F. Dalzell & R. Olegario (2004), *Rising Tide: Lessons from 165 Years of Brand Building at Procter & Gamble*, Boston, MA: Harvard Business School Press.

Easdown, G. & P. Wilms (2002), *Ansett: The Collapse*, Melbourne: Lothian Books.

Economic Analytical Unit (2005), *Australia and the United States: Trade and the Multinationals in a New Era*, Canberra: DFAT.

Economist (2004), 'Serial networker: Macquarie Bank', *The Economist*, 11 September.

Edwards, J. (1982), *Out of the Blue: A History of Reckitt & Colman in Australia*, Artarmon, NSW: Reckitt & Colman.

Eggertsson, T. (1990), *Economic Behaviour and Institutions,* Cambridge: Cambridge University Press.

Einstein, R. (2005), 'The Pepsi-fication of Penfold' [www.torbwine.com], 29 November 2005.

Eisenhardt, K.M. (1989), 'Agency theory: An assessment and review', *Academy of Management Journal*, **14** (1), 57–74.

Engineering Consulting Firms Association, Japan (2003), 'Overseas Activities of Members' [www.ecfa.or.jp/english/wh–osa.html], 19 April 2003.

ENR [Engineering News Record] (2005), *The Top International Design Firms,* **255**, 38–42.

Enright, M.J. & B.H. Roberts (2001), 'Regional clustering in Australia', *Australian Journal of Management*, **26** (Special Issue), 65–86.

Evans, J. & F.T. Mavondo (2002), 'Psychic distance and organizational performance: An empirical examination of international retailing operations', *Journal of International Business Studies*, **33** (3), 515–32.

Evans, P., V. Pucik, & J–L Barsoux (2002), *The Global Challenge: Frameworks for International Human Resource Management*, Boston: McGraw Hill Irwin.

Evans, S. (2006a), 'A pair of chronic laggards in the way', *The Australian Financial Review,* 15 February.

Evans, S. (2006b), 'Asian breweries may reap $200m', *The Australian Financial Review,* 2 May.

Evans, S. (2006c), 'Foster's warns of shake–out in the wine industry', *The Australian Financial Review*, 15 February.

Farquhar, I. (2002a), *Howard Smith Shipping: Enterprise and Diversity, 1854–2001*, Melbourne: Nautical Association of Australia.

Farquhar, I. (2002b), '"Rosie" and the ABC containerline N.V.', *New Zealand Marine News*, **50** (4), 169–83.

Farrell, J.J. (2003), *One Nation Under Goods: Malls and the Seductions of American Shopping*, Washington, DC: Smithsonian Books.

Ferguson, A. (1996), 'It's enough to break an Abeles man's heart', *Business Review Weekly*, 29 July, 23–5.

Ferguson, A. (1999a), 'Heady Times For CCA', *Business Review Weekly*, 16 April.

Ferguson, A. (1999b), 'Part Two: A Touch of Kunkel', *Business Review Weekly*, **21** (9), 78.

Ferguson, A. (2000a), 'Memo CCA: Take The Money', *Business Review Weekly*, 18 August.

Ferguson, A. (2000b), 'One Man's Fight To Find The Real CCA', *Business Review Weekly*, 1 December.

Ferguson, A. (2001), 'CCA Does A Philippines Deal', *Business Review Weekly*, 9 February.

Ferguson, A. (2003), 'Milk: Coke's Next Real Thing', *Business Review Weekly*, 10 July.

Ferguson, A. (2004), 'Coke with much more?', *Business Review Weekly*, 12 August.

Ferguson, A. (2005), 'Foster's big gamble', *Business Review Weekly,* 27 January, 12–17.

Ferguson, A. & D. James (2003), 'Secrets and traps of overseas expansion', *Business Review Weekly,* 5–11 June, 40–46.

Fernie, J. & S. Fernie (1997), 'The development of a US retail format in Europe: The case of factory outlet centres', *International Journal of Retail & Distribution Management*, **25** (11), 342–50.

Fieldhouse, D. (1978), *Unilever Overseas: The Anatomy of a Multinational 1895–1965*, London: Croom Helm.

Fitzpatrick, B. & E.L. Wheelwright (1965), *The Highest Bidder: A Citizen's Guide to the Problems of Foreign Investment in Australia,* Melbourne: Lansdowne Press.

Fleming, G., D. Merrett & S. Ville (2004), *The Big End of Town: Big Business and Corporate Leadership in Twentieth-Century Australia*, Cambridge: Cambridge University Press.

Flight Centre (2006), *FCL 2006 Half Year Results* [www.flightcentre.com.au/aboutus/investors/], 3 May 2006.

Forbes (2005), *The Forbes Global 2000* [www.forbes.com/2005/03/30/05f2000land.html], 10 August 2005.

Fortune (2003), *Fortune Global 500* [http://money.cnn.com/magazines/fortune/global 500/], 21 July 2005.

Fortune (2004), *Fortune Global 500,* [http://money.cnn.com/magazines/fortune/global 500/], 27January 2005.

Foster's (2005), *Annual Report* [www.fosters.com.au], 22 April 2006.

Fraser, W.H. (1981), *The Coming of the Mass Market, 1850–1914*, London: Macmillan.

Frost, D. (ed.) (1965), *The Broadcasting and Television Year Book 1965*, 8th edn, Sydney: Greater Publications.

Fung, J.G., E. Bain, J. Onto & I. Harper (2002), 'A decade of internationalization: The experience of an Australian retail bank', *Journal of International Financial Markets, Institutions and Money*, **12**, 399–417.

Garden, D. (1992), *Builders to the Nation: The A V Jennings Story*, Melbourne: Melbourne University Press.

Geringer, J.M., S. Tallman & D.M. Olsen (2000), 'Product and international diversification among Japanese multinational firms', *Strategic Management Journal*, **21**, 51–80.

Gestrin, M.V., R.F. Knight & A.M. Rugman (1998, 2001), *Templeton Global Performance Index*, Oxford: Templeton College.

GF (Goodman Fielder) (2003), *Annual Report 2002* [www.goodmanfielder.com.au/dir065/gfsite/gfLtd.nsf/Content/Investor+Relations+—+Annual+Report], 10 November 2005.

Ghemawat, P. (1991), *Commitment: The Dynamic of Strategy*, New York: The Free Press.

Ghemawat, P. (2000), 'Global advantage: arbitrage, replication and transformation', *Unpublished note,* Harvard Business School, Boston.

Ghemawat, P. (2001), 'Distance still matters: The hard reality of global expansion', *Harvard Business Review*, **79** (8), 137–47.

Ghemawat, P. (2003), 'Semiglobalization and international business strategy. *Journal of International Business Studies*, **34** (2), 138–52.

Ghemawat, P. (2005), 'Regional strategies for global leadership', *Harvard Business Review*, December, 98–108.

Ghemawat, P., D.J. Collis, G.P. Pisano & J.W. Rivkin (1999), *Strategy and the Business Landscape: Text and Cases*, Reading, MA: Addison-Wesley.

Ghoshal, S. (1987), 'Global strategy: An organizing framework', *Strategic Management Journal*, **8** (5), 425–40.

Ghoshal, S. & N. Nohria (1989), 'Internal differentiation within multinational corporations', *Strategic Management Journal*, **10** (4), 323–37.

Giebelhaus, A.W. (1994), 'The pause that refreshed the world', in G. Jones & N.J. Morgan (eds), *Adding Value. Brands and Marketing in Food and Drink*, London: Routledge, 191–214.

Gladstone, J. (2005), 'History of the Margaret River viticulture region: A personal perspective', *The Australian and New Zealand Wine Industry Journal*, **20** (6), 18–27.

Gladwell, M. (2004), 'The Terrazzo Jungle', *The New Yorker*, 15 March, 120.

Glaser, B. & A. Strauss (1967), *The Discovery of Grounded Theory: Strategies of Qualitative Research*, London: Weidenfeld & Nicholson.

Gluyas, R. (2001), 'Troubles brew but Foster's sees the light', *The Australian*, 23 October.

Godley, A. & S. Fletcher (2000), 'Foreign entry into British retailing, 1850–1994', *International Marketing Review*, **17** (4–5), 392–400.

Godley, A. & S. Fletcher (2001), 'International retailing in Britain, 1850–1994', *Services Industries Journal*, **21** (2), 31–46.

Goldsmith, R.W. (1969), *Financial Structure and Development*, New Haven and London: Yale University Press.

Goodfellow, N. (2000), 'Singapore buy extends OPSM's Asian push', *Courier Mail*, 13 January.

Goot, M. (n.d.), 'Askin, Sir Robert (Robin) William (1907–81)', Draft entry for D. Langmore (ed.), *Australian Dictionary of Biography,* vol. 17 [www.pol.mq.edu.au/publications/Askin.htm], 22 October 2004.

Gottliebsen, R. (1988), 'How PacDun's formula won', *Business Review Weekly*, 16 December, 66.

Gottliebsen, R. (2003), *10 Best and 10 Worst Decisions of Australian CEOs*, Ringwood: Viking.

Grant, R.M. (1987), 'Multinationality and performance among British manufacturing companies', *Journal of International Business Studies,* **18** (3), 79–89.

Grant, R.M. (1991), 'Porter's "Competitive Advantage of Nations": An Assessment', *Strategic Management Journal*, **12** (7), 535–48.

Gray, A.C. (1977), *Life Insurance in Australia: An Historical and Descriptive Account*, Melbourne: McCarron Bird.

Greenblat, E. (2004), 'New floats to stabilize Macquarie', *The Age*, 25 February.

Griffiths, A. & R.F. Zammuto (2005), 'Institutional governance systems and variations in national competitive advantage: An integrative framework', *Academy of Management Review,* **30** (4), 823–42.

Grigg, A. (2006), 'Master & Commander', *The AFR Magazine*, 31 March, 66–71.

Grosse, R. (2005), 'Are the largest financial institutions really "global"?', *Management International Review*, **45** (Special Issue 1), 129–44.

Grossman, D. (2006), 'Can Aussie wines gain traction above $10?', *Wine Business Monthly,* April, 58–62.

Group of Eight (2002), 'Research and Innovation: An Update. Benchmarking Australia's Investment in R&D' [www.go8.edu.au/policy/papers/2002/0918.pdf], 11 April 2006.

Gunn, J. (1995), *Taking Risks 1886–1994: A History of the QBE Insurance Group*, St Leonards, NSW: Allen & Unwin.

Gupta, A.K. & V. Govindarajan (1991), 'Knowledge flows and the structure of control within multinational corporations', *The Academy of Management Review,* **13** (4), 768–92.

Gupta, A.K. & V. Govindarajan (1994), 'Organizing for knowledge flows within MNCs', *International Business Review,* **43** (4), 443–57.

Gupta, A.K. & V. Govindarajan (2000), 'Knowledge flows within the multinational corporation', *Strategic Management Journal,* **21** (4), 473–96.

Haigh, G. (1999), *One of a Kind: The Story of Bankers Trust Australia, 1969-1999*, Melbourne: Text Publishing.

Halliday, J. (1994), *A History of the Australian Wine Industry,* Adelaide: Wine Titles.

Hammonds, K.H. (2001), 'Michael Porter's big ideas', *Fast Company,* 44 (March), 150.

Hanchett, T.W. (1996), 'U.S. tax policy and the shopping-center boom of the 1950s and 1960s', *American Historical Review,* **101** (4), 1082-110.

Hannan, M.T. & J. Freeman (1984), 'Structural inertia and organizational change', *American Sociological Review,* **49** (2), 149–64.

Hannen, M. (2001), 'Harvey Norman widens its global ambitions', *Business Review Weekly,* 9 March, 40–1.

Hannen, M. (2002), 'What A Bottler', *Business Review Weekly,* 17 January.

Hansard (1991), 'Mr Hatton', *NSW Legislative Assembly Hansard,* 24 September [/www.parliament.nsw.gov.au/prod/parlment/HansArt.nsf/0/ca256d11000bd3aa4], 22 October 2004.

Harley, R. (2005a), 'Lowy: full ahead on all fronts', *Australian Financial Review,* 10 November.

Harley, R. (2005b), 'Macquarie puts the world on its map', *Australian Financial Review*, 8 September.

Harrison, J. (2003), 'The Iron Ladies', *Ships in Focus Record*, No. 23 (March), 154–67.

Harvard Business School (1999), 'Westfield America', *Harvard Business School Case 9-899-260.*

Harvey Norman (2005), 'Corporate Profile – September 2005' [www.harveynorman.com.au/site/01/html/corp/companyprofile.htm], 3 May 2006.

Harzing, A.W.K. (1997), 'Response rates in international mail surveys: Results of a 22 country study', *International Business Review*, **6** (6), 641–65.

Harzing, A.W.K. (1999), *Managing the Multinationals: An International Study of Control Mechanisms*, Cheltenham, UK and Northampton, US: Edward Elgar.

Harzing, A.W.K. (2001), 'Of bears, bumble–bees and spiders: The role of expatriates in controlling foreign subsidiaries', *Journal of World Business*, **36** (4), 366–79.

Harzing, A.W.K. (2003), 'The role of culture in entry mode studies: From neglect to myopia?', *Advances in International Management*, **15**, 75–127.

Hast, A. (ed.) (1991), *International Directory of Company Histories*, Chicago and London: St James Press, Volume III, 'Health & Personal Care Products'.

Hatch Associates Pty Ltd (2001), *A Study of Key Global Supply Chain Operations in Australia*, Report prepared for the Department of State Development, Queensland, Brisbane.

Hayes, C.L. (2004), *Pop: Truth and Power at the Coca-Cola Company*, Hutchinson: London.

Hayward, W.S. & P. White (1928), *Chain Stores: Their Management and Operation*, New York: McGraw-Hill.

Hazel, D. (2001), 'Like father, like son', *Shopping Centres Today,* May [www.icsc.org/], 18 May 2006.

Hedlund, G. (1980), 'The role of foreign subsidiaries in strategic decision-making in Swedish multinational corporations', *Strategic Management Journal*, **11** (1), 7–22.

Henderson, B.D. (1979), *Henderson on Corporate Strategy*, Cambridge, MA: Abt Books.

Hennart, J-F. (2005), 'Some critical observations on the theory and methodology of the multinationality-performance literature', *Paper presented at the annual meeting of the Academy of International Business,* Quebec City, 9–11 July.

Hewett, J. (1993), 'The bank that's ahead of the pack', *Australian Financial Review*, 20 August.

Hewett, J. (2005), 'Shop till you drop: Lowy's on the prowl', *Australian Financial Review*, 31 August.

HIH Royal Commission (2003), *Report*, 3 vols, Canberra: AGPS.

Hill, C.W.L. (1994), 'Diversification and economic performance: Bringing structure and corporate management back into the picture', in Rumelt, R.R., D.E. Schendel & D.J. Teece (eds), *Fundamental Issues in Strategy: A Research Agenda*. Boston, MA: Harvard Business School Press.

Hill, C.W.L., M.A. Hitt, & R.E. Hoskisson (1992), 'Cooperative versus competitive structures in related and unrelated diversified firms', *Organization Science*, **3** (4), 501–20.

Hodgson, G. (1984), *Lloyd's of London: A Reputation at Risk*, London: Allen Lane.

Hoen, A. (2001), 'Clusters: Determinants and effects', *CPB Memorandum*, The Hague: CPB Netherlands Bureau for Economic Policy Analysis.

Hofstede, G. (1980), *Culture's Consequences: International Differences in Work-Related Values*. Beverley Hills, CA: Sage.

Holder, R.F. (1970), *Bank of New South Wales: A History*, Sydney: Angus & Robertson, 2 vols.

Holm, U. & T. Pedersen (eds) (2000), *The Emergence and Impact of MNC Centres of Excellence*, London: Macmillan.

Holm, U., A. Malmberg, & O. Sollvell (2003), 'Subsidiary impact on host-country economies: The case of foreign–owned subsidiaries attracting investment into Sweden', *Journal of Economic Geography*, **3** (4), 389–408.

Hood, N. & J.H. Taggart (1999), 'Subsidiary development in German and Japanese manufacturing subsidiaries in the British Isles', *Regional Studies*, **33** (6), 513–28.

Hooke, H. (1999), 'The flying winemakers', *Sydney Morning Herald*, 26 January.

Hooper, N. & S. Aylmer (2005), 'Going global finally pays dividends', *Australian Financial Review*, 23 November.

Hu, Y–S (1995), 'The international transferability of the firm's advantages', *California Management Review*, **37** (4), 73–88.

Hubbard, G. (2000), 'Village Roadshow: entertaining the world', in G. Hubbard, A. Morkel, S. Davenport & P. Beamish (eds), *Cases in Strategic Management,* New York: Prentice Hall, 307–18.

Hubbard, G., D. Samuel, S. Heap & G. Cocks (2002), *The First XI: Winning Organizations in Australia,* Milton, Qld: John Wiley & Son.

Huddart Parker (c.1926), *Huddart Parker Ltd, 1876–1926*, Melbourne: Huddart Parker.

Hughes, A. (2004), 'Westfield promises not to bully', *Sydney Morning Herald*, 18 June.

Hughes, H. (1967), 'Australians as foreign investors: Australian investment in Singapore and Malaysian manufacturing industries', *Australian Economic Papers,* June, 57–76.

Hyland, A. (2001), 'Macquarie's "filth" expansion plan', *Australian Financial Review,* 9 November.

Hymer, S. (1960), 'The international operations of national firms: A study of direct foreign investment', *Unpublished PhD dissertation*, Economics Department, MIT, Boston.
Hymer, S. (1976), *The International Operations of National Firms: A study of Direct Investment,* Cambridge, MA: MIT Press.
IBISWorld (2006), *Wine Manufacturing in Australia,* C2183: IBISWorld.
IMD (2004), *The World Competitiveness Yearbook*, Lausanne, Switzerland: International Institute for Management Development.
IMF (1995), *International Financial Statistics Yearbook*, Washington, DC: International Monetary Fund.
Industries Assistance Commission (1974a), *Annual Report*, Canberra: AGPS.
Industries Assistance Commission (1974b), *Pharmaceutical and Veterinary Products*, Statistical Handbook Review Inquiry No.14, Canberra: AGPS.
Industry Commission (1995), *Winegrape and Wine Industry in Australia: A Report by the Committee of Inquiry into the Winegrape and Wine Industry*, Canberra: AGPS.
Industry Commission (1996a), *The Pharmaceutical Industry*, Report No.51, Canberra: AGPS, 2 vols.
Industry Commission (1996b), *Implications for Australia of Firms Locating Offshore*, Report No.53, Canberra: AGPS.
Intellectual Property Research Institute of Australia (2004), *R&D and Intellectual Property Scoreboard, 2004*, Melbourne.
ISC (Insurance and Superannuation Commission)(various), *Annual Reports*.
Iverson, H. (ed.) (1963), *The Leaders of Industry and Commerce in Australia*, East Melbourne: Iverson Publicity Services.
Jackson, K.T. (1996), 'All the world's a mall: reflections on the social and economic consequences of the American shopping center', *American Historical Review*, **101** (4), 1111–21.
James, D. (1999), 'Australia's second chance', *Business Review Weekly*, 24 September, 68–75.
James, D. (2001), 'Local Coke', *Business Review Weekly*, 20 September.
James, D. (2005), 'Born global', *Business Review Weekly*, 1 December, 44–51.
James, G.F & R. Murray (1997), *The History of the SIO, 1914–1996*, Burwood: Chandos Publishing.
Jay, C. (1994), *The Coal Masters: The History of Coal & Allied, 1844–1994*, Sydney: Focus Publishing.
Jay, C. (1997), *Australian Expertise in Infrastructure,* Edgecliff, NSW: Focus Publishing.
Jefferys, J.B. (1954), *Retail Trading in Britain 1850–1950,* Cambridge: Cambridge University Press.
Jensen, M.C. (1986), 'Agency costs of free cash flow, corporate finance, and the market for takeovers', *American Economic Review*, **76** (May), 323–29.

Jensen, M.C. & W.H. Meckling (1976), 'Theory of the firm: managerial behavior, agency costs and ownership structure', *Journal of Financial Economics,* **3** (4), October, 305–60.

Jobson's (1969), *Jobson's Year Book of Public Companies of Australia and New Zealand,* North Sydney: Jobson's Financial Services.

Johanson, J. & F. Wiedersheim-Paul (1975), 'The internationalisation of the firm: Four Swedish case studies', *Journal of Management Studies*, **12** (3), 305–22.

Johanson, J. & J-E, Vahlne (1977), 'The internationalisation process of the firm: A model of knowledge development and increasing foreign market commitments', *Journal of International Business Studies*, **8** (1), 23–32.

Johnson, M. (2005), *Family Village Tribe: The Story of Flight Centre Ltd*, Sydney: Random House.

Johnston, S. (2005a), 'Firm strategy, subsidiary type and subsidiary autonomy in multinational corporations', Paper presented at the annual meeting of the *Academy of International Business*, Stockholm, 10–13 July.

Johnston, S. (2005b), *Headquarters and Subsidiaries in Multinational Corporations: Strategies, Tasks and Coordination*, Basingstoke: Palgrave Macmillan.

Jones, G. (1992), 'International financial centres in Asia, the Middle East and Australia: A historical perspective', in Y. Cassis (ed.), *Finance and Financiers in European History, 1880–1960*, Cambridge: Cambridge University Press, 405–35.

Jones, G. (1993), *British Multinational Banking, 1830–1990*, Oxford: Clarendon Press.

Jones, G. (1996), *The Evolution of International Business: An Introduction*, London and New York: Routledge.

Jones, G. (2005a), *Multinationals and Global Capitalism: From the Nineteenth to the Twenty-First Century*, Oxford: Oxford University Press.

Jones, G. (2005b), *Renewing Unilever: Transformation and Tradition*, Oxford & New York: Oxford University Press.

Jüttner, D.J. (1998), *International Finance and Global Investments*, 4th edn, South Melbourne: Addison Wesley Longman.

Kallunki, J-P., J. Larimo & S. Pynnonen (2001), 'Value creation in foreign direct investments', *Management International Review*, **41** (4), 357–76.

Karmel, P.H. & M.D. Brunt (1962), *The Structure of the Australian Economy*, Melbourne: F.W. Cheshire.

Kavanagh, J. (2001), 'We love your work', *Business Review Weekly*, 13 September.

Khanna, T. & K. Palepu (1999), 'The right way to restructure conglomerates in emerging markets', *Harvard Business Review*, July–August, 125–34.

Khanna, T. & K. Palepu (2005), 'Strategies that fit emerging markets', *Harvard Business Review*, June, 63–76.

Kiely, M. (1986), 'Alan Bond: Two-fisted marketing', *Marketing*, August.

Kim, W.C & R. Mauborgne (2005), 'Blue Ocean strategy: From theory to practice', *California Management Review*, **47** (3), 105–21.

Kimbell, D., A. Newby & D. Skalinder (2005), 'The big get bigger – but is it for the best?', *Euromoney*, **36**, 433.

King, S. (1999), *Leighton: 50 Years of Achievement 1949–1999*, St Leonards, NSW: Technical Resources.

Kingston, B. (1994), *Basket, Bag and Trolley: A History of Shopping in Australia*, Melbourne: Oxford University Press.

Kirby, J. (2003), *Gerry Harvey: Business Secrets of Harvey Norman's Retailing Mastermind*, Milton: John Wiley.

Kiwi (1951), *The Kiwi Story: The House of Ramsay, 1905–1951*, Melbourne: Kiwi Polish Co. Pty Ltd.

Kiwi (1962), *Kiwi International*, Melbourne: Kiwi Polish Co. Pty Ltd.

Kiwi (1966), *Kiwi International since 1906*, Melbourne: Associated World Public Relations.

Kluenker, C. (2001), 'Risk vs. conflict of interest: What every owner should consider when using construction management', *CM eJournal* (*Construction Management Association of America*), 1–18.

Knight, A.S. & T. Cavusgil (2005), 'Taxonomy of born-global firms', *Management International Review*, **45** (Special Issue 3), 15–35.

Knight, E. (2004), 'Time Amatil thought about dumping Korea', *Sydney Morning Herald*, 4 August.

Kobrin, S. (1994), 'Is there a relationship between a geocentric mind-set and multinational strategy?', *Journal of International Business Studies*, **25** (3), 493–511.

Kogut, B. (1985), 'Designing global strategies: Profiting from operational flexibility', *Sloan Management Review*, Fall, 27–38.

Kogut, B. & N. Kulatilaka (1994a), 'Operating flexibility, global manufacturing, and the option value of a multinational network', *Management Science*, **40** (1), 123–39.

Kogut, B. & N. Kulatilaka (1994b), 'Options thinking and platform investments: Investing in opportunity', *California Management Review*, **36** (2), 52–71.

Kogut, B. & H. Singh (1988), 'The effect of national culture on the choice of entry mode', *Journal of International Business Studies*, **19** (3), 411–32.

Kogut, B. & U. Zander (1993), 'Knowledge of the firm and the evolutionary theory of the multinational corporation', *Journal of International Business Studies*, **24** (4), 625–45.

Kohler, A. (1997). 'PacDun's make or break', *Business Review Weekly*, 14 April, 23–6.

Kolm, J.E. (1988), 'The chemical industry and Australian contribution to chemical technology', in Frank Eyre (ed.), *Technology in Australia*, Melbourne: Australian Academy of Technological Sciences and Engineering, 631–732.

Korporaal, G. (1986a), 'Painting the US red, white – and blue', *Business Review Weekly*, 21 February.

Korporaal, G. (1986b), *Yankee Dollars: Australian Investment in America*, Sydney: Allen & Unwin.

Korporaal, G. (2002), 'MacBank's silk road', *The Australian*, 7 May.

KPMG (1999), *Mergers and Acquisitions: A Global Research Report – Unlocking Shareholder Value*. New York: KPMG.

Kune, G. (1999), *Nothing is Impossible: The John Saunders Story*, Melbourne: Scribe.

Kunkel, T. (2001), *Brisbane Bourse Presentation*, Brisbane, 3 September.

Laird, P.W. (1998), *Advertising Progress: American Business and the Rise of Consumer Marketing*, Baltimore & London: Johns Hopkins University Press.

Lambiris, C. (1999), 'The struggle for growth: Australian SMEs, internationalisation and IPOs', *Unpublished Honours thesis*, Department of Management, University of Melbourne, Melbourne.

Langdale, J.V. (1991), *Internationalisation of Australia's Service Industries*, Canberra: AGPS.

Langfield-Smith, K. (1991), 'Carlton and United Breweries Ltd (B): The internationalization of the brewing industry', in G. Lewis, A. Morkel & G. Hubbard (eds), *Cases in Australian Strategic Management*, New York: Prentice Hall, 66–83.

Langfield-Smith, K. & G. Lewis (1993), 'Carlton and United Breweries (A): The Australian brewing industry', in G. Lewis, A. Morkel & G. Hubbard (eds), *Australian Strategic Management: Concepts, Context and Cases*, New York: Prentice Hall: 453–81.

Langmore, D. (1988), 'Ramsay, William (1868–1914)', in G. Serle (ed.), *Australian Dictionary of Biography, Volume 11, 1891–1939, Nes – Smi*, Melbourne: Melbourne University Press.

Lasserre, P. & H. Schütte (1995), *Strategies for Asia Pacific*, South Melbourne: Macmillan Business.

Laxon, W.A. (2002), *The Currie Line of Melbourne*, Melbourne: Nautical Association of Australia.

Laxon, W.A., I.J. Farquhar, N.J. Kirby & F.W. Perry (1997), *Crossed Flags: The Histories of the New Zealand Shipping Company, Federal Steam Navigation Company and their Subsidiaries*, Gravesend, UK: World Ship Society.

Lecky, S. (1988), 'PacDun's apparent switch is right on target', *Sydney Morning Herald*, 1 August.

Leser, D. (1990), 'An audience with Sir Peter Abeles', *Good Weekend*, 6 January, 26–32.

Lewis, G., K. Jarvie & T. Zalan (2004), 'Economic consequences of international diversification: FDI experiences of Australian firms', *Academy of International Business annual meeting*, Stockholm, July.

Lewis, G. & T. Minchev (2000), 'Creating value through international diversification: The case of the National Australia Bank', *Proceedings of the 2000 Annual ANZIBA Conference: The Role of Multinational Enterprises in the New Millennium,* Auckland, New Zealand.

Lewis, G., A. Morkel & G. Stockport (1999), 'Australia's and New Zealand's economic heritage', in G. Lewis, A. Morkel, G. Hubbard, S. Davenport & G. Stockport (eds), *Australian and New Zealand Strategic Management: Concepts, Context and Cases,* 2nd edn, Sydney: Prentice Hall of Australia, 393–408.

Lewis, G. & T. Zalan (2005a), 'Amcor (A) and (B)', in Ramburuth, P. & C. Welch (eds), *Casebook in International Business*, Frenchs Forest: Pearson Education Australia.

Lewis, G. & T. Zalan (2005b), 'Can Australia compete internationally? The old question revisited in the light of new evidence', *Asia-Pacific Business Review*, **11** (3), 309–26.

Li, P.P. (2003), 'Toward a geocentric theory of multinational evolution: The implications from the Asian MNEs as latecomers', *Asia Pacific Journal of Management*, **20** (2), 217–42.

LIC (Life Insurance Commissioner) (various), *Annual Report.*

Lin, N. (1999), 'Building a network theory of social capital', *Connections*, **22** (1), 28–51.

Lipson, N. & A. Walters (2006), *The Accidental Gangster: The Life and Times of Bela Csidei*, Sydney: Park Street Press and Media21 Publishing.

Log, *The Log*, quarterly, The Nautical Association of Australia.

Log, The (1980), 'Maritime Miscellany: Overseas', *The Log*, November.

Lopez, A. (1998), 'The return of a crony: Is Eduardo Cojuangco good for San Miguel?' *Asiaweek*, 24 July [www.pathfinder.com/asiaweek/98/0724/biz3.html], 6 June 2006.

Lovallo, D. & D. Kahneman (2003), 'Delusions of success: How optimism undermines executives' decisions', *Harvard Business Review*, July, 1–9.

Lowendahl, B.R. (1997), *Strategic Management of Professional Service Firms*, Copenhagen: Munksgaard International Publishers.

Lowendahl, B.R. (2000), 'The globalization of professional business service firms: Fad or genuine source of competitive advantage?', in L. Nachum & L. Aharoni (eds), *Globalization of Services: Some Implications for Theory and Practice,* London: Routledge, 142–62.

Lowndes, A.G. (ed.) (1956), *South Pacific Enterprise: The Colonial Sugar Refining Company Ltd,* Sydney: Angus & Robertson.

LRS (Lloyd's Register of Shipping) (1938), *Lloyd's Register of Ships 1938/39*, London: LRS.

Lubatkin, M., R. Calori, P. Very & J.F. Veiga (1998), 'Managing mergers across borders: A two-nation exploration of a nationally bound administrative heritage', *Organization Science*, **9** (6), 670–84.

Lumsden, A. (2004), 'Gaining from investment', *Paper presented at the Conference on Australia–United States Free Trade Agreement: New Opportunities & Impacts*, Canberra, 1–2 March.

Luo, Y. (2001), 'Determinants of entry in an emerging economy: A multilevel approach', *Journal of Management Studies*, **38** (3), 443–72.

Macfarlane, D. (1999), 'Ready to pounce on Asia: The man from Macquarie sees opportunities offshore', *The Australian*, 12 March.

Macquarie (2005), *2005 Financial Report* [www.macquarie.com], 7 December 2005.

Macquarie (2006), [www.macquarie.com].

Macquarie Bank (2005), *Annual Review* [www.macquarie.com], 7 December 2005.

Maddock, R. & I. McLean (1987), *The Australian Economy in the Long Run*, Cambridge: Cambridge University Press

Main, A. (2003), *Other People's Money*, Sydney: HarperCollins.

Maitland, E. & S. Nicholas (eds) (2002), 'Modeling multinationals from small, open economies', *International Studies of Management and Organization*, **32** (1), 3–15.

Mangos, N., P.W. O'Brien & R. Damania (2002), 'Is the interaction of international diversification and economic performance a linear relationship?' *JANZAM*, **8** (1), 21–31.

Mann, C.C. & M.L. Plummer (1991), *The Aspirin Wars: Money, Medicine, and 100 Years of Rampant Competition*, New York: Alfred A. Knopf.

Margo, J. (2000), *Frank Lowy: Pushing the Limits*, Sydney: Harper Collins.

Markides, C.C. & P.J. Williamson (1996), 'Corporate diversification and organisational structure: A resource-based view' *Academy of Management Journal*, **39** (2), 340–67.

Marsh, I. & B. Shaw (1999), 'Collaboration and learning in Australia's wine industry', *Wine Industry Journal*, **14** (5), 105–19.

Marsh, I. & B. Shaw (2000), *Australia's Wine Industry: Collaboration and Learning as Causes of Competitive Success*, North Sydney: Australian Business Foundation.

Martinez, J.I. & J.C. Jarillo (1989), 'The evolution of research on coordination mechanisms in multinational corporations', *Journal of International Business Studies*, **20** (1), 489–514.

Martinez, J.I. & J.C. Jarillo (1991), 'Coordination demands of international strategies', *Journal of International Business Studies*, **22** (3), 429–44.

Mascarehnas, B. & D.A. Aaker (1989), 'Mobility barriers and strategic groups', *Strategic Management Journal*, **10** (5), 475–85.

Maskell, P. (2001), 'Toward a knowledge-based theory of the geographical cluster', *Industrial and Corporate Change*, **10** (4), 921–43.

Mathur, I., M. Singh, & K.C. Gleason (2001), 'The evidence from Canadian firms on multinational diversification and performance', *The Quarterly Review of Economics and Finance*, **41** (4), 561–78.

Matsusaka, J. (1993), 'Takeover motives during the conglomerate merger wave', *RAND Journal of Economics*, **24** (3), 357–79.

McCormick (2006), [www.mccormick.com].

McDonell, R.J.F. (1976), *Build a Fleet, Lose a Fleet*, Melbourne: Hawthorn Press.

McGee, J. & H. Thomas (1986), 'Strategic groups: Theory, research, and taxonomy', *Strategic Management Journal*, **7** (2), 141–60.

McKay, M. (1974), *Cecil McKay: It Wasn't All Sunshine,* Melbourne: Hawthorn Press.

McKellar, N.L. (1977), *From Derby Round to Burketown: The A.U.S.N. Story*, Brisbane: University of Queensland Press.

McLaughlin, J. (1991), *Nothing over Half a Crown*, Main Ridge: Loch Haven.

McLean, G. (1990), *The Southern Octopus: The Rise of a Shipping Empire*, Wellington: New Zealand Ship and Marine Society.

McNair, W.A. (1937), *Radio Advertising in Australia*, Sydney: Angus & Robertson.

Mellor, W. (2006), 'Macquarie's Moss likely to leave a legacy of wholly holey holy dollars', *The Age*, 30 March.

Menzer, J. (2004), 'Global Expansion', in *Proceedings of the Seven Futures Conference*, Boeing Institute of International Business, St Louis University, Saint Louis, 76–89.

Menzies, H. (1988), 'Pacific Dunlop diversifies its way into America', *The New York Times,* 28 August.

Merck Sharp & Dohme (2002), *The Contribution of Merck Sharp & Dohme to the Australian Economy*, Technical report prepared for Merck Sharp & Dohme Australia Pty Ltd by Access Economics, Canberra.

Merrett, D.T. (1989), 'Australian banking practice and the crisis of 1893', *Australian Economic History Review*, **XIX** (1), 60–85.

Merrett, D.T. (1990), 'Paradise lost?: British banks in Australia', in G. Jones (ed.), *Banks as Multinationals*, London & New York: Routledge, 62–84.

Merrett, D.T. (1995), 'Global reach by Australian banks: Correspondent banking networks, 1830–1960', *Business History,* **37** (3), 70–88.

Merrett, D.T. (1998), 'Stability and change in the Australian brewing industry' in R.G. Wilson & T.R. Gourvish (eds), *The Dynamics of the International Brewing Industry since 1800,* London and New York: Routledge, 237–43.

Merrett, D.T. (2000), 'Australia's outward FDI in a comparative context: A case of constrained internationalisation?' *Proceedings of the ANZIBA 2000 Annual Conference: The Role of Multinational Enterprises in the New Millennium,* Auckland.

Merrett, D.T. (2002a), 'Australian firms abroad before 1970: Why so few, why those and why there', *Business History*, **44** (2), 65–87.

Merrett, D.T. (2002b), 'The internationalization of Australian banks', *Journal of International Financial Markets, Institutions & Money,* **12** (4–5), 377–97.

Merrett, D.T. (2002c), 'Australia's emergent multinationals: The legacy of having a natural resource intensive, small and closed economy at home', *International Studies of Management and Organization*, **32** (1), 109–35.

Merrett, D.T. (2002d), 'Corporate governance, incentives and the internationalization of Australian business', *Business History Conference,* Hagley Museum and Library, Wilmington, Delaware, US.

Merrett, D.T. & A. Seltzer (2000), 'Work in financial services industry and worker monitoring: A study of the Union Bank of Australia in the 1920s', *Business History*, **42** (3), 133–52.

Merrett, D.T. & G. Whitwell (1994), 'The empire strikes back: Marketing Australian beer and wine in the United Kingdom', in G. Jones & N.J. Morgan (eds), *Adding Value: Brands and Marketing in Food and Drink*, Routledge: London, 162–88.

Meyer, K.E. (forthcoming), 'Global focussing: From domestic conglomerates to global specialists', *Journal of Management Studies.*

Miles, D. (2000), 'Innovation: Unlocking the Future', Final Report of the Innovation Summit Implementation Group [backingaus.innovation.gov.au/docs/statement/isig%20report.pdf], 11 April 2006.

Miles, M.B. & A.M. Huberman (1994), *Qualitative Data Analysis: An Expanded Sourcebook*, 2nd edn, Newbury Park, CA: Sage Publications.

Minchev, T. (1999), 'F.H. Faulding & Co' in G. Lewis, A. Morkel, G. Hubbard, S. Davenport & G. Stockport (eds), *Australian and New Zealand Strategic Management: Concepts, Context and Cases*, 2nd edn, Sydney: Prentice-Hall of Australia, 564–92.

Minchev, T. & A. Lebed (1999), 'Foster's Brewing Group', in G. Lewis, A. Morkel, G. Hubbard, S. Davenport & G. Stockport (eds), *Australian and New Zealand Strategic Management. Concepts, Context and Cases*, 2nd edn, Sydney: Prentice Hall of Australia, 721–45.

Minerals Council of Australia (2004), 'Submission to the Senate Select Committee on the Free Trade Agreement between Australia and the United States', Submission No.440, [www.aph.gov.au/Senate/committee/freetrade_ctte/index.htm], 5 April 2005.

Mitchell, S. (2006), 'Can things get better at Coke?', *Australian Financial Review*, 6 February.

Morgan, B. (1959), *Apothecary's Venture: The Scientific Quest of the International Nicholas Organization*, London: Nicholas-Aspro.

Morkel, A. (1996), 'AMATIL Ltd' in G. Lewis, A. Morkel, G. Hubbard, G. Stockport, & S. Davenport (eds), *Cases in Strategic Management*, 2nd edn, Sydney: Prentice Hall Australia, 236–53.

Morkel, A. & T. Osegowitsch (1999), 'The international competitiveness of Australian business', in G. Lewis, A. Morkel, G. Hubbard, S. Davenport & G. Stockport (eds), *Australian and New Zealand Strategic Management: Concepts, Context and Cases*, 2nd edn, Sydney: Prentice Hall Australia, 409–22.

Morkel, A., T. Osegowitsch & G. Lewis (1999), 'International competitiveness: A strategic management approach' in G. Lewis, A. Morkel, G. Hubbard, S. Davenport & G. Stockport (eds), *Australian and New Zealand Strategic Management: Concepts, Context and Cases*, 2nd edn, Sydney: Prentice Hall Australia, 370–89.

Moynagh, M. (1981), *Brown or White?: A History of the Fiji Sugar Industry, 1873–1973,* Canberra: Australia National University.

Murphy, M. (1984), *Challenges of Change: The Lend Lease Story,* Sydney: Lend Lease Group.

Murray, J. (1999), *The Woolworths Way*, Edgecliff, NSW: Focus.

Myer, R. & M. Moncrief (2005), 'Macquarie's Universe: How big can it grow?', *The Age*, 22 October.

Myles Shaver, J. & F. Flyer (2000), 'Agglomeration economies, firm heterogeneity, and foreign direct investment in the United States', *Strategic Management Journal*, **21** (12), 1175–93.

Nachum, L. (1999), *The Origins of the International Competitiveness of Firms. The Impact of Location and Ownership in Professional Service Industries*, Cheltenham, UK and Northampton, US: Edward Elgar.

Nahapiet, J. & S. Ghoshal (1998), 'Social capital, intellectual capital, and the organizational advantage', *Academy of Management Review*, **23** (2), 242–66.

National Australia Bank (2004), *Annual Report*, Melbourne.

Nayyar, P.R. (1990), 'Information asymmetries: A source of competitive advantage for diversified service firms', *Strategic Management Journal*, **11** (7), 513–19.

Neufeld, E.P. (1969), *A Global Corporation: A History of the International Development of Massey-Ferguson Ltd*, Toronto: University of Toronto Press.

Nicholas Australia (annual), *Annual Report.*

Nicholas International (1976), *Annual Report.*

Nicholas Kiwi (1984), *Annual Report.*

Nicholas, S., A. Sammartino & E. Maitland (2003), *Do Multinational Enterprises Benefit Australia?*, Report prepared for the Committee for the Economic Development of Australia (CEDA), Melbourne.

Nicholas, S., A. Sammartino & E. Maitland (2005), 'MNE subsidiaries in Australia: Drivers of growth or harbingers of increasing disengagement?', *Paper presented at the annual meeting of the Academy of International Business*, Quebec City, 9–11 July.

Nohria, N., D. Dyer & F. Dalzell (2002), *Changing Fortunes: Remaking the Industrial Corporation*, New York: John Wiley & Sons.

NSW (2005), 'Facts and Statistics' [www.business.nsw.gov.au/factsReports.asp?cid=32&subCid=98], 20 December 2004.

NSW (2006), 'Sir James BURNS (1846–1923)', Parliament of NSW [www.parliament.nsw.gov.au/prod/parlment/members.nsf], 27 March 2006.

O'Connor, K. (1995), 'Changes in the pattern of airline services and city development', in J. Brotchie, M. Batty, E. Blakely, P. Hall & P. Newton (eds), *Cities in Competition: Productive and Sustainable Cities for the 21st Century,* Melbourne: Longman Australia.

Odell, J. (2005), 'Brand strength: Driving global growth for Australian wine', *2005 Australian Winegrape Conference*, 17 November.

OECD (Organization for Economic Cooperation and Development) (1991), *Bank Profitability: Financial Statements of Banks*, Paris: OECD.

OECD (2002), *Bank Profitability: Financial Statements of Banks*, Paris: OECD.

OECD (2005), *Country Report No. 78: Australia* [www.oecd.org/dataoecd], 29 November 2005.

O'Grady, S. & H.W. Lane (1996), 'The psychic distance paradox', *Journal of International Business Studies*, **27** (2), 309–34.

O'Halloran, F. (2004), 'CEO Viewpoint', *Journal of the Australian and New Zealand Institute of Insurance and Finance*, **27** (5), 9–10.

Ohmae, K. (1985), *Triad Power: The Coming Shape of Global Competition,* New York: The Free Press.

Oldfield, S. (2005a), 'Macquarie seeks Asian footprint', *Australian Financial Review*, 16 March.

Oldfield, S. (2005b), 'Macquarie Bank's best, brightest and the rest', *Australian Financial Review*, 15 October.

Oliver, D. (1973), *Bougainville: A Personal History,* Melbourne: Melbourne University Press.

O'Neill, G.L. (1999), *Executive Remuneration in Australia: An Overview of Trends and Issues,* AHRI Executive Remuneration Research Project, Neutral Bay, NSW: Australian Human Resources Institute.

Onto, J. & C. Thomas (1997), *Corporate Governance and Globalising Business: Reconciling Competing Pressures*, Melbourne: Egon Zehnder International.

OPSM (2003), *CEO's Full Year 2003 Results,* 27 August 2003 [www.opsmgroup.com/investor_information/ceo_presentations.htm], 3 May 2006.

Orica (2005), 'About Orica: History' [www.orica.com.au/BUSINESS/COR/orica/COR00254.NSF/Page?About_OricaHistory], 7 December 2005.

Osegowitsch, T. (2003), 'The relationship between global integration and performance in multinational professional engineering companies', *Unpublished doctoral thesis*, University of Western Australia, Perth.

Osegowitsch, T. & A. Sammartino (2006), 'Is regionalisation all there is? Revisiting the empirical evidence regarding the extent of internationalisation by large firms', *Working paper,* Australian Centre for International Business, University of Melbourne, Melbourne.

Osmond, R. & K. Anderson (1998), *Trends and Cycles in the Australian Wine Industry, 1850 to 2000*, Adelaide: Centre for International Economic Studies, University of Adelaide.

OTA (Office of Technology Assessment) (1987), *International Competition in Services*, Washington, DC: US Congress.

OTC (Overseas Telecommunications Commission) (1978–85), *Annual Reports*, Canberra: OTC.

Otterbeck, L. (ed.) (1981), *The Management of Headquarters Subsidiary Relationships in Multinational Corporations,* Aldershot, UK: Gower.

Ouchi, W.G. (1979), 'A conceptual framework for the design of organizational control mechanisms', *Management Science*, **25**, 833-48.

PA Cambridge Economic Consultants Ltd (1995), *Assessment of the Wider Effects of Foreign Direct Investment in Manufacturing in the UK*, Report prepared for the UK Department of Trade and Industry, Cambridge.

Page, B. (2003), *The Murdoch Archipelago,* London: Simon & Schuster.

Page, M. (1975), *Fitted for the Voyage: The Adelaide Steamship Company Ltd, 1875–1975*, Adelaide: Rigby.

Pangarkar, N. & S. Klein (2001), 'The impact of alliance purpose and partner similarity on alliance governance', *British Journal of Management*, **12** (4), 341–53.

Paperlinx (2005), 'Company History' [www.paperlinx.co.au/cpa/htm/htm_company_history.asp?page_id+101], 7 December 2005.

Papps, N. (2004), 'Westfield spends $8bn wooing shoppers', *The Advertiser*, 5 November.

Parker, J. (1991), 'The X factor behind TNT's share slide', *Australian Business*, 30 January, 24–5.

PCEK (Pappas, Carter, Evans & Koop/Telesis) (1990), *The Global Challenge: Australian Manufacturing in the 1990s*, Melbourne: Australian Manufacturing Council.

Pecchioli, R.M. (1983), *The Internationalisation of Banking: The Policy Issues*, Paris: OECD.

Pendergrast, M. (1996), *For God, Country and Coca-Cola*, Phoenix: London.

Peng, M.W., S-H Lee, & D.Y.L. Wang (2005), 'What determines the scope of the firm over time?: A focus on institutional relatedness', *Academy of Management Review*, **30** (3), 622–33.

Perkins, J.O.N. (1989), *The Deregulation of the Australian Financial System: The Experience of the 1980s*, Melbourne: Melbourne University Press.

Perlmutter, H.V. (1969), 'The tortuous evolution of the multinational corporation', *Columbia Journal of World Business* **4** (1), 9–18.

Pettigrew, A.M. (1990), 'Longitudinal field research on change: Theory and practice', *Organization Science*, **1** (3), 267–92.

Pinkstone, B. (1992), *Global Connections: A History of Exports and the Australian Economy,* Canberra: AGPS.

Pollard, I.A. (1988), 'A case study in adding value (with Frank Lowy)' in *Financial Engineering: Philosophies and Precedents*, Sydney: Butterworths, 8–16.

Porter, M.E. (1980), *Competitive Strategy: Techniques for Analyzing Industries and Competitors*, New York: The Free Press.

Porter, M.E. (1987), 'From Competitive Advantage to Corporate Strategy', *Harvard Business Review*, May/June, 43–59.

Porter, M.E. (1990), *The Competitive Advantage of Nations*, London: Macmillan.

Porter, M.E. (1996), 'What is strategy?' *Harvard Business Review*, November–December: 61–78.

Porter, M.E. (1998), *On Competition*, Boston, MA: Harvard Business Review Book.

Porter, M.E. & G.C. Bond (2004), 'The California wine cluster', Harvard Business School Case No 9-799-124, *Harvard Business School,* Boston.

Porter, M.E. & O. Solvell (2003), 'The Australian wine cluster: Supplementary information', note 9-703-492, *Harvard Business School*, Boston.

Potter, Ian & Co. (1972), *Australian Company Reviews 1972*, Melbourne.

Pratt, A. (ed.) (1934), *The National Handbook of Australia's Industries,* Melbourne: The Specialty Press.

Price, G. (2001), 'PacDun to death', *The Australian*, 11 December.

Pringle, I. (1996), 'CCA Ltd' in G. Lewis, A. Morkel, G. Hubbard, G. Stockport and S. Davenport (eds), *Cases in Strategic Management Australia and New Zealand*, 2nd edn, Sydney: Prentice Hall, 322–32.

Productivity Commission (2002), *Offshore Investment by Australian Firms: Survey Evidence,* Canberra: AGPS.

Pursell, G. (1968), 'Australian non-life insurance since 1909', *Economic Record*, **44** (108), December, 438–69.

Raftery, J., B. Pasadilla., Y.H. Chiang, E.C.M. Hui & B.-S. Tang (1998), 'Globalization and construction industry development: Implications of recent developments in the construction sector in Asia', *Construction Management and Economics*, **16** (6), 729–37.

Raines, P., I. Turok, & R. Brown (2001), 'Growing global: Foreign direct investment and the internationalization of local suppliers in Scotland', *European Planning Studies*, **9** (8), 965–78.

Ralph, J.T. (1979), *Pharmaceutical Manufacturing Industry Inquiry*, Report, Canberra: AGPS.

Rankine, B. (1996), *Evolution of the Modern Australian Wine Industry*, Adelaide: Ryan Publications.

RBA (Reserve Bank of Australia), 'Bank Assets' [www.rba.gov.au/historical_assets_individual_banks.xls], 22 March 2006.

RBA (1981), 'Overseas operations of Australian banks', *Reserve Bank of Australia Bulletin*, February, 415–19.

RBA (1987), 'Overseas operations of Australian banks', *Reserve Bank of Australia Bulletin*, December, 16–24.

RBA (2004), 'International banking statistics for Australia', *Reserve Bank of Australia Bulletin*, July, 18–24.

Reed, H.C. (1983), 'Appraising corporate investment policy: A financial center theory of foreign direct investment', in C.P. Kindleberger & D.B. Audretsch (eds), *The Multinational Corporation in the 1980s*, Cambridge, MA: MIT Press, 219–44.

Reina, P. & G.J. Tulacz (2001), 'Global firms increase their local presences', *ENR*, 23 July, 32–6.

Report of the Committee for Review of Export Market Development Assistance (1989), *Australian Exports: Performance Obstacles and Issues of Assistance*, Canberra: AGPS.

ResMed (2005), [http://resmed.com.au/portal/site/ResMedAU/index.?jsp], 7 December 2005.

Retail World (1993), *Grocery Industry Marketing Guide – 1993*, Rozelle, NSW: Retail World Pty Ltd.

Reuters (2000), 'Foster's seeks new growth with wine', *Reuters News*, 20 September.

Revell, J.R.S. (1980), *Costs and Margins in Banking: An International Survey*, Paris: OECD.

Ries, I. (1996), 'Two majors on the brink', *Australian Financial Review*, 15 May.

Ries, I. (1998), 'The jewel that cost a fortune', *Australian Financial Review*, 16 July.

Riley, D. (1992), *The Iron Ships: A Maritime History of BHP, 1885–1992*, Melbourne: BHP Transport.

Rimmer, P.J. (1970), *Freight Forwarding in Australia*, Canberra: Research School of Pacific Studies, Australian National University.

Rio Tinto (2005), [www.Riotinto.com].

Roberto, M.A. (2003), 'The changing structure of the global wine industry', *International Business & Economics Research Journal*, **2** (9), 1–14.

Roberts, B.H. & M.J. Enright (2004), 'Industry clusters in Australia: Recent trends and prospects', *European Planning Studies*, **12** (1), 99–121.

Roberts, C. (2004), 'Voyage to disappointment', *Business Review Weekly*, 4 March, 64–5.

Roberts, J. (1999), 'The internationalisation of business service firms: A stages approach', *The Service Industries Journal*, **19** (4), 68–88.

Roberts, J. (2001), 'Challenges facing service enterprises in a global knowledge-based economy: Lessons from the business services sector', *International Journal of Services Technology & Management*, **2** (3/4), 402–34.

Roberts, P. (2006), 'Is Australia just a quarry?' *Australian Financial Review*, 4 February.

Roche (2003), 'Company History' [www.roche.com/home/company/com_hist_intro/com_hist–1978.htm], 2 October 2003.

Rochfort, S. (2005), 'Petrol, Korea hurt CC Amatil', *Sydney Morning Herald*, 14 October.

Ross, E. (2005), 'In-house entrepreneurs', *Business Review Weekly*, 21 July.

Rugman, A.M. (2005), *The Regional Multinationals: MNEs and 'Global' Strategic Management*, Cambridge: Cambridge University Press.

Rugman, A.M. & C. Bain (2003), 'Multinational enterprises are regional, not global', *Multinational Business Review*, **11** (1), 3–12.

Rugman, A.M. & S. Collinson (2005), 'Multinational enterprises in the New Europe: Are they really global?', *Organizational Dynamics*, **34** (3), 258–72.

Rugman, A.M. & J.R. D'Cruz (2000), *Multinationals as Flagship Firms: Regional Business Networks*, London: Oxford University Press.

Rugman, A.M. & S. Girod (2003), 'Retail multinationals and globalization: the evidence is regional', *European Management Journal*, **21** (1), 24–37.

Rugman, A.M. & A. Verbeke (1990), *Global Corporate Strategy and Trade Policy*, London & New York: Routledge.

Rugman, A.M. & A. Verbeke (1991), 'Environmental change and global competitive strategy in Europe', *Research in Global Strategic Management*, **2**, 3–27.

Rugman, A.M. & A. Verbeke (1992), 'A note on the transnational solution and the transaction cost theory of multinational strategic management', *Journal of International Business Studies*, **23** (4), 761–72.

Rugman, A.M. & A. Verbeke (1993), 'Foreign subsidiaries and multinational strategic management: An extension and correction of Porter's single diamond framework', *Management International Review*, **33**, Special issue, 71–84.

Rugman, A.M. & A. Verbeke (2003), 'Extending the theory of the multinational enterprise: Internalization and strategic management perspective', *Journal of International Business Studies*, **34** (2), 125–38.

Rugman, A.M. & A. Verbeke (2004), 'A perspective on regional and global strategies of multinational enterprises', *Journal of International Business Studies*, **35** (1), 3–18.

Ruigrok, W. & H. Wagner (2004), 'Internationalization and firm performance: Meta–analytic review and future research direction' [www.uu.nl/content/WinifriedRuigrok.pdf], 18 January 2005.

Rumelt, R. (1974), *Strategy, Structure, and Economic Performance*, Boston, MA: Harvard Business School Press.
Sanders, W.G. & M.A. Carpenter (1998), 'Internationalisation and firm governance: The roles of CEO compensation, top team composition, and board structure', *The Academy of Management Journal*, **41** (2), 158–78.
Schedvin, C.B. (1992), *In Reserve: Central Banking in Australia, 1945–75*, St Leonards, NSW: Allen & Unwin.
Scherer, K. (2000), 'Coles Myer learns harsh Kiwi lesson', *New Zealand Herald*, 9 September.
Schmidt, L. & S. Lloyd (2003), 'Monsters of retail', *Business Review Weekly*, 13 November, 38–44.
Schreiner, J. (2005), 'The simple strategy of Torbreck Vintners: Old vines make bold wines', *Plan it Vancouver*, 23 May [www.planitvancouver.com/Articles/article0192–torbreck.html], 3 March 2006.
Scott, J. (2006), '2006 – is this the toughest time?' *Wine Industry Journal*, **21** (1), 81–2.
Scott-Kennel, J. (2004), 'Foreign Direct Investment to New Zealand', *University of Auckland Business Review*, **6** (2), 41–9.
Seeder, B. (2001), 'Macquarie set for European expansion', *Australian Financial Review*, 18 July.
Seltzer, A. & D.T. Merrett (2000), 'Human resource management practices at the Union Bank of Australia: Panel evidence from the 1887–1893 entry cohorts', *Journal of Labor Economics*, **18** (4), 573–613.
Seth, A. & G. Randall (2001), *The Grocers: the Rise and Rise of the Supermarket Chains*, 2nd edn, London: Kogan Page.
Seth, A. & G. Randall (2005), *Supermarket Wars*, Houndmills, UK: Palgrave Macmillan.
SFOCEA (Swedish Federation of Consulting Engineers and Architects) (2004), 'The Consulting Engineering and Architectural Groups: A Swedish and International Survey', Stockholm: Swedish Federation of Consulting Engineers and Architects.
Shand, A. (2002), 'Macquarie bank's big dealer: can he keep cutting it?', *Australian Financial Review*, 9 February.
Shand, A. & C. Ryan (2005), 'News: MacBank's mid-life crisis', *Australian Financial Review*, 5 December.
Sharma, D.D. (1991), *International Operations of Professional Firms*, Lund, Sweden: Studentlitteratur and Chartwell-Bratt.
Shaw G., L. Curth & A. Alexander (2004), 'Selling self-service and the supermarket: The Americanization of food retailing in Britain, 1945–90', *Business History*, **46** (4), 568–72.
Shoebridge, N. (1989), 'Amatil Split Good News for Coca-Cola', *Business Review Weekly*, 28 April.
Shoebridge, N. (1996), 'Officeworks hits the small-business nerve', *Business Review Weekly*, 29 April, 76.

Silver, E.S. (1999), 'Being all things, tackling all tasks', *Design Build,* August.

Simeon, R. (2001), 'Top team characteristics and the business strategies of Japanese firms', *Corporate Governance*, **1** (2), 4–12.

Sinclair, E.K. (1990), *The Spreading Tree: A History of APM and Amcor, 1844–1989*, North Sydney: Allen & Unwin.

Sinclair, J. (1987), *Images Incorporated: Advertising as Industry and Ideology*, London & New York: Croom Helm.

Skully, M.T. (1980), 'Foreign banking in New York City: The Australian bank agencies', *The Bankers' Magazine of Australasia*, December, 205–12.

Skully, M.T. (1987), *Merchant Banking in Australia*, Melbourne: Oxford University Press, 121–85.

Skully, M.T. (1997), 'Banks and financial institutions', in R. Bruce, B. McKern, I. Pollard & M. Skully (eds), *Handbook of Australian Corporate Finance*, 5th edn, Sydney: Butterworths. 15-61.

SMH, *Sydney Morning Herald*, daily, Sydney.

Smith, G.R. & A. Barrie (1976), *Aspro: How a Family Business Grew Up*, Melbourne: Nicholas International Ltd.

Smith, S. (2002), *From Club to Corporation: Motor Insurance and the Rise of Australian Associated Motor Insurers Ltd (AAMI), 1933–1999*, Melbourne: Australian Associated Motor Insurers Ltd.

Solomon, R. (1999), *Money on the Move: The Revolution in International Finance since 1980*, New Jersey: Princeton University Press.

South Australian Farmers Federation (2005), 'Submission to the Senate Rural and Regional Affairs and Transport Reference Committee', *Inquiry into the Wine Industry*, Adelaide: South Australian Farmers Federation.

Southcorp (1977), *Annual Report.*

Spector, R. (2005), *Category Killers*, Boston: Harvard Business School Press.

Stace, D. (1997), *Reaching Out From Down Under: Building Competence for Global Markets*, Sydney: McGraw Hill Australia.

Stephens, A.M. (ca. 1977), *The Stateships Story*, Fremantle: Stateships.

Stern, S. (1951), *The United States in International Banking*, New York: Columbia University Press.

Stevens, M.J. & A. Bird (2004), 'On the myth of believing that globalisation is a myth: or the effects of misdirected responses on obsolescing an emergent substantive discourse', *Journal of International Management*, **10** (4), 501–10.

Stevens, T.S. (m.s.), 'Scottish House: A History of McIlwraith, McEacharn & Company, shipowners, merchants and miners', Unpublished manuscript.

Stott, D. (1992), *Engineers in Company: BHP Engineering's First 25 Years 1967–1992*, North Sydney: BHP Engineering.

Strasser, S. (1989), *Satisfaction Guaranteed: The Making of the American Mass Market*, New York: Pantheon Books.

Strassman, W.P. (1998), *The Global Construction Industry*, London: Unwin Hyman.

Sullivan, D. (1994), 'Measuring the degree of internationalisation of a firm', *Journal of International Business Studies*, **25** (2), 325–42.

SvitzerWijsmuller (2006), 'Announcement', Media release, 3 July 2006 [svitzerwijsmuller.com], 11 September 2006.

Swaminathan, A. (1995), 'The proliferation of specialist organizations in the American wine industry, 1941–1990', *Administrative Science Quarterly*, **40** (4), 653–80.

Swedish Trade Council (1999), *Swedish Subsidiaries in Australia (HO, branches, agents)*, Sydney: STC.

Sykes, T. (1992), 'How Burns Philp hit Terra Firma', *Australian Business Monthly*, September, 84–9.

Sykes, T. (1994), *The Bold Riders: Behind Australia's Corporate Collapses*, Sydney: Allen and Unwin.

Sylla, R. (2002), 'United States banks and Europe: strategy and attitudes', in S. Battilossi & Y. Cassis (eds), *European Banks and the American Challenge*, Oxford: Oxford University Press, 53–73.

Tabart-Gay, J., & P.W. Wolnizer (1997), 'Business firms as adaptive entities: The case of the major Australian banks, 1983–94', *Abacus*, **33** (2), 186–207.

Taggart, J. (1993), *The World Pharmaceutical Industry*, London & New York: Routledge.

Taylor, P. (2005), 'Hungry Aldi to check out the CBD', *Herald–Sun*, 8 November.

Teece, D.J., G. Pisano & A. Shuen (1997), 'Dynamic capabilities and strategic management', *Strategic Management Journal*, **18** (7), 509–33.

Telstra (2005), [www.telstra.com.au].

Thomas, T. (1991), 'Macquarie sitting pretty', *Business Review Weekly*, 19 April.

Thomis, M.I. & W. Murdoch (1986), *From SGIO to SUNCORP*, Brisbane: SUNCORP Insurance and Finance.

Thompson, A. (1981a), *Australian Companies in Indonesia: Establishment and Operating Experience*, Melbourne: University of Melbourne, Asian Business Research Programme.

Thompson, A. (1981b), *Australian Companies in Thailand: Establishment and Operating Experience*, Melbourne: University of Melbourne, Asian Business Research Programme.

Thompson, A. (1983), *Australian Companies in the Philippines: Establishment and Operating Experience*, Melbourne: University of Melbourne, Asian Business Research Programme.

Thompson, A. & R. Muir (1982), *Australian Companies in Malaysia: Establishment and Operating Experience*, Melbourne: University of Melbourne, Asian Business Research Programme.

Thorburn, L., J. Langdale & J.W. Houghton (2002), '*Friend or Foe? Leveraging Foreign Multinationals in the Australian Economy*', Report prepared for Australian Business Foundation, Sydney.

Tichy, G. (2001), 'What do we know about success and failure of mergers?', *Journal of Industry, Competition and Trade*, **1** (4), 347–94.

Tjordman, A. (1995), 'European retailing: convergences, differences and perspectives', in P.J. McGoldrick & G. Davies (eds), *International Retailing:Trends and Strategies*, London: Pitman, 17–50.

TNT (2006), 'History' [www.tntlogistics.com/en/about_us/history/index.asp], 4 June 2006.

TNT (annual), *Annual Reports* (1977–87).

Todd, M. (2000), 'Amatil Rejects Push By Coke To Relinquish Asian Division', *Sydney Morning Herald*, 4 October.

Toll (2005), 'Milestones – 2006' [www.toll.com.au/milestone2000.html], 1 April 2006.

Toll (2006), 'SembLog Acquisition' [www.toll.com.au/Toll_SembLog_Acquisition_Proposal.html], 1 April 2006.

Toohey, B. (1989), 'Hawke and Abeles', *The Sunday Age*, 19 November.

Trade Law Committee (1979), *Australian Investment Overseas, Lines of Inquiry: The Results of a Research Project,* Melbourne: Australian Law Council Foundation.

Tschoegl, A.E. (2002), 'FDI and internationalization: Evidence from U.S. subsidiaries of foreign banks', *Journal of International Business Studies*, **33** (4), 805–15.

Tulacz, G.J. (1999), 'Reports measure world market', *ENR*, **243**, 12–13.

Tulder, R. van, D.A.F. van den Berghe & A. Muller (2001), *The World's Largest Firms and Internationalization*, Rotterdam: Erasmus University of Rotterdam.

Tweedie, S. (1994), *Trading Partners: Australia and Asia, 1790–1993,* Sydney: University of New South Wales Press.

United Nations (2003), *United Nations Statistical Yearbook*, New York: United Nations.

UNCTAD (United Nations Conference on Trade and Development) (various), *World Investment Report,* New York and Geneva: United Nations.

UNCTAD (1983), *Transnational Corporations in World Development*, Third Survey, New York.

Unwin, T. (1996), *Wine and the Vine*, London & New York: Routledge.

Upton, D. & R. Seet (1996), 'Pacific Dunlop China (A): Beijing', *Harvard Business School Case 9-695-029.*

US Bureau of Economic Analysis (2003), *Survey of Current Business*, November.

Veatch, N.D. (2001), 'Malls: It's all in how you count them', *Shopping Centre Directions*, **33** (2).

Vernon, R. (1966), 'International investment and international trade in the product cycle', *Quarterly Journal of Economics*, **80** (May), 190–207.

Vicziany, M. & S. Chatterjee (1999), 'Australian business attitudes to India in the late 1990s', in S. Neelemegham, D. Midgley & C. Sen (eds), *Enterprise Management: New Horizons in Indo-Australian Collaboration*, New Delhi: Tata McGraw-Hill, 135–56.

Vida, I. (2000), 'An empirical inquiry into international expansion of the United States retailers', *International Marketing Review*, **17** (4/5), 454–75.

Visy (2005), 'History' [www.visy.com.au/about/about_history.aspx], 7 December 2005.

Walker, B. & B. Walker (2000), *Privatisation: Sell Off or Sell Out? The Australian Experience*, Sydney: ABC Books.

Wall, J. (1988), 'Nicholas, Alfred Michael (1881–1937) and George Richard Rich (1884–1960)', in G. Serle (ed.), *Australian Dictionary of Biography, Volume 11 1891–1939, Nes – Smi*, Melbourne: Melbourne University Press.

Wallace, R.H. (1993), 'The business financiers: merchant banks and finance companies', in M.K. Lewis and R.H. Wallace (eds), *The Australian Financial System*, South Melbourne: Longman Cheshire, 214–48.

Walter, I. (1985), *Barriers to Trade in Banking and Financial Services*, London: Trade Policy Research Centre.

Wan, C-C (1998), 'International diversification, industrial diversification and firm performance of Hong Kong MNCs', *Asia Pacific Journal of Management*, **15** (2), 205–17.

Wasserstein, B. (1998), *Big Deal: Mergers and Acquisitions in the Digital Age*, New York: Warner Books.

Way, N. (2004a), 'Professions: Engineering's big overhaul', *Business Review Weekly*, 22 April.

Way, N. (2004b), 'Engineers get excited', *Business Review Weekly*, 2 September.

Wayland, R. (1994), 'Coca-Cola versus Pepsi-Cola and the soft drink industry', *Harvard Business School Case* 9391-179. Boston.

Webb, R. (1988), 'PacDun expansion has a new nucleus', *Australian Financial Review*, 24 August.

Welch, L. & R. Luostarinen (1988), 'Internationalization: Evolution of a concept', *Journal of General Management*, **14** (2), 34–55.

Were, J.B., *Kiwi International 1950–1970*, University of Melbourne Archive, Accession 100:17, Box 346.

Were, J.B., *Nicholas Kiwi 1970–1984*, University of Melbourne Archive, Accession 100:17, Box 767.

Wernerfelt, B. (1984), 'A resource-based view of the firm', *Strategic Management Journal*, **5** (2), 171–80.

Westfield Holdings (2000), *The Westfield Story: The First 40 Years*, Sydney: Armstrong Miller & McLaren.

Westfield (2005), [www.westfield.com.au].

Westfield (2006), [http://westfield.com/corporate/about], 18 May 2006.

Wetherel, P. (1988), 'The unsung brewer', *Australian Business,* 26 October.

WGCA & WFA (1994), 'Sustaining success: Policies to achieve the potential of the Australian winegrape and wine industries', *National Industry Submission to the Committee of Inquiry into the Winegrape and Wine Industry*, Industry Commission, Canberra.

White, R.E. & T.A. Poynter (1984), 'Strategies for foreign-owned subsidiaries in Canada', *Business Quarterly*, **48** (4), 59–69.

Wilkinson, B.A. & R.K. Willson (1981), *The Main Line Fleet of Burns Philp*, Canberra: Nautical Association of Australia.

Wilkinson, M. (1987), 'Flying high: Sir Peter Abeles', *Four Corners*, 2 November [www,vision.net.au/~apaterson/politics/4cnrs_abeles.htm], 14 October 2004.

Williamson, O.E. (1985), *The Economic Foundations of Capitalism*, New York: Free Press.

Williamson, P.J. (2004), *Winning in Asia: Strategies for Competing in the New Millennium*, Boston, MA: Harvard Business School Press.

Wittington, R., M. Mayer & F. Curto (1999), 'Chandlerism in post-war Europe: Strategic and structural change in France, Germany and the U.K., 1950–1993', *Industrial and Corporate Change*, **8** (3), 519–51.

Wolf, G. (1997), 'Kmart Corporation', in T. Grant & J.P. Pedersen (eds), *International Directory of Company Histories*, Chicago: St. James Press, **18**, 283–87.

Wood, L. (1997), 'Burns Flips', *The Age,* 8 November.

Woodhead, L. (2003), *War Paint: Miss Elizabeth Arden and Madame Helena Rubenstein: Their Lives, Their Times, Their Rivalry*, London: Virago Press.

Woolworths (2005), 'Woolworths announces acquisition of Foodland New Zealand business plus 22 Australian stores', 25 May [www.woolworthslimited.com.au/news/mediareleases/index.asp], 3 May 2006.

World Bank (2005), *World Bank Development Indicators 2003* [www.worldbank.org/data/wdi2003/index.htm], 25 March 2006.

Wright, C. (2000), 'From shop floor to board room: The historical evolution of Australian management consulting, 1940s to 1980s', *Business History,* **42** (1), 85–106.

Wrigley, L. (1970), 'Divisional autonomy and diversification', *Unpublished doctoral thesis*, Harvard Business School.

Yeaple, S.R. (2003), 'The complex integration strategies of multinationals and cross country dependencies in the structure of foreign direct investment', *Journal of International Economics,* **60** (2), 293-314.

Yetton, P., J. Craig, J. Davis & F. Hilmer (1992), 'Are diamonds a country's best friend?: A critique of Porter's theory of national competition as applied to Canada, New Zealand and Australia', *Australian Journal of Management*, **17** (1), 89–119.

Yetton, P., J. Davis & P. Swan (1991), 'Going international: Export myths and strategic realities', *Report to the Australian Manufacturing Council*, Randwick, NSW: Australian Graduate School of Management.

Yong, C.F. (1977), *The New Gold Mountain: The Chinese in Australia, 1901–1921*, Richmond, SA: Raphael Arts.

Young, O. (2005), 'Australians blind to Asia's lures', *Australian Financial Review*, 4 July.

Young, S., C. Huang & M. McDermott (1996), 'Internationalization and competitive catch-up process: Case study evidence on Chinese multinational enterprises', *Management International Review*, **36** (4), 295–314.

Zaheer, S. (1995), 'Overcoming the liability of foreignness', *Academy of Management Journal*, **38** (2), 341–63.

Zalan, T. (2003), 'Internationalisation of Australian firms: Toward a theory of international failure', *Unpublished doctoral dissertation,* Flinders University of South Australia, Adelaide.

Zimmerman, M.M. (1955), *The Super Market: A Revolution in Distribution*, New York: McGraw-Hill.

Index